The
Red Hills
of
Florida
1528–1865

The
Red Hills
of
Florida
1528–1865

Clifton Paisley

The University of Alabama Press
TUSCALOOSA AND LONDON

Copyright © 1989 by
The University of Alabama Press
Tuscaloosa, Alabama 35487–0380
All rights reserved
Manufactured in the United States of America

Library of Congress Cataloging-in-Publication Data

Paisley, Clifton L.
 The Red Hills of Florida, 1528–1865

 Bibliography: p.
 Includes index.
 1. Red Hills (Fla.)—History. I. Title.
F317.R43P35   1989   975.9'8   88–5767
ISBN 0–8173–0412–6 (alk. paper)

British Library Cataloging-in-Publication Data available

SECOND PRINTING 1990

To
my granddaughter, Alice,
and
my grandsons, Brendan and Ryan

Contents

Contents

Preface

"The Red Clay Hills of North Florida" was the name that R. E. Rose, Florida state chemist seventy-five years ago, gave to a region that provides the setting for this book. Pamphlet after pamphlet, including *The Lands of Leon*, published in 1911, sought to interest "the intelligent northern immigrant" in taking over the then worn-out cotton fields of Leon, one of five counties in this region, and making them prosperous farms. The invitation to come south was finally accepted principally by wealthy northern industrialists who, instead of cultivating the land, turned the red hills into what the late very colorful politician Jerry Carter called "pa'tridge pastuahs." I devoted some attention to these gentry and their winter hunting preserves in *From Cotton to Quail* (1968).

It was evident to me that the Red Hills—in Leon and its neighboring counties Gadsden and Jackson to the west and Jefferson and Madison to the east—had attracted people like a magnet, the cotton planters long before quail planters and the Spanish explorers and missionaries before them. Everywhere I have lived, nearby footprints of the past have been an attraction, whether on the site of the Civil War Battle of Prairie Grove, Arkansas, or at Nashville, Tennessee, where the footprints were those of Andrew Jackson and Frank James. In Tallahassee, where the Jacksonville *Florida Times-Union* assigned me as capital correspondent in December 1954, I found footprints that went back much farther than they had in any place I had ever lived. The newspaper indulged me in my suggestion that I go down to St. Marks and look for the ruins of an old stone fort that the English had found in 1763 when they took over Florida for twenty years. I was sure present-day people knew little or nothing about it.

So on a pleasant Saturday in October 1955, Charles H. Schaeffer of the State Park Service and I rowed the half mile downriver from the wharf to where the St. Marks and Wakulla rivers come together to "rediscover" San Marcos de Apalache. The Park Service already had dreams of acquiring the site and digging what was left of the fort from a jungle of cedar, palmetto, and hackberry trees. American settlers had had many buildings to build, including a lighthouse, and the fort had been cannibalized so that its finely cut limestone blocks, even those of the vaulted ceiling of the "bombproof," could be used to build these structures. We were able to trace an outline of the fort from the mounded earth, but the only visible part was a length of stone wall rising on the Wakulla River side about where old plans showed the northwestern bastion to have been.

My only information about the fort came from a piece written by the late Mark F. Boyd in the *Florida Historical Quarterly*. My family and I lived across the street from Dr. Boyd on East Sixth Avenue, and so I went to see him for additional details. What I remember principally about the interview was his insistence on precision. When I mentioned a "stone wall," he corrected me; it was a "rubble wall." He was a physician and was just as clinically incisive in his writing. After starting research for *The Red Hills* some fifteen years ago, I discovered that over the course of about twenty years Boyd had brought together, principally in the *Quarterly*, what amounts to a documentary history of this region. The area was under the Spanish flag for more than three hundred years, and Boyd himself translated many of the documents. Although he never, to my knowledge, used the term "Red Hills," he ably documented this region and its coastal approaches, and I am more indebted to him than to any other historian.

Those who have assisted me in my inquiry include first and foremost my wife, Joy Smith Paisley, who has always shared my enthusiasm for the region and its history. She is responsible for a survey that was completed in 1978—but should have been made half a century earlier—of the plantation and rural family and church cemeteries of Leon County. Her book, *The Cemeteries of Leon County, Florida*, records information on the stones in about seventy old cemeteries, including information about the only known grave of a Revolutionary War veteran. Joy has backed me all the way, offering suggestions, reading copy before and after completion of a fresh typescript, encouraging me with her enthusiasm for the project. Our daughters, Mary and Elizabeth, have also lent their support and talents in various ways.

Many others have assisted me. I will mention particularly those who have read and made suggestions about parts of the book during various stages of revision: in Tallahassee, LeRoy Collins, James N.

Eaton, Mary Louise Ellis, Charles W. Hendry, Jr., the late Lou Whit-field (Mrs. J. Frank) Miller, John H. Moore, the late George Lester Patterson, and the late Amy Goodbody (Mrs. George Lester) Patter-son, William W. Rogers, Dr. Fred B. Thigpen, Louis Daniel Tesar, and the late Sally Lines (Mrs. Edward) Thomas; elsewhere in Florida, the late Edwin B. Browning, Madison; Floie Criglar (Mrs. John C.) Packard, Marianna; Esther (Mrs. Frederick W.) Connolly, Monticello; and Lee H. Warner, Sarasota; and outside of Florida, Amy Turner Bushnell, Mobile, Alabama; Linda Ellsworth, Philadelphia, Pennsyl-vania; and Robert A. Matter, Seattle, Washington. I also thank Susan Hamburger, Tallahassee, for expertly typing the manuscript, and James R. Anderson, Jr., and Peter A. Krafft, Tallahassee, for expertly drawing the maps.

Tallahassee, Florida   CLIFTON PAISLEY

The
Red Hills
of
Florida
1528–1865

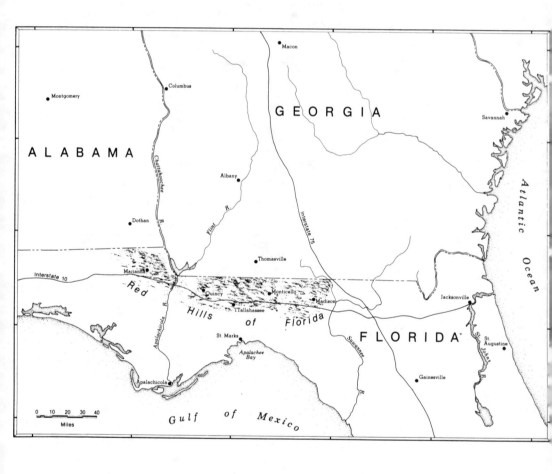

1

Piedmont Florida

The motorist who is southward bound through Georgia leaves the mountains north of Atlanta but enjoys a replica of them in the hilly-to-rolling Piedmont and in what are sometimes called "the Red Hills of Georgia." At Albany the hills seem to have been left behind, and much of the drive toward Tallahassee on U.S. 19 follows a straight and level stretch. Below Thomasville and near the Florida line, one expects U.S. 319 to drop down farther to the sandy, flat coastlands—for the Gulf of Mexico is only fifty miles away—but the land wrinkles up again, and one sees more hills and valleys for twenty miles than appeared in one hundred miles of Georgia. Where the earth has been gashed, as in road cuts, the traveler also notices the red clay familiar from the Georgia hills and mountains.

Our upcountry motorist is now in the Red Hills of Florida, a region that is the setting for this narrative. Travelers from the earliest times have commented on the beauty of the region, on its hill-and-valley character, with an abundance of lakes and springs and a vegetation indicating naturally rich soils. Sidney Lanier, a late nineteenth-century visitor, called this strip of land extending for 150 miles along the border of Alabama and Georgia "Piedmont Florida." Never more than twenty-five miles wide, the hill country occupies the northernmost parts of the counties of Jackson, Gadsden, Leon, Jefferson, and Madison in Florida. There are higher elevations in the Panhandle and Peninsula of Florida, but nowhere is the up-and-down character of the land more impressive. After Lanier's train had crossed the Suwannee River, he discovered "a country differing wholly in appearance from the lumber and turpentine regions of Duval, Baker, Columbia and Suwannee counties" through which he had passed on the way from Jacksonville, a region having, said he, "as fair a set of arable hills as one could wish to see."[1]

The New England naturalist Bradford Torrey, making this rail trip in 1893, noted the same change from level country to hills and "from white sand to red clay."[2] Entering the region from the west in June 1827, the Right Reverend Michael Portier, Catholic bishop of Alabama and Florida, found an overnight haven from the pine forests of the Panhandle in what is today called Orange Hill in Washington County. This was only a foretaste, though, of what Portier found in the "Chipola country" in Jackson County twenty miles farther along, with its reddish soils, rolling lands, cool brooks and fine hardwood forests. Finding this land after passing through "interminable tracts of stunted pine trees" was "like escaping suddenly from the infernal Taenarus into paradise."[3]

The novelist Maurice Thompson described a trip of thirty-five miles by hack from Thomasville, Georgia, to Tallahassee in 1880 during which the road left level sandy pinelands for the hill country. He found around Tallahassee "a region at once the most fertile, the most picturesque and the most salubrious to be found south of the North Georgia mountains."[4] The road taken by Thompson is still called the Thomasville Road but as U.S. 319 is today a busy thoroughfare in places four lanes wide. A better introduction to the natural setting of the Red Hills is by way of the Meridian Road five miles to the west via State Road 12.

Hardwood forests press against the twenty-foot-wide asphalt strip of Meridian along the seventeen-mile drive into Tallahassee. Although there are many, many pines, one is now likely to see white-trunked beeches, oaks and hickories of many kinds, sweetgums, tulip poplars, and dogwoods, with an understory of sumac, wild plum, French mulberry, haw, and elder. In winter these forests are stark and bare except for the shiny-leaved magnolias and hollies, and the open ground is as brown as a Tennessee sedgefield. The brown fields turn as white as a Vermont snowdrift on a sharp, frosty morning, but it is often summertime in the afternoon. Wealthy northerners who bought up the worn-out cotton lands at the turn of the century and turned them into "quail plantations" showed local people the charm of these winter woods. In the spring the light greens of hickories and gum join the duller tones of evergreens, but as summer wears on, all of the greens become subdued, muted also by the dark limbs and massive trunks of the live oaks. These with their ever-present Spanish moss—great streamers of it almost reach the ground—appear in increasing numbers. When fall comes, the woods light up with a merry medley of reds, purples, and yellows, showing outlanders how much autumn color can be found even in Florida.

Meridian Road rises and falls in gentle slopes from elevations of 100 feet above sea level along the western end of Lake Iamonia to 240 feet along the eastern side of Lake Jackson. Nearby, just off Orchard Pond Road, is a peak of 279 feet less than three-fourths of a mile from a backwater of the lake called Mallard Pond, surface eighty-seven feet.[5] For the most part, Meridian runs straight along the zero meridian of the 1825 land surveys. An observant botanist-geographer, Roland M. Harper, marveled in 1914 at the way road builders in Leon County often ran the roads straight regardless of hills, traveling across rather than around them. The red clay stuck together so well that the deep, perfectly vertical sides of the roadways stood in place for years, becoming covered with a gray-green lichen that Harper had rarely seen elsewhere.[6]

Six miles south of State Road 12, as Meridian begins to cross the higher ridges, these road cuts with their crust of lichens sometimes rise in sheer walls of eight or ten feet. There is no evidence of agriculture today, but the deep road cuts now provide a telltale sign of the agriculture of 1850, when Leon County grew more than a third of all the cotton grown in Florida.[7] In taking the cotton to market, six-mule-team wagons bearing two or three tons of baled cotton were the real road builders, wearing roads like Meridian to their present level. Live oaks along the sides grew large, their limbs and branches intertwining over the roadway, shading the lichen-covered banks, and providing a pleasant canopy for the summer traveler. This canopy ends just to the south of Maclay School, and the traveler also sees fewer of the interesting gray-green banks, for modern road builders favor slanted rather than vertical side ditches, and the lichens refuse to grow on banks that bake in the sun.

The drive is nevertheless pleasant as Meridian proceeds into Tallahassee and joins the Thomasville Road. On Monroe Street the traveler ascends a gentle slope to the restored "old capitol," eighteen miles from the Georgia line. At the intersection of Adams Street, a block to the west, and Pensacola Street is the twenty-two-story "new capitol," built during the 1970s. It was here, from a porch of the City Hotel, that Lanier looked out on the hill country and, reminded of the fertile hills around Macon, Georgia, his old home, felt prompted to speak of "Piedmont Florida."[8]

The land at the base of the two capitols is 215 feet above sea level, but just to the south it falls off steeply to less than 100 feet. The traveler is at the edge of the Red Hills and from the glassed-in observation deck at the top of the new capitol surveys a vast stretch of level pineland. The horizon to the south shows no evidence of the blue waters of the Gulf, but on a very clear day a guide may identify a pinpoint on the horizon as the St. Marks lighthouse.

Geologists call the drop of land separating the Red Hills from the coastal lowlands the Cody Scarp. Rarely is the escarpment as pronounced as it is near Tallahassee, but it extends eastward to the Withlacoochee River, a tributary of the Suwannee, and westward to the Apalachicola, with some manifestations beyond.[9] Back on Monroe Street, one can drive southward toward St. Marks to look at the lowlands. The drive descends a steep grade which is the valley of an ancient stream that here cuts through a southward-tending thrust of the Scarp as it comes from the west. A stream—still evident as a drainage ditch on Franklin Boulevard—flowed around the southeastern corner of early Tallahassee and, south of that hamlet, dropped in a sixteen-foot waterfall called "the cascade" into a rock sink.[10] The ancestor stream formed the first valley across which Monroe Street now runs, and a second was formed by a stream, now also a drainage ditch, that flowed through Indian Head Acres and along Orange Avenue. Near present-day Monroe Street these waters were used by George Washington Scott, a nineteenth-century planter (and later founder of Agnes Scott College), to turn a sixteen-foot waterwheel that powered a cotton gin and corn-grinding machinery, giving the flow here the name "Scott's Ditch."[11]

The motorist is still in the Red Hills as the roadway rises from the second valley. A detour via Paul Russell Road some two miles south of the old capitol takes the motorist to a high ridge on the eastward-running course of the Cody Scarp. The view of residents with houses here has been about the same as that from the top of the capitol. Although the lighthouse cannot be seen, the glow from its light has been discernible on clear nights.[12] Lookouts at the seventeenth-century mission of San Martín de Tomoli here had this same view of the flatlands, as did John McIver, an early Leon County settler who built his house in the ruins of this mission.[13]

Back on the Woodville Highway, the motorist is at an elevation of about fifty feet above sea level where Old Tram Road strikes off to the southeast near the base of the Cody Scarp. A drive southward crosses increasingly low shorelines of Pleistocene times. White sands everywhere replace the red and yellow clays and dark topsoils of the hills. Longleaf pine still grows in small natural stands from a floor of wiregrass that has never felt the touch of a plow. But the forests often are of even-age slash pines, standing in military ranks, the universal imprint of the pulp paper industry. Where these trees have been cut down, ragged-looking turkey oaks have taken their place. Beyond

Woodville, as the elevation falls almost to sea level, these lowlands become a "watery wilderness."[14]

Geologists explain that the Red Hills comprise an accumulation of clays, sands, and other rock fragments deposited on a limestone bed that were washed down from the Appalachian Mountains beginning about 20 million years ago, following an uplift of these mountains. Originally the clayey sands formed a level plain about three hundred feet above present sea level. The runoff from heavy rains—today this coastal area averages about sixty inches a year—carved the plain into the hills and valleys seen today, while at the Cody Scarp these uplands were sheared off abruptly and worn down, most likely by several higher stands of sea level. East of the Ochlockonee River, which divides Leon County from Gadsden, some of the deeper valleys were eroded enough to reach the most recent of several layers of underlying limestone, a brittle and sandy stratum called the St. Marks formation. Acids in the downward-percolating surface waters dissolved portions of the bedrock, creating fissures and caves. Streams flowing through these valleys then entered underground passages.[15] Some geologists maintain that the large Lakes Iamonia, Jackson, and Lafayette in Leon County, and Miccosukee on the border of Leon and Jefferson counties, were at one time streams and that their beds, made deeper and broader by erosion and collapse of the underlying caves (sinkholes), became lakes.[16] All still have sinkholes and, in the absence of man-made dams and other structures, become "disappearing lakes" that during very long and continued dry spells shrink to a third of their normal size.

In Gadsden and Liberty counties west of the Ochlockonee, the limestone bedrock subsided in the distant past into a coastward-sloping trough, and this trough accumulated more of the Appalachian fragments than the counties to the east. Streams have never been able to penetrate these deep clays and sands far enough to reach the bedrock.[17]

Jackson, the westernmost Red Hills county, has still another geological history. The northern part is assigned to what has been called "the Marianna River Valley Lowlands," but these lowlands consist of rolling land between 100 and 170 feet above sea level. In ancient times broad rivers—the ancestors of the Chattahoochee-Apalachicola system—left their deposits and eroded them more evenly and thoroughly, forming a lower plain than east of the river before valleys were carved by smaller streams. Older bedrock is nearer the surface, and the more recent erosion has carved out numerous, now relatively dry, underground caves, for example the Florida Caverns near Marianna. Sandy remnant hills in the southern part of the county stand at much higher elevations, but the hills in northern Jackson County are linked with the Red Hills parts of four counties east of the Apalachicola.[18]

William Bartram, who wrote so enchantingly about the Alachua country and the valley of the St. Johns River, never saw the Red Hills in his travels of 1774, but the keenly observant botanist and geographer Roland M. Harper is a good substitute in recording the native plant life. Noting topography and soils as well as trees, shrubs, and herbs, Harper left a record of what he saw in 1914 from west to east.[19]

In the central and northwestern part of Jackson County, on both sides of the Chipola River, Harper found in what he called the "Marianna Red Lands" one of the richest soils in Florida. There was a tendency here toward dense forests of oaks, magnolias, sweetgums, beeches, and hollies, with rather more cedars, maples, walnuts, and redbuds than he had found elsewhere in northern Florida. Longleaf pines were found in considerable numbers on sandy uplands, in addition to blackjack oaks, but loblolly or "old field" pines were more frequent than longleaf.[20] The eastern side of the county, except for the floodplain of the Chattahoochee and Apalachicola, was a place for naval stores and lumber enterprises, and only 15 percent of this "lime sink or cypress pond" region lay in improved lands. Harper guessed that longleaf pines comprised 60 percent of the original stand of timber. These pines in 1914 stood in forests that were "so open that a wagon could be driven through them almost anywhere." Fire burned through the woods nearly every year, assuring the survival of the longleaf.[21]

To the east the floodplain of the Apalachicola provided rich land for farming that, however, could be undertaken only with great peril because of the spring floods; the Apalachicola near the forks sometimes changed its level by thirty feet in a short time. Harper noted that all other Florida rivers originated in the coastal plain but that the Chattahoochee, flowing "out of the hills of Habersham, down the valleys of Hall," came all the way from the Blue Ridge, bearing melting snows of spring thaws. Like many botanists before him, Harper was fascinated with the plant life on the eastern shore of the Apalachicola. Much of it was the same as that in northern climes. On this eastern shore a high ridge extended northward into Georgia along the eastern side of the Flint River, but in Florida tributary streams had cut this ridge into many precipitous valleys. The Apalachicola River on the western side and the rugged topography of this area combined to protect it from fire. Probably, said Harper, it had suffered fewer wildfires than any other part of Florida, and humus lay deep on the forest floor. The botanist-geographer was awed by the high bluffs: "Aspalaga Bluff, in Gadsden County, rises about 175 feet in a distance of a quarter of a mile from the water's edge, and Alum Bluff, in Liberty County, has a very precipitous face about 160 feet high, which is perhaps the most conspicuous topographic feature in all Florida."[22]

East of the steep hills and valleys of Gadsden County were what Harper called the "West Florida Pine Hills," which greatly resembled the pinelands of the Panhandle far to the west and did not offer the best land for farming.[23] In contrast, eastern Gadsden County had excellent land, part of the "Middle Florida Hammock Belt." Here, although longleaf pine still was the dominant tree, Harper found a stronger mixture of shortleaf and old field pines, as well as hardwoods such as magnolias, and there was more farming than in western Gadsden County.[24]

The "Tallahassee Red Hills" in Leon County east of the Ochlockonee, like the Marianna Red Lands in Jackson County, had "richer, redder soils, more hilly topography, [and] a scarcity of longleaf pine" when compared with lands to the east and west. And although Leon County was more hilly than any other place Harper had encountered in Florida, it had "almost no bluffs, ravines or hills too steep for wagons to climb." Gullies were rare and farmers frequently ran furrows up the side of a hill without fear of erosion. The drier uplands appeared to have been covered originally with comparatively open forests of shortleaf pine, red oak, hickory, dogwood, and other hardwoods. On sandier soil near the center of these uplands, there were limited areas of longleaf pine forest. On some hillsides and richer uplands dense forests of hardwoods were found, with a considerable accumulation of humus. Among pine trees, the shortleaf was the most prominent; the old field pine came next. These together might comprise a third of the arboreal cover, while the remaining two-thirds was made up largely of sweetgum, dogwoods, red oaks, live oaks, water oaks, magnolia, wild cherry, hickories, post oaks, and other hardwoods, with hardly a corporal's guard of longleaf pine. Harper found evidence aplenty "that this region has been longer and more extensively cultivated than any other area of the same size in Florida," part of this evidence being the large number of weeds in old fields and on roadsides and railroad rights-of-way. The land had been cultivated by Indians long before the white man came.[25]

The typical vegetation of Leon County's red hills extended over the Georgia line and into Jefferson County. But Harper noted that most of the rolling lands of Jefferson and Madison counties were typical of what he called the "Hammock Belt" of eastern Gadsden County.[26] "Tallahassee Red Hills," the name Harper gave to the 340 square miles of rich lands that were principally in Leon County, was shortened by geologists to "The Tallahassee Hills," which they defined as covering all of the rolling country between the Withlacoochee and the Apalachicola. In this history I treat the Red Hills of Florida as extending across the wide Apalachicola—just as Lanier did in describing Piedmont Florida—to include the old "Chipola country" around Marianna. This hilly region, clinging to the Georgia line for most of its length, seems more like a southern intrusion of the Peach State than a part of the Sunshine State. But although its five Florida counties resemble their neighbors just across the line, they seem even more akin to the Georgia of the Piedmont or to the Red Hills of Georgia that extend from the area of Houston County to Stewart County and then southward along the Chattahoochee River to Early County, Georgia.[27]

Except for the Apalachicola, which runs one hundred miles and empties into the Gulf with a flow of 24,700 cubic feet per second, making it the twenty-third largest river in the United States,[28] this is not a region of large or important rivers. The Withlacoochee on the eastern side and Holmes Creek on the western are tiny streams, while the Suwannee into which the Withlacoochee flows is less than half the size of the Apalachicola.[29] All of the other rivers are small: the Chipola, with headwaters above the Alabama line, flows through Jackson and Calhoun counties before joining the Apalachicola in Gulf County; the Ochlockonee begins its lazy journey in Worth County, Georgia, gains some size from Gadsden County streams, and empties into the west side of Apalachee Bay in a wide estuary. The St. Marks, rising in northeastern Leon County, never reaches a respectable size until, at the Natural Bridge, it is fed by large springs, after which it is joined by the Wakulla before flowing nine more miles to Apalachee Bay. The Aucilla, rising just above the Georgia line and running between Jefferson and Madison counties, becomes a formidable river— at least to cross—only because of the wide swamps along much of its length, then in the lower reaches, below Nuttall Rise, receives some of the waters of the Wacissa to the west. The region is more a country of lakes than rivers, and the Florida Division of Water Resources has counted six hundred that either are named lakes or are as large as ten acres, half of the entire number being in Jackson County. The largest lake of all, Miccosukee, covering 6,226 acres, is shared by Leon and Jefferson counties, while Leon alone has the large lakes Iamonia, Jackson, and Lafayette.[30]

With more hardwood forests than other parts of Florida, the Red Hills also, before the widespread use of fertilizers, enjoyed a reputation for having better soils. Orangeburg sandy loams, found principally on higher ground, and Norfolk soils have been the most favored for crop production and give the area a richness for cultivated crops that has made it the envy of counties to the east and west.[31]

Cooled by the breezes and rains from the Gulf in the subtropical summers and warmed by the Gulf in the frosty winters, with their rich soils, interesting terrain, woods full of game, broad lakes and rivers full of fish, and many crystal springs, the Red Hills of Florida seemed likely to attract a large population, especially of farmers. This they did long before they were discovered by the white man on the journeys of Pánfilo de Narváez and Hernando de Soto in 1528 and 1539.

2

The Nation of
Apalachee, Narváez,
and De Soto

The most popular resort near the Red Hills since the early settlement of Tallahassee has been Wakulla Springs, sixteen miles south of town. Here a tremendous flow from the Floridan Aquifer boils up out of a cave and forms a deep basin, the water then flowing away as a full-sized river to the Gulf. Visitors through the years, including Sidney Lanier, have floated face down on the surface of the basin and on a clear day have been able to follow the descent of a dime one hundred feet to the limestone bottom. Not until a sparkling day in April 1850 did a newcomer to Tallahassee, twenty-year-old Sarah H. Smith of Fayetteville, North Carolina, identify large bones and tusks long seen on the bottom as those of a mastodon.[1] And not until 1930 was the full skeleton of a mastodon retrieved from the bottom. The skeleton was displayed for years in the office of the Florida Geological Survey and was eventually taken apart. It did not see the light of day again until May 1977, when, reassembled and standing eight feet eleven inches high at the shoulder, it was erected near the entrance of the new Museum of Florida History, where it is a formidable presence that sometimes sends frightened youngsters into the arms of their mothers.[2]

No one up to and including Geological Survey Director Herman Gunter, who wrote about the retrieval of the Wakulla skeleton in 1941, associated mastodons with the first presence of man in Florida. However, during the 1930s, discoveries near Clovis, New Mexico, triggered a nationwide effort to date the earliest appearance of man in a locality by his encounter with a mammoth or mastodon. Florida began to figure in this man-and-elephant hunt in 1941 when long, pointed artifacts made of bone or ivory retrieved from the Ichatucknee River, which also abounded in mastodon bones, were found to be "typologically the same" as bone points associated with Clovis kills. Florida appeared to have had big game hunters ten or more millennia ago.[3]

At Silver Springs in Marion County, the archaeologist Wilfred T. Neill found a large "Clovis-like" stone point, the "Suwannee," at the bottom of eight feet of strata marking several prehistoric hunting camps, showing the Suwannee to be the earliest lithic point in Florida and contemporary with the mastodon.[4] Neill then explored the idea that, at a time near the end of the Ice Age when sea level was 80 to 135 feet lower than it is at present (the sea's water being locked up in polar ice), and when the water table was also much lower and watering places fewer, the great springs and sinks of the present lowlands of Florida had been water holes for big game. Mastodons came to them for a drink, and hunters followed for a kill. That Silver Springs did, apparently, provide such a watering place, and was also the resort of ancient hunters, was suggested by the find within a cave of the main spring, in mud on a ledge of the cave near its entrance and thirty-five feet beneath the water surface, of a fragment of a mastodon tooth and a Suwannee point. The ledge would have been above water in ancient times and overlooking a water hole.[5]

Until 1954 Wakulla Cave had never been explored beyond its sunny underwater entrance. In that year six graduate students at Florida State University began an exploration using scuba gear. From a ledge above the cave entrance thirty feet below the surface of the basin, the divers dropped to the floor of the cave 103 feet below the surface. The sandy floor sloped abruptly for 200 feet to a depth of 180, then leveled off at about 200 for the next 300 feet. Large and small fragments of limestone, which had apparently broken off from the high ceiling, littered the floor here. In the litter were found bones of mastodon, sloth, deer, and mammoth, all extinct species from the Ice Age. In the midst of the litter the divers retrieved only a few flint points, including the Suwannee, but there was a vast array of bone points, six hundred of them, and some of these greatly resembled the points from the Ichatucknee River. Near the deposits of animal bones and artifacts they found some charcoal, leading them to call this place "the camp fire."[6]

Unlike the Silver Springs cave, Wakulla Cave appeared to have no part that had been dry land at a time when man could have been there. It was therefore thought that the bones and artifacts had reached their position from the cave-in of a sinkhole—and indeed there is a sinkhole on the surface directly above. Some of the divers, including Garry Salsman and Wally Jenkins, returned to the Springs for dives during the 1960s and 1970s, commuting from their homes in Panama City. Jenkins estimated in 1974 that he had made 160 dives in all. The idea that the bones and artifacts had come from the sinkhole was suddenly dashed one day in 1972. Two divers, carrying heavy weights used to speed the seventy-foot drop at the cave entrance, decided that the water was too murky, dropped their weights twenty feet from the bottom and returned to the basin outside. Before surfacing they saw the normally clear water cloud up suddenly with silt and discovered later that the weights had somehow dislodged an eight-foot vertical section of the cave entrance and a giant landslide had littered the level area inside with sand and additional prehistoric bones and artifacts, along with charcoal, Coke bottles, and pennies. The litter they had found earlier was evidently from an earlier landslide.[7]

It remained for C. J. Clausen and others, continuing the underwater research that interested Neill, to document the presence of Paleo-Indians (although not necessarily mastodon hunters) in Florida as early as 12,000 years ago. Clausen and his colleagues found, deep within a sink called Little Salt Spring in Sarasota County, an extinct giant land tortoise impaled with a pointed wooden stake that was dated by carbon 14 at 12,030 years before the present.[8]

The ancient hunters whose weaponry has been found at Wakulla Springs along with the bones of Ice Age mammals seem not to have been interested in the Red Hills. The same kind of artifacts and bones have been retrieved in equally large numbers by amateur archaeologists from the lower reaches of the Chipola, St. Marks, Wacissa, and Aucilla rivers, all running south of the Red Hills.[9] The only Paleo-Indian site so far recorded in Leon County is the Johnson Sand Pit Site on the edge of the Cody Scarp overlooking a relic channel of the Ochlockonee River.[10] Following the Paleo-Indians were hunters of the Archaic Period, 8000 to 1000 B.C., and although these were somewhat more partial to the Red Hills, their projectile points and camps have been found as frequently in the lowlands.[11]

 After these Indians in this northwestern part of Florida, the first settled communities were along the Gulf coast beginning sometime before the birth of Christ. Except for limited hammock lands near the shores of estuaries, there was no land for farming, and these hunter-gatherers lived on the land animals they hunted, the plant foods they could gather, and the shellfish that abounded in the shallows. The coastal Indians included those of the Weeden Island culture, from between A.D. 400 or 500 to A.D. 900 or 1000, which was subject to several inland influences.[12] Some of the Weeden Islanders had somehow learned enough about corn culture for evidence of this knowledge (an impression of a corncob on an earthen cooking vessel and grains of corn in food wastes) to be found in the house of one family, part of an extensive community, at a site dug in 1973 by Jerald T. Milanich. This, called the Sycamore site, was, significantly, in the middle of the Red Hills. The house stood in the Torreya Ravines that were so dear to Roland Harper, near an abutment of the Interstate 10 bridge over the Apalachicola River, in Gadsden County. The site, carbon-dated to A.D. 860, showed Milanich a connection with "the Cartersville peoples" up the Chattahoochee River Valley in the Georgia Piedmont. There was a "heavy utilization of the natural resources of the Torreya woodlands" habitats that greatly resembled the forested Piedmont, and the site had "only one artifact of coastal origin."[13]

The Weeden Island culture soon disappeared, though, perhaps from the pressures of a growing population that demanded better farming.[14] It was succeeded in the Red Hills by a cultural tradition called the Mississippian that had long exploited the secrets of intensive corn agriculture. This culture was present in the Mississippi Valley by about A.D. 900, having apparently come from Mexico, and rapidly spread westward and eastward. By 1000 A.D. it had reached the Lamar-Macon Plateau in Georgia, and it seems to have appeared in Florida some time between 1000 and 1200 A.D. around the forks of the Chattahoochee and Flint rivers only half a dozen miles north of the oval-shaped Torreya Ravines house. Based on a farm economy that accommodated large populations, a division of labor, and social stratification—with commoners, lords, and a ruling chief who held considerable power—the Mississippian culture was also characterized by territorial federations made up of several towns. Each federation had a central political capital and religious and ceremonial center. Towns were permanent and sometimes large and their most characteristic physical structures, which often remain today, were large earthen mounds of flat-topped pyramidal form, upon which were erected the temples of the priests and rulers and the houses of these important men.[15]

In Florida, this culture gained the name of Fort Walton. Its manifestations have been found far down the Apalachicola River but principally near the large lakes in Leon County, reaching into Jefferson County. There is a mound just to the north of Lake Lafayette, and the highest of all, called the Letchworth mound, just south of Lake Miccosukee at the edge of Jefferson County, stands forty-six feet high. But the principal cluster of mounds is on Lake Jackson, and this was evidently the "capital" of a political and religious federation extending over a considerable area. On the western edge of Meginniss Arm, just north of Tallahassee, the Lake Jackson complex originally had seven mounds, six of the ceremonial type. There is evidence of a trade in whelk and other shells from the Lake Jackson site that circulated through a broad Mississippian region extending from Etowah in Georgia to Spiro in Oklahoma. Lake Jackson was at the southeastern corner of this vast complex and only a thirty-mile walk straight down what later became the Shell Point Road to the sandy and shell-laden beaches of the Gulf.[16]

The principal mound, now in a state park, is 36 feet high and measures 213 by 157 feet at the base. The level top measures 100 feet across. From this elevation lookouts could scan the southern half of Lake Jackson and communicate with a smaller mound across the lake at Rollins Point, which had the remainder of the lake in view. Gordon R. Willey made a preliminary dig at Lake Jackson in 1940, and John Griffin a dig in 1947. Griffin noticed enough difference in the pottery to show that a cultural change had been under way while the mounds were in use.[17]

In 1975–1976 another dig was made, under the following circumstances. A friend called the archaeologist B. Calvin Jones about a copper artifact found in some fill dirt that had just been placed on his Tallahassee yard. The artifact proved to be a small copper ceremonial axe head, or celt. It was traced to dirt that had come from a sixteen-foot-high mound on private property that the owner was beginning to raze. Jones obtained permission to dig the mound and did so between November 1975 and February 1976. He dug through twelve successive floors of wooden houses below which were graves of priests or chieftains who had apparently lived in the houses and who wore all of the paraphernalia of their rank into the grave. Pieces of logs showed carbon-14 dates from about A.D. 1200 to 1500. Five skeletons in the deepest graves wore copper breastplates embossed with a dancing human figure identical to that found at Etowah, while copper celts suggested Spiro. The Lake Jackson assemblage connected the Indians here unmistakably with the "Southern Cult," or ceremonial complex, that accompanied the Mississippian culture through the Southeast.[18]

The mound-building Indians after three hundred years suddenly disappeared, as though from a devastating military defeat. Did commoners, or minor barons, dictate their Magna Charta and then depose the lords of the mounds? Did a strike (in a very literal sense) of their shell workers and carriers undermine their economy? Whatever happened, by the time the Spaniards—having completed the conquest of Mexico and having begun that of Peru—had arrived to begin the conquest of Florida, these Indians' place in the Red Hills had been taken by a tribe called the Apalachee. Chroniclers of the expeditions of Pánfilo de Narváez in 1528 and Hernando de Soto in 1539–1540 and missionaries after them have left descriptions of the Apalachee. We know more about these Indians than we do about any of their predecessors.[19]

Members of the Muskhogean linguistic family, the Apalachee settled on the uplands between the Ochlockonee River and Aucilla River. On the north, their farms and habitations appear not to have extended much, if at all, farther than the Georgia line. On the south, their towns, or those allied with them, went to the Gulf coast, but the lowland towns were few in number, limited to hammock lands that would support the culture of corn, beans, and squash. The province of Apalachee was largely confined to the highlands of just two present-day Florida counties, Leon and Jefferson.[20]

The Apalachee were ruled by chiefs and nobles as their predecessors had been. Yet the Apalachee had little of the love for display, luxury, and ceremony that was exhibited by the royalty of Lake Jackson, and rather than building on mounds, they placed the houses of their chiefs on natural hilltops, where many of their towns were also located. Archaeological evidence confirms that the Apalachee built their houses and towns on higher elevations.[21]

Each of the towns had its own chief, or cacique, who lived off the tribute paid by the farmers of the neighborhood. The Catholic bishop of Cuba, Gabriel Díaz Vara Calderón, visited Apalachee in 1674–1675 and wrote: "In April they commence to sow, and as the man goes along opening the trench, the woman follows sowing. All in common cultivate and sow the lands of the caciques."[22] Early Spanish friars considering the missionization of Apalachee estimated the population at 30,000 or 34,000, and there were said to be 107 towns. Some ethnologists consider these estimates much inflated, but Milanich and Charles H. Fairbanks believe that the population of Apalachee at the time of first European contact was "at least 25,000."[23]

Houses of the common people were round, built of poles and thatched with palmetto leaves or grass, with a door only 2.8 feet high. Inside was a raised shelf along the wall which was used as a bed, "with a bear skin laid upon it and without any cover, the fire they build in the center of the house serving in place of a blanket." Outside the house a granary "supported by twelve beams" was used to store the corn crop. The plaza of the mounds people survived, and the principal building in every considerable village was the council house. Constructed of wood and covered with straw, "round, with a very large opening in the top," it was a public building built to accommodate two thousand to three thousand persons, said the bishop. "They are furnished all around the interior with niches called *barbacoas*, which serve as beds and seats for the caciques and chiefs, and as lodgings for soldiers and transients. Dances and festivals are held in them around a great fire in the center. The missionary priest attends these festivities in order to prevent indecent and lewd conduct, and they last until the bell strikes the hour of *las ánimas*."[24] The extraordinary size of the council houses was confirmed in a 1985 archaeological dig by Gary Shapiro at San Luis in present Tallahassee. Shapiro found evidence of a round structure 120 feet in diameter. Some of the support poles were twenty inches thick and had been inserted 6 feet into the ground.[25]

Corn was the principal crop of the Apalachee, and like Central Americans, they used alkali cooking techniques that made the small amount of the protein lysine in corn available. "Their ordinary diet consists of porridge which they make of corn with ashes, pumpkins, beans which they call *frijoles*, with game and fish from the rivers and lakes," wrote the touring bishop in 1675. The beans, fish, and meat—the last taken in winter hunts—provided additional protein for a larder that depended principally on corn.[26] The most notable of all their accomplishments was their horticulture, which, according to Bishop Calderón, was sufficient in 1675 to supply the several hundred residents of St. Augustine, who could produce but little corn in the nearby sands and then only with much labor. "Thus the inhabitants are compelled regularly to depend for their sustenance upon the products of the province of Apalache," he said.[27]

Pánfilo de Narváez, the first European to explore Florida, never discovered the abundance of Apalachee's farm economy, for he never quite reached the Red Hills. He did, however, discover another noteworthy characteristic of the Apalachee, namely a fierce determination to defend their homeland against any outsiders daring to trespass on it. Narváez and three hundred men, with forty-two horses, landed at Tampa Bay on 14 April 1528. Hearing about "a province called Apalachen in which there was much gold" as well as food, Narváez led a march across the flatwoods up the Florida peninsula. On 25 June the expedition came to a town called Apalachen, but it was a miserable little place of forty houses in the midst of dense woods and large lakes. The country thereabouts was nothing like the fertile farmland the Spaniards expected, nor was there any gold, yet when they inquired of the natives they were told that Apalachen was the most populous town of the province and that to the north the land was "little occupied" and full of "great lakes, dense forests, immense deserts and solitudes." But, said the natives, toward the south was the town of Aute, "the inhabitants whereof had much maize, beans and pumpkins, and being near the sea they had fish."[28]

It is difficult to guess where Apalachen was, but plainly it was in the lowlands, perhaps in the vicinity of the former community of Walker Springs about eight miles south of Lamont, a town only allied with Apalachee or an outlying village. On the journey of nine days that the party now took to the west and south, the Spaniards evidently never saw the Cody Scarp that marked virtually the southern boundary of Apalachee. The journey led across territory so wild and difficult that even the Indians shunned it. At the outset, though, the warriors of Apalachee, probably from the great town of Ivitachuco on the edge of Iamonia Lake, came out to interdict their passage across a chest-deep lake and impressed the Spaniards with their military prowess. Said the account of Alvar Nuñez Cabeza de Vaca: "Some of our men were wounded in this conflict, for whom the good armor they wore did not avail." The Indians' bows were as thick as the arm and these "they will discharge at two hundred paces with so great precision that they miss nothing."[29]

Aute, the objective of their journey, appears to have been in the vicinity of Wakulla Springs or Crawfordville. They did not tarry here, but hopeful of being picked up by one of the five vessels that had been dismissed after the landing at Tampa Bay, they pitched their camp on the edge of an inlet of Apalachee Bay, probably Oyster Bay. Hopes of a rescue dimmed through the summer, and fifty men died of hunger or disease, others from the arrows of Indians. Finally the men, killing one of the ten remaining horses every third day for food and using their skin for water bottles and their tails and manes for ropes and rigging, built five crude rafts in which they set out from what came to be called the Bahía de Caballos for the Mexican coast. Only four survivors arrived, eight years later, in the settlements around Mexico City.[30]

The next explorer, Hernando De Soto, one of the principal lieutenants of Francisco Pizarro in the conquest of Peru, landed with six hundred men and three hundred horses on the last day of May 1539, not far from the place where Narváez had landed at Tampa Bay. Like Narváez, De Soto headed for Apalachee, but his route lay more inland, along a ridge of highlands that is today called "the lake country" and that in 1539 supported several prosperous towns of the Timucuan

Hernando De Soto, the first European to visit the Red Hills, wintered in 1539–40 at a site in the middle of present Tallahassee. (From an eighteenth-century engraving, courtesy of Florida State Archives)

confederation. Unlike Narváez, De Soto encountered large populations and found bitter opposition from these agricultural tribes before ever reaching Apalachee.[31]

After De Soto crossed the Suwannee, he clearly entered the Red Hills of Florida (as Narváez had not). The entry into these lands that rise in Madison County from the low pinelands to the south and east

is signaled in the account of Rodrigo Ranjel, De Soto's private secretary, who reported that they "passed by a high mountain."[32] In
the deserted town of Osachile, the principal settlement of a Timucuan
province that is often called Yustaga, in the vicinity of Sampala Lake,
were found good supplies of maize, beans, and pumpkins, produce
that was more in evidence here than anywhere else the Spaniards
had been in Florida.[33] The Spaniards had heard of the fertility of
Apalachee and of the military prowess of its warriors, who "would
shoot them with arrows, quarter, burn and destroy them." It was
now late in September and the Spaniards were determined to press
on toward Apalachee "and if it were as fertile as it had been represented, to pass the winter there."[34] Crossing an unpopulated wilderness lying between Yustaga and Apalachee, they came to the Asile
(Aucilla) River. The army aimed for Asile, a town that one chronicler,
Luys Hernandez de Biedma, factor of the expedition, described as
being "on the confines of Apalachee"[35] and another, Ranjel, as being
"subject to Apalachee."[36] Archaeological evidence seems to indicate
that Asile, at least in later mission times, stood on the western side
of the river about four miles south of present Lamont.[37] Somewhere
in this vicinity De Soto made his crossing. The rains had swollen the
river, normally with a forty-foot channel, and it was now more than
a mile wide, spreading across the forest on both sides.[38]

The Spaniards camped at Ivitachuco, whose inhabitants had fled,
leaving the town burning. On the next morning, the army set out for
Iniahica, the principal town of Apalachee, traveling through "great
fields of corn, beans, squash and other vegetables which had been
sown on both sides of the road and were spread out as far as the eye
could see across two leagues of the plain."[39]

Garcilaso reported there was a last-ditch stand of the Apalachee at
a "deep ravine filled with water,"and it was four leagues (10.4 miles)
from this point to Iniahica.[40] This, the site of De Soto's winter encampment of 1539–1540, has been known to have been in or near
Tallahassee, but only in March 1987 was the first archaeological evidence found to mark the site. B. Calvin Jones discovered a single tiny
link of chain mail in a test hole and during an intensive dig in the
spring and summer located several hundred others, fourteen of them
still forming a tiny piece of armor. The dig uncovered the foundations
of a building measuring twenty-eight by thirty feet that appeared to
be of European construction. It was rectangular, while the Indians
built round houses, but unlike the later mission churches and convents, it apparently lacked hinges, locks or other hardware, or white-
wash, all of which were used in the missions. Quantities of olive jar

Archaeologist B. Calvin Jones, who discovered the Spanish site on Lafayette Street, was about to complete a dig in July 1987 before bulldozers cleared the way for an office complex. (Photo by Clifton Paisley)

sherds were found in and around the building and were thinner walled than the olive jars of later mission times. In July a copper four-maravedi piece minted near the time of King Ferdinand and Queen Isabella was found, followed by several other coins and by the one-and-a-half-inch iron point of a crossbow bolt. Quantities of blown glass beads used in early sixteenth-century trade with the Indians, along with faceted chevron beads with tints of red, white, and blue, were also found. Fragments of human skeletons were found, bones of pigs (the Spaniards drove a herd of pigs), and in a contemporary cistern the tooth of a horse.[41]

The site, on Lafayette Street a mile east of Florida's capitol, had been chosen for an office complex whose construction was postponed while the dig went on. In July, bulldozers moved onto one part of the dig, and a concrete floor was soon in place. In September the archaeologists had to move away from the acre or more of land reserved for the office complex. The site is on a ridge of land two hundred feet above sea level that forms a watershed between the St. Marks and Wakulla rivers, in a heavily built-over part of Tallahassee. Jones is convinced that this is the site of Iniahica and that in traveling to it De Soto took a route to the south of Lake Lafayette.[42] Probably he traveled along U.S. 27 and the Old St. Augustine Road. If so, and if the St. Marks River is the "deep ravine," the distance, 10.7 miles, closely matches Garcilaso's 10.4 miles. Interestingly, a mile or so east of the site high red clay banks mark the location of a mid-nineteenth-century plantation called "De Soto."[43]

Iniahica was ideally located for the principal town of the Apalachee. From it the Indians could walk straight south to the juncture of the St. Marks and Wakulla rivers and the "fishing near the sea" that they enjoyed. In no hurry to reveal this route to the Europeans, the Indians directed the Spaniards to reach the sea by way of Aute, the town visited by Narváez. The Spaniards therefore traveled along "a very excellent road, both wide and flat"—apparently the same one used by the mounds people in pursuit of their shell business, following today's Crawfordville, Wakulla, and Shell Point roads to the edge of Apalachee Bay. Here the party led by Captain Juan de Añasco came on Narváez's unhappy encampment, still marked after eleven years by skulls and headpieces of horses, charcoal from a forge, logs carved as mortars, and a few crosses carved on trees.[44]

The Spaniards left their winter camp in March 1540. Throughout their journey across the South, members of the De Soto expedition recalled "the bellicose province of Apalachee."[45] Garcilaso's final tribute to the horticultural skill of the Apalachee was his statement that

Among hundreds of artifacts that marked the site as that of De Soto's encampment in the principal town of the Apalachee Indians, Iniahica, were a four-maravedi piece, the iron point of a crossbow bolt, and many links of chain mail. (Florida Division of Historical Resources)

the whole Spanish army, along with their Indian servants, fifteen hundred persons, and more than three hundred horses, during the five months' encampment "fed upon the foods which they gathered when they first arrived there; and when they needed more, they found it in neighboring hamlets in such quantity that they never went so far as a league and a half [four miles] from the principal village to obtain it."[46]

3

The Cross
in the Hills

For nearly a century after the departure of De Soto from Iniahica, Spain ignored Apalachee, "tierra fertil y de gran cosecha de maiz y otras cosas." St. Augustine was settled in 1565, and missions were set up in the hinterland of this presidio.[1] The missionaries, of the Franciscan Order, were full of Christian zeal, not only to win converts but to see that these converts followed a strict code of conduct. "Being pregnant, have you killed the unborn child or wished to kill it by taking some drink or striking yourself or squeezing your belly to choke it as you used to do?" read a confessionario used by the friars in Timucua. "Have you some [black female] slave or servant as your mistress?" The Franciscans were also anxious to stamp out every vestige of heathenish superstition. The confessionario proposed asking: "Have you believed that when the blue jay or another bird sings, that it is a signal that people are coming or that something important is about to happen?"[2]

Yet while opposing magic and superstition, some of the friars were quick to believe in miraculous occurrences when these promoted the Christian faith. Fray Martín Prieto traveled in 1606 to Potano, the Timucuan district in the neighborhood of present Gainesville, preaching the word of God and erecting churches where there had been only one convert before he arrived. At the town of Santa Anna, Prieto insisted on visiting a very old cacique who as a boy had been captured and held by De Soto and thus had acquired a lifetime hatred of Spaniards and Christians. When Prieto went into his house, the old man lost his temper and ordered him beaten and thrown out. Prieto related ten years later: "At that moment there was a thunderclap . . . , accompanied by so strong a wind that . . . there remained neither a house nor a barn standing. . . . Only a cross and a church in which mass had been said remained standing." Within six days he baptized

this chief and four hundred other persons.[3] Prieto now carried the
gospel to Utina north of this district. Utina then being at war with
Apalachee one hundred miles to the west, Father Prieto determined
to go to Apalachee to end the conflict; he would carry the gospel
there. In the middle of July 1608 he set out, accompanied by 150
Indians from Potano and Utina. The cacique of Ivitachuco, the most
important among seventy chiefs who had assembled in this town,
along with a large number of other Indians, agreed to the peace plan.
The missionary and the delegation from Potano and Utina were guests
for six days. When they left, the Apalachee instructed the chief of
Iniahica to accompany them to St. Augustine "and in the name of
all, give obedience to the governor" as the representative of the king.[4]

But not until 15 November 1633 was Florida governor Luis de Horruytiner able to inform the king that two friars, Pedro Múñoz and
Francisco Martínez, had entered Apalachee on 16 October and
founded the first mission.[5] Governor Horruytiner soon encountered
the problem of relaying supplies to missionaries who were nearly two
hundred miles away from St. Augustine. Although Apalachee had
an abundance of corn, Spanish friars much preferred wheat flour,
which could be made into the bread familiar to them in Spain.[6] There
were other things to transport also. As Franciscans, the friars were
obligated to live on alms, and since Florida had no gold or any other
wealth, the King had decreed that each was to receive from royal
funds three reales a day in clothing, medicine, and other necessities
along with wine and other furnishings for the mass. The friars called
these "the alms which your majesty gives us."[7] At first the supplies
were carried by Indians on their shoulders, but in 1637 Horruytiner
sent a *fragata* to Cuba, where it was loaded with needed supplies.
The ship's arrival in Apalachee Bay gave great pleasure not only to
the friars but also to the Indians, who celebrated with fiestas.[8] However, in 1639 Apalachee with its rich grain and vegetable fields became
more of a supplier than a receiver of necessities; with St. Augustine
suffering one of its frequent food shortages that year, a fragata sailed
from the presidio to Apalachee Bay, eight hundred miles away, and
returned with corn and other edibles. Thereafter St. Augustine came
to depend on Apalachee for much of its food supply.[9]

Apalachee still had only two friars as late as 1639, but there were
one thousand converts. There was one very notable conversion that
year, of the cacique of Cupahica, lord of two hundred vassals. This
cacique went to St. Augustine to be baptized and took the Christian
name Balthazar. He returned to Apalachee with a Franciscan father
who may have founded the mission of San Damian de Cupahica, later

called Escambi, whose site has been found a mile west of the Old Bainbridge Road near Tallahassee along the side of Interstate 10.[10] Possibly at this time, and certainly within a few years, San Luis de Talimali, the headquarters of the mission system of Apalachee, was founded as a mission. San Luis and Cupahica appeared on a list of the nine Apalachee missions in 1655.[11]

San Luis stood on a high hill two miles south of Cupahica and about the same distance west of present uptown Tallahassee. On the western edge of Apalachee, San Luis overlooked the valley of the Ochlockonee River, standing guard against danger from the west. At the same time it was near the sea approaches through what became the port of St. Marks, which was already being visited by vessels from St. Augustine and Havana. While Iniahica, the one-time capital of Apalachee, was directly north of St. Marks, San Luis was three miles west of Iniahica and was reached from the port by a road slanting a little to the west of north, even as the St. Marks–Tallahassee road runs today. In mission times St. Marks was also connected with San Luis by a secret canoe route. This proceeded up the Wakulla River and thence to within a few miles of San Luis, as indicated by a remnant stream valley that today links Lake Munson with the Wakulla.[12]

Missions were established in the western part of Timucua, about the same time as in Apalachee, and by 1675 these, in Madison County, included San Pedro y San Pablo de Potohiriba, Santa Elena de Machaba, and San Mateo de Tolapatafi. Another mission was established on the Asile River. Mark F. Boyd, a transplanted native of St. Paul, Minnesota, who came to Tallahassee in the 1930s, compiled Spanish documentary sources and began a search for the Apalachee missions, of which there were thirteen in 1675. Until he began his studies, only the site of San Luis in the present city of Tallahassee was known. The archaeologist B. Calvin Jones, using documents provided by Boyd, established most of the other locations in archaeological digs during the late 1960s and 1970s.[13]

In 1675, at the time of a visit by Gabriel Díaz Vara Calderón, bishop of Cuba, the Apalachee mission chain stretched westward from San Lorenzo de Ivitachuco, with a population of 1,200 (but a one-time population of 2,500) on Iamonia Lake, almost on the edge of the Cody Scarp.[14] The next mission to the west was Nuestra Señora de la Purisssima Concepción de Ayubale (800) two miles south of present-day Waukeenah.[15] The missions continued in present Jefferson County, with San Francisco de Oconi (200), San Juan de Aspalaga (800), and San Joseph de Ocuya (900). The last was near the crossing of Burnt Mill Creek by U.S. Highway 27, some three miles north of the com-

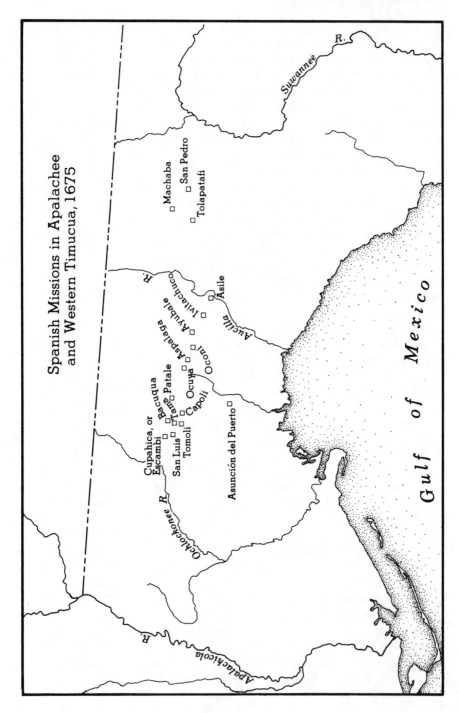

Spanish Missions in Apalachee
and Western Timucua, 1675

Suwannee R.

Machaba
San Pedro
Tolapatafi

Ivitachuco R.

Asile
Ayubale
Aspalaga
Occoni
Cupahica, or
Escambi
Bacuqua
Tame Patale
Ocuya
San Luis
Capoli
Tomoli

Asunción del Puerto

Aucilla

Ochlockonee R.

Apalachicola R.

Gulf of Mexico

munity of Cody, for which the Cody Scarp was named. The sites of Aspalaga and Ocuya were on the early American road that is now called "the Old St. Augustine Road."[16]

If the line of missions had continued westward in Leon County along this road, it would have reached San Luis, the principal mission, by a route south of Lake Lafayette. Instead the line now bent sharply to the northwest, heading north of Lake Lafayette. In ten miles was San Pedro y San Pablo de Patale (500) on a beautiful hilltop on Buck Lake Road. The mission line now traveled due west along the line of present Buck Lake Road and Tharpe Street, passing San Antonio de Bacuqua (120) in five miles and coming in five more to Cupahica, or Escambi (900), just to the north of this line and San Luis (1,400) just to the south of it. San Luis was connected directly with St. Augustine by the St. Augustine Road and was also in communication with a cluster of four nearby missions, these being south of Lake Lafayette.[17]

According to Jones, the largest and most prominent building in a mission compound was the church, typically thirty-five by seventy feet in dimensions. The convents were a third as large, both being of rectangular construction, these buildings rising, as did houses of the Apalachee Indians, from a floor of sun- or fire-hardened red clay. Walls of churches and convents were built of "wattle and daub"— mud or plaster applied to a lattice frame between the wooden posts supporting the roof—and the roof was gabled and thatched. The churches and convents were European in appearance, constructed with iron nails, hinges, and locks, and the structures were white-washed, so that they stood out on a hilltop, on which also spread the surrounding village of low, thatched houses.[18] The churches and convents were the centers not only of religious study and worship but of instruction in the Spanish language and Spanish arts.

As important as these were the great council houses, sometimes just across the town plaza, where Indian law and Indian tradition held sway. San Luis was acquired by the state of Florida in 1984. The first discovery in an archaeological dig there was the foundations of a council house. The council house on the other, eastern, side of Apalachee at Ivitachuco must have been even more impressive, the meeting place no doubt of the great assembly that witnessed the peace pact between Apalachee and Utina in 1608.[19]

At the time of Calderón's visit, the Florida missions were in their Golden Age. Two-thirds of the 13,152 Christian Indians in Florida were in Apalachee, the others in Timucua and Guale to the east. Everywhere the Spanish friars had succeeded in converting the Indians to the Christian faith and also in teaching them the Spanish language and Spanish arts. But the Spaniards made a series of mistakes, particularly in Apalachee, that, combined with English rivalry for empire, resulted in the destruction of the Apalachee missions only three-quarters of a century after their founding in 1633.

The first blunder occurred in 1647, when Governor Benito Ruíz de Salazar Vallecilla established his short-lived "Asile hacienda and wheat and maize farm" in the vicinity of the town of Asile. The cacique of Asile would never have tolerated this farm except that, as critical friars pointed out, "the powerful hand of the governor" lay behind it. Cows trampled Indian crops, and the principal enterprise, the cultivation of wheat, was almost impossible in the Red Hills, as American experience showed through the mid-twentieth century. The principal complaint against the enterprise was that Indians were used as burden bearers, carrying heavy tools and equipment from St. Augustine. A bloody revolt broke out in Apalachee. Seven of the eight churches and convents were burned, and three friars were killed. The deputy governor in command of soldiers in Apalachee was also killed, along with his family. The Spaniards garroted twelve leaders of the rebellion and condemned many others to forced labor in St. Augustine.[20]

The penalty of having to work without pay on the St. Augustine castillo—a series of wooden forts that always seemed to need repair and a stone one that needed to be built—was applied freely to delinquents. Even when the work was for pay, the wages were as little as one real a day, and hunger, disease, and frequently death accompanied assignment to St. Augustine. The Indians, particularly in the western pueblos, detested this work because they had to abandon their own crops and leave their families, sometimes for as long as a year. They dreaded the long trip to St. Augustine, a journey of from 170 to 220 miles if they traveled from Apalachee, always on foot and frequently with their food supply on their backs, for St. Augustine was nearly always short of food.

The issue of carrying loads to St. Augustine resulted in a second revolt in 1657, this one in Timucua. This rebellion hardly touched Apalachee, although during the eight months it continued, the friars in Apalachee, greatly alarmed, fought the St. Augustine establishment with condemnation and a dose of civil disobedience. The revolt was brutally put down, and eleven chiefs were executed.[21]

In addition to providing cheap labor, the Indians of Apalachee increasingly took on the duties of "surrogate Spaniards" with military assignments. As Herbert Bolton, the great historian of the Spanish borderlands, said of the colonial and mission policy adopted by Spain: "Lacking Spaniards to colonize the frontier, she would colonize it

Beads often were the most valuable possessions of Apalachee mission Indians in graves like these in church cemeteries extensively dug by archaeologists in the 1970s. (Courtesy of B. Calvin Jones)

with the aborigines."[22] The Indians of Apalachee became a Spanish militia, seeing some practice as soldiers in settling some of their own disputes. In 1677 they traced to the Chiscas (Euchee) living one hundred miles to the west some misdeeds by roving bands, and 30 arquebusiers and 160 archers attacked the Chisca stockade in the middle of the night, not even sparing women and small children.[23]

In the late seventeenth century, though, the Indians' principal military duty became taking the field for the glory of the king in a war of empire with the English. The English settled Jamestown, Virginia, in 1607 and in 1670 came dangerously close to Florida missions by founding Charles Town, South Carolina. The English there established a trade with the Creek Indians, settled in several villages at the falls of the Chattahoochee River, only about one hundred miles from Apalachee. The Spaniards, claiming this territory as their own, now attempted to missionize the Creeks, but when four Creek towns showed their unwillingness to have missions, a rash Spanish commander, Lieutenant Antonio Matheos, burned these towns. Now there was a wholesale desertion of the Apalachicolas—the Spanish name for the Lower Creeks. Many Creeks now moved across present

Georgia to the Ocmulgee River, and the area became the center for slave taking and other raids on Florida mission villages.[24]

Meanwhile the Spaniards strengthened their Florida defenses against this increasing presence of San Jorge, as they called the Charles Town establishment. There had been several wooden forts at St. Augustine, and in 1672 work began on the great stone castillo. This construction was only another aggravation for the Apalachee, three hundred of whom were sometimes housed there to work on the fort. The Spanish also built a wooden fort of sorts at the forks of the St. Marks and Wakulla rivers, whitewashed so that it would resemble a stone fort. This ruse did not fool a pirate band that, on the night of 20 March 1682, sent two pirogues ashore and surprised the few Spaniards there, captured and held them for a fortnight, looted and then burned the fort, and in a leisurely manner sailed out to sea.[25]

Finally the Spaniards in 1696–1697 built a blockhouse of massive timbers at San Luis de Talimali. It was surrounded by a high palisade wall with a moat outside. On top of the blockhouse the Spaniards installed eight cannon. The work turned this headquarters village of the Apalachee missions into a strong outpost. Palisade walls were built around some other missions, making these also defensible. Even in the building of the blockhouse the Spaniards blindly continued to offend and mistreat the Indians. The peons cut and hauled the big logs to the mission hilltop and provided the labor to build the blockhouse, whose construction dragged on for months. Since they had "volunteered" their labor, they were paid nothing for the work. They were merely provided with tools and the corn necessary to sustain them.[26]

Meanwhile permission had been given a few favored families in the St. Augustine bureaucracy to establish cattle ranches in Apalachee, particularly the San Luis area. These ranchers particularly irritated the Apalachee. Creoles, *hidalgos* whose salaries as treasury officials did not support the lifestyle demanded of the gentlemanly class, these ranchers became Florida's landed gentry. The Florencia family and its in-laws and friends were the principal operators of the nine ranches in Apalachee. Descended from a Portuguese pilot who came to Florida in 1591, the family provided most of the deputy governors assigned to Apalachee. One of them was killed with his family in the 1647 revolt. The Florencias considered Apalachee "a private fief."[27]

According to a complaint addressed on 12 February 1699 to the king by Don Patricio de Hinachuba of Ivitachuco, principal cacique of Apalachee, and Don Andrés, the cacique of San Luis, Indians after completing their work on the fort were kept busy, still without pay, building houses for Diego and Francisco Florencia, brothers-in-law of the lieutenant governor in command at San Luis, Captain Jacinto Roque Pérez, who with other Spanish settlers lorded it over them on the ranches.

As for Pérez, said they: "We receive considerable injury to our fields from his cattle, as well as from those of Diego Florencia and Francisco Florencia, his brothers-in-law, who reside with him." Moreover, Juana Caterina, wife of Pérez, and sister of the Florencias, "gave two slaps in the face to the cacique of the Indians of San Luis, because he had not brought her fish on one Friday, and obliged the village to furnish six Indian women for the grinding every day without payment for their work." She also wanted an Indian to come every day with a pitcher of milk for the house of Pérez.[28]

The same group of well-connected *criollos* had so angered the chief of the village of Tama, a skilled tanner, that he had fled and joined the English at San Jorge; the Spanish had required him to prepare skins for them without paying him. Everywhere the Apalachee were running away, many of them to San Jorge, to escape from the oppression of the ranchers, whose cattle were frequently in the villages, "with no effort to remove them to their ranches."[29]

Yet these Apalachee, irritated by mistreatment and now only half loyal to the Spanish cause, were those sent out, some armed only with bow and arrow, against the gun-carrying allies of the English, to punish raids on Timucua that were being made with ever greater frequency. After one such raid in 1702, eight hundred Apalachee set out with a few Spanish infantrymen under the command of Captain Don Francisco de Uriza to attack the Apalachicola. English allies learned of the plan and led five hundred Apalachicola to a big bend of the Flint River (then called the Pedernales), surprised the Florida invaders, routed them, and sent the survivors back to Apalachee.[30]

By this time the succession of the Spanish crown from a Hapsburg to a Bourbon, Philip of Anjou, had touched off a war that in Europe was called the War of the Spanish Succession, lasting from 1701 to 1713. Spain's old enemy France, finally settling on the Gulf coast, now became a somewhat wary ally of Spain as well as the principal rival of San Jorge. The Spaniards and French now planned military actions against the English, but the Carolinians struck next. Governor James Moore of South Carolina led an expedition by sea against the Spanish presidio St. Augustine. Unsuccessful in this, Moore raised another large force in December 1703 at his own expense, crossed south-western Georgia, and entered Apalachee.[31]

Following somewhat the route of U.S. 19, Moore's party of fifty whites and one thousand or more Creek Indians crossed almost the entire extent of the Red Hills from north to south without being de-tected and at dawn on 25 January 1704 entered the mission village of Ayubale, some twenty-three miles east of San Luis. The English took a position beside the great council house and stockade. No Spanish soldier was around, but the brave young parish priest, Fray Angel de Miranda, mobilized a force barely numbering fifty Indians in the church, with as many women and children also present. Assault after assault was made against the door but Miranda held out for nine hours, until his ammunition was exhausted. After that the church was burned and the priest and his small army captured. On the fol-lowing day Moore's forces had a much easier time defeating a force of thirty Spaniards and four hundred Apalachee Indians who arrived from San Luis.[32]

Altogether the Spanish and Apalachee forces in two days lost more than two hundred dead and wounded. The worst fate of all was reserved for forty Indian defenders who, over the protest of Father Miranda, were tied to stakes and burned to death by Indians of Moore's party. Most were burned quickly, but a worse fate was re-served for such leaders as Antonio Acuipa Feliciano and Luis Dom-ingo of San Luis, who, according to one witness, were burned "little by little" all day. After resting from the battle Moore now visited at least half a dozen other Indian villages, five of which were destroyed. Ivitachuco, according to his account, purchased its freedom with the church plate. Moore's biggest haul was in prisoners, including many women and children who were taken as slaves. By his own account Moore's losses in men killed were only four whites and fifteen In-dians.[33]

The stronghold of San Luis still stood, however, and Ivitachuco, Patale, Escambi, and Aspalaga were still intact. The province had been given such a scare, however, that there were now many more de-sertions. Fulano, an Indian of the village of Patale, was one of the deserters. He five months later assisted a second party of Carolina raiders that consisted entirely or almost entirely of Creek Indians. Fulano led some of these to the door of the Patale convent on the night of 23 June 1704. He called out to the padre in charge, Fray Manuel de Mendoza, in a familiar voice: "Good, you may open,

Father. . . . We will do you no harm." Mendoza came to a window, opened it, and was killed by a gunshot. The invading force then burned the convent, captured villagers, and encamped on the site to prepare for raids in the next few days on other missions, even San Luis.[34]

Adjutant Manuel Solano, now in charge at San Luis, led forty-three Spaniards, ninety-three Indians armed with guns, and sixty Indians armed with bows and arrows on an expedition to Patale on the night of 3 July. A force from Ivitachuco was to meet them a league away from Patale, but this force had not arrived when the fighting began the next day. There was a wholesale retreat of the San Luis force and many were captured. Spanish soldiers were among the seventeen persons who were bound to stations of the cross in Patale and set afire.[35]

Of the burning of Balthazar Francisco, a soldier from the Canary Islands, one witness reported: "They cut out his tongue and eyes, cut off his ears, scalped him, and put a crown on him, which in Indian style is placed on the Indian warriors when they dance . . . , slashed him all over and placed burning splinters in the wounds; and as soon as they set him afire, they mocked and insulted him, laughing on hearing what the said Balthazar Francisco told the pagans in the Spanish and Apalachian languages while he called on the Most Holy Virgin to help him."[36]

Although the San Luis blockhouse had never been attacked during the two raids, the Spaniards burned it and left. Missionaries deserted whatever missions remained, and surviving Apalachee resettled near St. Augustine or traveled westward to Pensacola and Mobile. Those traveling east included the principal chief of Apalachee and headman of Ivitachuco, Don Patricio de Hinachuba, and all of his village. As Amy Bushnell described him in an article lovingly entitled "Patricio de Hinachuba: Defender of the Word of God, the Crown of the King, and the Little Children of Ivitachuco," this prince of Apalachee emerges as the first hero of the Red Hills. He was, she said, "a devout son of the Church who did not let the friar run his town, a brave captain who fought no unnecessary battle, and a loyal supporter of the Crown whom the Spanish could not take for granted." But Hinachuba and his party were harassed by bands of the English allies the Creeks, and soon they were all dead.[37]

A week and two days after the battle of Patale, a council of war at St. Augustine reported that the Apalachee, who had recently numbered eight thousand in fourteen villages, were now reduced to only two hundred persons, and these wished to leave. Neighboring parts of Timucua were depopulated by raids during the next few years. The Red Hills became a deserted place, with only the ruins of villages and mission compounds, along with the "old fields" of Apalachee horticulture, to mark the place where there had once been a prosperous province.[38]

4

The Old Fields
of Apalachee

When Lieutenant Diego Peña traveled from St. Augustine to the Lower Creek country in 1716, he did not encounter a soul in Apalachee. However, the destruction of the missions had brought an unfamiliar animal, the bison, even to the once populous San Luis area where, on the shore of Lake Jackson, his party also encountered many cattle from the one-time ranches. A melancholy note entered the soldier's journal as his party crossed Ivitachuco Swamp and visited the ruins of Ayubale and Patale. The final downfall of Apalachee occurred at Patale. When Peña reached the hilltop here on 6 September, he noted that at this spot "the Rev. Father Fray Manuel de Mendoza sacrificed his life." The last Spaniards to visit Patale before Peña had evidently been in a search party that, following the battle of 4 July 1704, found Mendoza's body "beneath a fragment of mud wall and burned wattle" of the convent. In 1971 when archaeologist B. Calvin Jones dug the ruins of Patale, a student assistant uncovered a long beam just, perhaps, as it had fallen on or been lifted off the body of Father Mendoza.[1]

Peña's instructions were to invite Creeks who had returned to their old homeland on the Chattahoochee to come to Apalachee and establish villages. There was reason to believe that some would be interested in doing so, for they had now been defeated and humiliated by the English in the Yamassee War of 1715. To encourage the repopulation of Apalachee, Captain Joseph Primo de Rivera arrived at St. Marks with sixty men in 1718 with instructions to build a fort to house one hundred men, a storehouse for supplies, and a powder house. But there was no onrush of settlers, and in 1728 there were only two towns in Apalachee, including San Juan de Guacara near the fort.[2]

Beginning about 1750 Spain began building a stone fort at St. Marks,

using great blocks of limestone mined near the site. At the time that
Spain, a loser in the Seven Years' War, turned Florida over to Great
Britain in 1763, the fort was still far from complete. However, there
was a massive bombproof with walls four feet thick and arched ceilings divided into four rooms of twenty-one by thirty-one feet that
were fifteen feet six inches high. These casemates on the landward
side joined a massive stone wall that then extended westward to a
bastion at the shore of the Wakulla River. The bombproof had been
built halfway between the Wakulla and St. Marks rivers some 150 feet
from where the rivers joined. The Spaniards had expected to extend
the stone wall to the St. Marks River, but this extension was never
made. However the wall lay behind a wide moat connecting the two
rivers, and a high wooden palisade back of this extended to the St.
Marks and southward to enclose a compound with several wooden
buildings, finally connecting with the bastion on the northwest corner
of the fort. The fort could accommodate a garrison of one hundred
soldiers who could not be dislodged as long as supplies could be
received by sea, particularly when the men retreated to the interior
of the bombproof.[3]

But the sixty British soldiers and sailors who garrisoned Fort St.
Marks in 1764 found as dreary and uncomfortable a place to live as
could be imagined, and in 1769 Great Britain withdrew the garrison.[4]
English cartographers left us much valuable information about the
Red Hills north of St. Marks, having tramped over these highlands.
A 1767 map notes about the "Old Fields" at the edge of the Cody
Scarp: "Here the land begins to become pretty good."[5] A map of
1778 has a wealth of additional detail.[6] These English mapmakers
showed for the first time the existence of two named Indian towns,
Tallahassa Taloofa, or "Tonaby's Town," and Mikasuki, or "New
Town." The 1767 map shows a "path" leading directly northward
from the fort that after several miles forks, the right branch then
traveling in a northeasterly direction toward Mikasuki on a lake that
still bears the name Miccosukee. The forks of the road are in the
vicinity of a landmark shown on the map as a "well in the solid rock
six fathoms deep about 30 ft in diameter & 20 ft below the surface of
the ground," these dimensions marking it as what is today called the
"Natural Well" a mile southeast of Woodville and has been known
to generations as a picnic site.[7]

The western branch of the road fork at Natural Well leads northward and, following a course that appears to approximate present
Meridian Road, passes on the left a "pond" that appears to be present-
day Lake Ella. Thereafter it joins a path toward the west that im-

Part of the four-foot-thick stone wall of a long bombproof is almost all that remains of Fort St. Marks that was built shortly before the Spaniards turned Florida over to Great Britain in 1763. Student archaeologists are shown digging out the wall in 1965. (Courtesy of Florida State University)

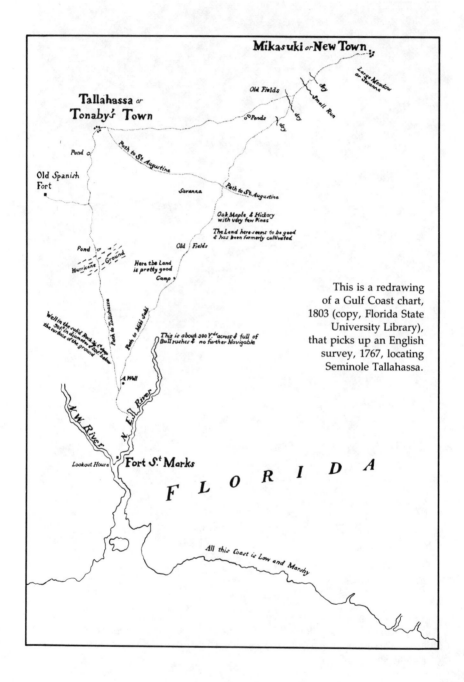

This is a redrawing of a Gulf Coast chart, 1803 (copy, Florida State University Library), that picks up an English survey, 1767, locating Seminole Tallahassa.

mediately brings the traveler to Tallahassa Taloofa. This map and that of 1778 with additional detail make it almost certain that Tallahassa lay on the broad flat hilltop in the northern part of present Tallahassee on which the Northwood and Tallahassee Malls were built, a hilltop reaching one of the highest elevations in Tallahassee, approximately 230 feet above sea level, in the vicinity of Albertson's store.

The Stuart-Purcell map informs us that in 1778 Tallahassa Taloofa had thirty-six houses, a square, sixteen families, and thirty gunmen and that the headman was still Tonaby. Meanwhile Mikasuki, its neighbor eighteen and one-half miles to the northeast, had become the more important town. Mikasuki had sixty houses, a square, twenty-eight families, and seventy gunmen, and the headman was Senetahago (Kinhagee).[8]

By his own account Tonaby, the founder and chief of Tallahassa Taloofa, was a loyal ally of the Spaniards before Florida became a British possession in 1763 and continued his loyalty in the 1770s, when he appears to have been the most important chief in the Red Hills. Tonaby was one of the Florida Indians, ultimate successors to the Apalachee and Timucuans, who were sometimes called "the wild ones" or "runaways" from the Creek Confederation. Although they long retained some loyalty to the Creek Nation, they came to be known as the Seminoles.[9]

Tonaby was born in the principal Lower Creek town of Coweta, according to his own account, and accompanied his father on a visit to St. Augustine between 1718 and 1734 as a boy of nine or ten. From the time he learned to handle firearms, Tonaby served the Spanish commandant at St. Marks for twenty years, carrying letters to and from the garrison. Finally—and presumably not long before the English came in—he established a village that, instead of being in the flatlands, was in the Red Hills. By his account, as understood by the Spaniards in 1777, the village was "on the site of San Luis de Talimali," although, as we have seen, Tallahassa was actually two miles northeast of San Luis, on an even higher hilltop.[10]

After the American Revolution broke out, Tonaby, a Uchise Creek who by now was the principal spokesman for the Creek villages of Apalachee, began to show his friendship with Spain. Far to the east, the Seminole chief Cowkeeper, an Oconi Creek, remained a confirmed loyalist. His braves took the field on several occasions to help put down the American revolt that the English colony of Florida had never joined. In contrast to Cowkeeper's Oconi Indians, Indians of the Mikasuki and Tallahassa settlements remained neutral, heeding the advice of the American Indian agent George Galphin that they should stay out of "the white man's war."[11]

Tonaby, however, went even further and attempted to make an Indian alliance with the Spaniards, who although neutral for most of the war, eventually entered it as enemies of the British. Creeks of the lower villages of the Creek Confederation maintained some contact with Spaniards during the British period, and on 13 December 1777, Tonaby and eleven of his followers were carried by a Spanish fishing boat to Havana for talks with the Spaniards. Tonaby saw an important official and sometime resident of Florida, Juan Joseph Eligio de la Puente, and boldly asked the Spaniards to repossess the fort at St. Marks and, if not that, at least to provide him with a Spanish flag that he could raise over the now vacant fort "in order that all who see it will know that castle belongs to the Great King of Spain." He promised "to defend it until the last drop of his blood is shed," according to Puente. Despite the Spaniards' wish to embarrass the British in any way they could, they were hardly interested in going to the extremes suggested by this big-talking chief. And so the suggestion of taking over Fort St. Marks was rejected. However, Puente seems to have granted Tonaby's request for a Spanish flag.[12]

As a result the banner of Spain shortly began to fly in the plaza of the Seminole town of Tallahassa, a surprising sight to a recruiting agent in the service of His Majesty King George III who showed up on the morning of 6 August 1778. Lieutenant David Holmes was making the rounds of the lower villages to recruit reluctant Creeks for a Loyalist campaign to the east. Holmes first demanded that Tonaby haul down the Spanish flag and substitute the Union Jack. The chief was hardly prepared to do anything else, and his ardor for combat with the English had cooled. He hedged when he was asked to join the expedition, however. His men would do whatever their neighbors the Mikasuki did. So Holmes now went to Senetahago—usually known as Kinhagee—who was to lead the Mikasuki band for another forty years. Kinhagee agreed to the expedition. Forty-one warriors from Mikasuki and twenty-six from the Apalachee Old Fields (Tallahassa) were among a band of one hundred that made what was evidently an uneventful and unimportant expedition to the Altamaha River to help Loyalists fend off an American threat to St. Augustine.[13]

Otherwise the long war hardly touched the neutralists of Apalachee. Tonaby disappeared from view, and Kinhagee became the leader. Afterward, when Spain repossessed Florida, Creeks of the lower villages, having traded with the English, were willing to support the Spaniards, provided that they could obtain trade goods that were the equivalent of those that had been supplied by Britain. During the English period the Indian population of Old Apalachee and its environs had increased substantially. Spain, in possession of Florida and with an "Indian problem," and now aware of the value of trade in maintaining friendly Indians along Florida's border, turned over a virtual monopoly of Indian trade to a British-American firm, Panton, Leslie and Company. In 1784 this company set up a trading post on the western shore of the Wakulla River four miles from the fort, leaving it in the hands of Charles McLatchey.[14]

Panton, Leslie expanded its trade to the Upper Creek settlements in central Alabama, and the Indians there began to trade with a Panton store in Pensacola. The firm even traded to some extent with Choctaws and Chickasaws to the west. Big profits were now returned to the company, and the Spaniards for a time enjoyed friendlier Indian relations than ever. In time, however, the Creeks began to grumble about high prices. Coupled with this complaint, particularly in the lower villages, was anger against Alexander McGillivray, the principal Creek chief and mainstay of Panton; McGillivray had quietly signed a treaty with the new United States of America in 1790 that established a boundary line, unpopular with the Lower Creeks, between the Creeks and the state of Georgia.[15]

Capitalizing on the unpopularity of both McGillivray and Panton, Leslie, a young Marylander, William Augustus Bowles, landed in Florida in 1791 with ambitions of organizing the Creeks into a borderland nation. A Loyalist during the Revolution, Bowles had fought a losing battle against the Spaniards in the Battle of Pensacola while still in his teens. He lived among the Creeks for a time and married the daughter of a borderland micco, Perryman. After an absence from Florida and one unsuccessful return in 1788, Bowles now, with the backing of British merchants in the Bahamas who dreamed of breaking the Panton monopoly, set up a ramshackle store near the broad mouth of the Ochlockonee River a few miles from St. Marks. Mustering support from Creek villages, Bowles had himself declared the "Director General" of what was called "the Nation of Muskogee." He not only challenged the leadership of the now dying McGillivray but declared that the treaty line agreed upon by him should never be run.[16]

Bowles's Nassau backers failed, however, to provide him with trading goods that had already been promised the Indians. He decided upon a bold stroke. On 16 January 1792, Bowles and an aide, William Cunningham, with several other white men and perhaps one hundred Indians, presented themselves at the Panton store near St. Marks and demanded its surrender. There was nothing to do but comply, and guns, blankets, shirts, and boots were passed around. Some fifteen thousand dollars' worth of additional goods were held for later distribution. William Panton stormed in a letter to his Indian friend and protector, Alexander McGillivray: "I demand the Life of that Villain Bowls," or that he be delivered to the Spaniards for trial. At the first opportunity Bowles was seized and packed off for imprisonment in Havana, Spain, and the Philippines.[17]

While Bowles was in prison, an even more unpopular boundary line was agreed upon in the Pinckney Treaty of 1795 between Spain and the United States. This line split the lower Creek settlements near the forks of the Chattahoochee and Flint rivers, setting the Georgia-Florida border near its present location and opening more Creek hunting land for American settlement. In 1799 the American surveyor Andrew Ellicott ran this line eastward from the Mississippi River, but when he reached the forks of the Flint and Chattahoochee, he found Kinhagee and a party of Mikasuki barring a further advance. Ellicott abandoned the survey for the time and retreated to the mouth of the Apalachicola, where, in September 1799, he encountered, of all men, the terrible Mr. Bowles. Having escaped from prison, Bowles had returned to Florida by way of England and now claimed the support of Britain's might in achieving greater goals. He had approached St. George Sound aboard a British sloop, the *Fox*, which was loaded with munitions and supplies. The vessel foundered and sank off the eastern tip of St. George Island, giving it the name Fox Point, but this mishap did not deter Bowles, who boasted to the American surveyor that he intended to capture Fort St. Marks from the Spaniards.[18]

Bowles reorganized the forces of Muskogee and established a "capital" in the hometown of his friend Kinhagee. Here at Mikasuki in the spring of 1800, Bowles and Muskogee declared war on Spain, and on 9 April the Fort St. Marks commandant, Thomas Portell, could scarcely believe what his eyes now told him—the Indians emerging from the pine forest approaches to the fort wore war paint! Shortly they numbered seven hundred or more, while Bowles himself—who held an old commission as general in the British army—and a handful of white followers were also on hand.[19]

To Bowles's demand that the fort be surrendered, however, Portell returned a haughty "no." With twelve fair-sized cannon and eighty-eight men behind walls that had never been breached, the commandant felt secure against the motley force that faced him, even though the Spaniards were badly outnumbered. Week after week a siege went on, and Portell began to be more polite. He was more than sixty years old and nearing retirement, only recently having been assigned to St. Marks after service on the Mississippi River in the vicinity of Memphis. With him in the fort was Señora Portell, who may by this time have regretted having scolded Kinhagee; sometime earlier at a conference with the commandant the chief had been ordered by this fastidious lady to take his smelly pipe from his mouth. Finally the unlucky Portell, after five weeks and the Indians' capture of two supply vessels sent to sustain the Spaniards, surrendered Fort St. Marks on 19 May 1800. All of the occupants boarded small vessels and sailed off to Pensacola, where the commandant was imprisoned and sent to Havana to await trial for having so ingloriously given up the fort. In the fort meanwhile the flag of Muskogee, a brilliant sunburst on a field of blue, was hoisted, to the accompaniment, no doubt, of Indian war whoops and English huzzahs.[20]

But Bowles held the fort for only a month. A small Spanish fleet arrived from Pensacola in mid-June, and after a ninety-minute bombardment the fort was Spain's again. Bowles escaped and was soon directing a Muskogee "navy" that harassed Spanish shipping. The American government was becoming more restive by the minute at the activities of this bold adventurer on the southern frontier. Alexander Hawkins, an American Indian agent, finally proved to be Bowles's undoing. While attending a conference of the Creeks at Hickory Ground in Alabama, Bowles was captured and bound through the machinations of Hawkins and was turned over to the Spaniards. In Havana's Morro Castle, where the St. Marks commandant Portell was also imprisoned to await trial, Bowles died on 23 December 1805.[21]

5

Andrew Jackson's
Leisurely "Wolf Hunt"
in the Red Hills

Relative quiet returned to the Red Hills after Bowles's downfall. But the bitter memory of the robbery of the store of Panton, Leslie rankled in the heart of William Panton, the principal partner in the firm. Immediately following the robbery in 1792 he added the firm's losses in this looting to store debts owed by the Creeks and hit upon the idea of collecting the combined debt by persuading the Indians to cede land. He first tried to obtain this land within American boundaries. This notion was rejected outright by the Creeks, who lived principally in Georgia and Alabama; they ridiculed the idea of having to pay for robberies "committed by Bowles and his Seminoles" in Spanish Florida. Meanwhile in 1800, at the time Bowles took St. Marks fort, his Indians raided and looted the store a second time, and Panton, Leslie withdrew from St. Marks.[1]

Forbes & Company, succeeding Panton, Leslie, was finally permitted by Spain to recoup the losses by obtaining 1,500,000 acres of land, called the Forbes Purchase. Almost entirely worthless for agriculture and all below the Cody Scarp, the big acreage extended from the St. Marks to the Apalachicola River. Forbes established a trading post at Prospect Bluff, twenty-five miles from the mouth of the Apalachicola, on the east side, and left it in the hands of the traders William Hambly and Edmund Doyle, who for a time seem to have been the only white residents in this part of Florida except for the Spanish garrison at St. Marks.[2]

During the Napoleonic wars Spain came under the virtual control of Great Britain, and with the outbreak of the War of 1812, English Major Edward Nicolls stirred up a hornet's nest of anti-American Indian activity in the Florida borderlands. Rebel Red Sticks among the Alabama Creeks fled to the Florida Panhandle by the hundreds after their defeat by General Andrew Jackson at Horseshoe Bend in

1814, and Nicolls recruited them to continue their hostility.[3] His most provocative act, following the end of the war in 1815, was to leave a vast store of powder, guns, cannon, and other military supplies in a fort he had built at Prospect Bluff, and this immediately fell into the possession of three hundred blacks, some of them runaway slaves from American plantations. Called "the negro fort," this installation blocked American plans for supplying a new fort that the United States built near the forks of the Chattahoochee and Flint rivers just above the Florida line—for it was planned to supply the fort from New Orleans by way of the Apalachicola River through Spanish Florida. Elimination of the Negro Fort, now a necessity, was accomplished in 1816 when one lucky shot from an American gunboat with a cannonball heated red hot in the range landed in the powder stores. The explosion killed 275 occupants.[4]

The destruction of the Negro Fort brought quiet briefly to the Florida Indian frontier. The army withdrew for a time the garrison that had been stationed at Fort Scott. There was talk of annexing Florida to the United States, and friends of General Andrew Jackson at Nashville invested in land near Pensacola. However, resentment grew among Indians, especially the Red Stick Creeks, at the loss of their lands in the Treaty of Fort Jackson. General Jackson had dictated this treaty to a small, captive delegation of Creeks not representative of the nation, and in it some 20 million acres of Creek lands were signed away. These extended down through Alabama to the Florida line and in an L shape, then ran in a seventy-mile-wide strip across the southern extremity of Georgia, below the principal Lower Creek villages. The lands were opened up for American settlement, bringing increasing trouble to the frontier. Borderland Indians particularly disliked the presence of Fort Scott on some of this land.[5]

Before leaving Florida in 1815, Colonel Nicolls had seized upon an idea that the new Treaty of Ghent ending the War of 1812 had superseded the land cession in the Fort Jackson treaty, and he encouraged the Red Sticks in believing that Great Britain would help the Creeks regain this land. Nicolls took with him to England the Indian Hillis Hadjo, also called Francis the Prophet, leader of the Red Sticks now in Florida. In England Francis was presented with a commission and the uniform of a brigadier, was hailed as "the patriot Francis," and in a great show of friendship was given an audience with the prince regent. When he returned to Florida in 1817 after several months, Francis called a meeting at Tallahassa to make known a message said to be from the prince regent. Francis believed that the British Crown was now going to assist the Red Sticks militarily in recovering the treaty lands—even though Britain had no intention of doing so.[6] A newcomer to Florida, the Scotsman Alexander Arbuthnot, joined Francis in protesting the terms of the treaty. From a base in the Bahama Islands, this merchant had set up a trading store on the edge of Ochlockonee Sound. The twelve chiefs who later authorized the Scot to speak for them included the Red Sticks Hillis Hadjo and Peter McQueen, Chief Kinhagee of Mikasuki on the Florida side of the border, and Chief Neamathla of Fowltown, above the line in Georgia, a village of sixty warriors less than fifteen miles east of Fort Scott.[7]

The Treaty of Fort Jackson had taken away the land on which Fowltown stood. Since this treaty land was opened for settlement, it brought the American frontier nearer also to Mikasuki across the Florida border. Indians had sometimes made known their anger by stealing cattle, firing cabins, and murdering the settlers. However, according to former Georgia governor David B. Mitchell, who succeeded Alexander Hawkins as Indian Agent on his death in 1816, aggression was equally frequent on the part of whites. When Major General Edmund P. Gaines, the military commander for this region, demanded that murderers of a woman and two children in the St. Mary's River area in southeastern Georgia be turned over to the American authorities—these murders having been traced to a war party from Mikasuki—Chief Kinhagee replied on 11 September 1817 in a letter which had been shown to nine other border chiefs saying that in three years whites had killed nine or ten Indians, while the Indians in retaliation had not killed as many whites. "The white people killed our people first, and the Indians then took satisfaction. There are yet three men that the red people have never taken satisfaction for." The letter was sent to Washington as an indication of Indian belligerence. The Indians, said Gaines, "admit by necessary implication, that they have killed seven of our citizens."[8]

President Monroe reacted by directing that a large force be stationed at Fort Scott again and that the Indians be required to make reparations for any killings. If no reparations were made, then, if they were on treaty land, they must be moved. He advised, however, against crossing the Florida line.[9] At this juncture a provocative gesture occurred on the treaty land in the village of Fowltown. Major D. E. Twiggs, in command at Fort Scott before the arrival there of General Gaines, reported that Neamathla, chief of Fowltown, had told him "that if ever a detachment of United States troops crossed the Flint river he would resist them by force. He also cautioned me not to turn over there, either horses or cattle, nor to get any timber from off the land as he was determined it should not be done except by force." Twiggs told his superior, General Gaines, he had no doubt that Neamathla and his allies in Florida would "commence hostilities" if the Flint were crossed, "and they have 2,700 warriors."[10]

Gaines, arriving at Fort Scott on 17 November, sent a message to Neamathla, asking him to come in for a talk. Neamathla refused, adding that all he had to say he had said to Twiggs. Gaines now directed this officer to go to Fowltown with a detachment "and remove them." If there was any resistance, he was to "treat them as enemies." On 21 November 1817, Twiggs and three hundred soldiers showed up at Fowltown before dawn and were fired on "without effect," according to the official report. Then the Americans "briskly returned" the fire, killing five Indians, including one woman, and wounding many others. There was still another attack with other deaths, and the Indians fled to the swamps, some going then to Mikasuki. Twiggs searched Fowltown and in Neamathla's hut found the scarlet coat of a British uniform along with a note from Major Nicolls calling Neamathla a "friend of the British." The town was burned.[11]

Tempers now boiled in the Indian towns around the forks. The black drink was passed around, and red war poles went up. Nine days after the attack, a band of Indians lying in the bushes along the Apalachicola River just below the forks waited until a barge loaded with forty soldiers from Fort Scott, the wives of seven of them, and several small children, rowed near the shore. Then the Indians fired volley after volley at close range. All but five in the barge were killed and scalped or bound and carried off; the dead included the leader, Lieutenant Richard W. Scott.[12]

On 26 December 1817, Secretary of War John C. Calhoun wrote General Jackson at Nashville, ordering him to assemble and march his forces to Fort Scott. Old Hickory was ready enough to do so. His response to "the Scott massacre" had been: "Should . . . their hostility continue, the protection of our citizens will require that the wolf be struck in his den." Quickly mustering several hundred Tennesseans, Kentuckians, and regulars, Jackson marched to Hartford, Georgia, where nine hundred Georgia militia joined the army, as fifteen hundred Lower Creek warriors from the main Confederation soon did also. Many of the mainstream Upper and Lower Creeks had been as distressed as the Red Sticks by the Fort Jackson treaty, for their land as well as that of the rebel Red Sticks had been taken away for the benefit of the advancing American frontier. Now, however, the Creeks seemed to have dropped this issue and seized the opportunity to punish the Red Stick rebels and enforce Creek law among the rebellious Seminoles. Jackson's orders sanctioned a military campaign across the Florida border, and Washington left what he might do there up to the general whom Indians called "The Sharp Knife." Old Hickory lost no time, after arriving at Fort Scott, in crossing the Florida border. Evidently his reputation as a fighter preceded him, for the army marched one hundred miles in Florida before encountering more than a handful of hostiles.[13]

Captain Hugh Young, the topographical engineer accompanying General Jackson, proved invaluable in mapping out the route of the march. His knowledge and skill enabled him to leave a description of the topography, soils, vegetation, and Indian population of the Red Hills that is invaluable. Most of the Indians were now concentrated in the Mikasuki villages which, according to Young, had 160 warriors and perhaps eight or nine times as many women and children, for a total population of about 1,400. These were still mainly Hitchiti speaking, and Young indicates that the other Hitchiti speakers in this region included the Fowltown Indians with thirty or forty warriors. These and a few Uchees now lived near the Mikasuki people. Young said several Muskogee-speaking Indians were in the Apalachicola River valley: the Ocheesees at a bluff of the same name, with twenty-five warriors; the Ehawhohasles twelve miles below Ocheesee, with fifteen to twenty warriors; and the Tamatles seven miles above Ocheesee, with twenty-five warriors. The Indians of Tallahassa, now with only fifteen warriors, were commanded by a chief named Okiakhija, who was described as "worthless, dishonest and inveterately hostile." But until the army reached the neighborhood of Mikasuki, the Indians scattered at the approach of Jackson. The only big concentration of Seminoles apart from those at Mikasuki was in Boleck's Town on the Suwannee River, and near them were some two hundred Negro allies.[14]

Jackson's first move was not toward the enemy towns but toward a food supply for his army, now with a force of eight hundred volunteers and regulars, including some men already at Fort Scott, nine hundred Georgia militia, and some Creeks. They were down to only three more days of rations. Jackson had arranged for vessels to bring food to Apalachicola Bay and then upriver, and so at noon on 10 March, only a day after arriving at Fort Scott, he turned his army southward into Florida and toward this food supply. Marching along the east side of the Apalachicola, the army came on 16 March to Prospect Bluff. There Lieutenant James Gadsden, Jackson's aide-de-camp and engineer, was directed to build a fort where the Negro Fort had stood. Having now intercepted the food supply, the army rested

Andrew Jackson, known to the Indians as "Sharp Knife," led an army of 3,000 through the Red Hills in March and April 1818 in what came to be called the First Seminole War, the Seminoles having replaced the Apalachee here. (Photographed from Benson J. Loring, *The Pictorial Fieldbook of the War of 1812* [New York: Harper & Brothers, 1869], p. 1020)

here for ten days while the fort, named Gadsden for its builder, was being erected.[15]

The army then set out on 26 March for the Mikasuki towns, crossing the flat pinelands and swamps of present Liberty County. On 29 March it reached the Ochlockonee River, here running fifty-six yards wide between high banks, the one on the east rising to what still is called Jackson's Bluff. Nineteen canoes were built. By 8:00 P.M. of the twenty-ninth more than half of the army had crossed, the remainder getting over the next morning in time for the whole army to resume its march at 11:00 A.M. on 30 March. Heading along the course of present State Road 20, the march for several miles crossed the Oke-fenokee Dunes, then entered the Red Hills. Young's account now begins to fill with superlatives as he describes this rich farming country. The land was "fertile with a growth of oak and hickory." The army camped for the night at a pond that was just four miles from Tallahassa.[16]

This encampment appears to have been in the lowlands along West Tharpe Street, about four miles west of North Monroe (U.S. 27). There is no pond here today, but water flows southward through several drainage ditches. The army marched toward Tallahassa on 31 March. "Four miles to Tallehassa T," wrote Topographical Engineer Young, "through an excellent body of land, the soil adapted to any kind of culture growth, oak and hickory." There was a "small miry branch near the village," said Young, and beyond it: "The town was hand-somely situated on a hill and consisted of ten or twelve houses with a large clearing cultivated in common." Today this hill has been se-verely bulldozed and scraped down in places by the building of the Northwood and particularly Tallahassee malls. The one place on the hilltop with a sweeping view to the west is at the intersection of U.S. 27 and John Knox Road. Knox Road here becomes Monticello Drive, which falls steeply off the hilltop to what was evidently the "miry branch," now a drainage ditch running along Boone Boulevard to-ward Lake Jackson. Beyond the ditch Monticello Drive runs straight up a hill beyond. Standing today at U.S. 27 and Monticello—although Jackson seems to have marched a little to the south of this point— one can picture Jackson's army as it came into view. The army doubt-less marched three abreast to guard against surprise attacks in the manner of the Creek campaign of 1813–1814.[17]

The army did not march, however, until a company led by Major D. E. Twiggs, accompanied by two hundred Indian warriors, had gone ahead to scout the town, the first thought likely to offer resis-tance. The people of Tallahassa, said Young, "have neither arts nor cattle, but their land is excellent and gave them fine crops with very little labour." However, Twiggs found the town deserted, its inhabitants having fled "some days before." The main body of the army now marched, passing through the village at noon and then pressing on toward Mikasuki eighteen miles away.[18]

On the way to the Mikasuki villages, the army encountered the same kind of land that it had seen just west of Tallahassa. The villages lay beside a lake that was twelve to fourteen miles long, north to south, and two or three miles wide. The surrounding land was "fertile and of beautiful aspect," wrote Young. "Here the Indians raised abundance of corn, rice, potatoes, peas, beans, and gound nuts—the soil yielding plentiful crops without much labor of cultivation. They had immense droves of cattle and hogs roaming through the woods, and the abundance of game gave them plenty of venison and skins. They also raised numbers of small but hardy horses." Their agriculture was "of the simplest kind. The looseness of the soil obviated the necessity of heavy labour and the work of a few hoes soon opened a field and prepared a crop." The Mikasuki were still under the leadership of Kinhagee, then about seventy or eighty years of age. But while this chief exercised political control, the war chief was Coche-Tustenuggee, "a brave man and a better soldier than Kinhega."[19]

The American army encamped a few miles from the Mikasuki villages and here was joined by a four-hundred-member contingent of Tennessee Volunteers tardily reaching the theater of war. It was also joined by a fifteen-hundred-man force of friendly Creeks commanded by their chief, William McIntosh, now commissioned an American army brigadier general. Jackson's army of thirty-three hundred men was the largest military force ever to march across the Red Hills before or since. Against this force were opposed an estimated twelve hundred warriors (not Twiggs's estimated twenty-seven hundred), and these were never available in sufficient strength at any one place to offer serious resistance to Jackson.[20]

Only a small band of Mikasuki had dug in a mile and a half west of the villages when on 1 April Jackson's army reached the place, a point of land extending into a swamp. For a while the hostiles returned brisk rifle fire directed from two flanks, and then the Indians retreated, leaving fourteen dead. When the Americans marched into the main Mikasuki village, it was deserted. The army burned three hundred houses, rounded up a thousand head of cattle and took three hundred bushels of corn. "Every indication of a hostile spirit was found in the habitations of the chiefs," Jackson reported. "In the council houses of Kinhaje's town, the king of the Mekasykians, more than fifty fresh scalps were found, and in the center of the public square, the old red stick's standard, a red pole, was erected, crowned with scalps, recognized by the hair, as torn from the heads of the unfortunate companions of Scott." The body of the old Chief Kinhagee was found after the Mikasuki action. His death brought to an end a regime that had begun forty years before.[21]

The army marched southward toward St. Marks on 5 April, perhaps via the old Spanish road that traveled past the Natural Well, reaching the fort on the evening of 6 April. The next day Jackson took this stronghold from the hands of the protesting Spanish commandant, Don Francisco Caso y Luengo.[22] Two more military objectives remained, Suwannee Old Town, where Chief Boleck (or Bowlegs) presided, and the Negro town nearby. These lay 107 miles to the southeast, across many swamps and palmetto thickets, and on 9 April an army of whites and Indians started the five-day march. On the night of 12 April, in the vicinity of Econfino Creek, the sound of lowing cattle and barking dogs signaled the nearness of hostiles. On the morning of 13 April, the next day, McIntosh and his Creeks set out in pursuit. It turned out to be the band of the Red Stick chief, Peter McQueen. This party of two hundred was pursued for three miles in a running battle. Thirty-seven of its warriors were left dead on the field, while Jackson's force lost only three men killed. The Suwannee River villages were deserted when the Americans marched in. The army now returned to St. Marks, arriving on 25 April. The Georgia militia and McIntosh's Creeks were released to return to their homes.[23]

McQueen, who escaped to the coastal swamps following his band's encounter, was luckier than his fellow Red Stick, Francis. Francis appears to have continued at his home on the south bank of the Wakulla River, a few miles from St. Marks, almost until the arrival there of General Jackson. When Jackson had left Prospect Bluff for Mikasuki he had instructed Captain Isaac McKeever of the navy to sail eastward, searching the coast for hostiles, "white, red or black." Along the way McKeever picked up the traders William Hambly and Edmund Doyle who, like their former employer, Forbes & Company, had changed like chameleons from loyalty to Spain, then Great Britain and now the victorious United States. In 1817 Hambly, especially, began to inform the Americans of the Indians' every movement. After the Fowltown incident a band of Indians, including some from Fowltown, visited the homes of Hambly and Doyle on the Apalachicola River and made both men prisoners. Death seemed to be in store for them, but instead they were imprisoned, first at Mikasuki, then at

Suwannee Old Town, and finally they were placed in the custody of the Spanish commander at St. Marks. They somehow escaped from the fort and sought greater safety from the Indians aboard McKeever's vessel. According to the diary of a Tennessee officer in Jackson's army, J. B. Rodgers, they helped design a stratagem for capturing the Prophet Francis, telling McKeever about this Indian's "ardent desire for, and constant expectation of the arrival of supplies to carry on the war against the United States." The captain therefore conspicuously displayed the Union Jack above his ship while it lay at anchor near the mouth of the St. Mark's River.[24]

The ruse worked. A canoe bearing Hillis Hadjo, and a fellow Red Stick, Himollemico, soon pulled alongside McKeever's ship, after having been paddled ten miles across the bay. On this very day, 6 April, but a few hours later, Jackson arrived at Fort St. Marks. McKeever greeted the Indians cordially and took them below decks for a drink. Here they were seized, bound, and taken ashore. Upon arriving, Jackson lost no time in ordering that the Prophet Francis and his companion be hanged without any trial. This summary sentence has troubled Jackson biographers and historians. Himollemico, they say, was a scoundrel who may have deserved this fate—he had led the massacre of the Scott party. But Francis had most of the virtues that Americans valued—courage, dignity, compassion, and the rest. He was, as one Jackson biographer reported, "humane in his disposition, by no means barbarous—a model chief." His manners were pleasing, he conversed well in English and Spanish, and he was a man of comfortable wealth, with property that included a number of slaves. The only thing Jackson had against him was that he was also a Creek patriot, opposing the march of Manifest Destiny—but patriotism was also a virtue. Instead of placing Francis before a firing squad, and thereby giving him a death more honorable, Jackson decreed that he should receive the execution of a villain. So on 8 April, Himollemico, "morose and taciturn," and Francis were hanged. Francis was tied up—despite his protest that this measure was not necessary—and shortly afterward this "handsome man," slender, six feet tall, and now about forty, swung in the air, wearing the gray frock coat that had been given to him in England.[25]

The Indians nearby who witnessed this terrible event probably included Francis's daughter, Milly (also called Malee). A girl of about fifteen or seventeen, this black-haired beauty was celebrated in the St. Marks compound for her charm and intelligence. She reacted with sorrow three weeks later when two British nationals were put to death. One of them was the Scottish trader Alexander Arbuthnot, now about seventy years old. He had constantly befriended the Indians, had taken their complaints to American authorities, and also, toward the end of the Jackson campaign, had warned Boleck of the impending march on Suwannee Old Town. A fourteen-member military court of Jackson cronies found Arbuthnot guilty of aiding the Indians and sentenced him to be hanged. Richard C. Ambrister, thirty-three, a captain in the British Marines and a wounded veteran of the Battle of Waterloo, was far less involved in what was considered anti-American activity. He was tried by the same court, was also found guilty, and was sentenced to death. Relenting, the court then changed the sentence to fifty lashes and a year in prison, but Old Hickory would have none of this clemency and approved the original sentence. On the morning of 29 April, Ambrister was the first to be marched outside the fort gate, to be shot by a firing squad at the edge of a freshly dug grave that shortly received also the body of Arbuthnot, who was hanged for twenty minutes from the yardarm of his own vessel, his white flowing hair and black suit presenting a memorable silhouette.[26]

The diarist Rodgers said Francis' Town was three miles from the fort. Milly, knowing English and Spanish like her father, had served the young officer Ambrister as interpreter. But there was a stronger tie between Ambrister and Milly. The officer lived at Francis's house, and Milly was "extremely, though chastely, intimate" with him. After Ambrister's death it was said by the Spanish commandant's family that Malee "went to their house and there gave full vent to her feelings."[27]

A few weeks earlier, Milly had saved the life of a frightened Georgia militiaman who was about to be shot and had been captured by her father's warriors, stripped naked, and tied to a tree. The story was circulated widely in the United States, and she became known as "the Florida Pocahontas." Later Milly was removed along with other Florida Seminoles to the Indian Territory, where she settled among the Creeks near Muskogee. She died of tuberculosis in 1848, too early to receive the ninety-six-dollar pension provided by Congress in 1844, along with a medal, but after hearing about them. Both were the result of efforts by Army Colonel (and later Major General) Ethan Allen Hitchcock, who visited her in 1842 while investigating fraud in contracting for supplies in the Indian Territory.[28]

Jackson's army, reduced to twelve hundred after the Suwannee campaign, hardly rested at Fort Gadsden. Listening to the tattletale Hambly's story that fugitive Indians were being protected in Spanish Pensacola, Jackson began a march on 10 May toward this capital of

West Florida. He took over and briefly held the fortifications there, then returned to Nashville with his old ambition of possessing the Floridas for the United States practically an assured reality. Now home from the "wolf-hunt," the crusty Tennessean boasted that the Indians "have not the power, if the will remains, of again annoying our frontier." Certainly such would appear to have been the case: Jackson's big army, with minimal losses of its own, had killed one hundred or more Indians, had burned more than six hundred houses, had driven off hundreds of cattle, and had scattered the populations of the old border towns in Florida.[29]

Captain Young's "Topographical Memoir" reads like a real estate salesman's brochure inviting people all over the United States to come to a soil-rich region that was still Spanish territory. The soil of the Apalachicola River bottom, according to Young, "equals that of the Mississippi," while the Apalachicola's tributary, the Chipola, "runs through the finest body of land in the southern country." The Red Hills presented in many places "an aspect of most prepossessing beauty—a surface gently rolling, fine large timber, good water and generally deep red soil with strength and fertility equal to any kind of culture. It would be unfair to estimate the prospective agricultural importance of this country from the crops of the Seminoles. The Indians make no experiments, having few wants, and despising luxuries, they prefer raising a sufficiency of corn and potatoes to the labour of a trial which might have proved the aptitude of their soil for cotton and sugar." Neither had been tried here, Young declared, but both would succeed.[30]

Young, moreover, was the very first writer about this region to remark insightfully regarding the geography of the Red Hills that the region lay near the sea with its shipping lanes. Proximity to the sea had been important to the mound builders at Lake Jackson, to the Apalachee Indians at Iniahica, to the Spanish missionaries at San Luis, and perhaps to the Seminole Indians at Mikasuki and Tallahassa Taloofa. But Young, with the mind of an economic geographer, first called attention to the way in which the Gulf takes a huge bite of land below the hills in the form of a crescent with its points at Cape San Blas and the mouth of the Suwannee River. At the old Spanish port of St. Marks at the middle of this crescent, the fertile hills were less than twenty miles away, so that the fertile cotton-growing region lay very close to shipping.[31]

Young's report was not made available to the public; it gathered dust for more than one hundred years in the archives of the Corps of Engineers. But two thousand American soldiers, Tennesseans,

Kentuckians, and Georgians, as well as regulars with homes to the north of these states, had been exposed to the pleasant uplands during two months of the year, March and April, when they are at their most attractive. The Florida War was not a strenuous one, and these soldiers had time to enjoy the Red Hills. Theirs was the first "Springtime Tallahassee Parade."[32] Some of these soldiers would return, and many others who would learn about this country would soon come as settlers.

6

The Spring Creek
Trail

Following what he called Jackson's "luxuriant frolic" in Spanish Florida, U.S. Attorney General William Wirt proposed "the temporary occupation" of Texas.[1] The South Carolinian James Gadsden, fresh from the Florida campaign as aide-de-camp to Old Hickory, suggested a more permanent occupation of Florida alone, calling Jackson's attention, in a report on 1 August 1818, to the military advantages and saying that, north of St. Marks, "an extensive and rich back country" would "invite a populous settlement."[2] A treaty transferring Florida to the United States was signed only seven months after Gadsden's report but because of delays in Spain was not finally ratified until 22 February 1821, after which, on 17 July, the United States took possession of the territory.

The start of a "populous settlement" did not wait for ratification of the treaty. Between 1819 and 1821 a community of thirty-one families was formed, not in the hills immediately north of St. Marks, but across the Apalachicola River in what is presently the northwestern corner of Jackson County. Holmes Creek is the western boundary of the county here. In the uplands, rising from the creek bottom, the topsoil with every spring plowing lights up a bright red, the same color as the subsoil. Farmers around here swear that this soil, which with the fresh green crops give a Christmas-in-May appearance to the land, is in every way as good as the brown soils covering most of the Red Hills.[3] From these uplands, and from some just across the border in Alabama, flow several springs that form Spring Creek. This, after flowing eastward for a mile or so in Alabama, crosses the Florida line. The creek flows south for a mile, then southeast for another, then northeast for four or five more miles to cross the Alabama border again and become a tributary of the Chipola River. Alabamans today scarcely notice the tiny stream as they speed over it a mile south of

the state line along U.S. Highway 231 on the way to their favorite
Florida beach resort, Panama City.

Our information today about the 31 heads of household and their
families, perhaps 150 persons in all, who settled along the Florida
course of Spring Creek, principally in 1820 and 1821, is contained in
an old record book of the Florida Land Claims Commission. The hand-
writing of the clerk records the testimony of settlers who swore that
they had settled on a tract and were cultivating it on 17 July 1821
along with the testimony of witnesses. Any settler who was twenty-
one years old and the head of a family at the time was then enabled
by an act of Congress to claim the land as his own up to a maximum
of 640 acres.[4] The testimony, recorded in 1824, often provides clues
to the location of these early settlers within the Spring Creek community, while early public land purchases suggest the location of
other settlers, for instance the Williams brothers, John and Owen.
John had land at the Alabama line just over two miles west of Highway
231, and Owen about two miles to the south along the course of a
small stream joining Spring Creek from the south as it bends to the
southeast.[5]

John Williams's land was at the Alabama line, and James Falk and
William T. Nelson cultivated theirs near him, all west of Spring Creek
as it flows south. On the west side also was Abraham Philips, whose
neighbor to the south was Benjamin Hamilton, his claim joining that
of Owen Williams on the south. Owen Williams had two neighbors
not far west of him, Micajah Cadwell and Joseph Parrot, but there
were several settlers still farther west, among them John Ward and
south of him Nathan A. Ward, with William Philips to the south of
Nathan. There was a third Ward in the settlement, James. Nathan
Ward's claim on the west adjoined that of Andrew Farmer, who described his land as being on Holmes Creek, as was that of Robert
Thomas. Farmer and Thomas can be considered part of the Spring
Creek community. Well to the south of Owen Williams was the claim
of John Hays.

On the east side of Spring Creek, as it flows from the Alabama line,
and about halfway to the first bend, was the land of Samuel C. Fowler.
Below him were Nathaniel Hudson and Wilie (or Wiley) Blount. For
three-fourths of a mile, Spring Creek takes a southeasterly course,
then bends northeast. It is joined at the latter bend by a substantial
flow of water in a branch that begins in present Campbellton. The
settler of the land where this stream enters Spring Creek was Moses
Brentley, or Brantley (Brantley Pond appears to perpetuate this name),
with Robert Thompson to the south of him and on the east side of

the branch. Settlements continued eastward along the south shore of Spring Creek with Guthrie Moore, Stephen Daniel (whose land was at the present U.S. 231 bridge), John Gwinn, and John Jones. North of Daniel was Allaway Roach, and settlers on the north side of Spring Creek included Henry Moses, Joel Porter, and Simeon Cook. As the settlements continued, that of James C. Roach was at the Alabama line, while a neighbor there was John Smith, below him on Spring Creek. Presley Scurlock claimed land "on Spring Creek of the Chipola," although early land records bring him no closer to the settlement than the western edge of Waddell's Mill Pond.

Nothing in the record shows where these Spring Creek settlers came from or just who they were, but they and a good many other early settlers in Jackson County were probably in a backwash from a flood of Georgians trying to obtain Alabama lands opened up by the Treaty of Fort Jackson. A land office was opened in 1817 at Milledgeville, the capital of Georgia, to sell these Alabama lands. Land sales began in August 1817, the first land to be sold being around present Montgomery in the heart of the Alabama Black Prairie, a prime cotton soil. Squatters already present could, of course, bid on land that they had settled—provided they could get to the Milledgeville land office two hundred miles away. Few of these or other small farmers, though, could outbid speculators or more substantial planters.[6]

Farmers frustrated in their attempt to settle the Alabama blacklands and river bottoms could, of course, turn to the strip of Georgia below present Albany that was also in the Fort Jackson treaty, but most of the southern Georgia treaty lands were regarded as a worthless "pine barren."[7] Many of the Georgians who moved to Alabama and then to Florida were only a generation away from North Carolina. Such was the case with the family of John and Owen Williams, one of the best-known families in Jackson County today, whose widely attended reunion is held annually near Graceville on the edge of the Spring Creek community. Their father, Frederick Williams, moved from Duplin County, North Carolina, to Bulloch County, Georgia, in about 1793, and some members were in Conecuh County, Alabama, in 1819.[8]

Spring Creek seemed fair ground for settlement to these and other Florida "sooners"—a rolling country of many oaks, hickories, magnolias, and beech trees, the sort where cotton could be grown. However, all of the settlers, at least at first, were only subsistence farmers, and none of them grew cotton. At most they had cleared and were cultivating as many as forty acres but more often between ten and fifteen, while few used slave labor. Life was bitterly difficult in this

log cabin frontier. By the latter part of 1824, four of the settlers—
Nelson, Brantley, Porter, and Gwinn—had died, and their widows
filed claims for the land. Others disappeared from view in the first
years of the Florida territory. When a special census was made in
August 1825, only sixteen of the thirty-one were counted in Jackson
County.[9]

The 1825 manuscript census adds only fragments of information
about the sixteen Spring Creek "survivors." Nine of the heads of
household owned no slaves (Hudson, Parrot, Cook, Allaway Roach,
John and Nathan Ward, John and Owen Williams, and Robert
Thomas) and evidently still depended on members of the family,
numbering from three to thirteen, for much or all of the labor.

The thirty-one Spring Creek families were among sixty-two families
or individual claimants shown in Land Claims Commission Record
Book 2 to have settled in Jackson County before the change of flags.
Six took up land to the east of the Spring Creek settlement, on or
very near the Chipola River: Robert Sullivan, Hugh Robertson, James
Dennard, Joshua Scurlock, John Hopson, and Jonathan Hagan. Two
others claimed land at the Big Spring (presently called Blue Springs),
several miles northeast of present Marianna: William Pyles and William McDonald, his claim being "for the benefit and advantage of
Charles Trippe," to whom he had sold the title.

McDonald earlier, in 1820, had settled on the Chattahoochee River,
whose west bank together with that of the Apalachicola River, next
to Spring Creek, saw the greatest number of settlers before the change
of flags, seventeen in all.[10] From the vicinity of Conchatty Hatchy or
Red Ground Creek near the Chattahoochee the settlers included James
Irwin, James Brown, Joseph Brooks, William Brown, William H. Pyke,
Allis Wood, William Chamblis, Adam Kimbrough, and George Sharp.
Adam Hunter claimed land on the Apalachicola, apparently somewhere west of the forks, and downstream were Charles Barnes, John
H. King, Reuben Littleton, Lovin McClinton, and, at Ocheesee Bluff
a dozen miles south of the forks, Thomas C. Richards and a kinsman,
Stephen Richards. Stephen Richards is better known in Florida history
than any of the sixty-one other early settlers in Jackson County, for
he served in the early years of the territory as an interpreter for talks
between American agents and Indian chiefs. We can trace this family
from France through England to North Carolina. A native of North
Carolina, Stephen moved to Georgia as a child and was in his teens
at the time of the War of 1812. He enlisted in a militia company
commanded by Captain West Whitaker in the regiment of Major John
H. Broadnax.[11] Others settled to the west and south in present-day

counties that were at first part of Jackson. These were Eli Scurlock, John Bush, David Durgan, Samuel Story, John Guerra, Joseph Cobb, and Daniel Lyran.

When the 1825 census was taken, Jackson County had been reduced to its present size, except that it included an almost vacant portion which is now Calhoun County. However, the approximately 300 persons in sixty-two households who were present in 1821 had increased to 2,156 persons, as shown by this special census.[12] The manuscript census shows not only the heaviest early American settlement of the Red Hills in Jackson County but a change from subsistence farming toward plantation agriculture, with a large number of black slaves, 808, or 37 percent of the total population. That cotton was beginning to replace subsistence farming in Jackson County even before the transfer of flags is evident from an item in *Niles' Register* on 1 June 1822. It reported that the brig *William and Jane* had arrived at New York from Apalachicola Bay loaded with 266 bales of cotton, "the product of the first seed ever planted in the neighborhood, which has succeeded beyond expectation." Cotton was to be planted especially in the rich Chipola country, which could wagon its crop to steamboats on the Chattahoochee or barge it down the Chipola River to the Apalachicola. By the 1824–1825 crop season, the port at the mouth of the Apalachicola was expecting to ship eight hundred bales of cotton.[13]

The Spring Creek settlement itself was changing and adapting to the South's increasing interest in cotton. Some of the early settlers had begun to drift away. Settlement, more and more of it permanent, expanded the old Spring Creek community to the south, this part becoming the town of Campbellton. Enough settlers had moved into this area for what was called Bethlehem (later Campbellton Baptist) Church to be opened on 12 March 1825, the second Baptist church in all of Florida.[14] (It still holds services in a building constructed, it is said, in 1858.) A Jackson County map on which are plotted 1826 and 1827 sales of public land is black with purchases in the Spring Creek–Campbellton area and along much of the route of U.S. 231 to the junction with State Road 73. The settlements extended east from U.S. 231 across the Chipola River and from the vicinity of Florida Caverns State Park to Blue Springs.

The 1825 census reveals that 19 of the 213 heads of household in the county owned 15 or more slaves. Forty or more were owned by Jacob Robinson, one of four brothers from Jefferson County, Georgia,[15] Jonas Daniel, and Joseph W. Russ, one of three brothers from Brunswick County, North Carolina.[16] The 19 with 15 slaves or more owned 447 of the 808 slaves in the county. Thus at an early date this county set a pattern for the remainder of the Red Hills, with a community of large and moderate-sized slaveholders, many of whom also had a considerable acreage of farmland, that would dominate politics, social life, and business. Of the 213 heads of household, however, 118 had no slaves at all. Jackson County would continue for much of the antebellum period with a large number of small farmers and a relatively small black population.

The county also remained for a time a rough frontier, with occasional flareups of violence of the kind reported by the *Pensacola Floridian* on 30 August 1823: "On the night of Tuesday, the first of July, Dr. John H. Keddie of Chipoli, Jackson County, was murdered in his bed by a gun fired through an aperture in the chimney of his house, the contents of which lodged in his head and knee and killed him instantly." The culprit was apparently never caught. Following another murder two years later, justice moved swiftly. John Carroll was tried in Superior Court for the murder of Mrs. Elvira B. H. Northrup, with attorneys Webb, Call, and Stone representing the prosecution and Allen, Baltzell, and Gordon the defendant. Carroll was found guilty and on 27 January 1826 was hanged in what the *Pensacola Gazette and West Florida Advertiser* called the first administration of capital punishment in the new territory of Florida.[17]

The county remained a rural and agricultural society, with no formally organized towns, for several years. In 1822 the Florida Territorial Council designated Big Spring as the site for a superior court that would hold sessions twice a year.[18] The next year there was still no town, and in an election for congressional delegate the voting took place in one precinct at the house of the Spring Creek settler Owen Williams, with Williams as one election judge and John Smith, another Spring Creek pioneer, as the other. Forty votes were cast here and thirteen at the house of Thomas Russ in what was called the Chipola area, with Russ and William G. Mooring as election judges.[19] The County Court met on 18 April 1825 at "the house of the widow Hull" in the Chipola settlement.[20] The organized town of Webbville shortly emerged nearby but then became a ghost town after Marianna, settled late in the 1820s, won a bitter battle to become county seat.[21]

In Gadsden County across the Apalachicola River, a much smaller number of newcomers settled before this became American territory. This early settlement acquired a distinct character thanks to Henry Yonge, who was forty-three when he arrived in June 1819 to look over land on the east side of the Apalachicola River at a point called "The Cutoff." From a family in colonial Georgia, Yonge put more than twenty hands to work in 1820 on his Apalachicola River plantation, clearing and cultivating twenty acres and constructing farm buildings. His efforts here were a complete failure. There was much damage from flooding, while the work force became ill in the un-healthful river bottom. After two years Yonge transferred his planting interests to the east side of Gadsden County, also on Forbes Purchase land. His home called Retreat appeared on a May 1824 map about five miles west of the present community of Midway on the west side of Little River.[22]

Thereafter the records show Yonge in the role of peacemaker in a bitter dispute between the rival politicians Richard K. Call and Joseph M. White that seemed to be leading to a duel (1825) and as a colonel in the local militia (1827);[23] as head of a household of eleven white persons and twelve Negro slaves (1830 census);[24] and as the proud parent (or grandparent) of Samuel C. Yonge, who won a premium as a merit scholar at the Quincy Academy (December 1831).[25] On 5 February 1833, Henry's second wife, Ann, died, four months after the birth of her thirteenth child.[26] Having devoted much of his income to educating his family, Yonge was poor when he died a year later. The sheriff of Gadsden County already had levied on and put up for sale his two plantations, the four hundred acres on the Apalachicola, and the "home place."[27] But although his planting in Gadsden County failed to make Yonge rich, it did educate his family; Henry Yonge therefore left to Florida a vast estate of "human capital." A son, Chandler Cox Yonge, born in 1818, studied law in Quincy after getting a degree from the University of Georgia and began his long career as secretary of the Florida Constitutional Convention in St. Joseph in 1838. Thereafter he practiced law for many years in Marianna and then in Pensacola, where he died in 1889. Chandler's son Philip Keyes Yonge after achieving a substantial fortune in the lumber business made many contributions to education, serving for years on the Board of Control for higher education. His great interest in Florida history was recognized in the P. K. Yonge Memorial Library of Florida History at the University of Florida. Julien C. Yonge of another generation was editor of the *Florida Historical Quarterly* from 1924 to 1956.[28]

The bookish cast of the family is shown in an old Gadsden County probate file of another son of Henry Yonge, Henry Fernando Yonge, who died in October 1834 at almost the same time as his father. Only twenty-three, he had just begun the practice of law in Quincy. His personal possessions were few but included a much-prized violin, a gift from his father, and a book collection of exceptional interest. When word had circulated around Gadsden County that the Yonge library was for sale, a dozen or more residents came to the courthouse to make purchases: David L. White, *The Federalist*; J. R. Harris, *Ainsworth's Dictionary*, a French grammar, a volume of poetry by Lord Byron, and other books; Bryan Croom, *Goldsmith's Works* and Hallam's *Middle Ages*; Robert Forbes, Bourienne's *Napoleon*; R. H. M. Davidson, *Travels in Germany, American Speeches*, and Taylor's *Enquiry*; J. M. Nixon, a volume of *The Spectator*; Jesse Gregory, *DeStael on the French Revolution*. Other sales included works of Shakespeare, Bacon, and Scott and novels by Sterne, Fielding, and Bulwer-Lytton.[29]

"The Cutoff" is a place name no longer familiar, but we can locate it from the record of John Tanner, another settler, as having been in the vicinity of Bristol in Liberty County. Tanner took up land twenty-four miles south of the forks and on the east side of the river "near the Cutoff." He died, and the claim fell to his widow Elizabeth and her brother William S. Pope as next friend of two minor children. None of the family stayed here. After laying out a town called Mount Vernon at the forks, Mrs. Tanner and Pope moved to land several miles to the west of the forks in Jackson County.[30]

Another settler in the same Bristol area was William Ellis, who migrated from McIntosh County, Georgia, and made crops in 1820 and 1821 "a mile below the Cut-Off." Like the others he was evidently unsuccessful and moved from the west to the east side of Gadsden County to settle four miles west of an Ochlockonee River crossing. In 1824 he was found here "with a large family."[31] John Collins followed the same course and had finally settled by 1824, a mile south of Colonel Yonge's Retreat. He died in 1828. His will, signed with a mark, left seven Negro slaves and eighty head of cattle to his widow Sarough and four children.[32]

John Carnochan of Savannah, whose family had become part owners of the Forbes Purchase, was able to choose some of the better land on the Apalachicola, well upstream from Henry Yonge. Here, according to the witness Edmund Doyle, who appeared before the Land Claims Commission, Carnochan pioneered the introduction of Sea Island, or black seed, cotton in this part of Florida, along with sugarcane. In April 1820 he sent a gang of twenty blacks to the site and himself arrived in September. Carnochan is said to have spent "a great deal of money" making various improvements, including the construction of a sugar mill with copper boilers, the only equipment of this kind anywhere around. But according to his own account in 1824, "a large and valuable gang of slaves have not for the four years 1820, 1821, 1822, 1823, paid their own and plantation expenses."[33]

By far the largest planter among the early settlers was Jonathan Robinson, who appears to have arrived in the spring of 1822, for a visitor to his plantation in October 1823 found that Robinson had tried the soil for two crop seasons. The visitor was Dr. W. H. Simmons of St. Augustine, one of the two commissioners who had been directed to select a site for a territorial capital. He reached the plantation by a road from St. Marks that crossed the Ochlockonee River and then its tributary, Little River. The land did not seem too good for cultivation until he reached the other side of Little River, "to which we crossed by a handsome plank bridge," as Simmons wrote in his journal. Then the soil "did not vary until near Judge Robinson's, when it became a red loam, resting on clay." Here Robinson's planting "evinced the raciness of a new and fertile soil," with a crop of long staple cotton "superior to any I have ever seen," the stalks growing ten to twelve feet high and some of them fifteen, "yet all were loaded with forms and opened freely. Some rice and cane had been planted, which also flourished well."[34]

Little is known about Robinson's origin, but he is thought to have been a native of North Carolina. Descendants have picked up his trail, before he came to Florida, in southeast Georgia. Like other settlers in this part of Gadsden County, he apparently reached it by vessel from a southeastern Georgia port to St. Marks. Perhaps he was even aboard the schooner *Harmony*, which brought "passengers and a cargo of sugar cane plants, sugar boilers, cotton seed and plantation instruments" from Darien, Georgia, to St. Marks in the spring of 1822.[35] Robinson's house was on the north side of a road (County 65B) angling southwestward and then straight west that is sometimes still called "the Federal Road," the link between Tallahassee and Pensacola in territorial times. The site is marked today only by the family cemetery in which Robinson is buried. His tombstone reads: "Sacred to the memory of Mr. Jona. Robinson who departed this life Sept. 15 1838 Ae 68."[36]

Robinson's plantation, stretching northward to within two or three miles of Quincy, covered about three thousand acres. His slave force was sixty-nine in 1830. Sarah Ann, his daughter, married John Lines from Liberty County, Georgia, who died in December 1831 from a fall from a horse, leaving the widow and eight children. The widow inherited the Robinson place. It was subsequently called "the Lines place" and was for a long time the best-known plantation in the county.[37] Some two miles east of Robinson was Sherrod McCall, a native of South Carolina. McCall and Robinson were the most substantial planters in the vicinity when a meeting place was needed in 1824 for the Territorial Council in the new territorial capital, Tallahassee. They were engaged to bring hands the twenty miles to the site and construct three log buildings to serve as a temporary capitol. Unlike Henry Fernando Yonge, who was a witness when McCall made his will, McCall was not a bookish man. He left only "a lot of books," worth seven dallars, but he was a man of quiet dignity and eloquence, as evidenced by his instructions for his funeral: "I desire that my body be interred in a decent Christian like manner, without parade or ostentation."[38]

One very early settler was a "Dr. White" who was said to live on a plantation to the west of Robinson at the time of the Simmons visit. White's house was a mile north of Forbes Purchase and south of Quincy on State Road 267 just before this road passes under Interstate 10.[39] During the four decades that White lived here, he was unmatched in all of the Red Hills for his energy and a diversified array of talents. "Slept here" is more appropriate for David L. White's residence, for much of the time he was "on the road." Originally of Bladen County, North Carolina, he was in Putnam County, Georgia, in 1820. White was a Methodist minister, physician, and magistrate and, apparently having much energy to spare, conducted during the 1830s a business, managing work forces on plantations throughout the county. His own farm was practically an experiment station. All of these activities appear in the diary that he kept, which was found on the floor of his now abandoned house early in the twentieth century during a moonshine raid: "Off for Quarterly Meeting, to Dr. Nicholson's at Concord. . . . Opened Sister Degraffenreid leg in two places, off for home, arrive for supper. . . . Robinson will proved and qualified. . . . Clear, listing for corn and clearing at Yonge place. . . . Plant Egyptn cotton seed sent me by Mrs. Morat [Murat?]."[40] Dr. White did rest some, at least in his old age, and when he did so it was likely to be at the end of a cane pole. And so in the early spring of 1862, at the age of eighty-two, and having rushed the season by changing into his light Nankeen suit, he wet his line in Mrs. Lines's mill pond, lingering until the cool of the evening. Stricken with congestion, he died before the dawn of the next day, 5 April.[41]

Early sales of public land, beginning in 1826, show a pattern of settlement, almost all of it north of the largely barren Forbes Purchase and of present Interstate 10. The heaviest settlement of all was around Quincy. In contrast with Jackson County, Gadsden almost immediately established an urban center, Quincy, designated as the county seat on 10 May 1825. It shortly became a place of comfortable houses, serviceable stores, and pleasant churches as well as a good school, the Quincy Academy. Quincy remained a small town, though, and the county remained overwhelmingly rural and agricultural into the twentieth century.[42]

The early settlement of Gadsden County showed a strong flow from North Carolina to Georgia and then to Florida, sometimes with a generation between the Old North State and the Sunshine Territory. A stronger flow than is apparent in Jackson County was from South Carolina to Georgia to Florida. Telfair County in the Georgia coastal plain was a favored stopover place. Within a vast domain of longleaf pines growing out of wiregrass, this part of Georgia was not the best place for farming. Still, the hardy wiregrass, as indifferent to fires as were the pines, made wonderful feed for cattle. There was also, according to the geographer George White, plenty of lighterwood, "the poor man's fuel."[43]

Gadsden County had better land, and this fact was evidently known to Cullen Edwards. Edwards was born about 1770 in North Carolina, moved to Montgomery County, Georgia, before the turn of the nineteenth century, and was in Telfair when this county was created in 1807. Cullen and his sons (John, William, Thomas, and Samuel) had settled in Gadsden in time for all five to be impaneled for the grand and petit juries selected at the first session of county court in 1824.[44] Another North Carolina family that came by way of Telfair County was the Love family, members of which settled among other Presbyterians around Philadelphia Church. Daniel and Alexander Love and their families crossed the Florida line (according to family tradition) on 5 February 1823. A brother, John Love, had been in Florida before this, as had their sister Jane Love and her husband Archibald Smith.[45] Two natives of Chester County, South Carolina, the brothers William and Patrick McGriff, sold adjoining farms on the border of Laurens and Pulaski counties, Georgia, in 1824 and established plantations side by side south of the community of Scotland in Gadsden County.[46]

Malcolm Nicholson, born in North Carolina in 1799, moved with his father to South Carolina, received a medical education there, and practiced in Burke County, Georgia, on the South Carolina line. His practice was said to be lucrative, but when he was in his thirties he left it because of his health, hoping to retire from medicine. Nicholson bought land eventually totaling more than two thousand acres west of present-day Havana and built a comfortable house with a dogtrot that remained in the family until the 1970s, when it was sold and restored. But the "peaceful vocation" of this planter "was often interrupted by calls for succour from the afflicted, far and near," according to Nicholson's newspaper obituary, which called him a pioneer of Florida medicine.[47]

No manuscript census of 1825 remains to give details about individuals in Gadsden County, but the total population was 1,374,813 white persons and 581 blacks. The 1830 census shows several quite large slaveholders: Malcolm Nicholson, fifty-one; William McGriff, fifty-two; Jonathan Robinson, sixty-nine; John Carnochan, sixty-three; Bryan Croom, sixty-three; and Thomas Preston, eighty-eight. Following in the footsteps of Jackson County, Gadsden carried the Red Hills much further toward their destiny as a remote Florida province of the South's great Cotton Kingdom.[48]

7

The Complaint of Neamathla

The most attractive cotton soils of all lay east of the Ochlockonee River along the banks of four large lakes, Iamonia, Jackson, Miccosukee, and Lafayette, and between them. This country, once the center of the agricultural activities of the Apalachee, was also nearer to the principal cotton port of New York than any other farmland in Florida, for after the hills stopped eighteen or twenty miles from the Georgia line, the port of St. Marks was only as many more miles away across the flat sands.

There was one obstacle to settlement, though, when the change of flags occurred on 17 July 1821: the Indians who had been humbled and whose homes had been burned and villages destroyed in 1818 were still present in large numbers in this part of present Leon County. Andrew Jackson, whose ideas about the place of Indians in relation to Manifest Destiny were well known, was immediately placed in command of the new territory. President Monroe appointed him governor of Florida with almost dictatorial powers of organizing and running the territory. He arrived in Pensacola on 17 July 1821 with his wife, Rachel, who during the four or five months they spent in Pensacola was much discomfited by the drinking, gambling, Sabbath breaking, and vice in this one of the two capitals of Florida.[1]

Jackson pounced on the Indian problem. In a series of "Friends and Brothers" communications, he sought first to ascertain the strength and distribution of the Seminoles in Florida, particularly in the soil-rich area just beyond the Ochlockonee that remained out of reach of the beneficent hand of the American cotton planter. The effort shortly brought him in contact, ironically, with that Marshal Foch of Fowltown, Georgia, whose "ils ne passeront pas" stance had set off the Florida War of 1818. Neamathla, the head man at Fowltown, disappeared after his confrontation with Major Twiggs in 1817, and we find nothing about him as an actor in the War of 1818. Now, though, he lived among and spoke for the so-called Fowltown settlements, fragments of the Georgia population, around the burned Seminole village of Tallahassa, also for most of the scattered Mikasuki. Moreover, he would soon speak for all of the Indians of Florida.[2]

Neamathla traveled in September 1821 the 200 miles to Pensacola to see Jackson. He was accompanied by John Blount, a "friendly Indian" who had aided Jackson in the Creek War in Alabama and in the First Seminole War in Florida and who now lived at Iola or Iolee south of present Blountstown; Mulatto King, the head man at Coconokla on the west side of the Apalachicola River four miles south of the forks; and the Ocheesee settler Stephen Richards, the interpreter. The cagey Neamathla told Jackson only half of the story about the number, population, and headmen of the Seminole villages, failing even to mention his own village, Cahallahatchee, three miles east of present Tallahassee. Neamathla said he knew of fifteen towns and their chiefs and placed the Seminole population at "about 2,000."[3]

It was soon ascertained, however, that there were thirty-seven towns and a population of 4,883, perhaps 2,000 of the number in some twenty-six towns on or west of the Suwannee River. In present Leon County were Hiamonee on the east side of the Ochlockonee River five miles from the Georgia line and not far from it Tuckagulga, or Ben Burgess' Town. Three miles southeast of Neamathla's town was one with the same name as Tonaby's Tallahassa; the Americans spelled the name "Tallahassee." Chefixico, the chief, had one hundred followers. Four miles to the east was Welika. Farther east, near the border of Leon and Jefferson counties, lay Yumersee at the head of the Samulga Hatchee River [Burnt Mill Creek], with Alouko and Wasupa nearby. The large town of Mikasuki had been broken up into fragments in the 1818 war. Some of the Mikasuki band now lived ten miles to the east at Etotulga, while others were at Hatchcalamocha near Drum Swamp, both in Jefferson County. Much of the Mikasuki population had fled to the vicinity of present Greenville in Madison County to establish New Mikasuki, while Topananaulka was three miles west of this town and Ahosulga five miles south.[4]

It was never for a moment contemplated that Indians occupying the rich farming lands of northern Florida, whether east or west of the Suwannee River, would be allowed to remain for long. In the conference with Governor Jackson, Neamathla responded to his questions about population only after the question of removal, of interest to all three chiefs, had been discussed. Jackson told them that the president "is anxious to have them collected together at some one point, where he can protect them, either within the limits of your old nation the Creeks or at such other point where they can all be together." Neamathla accepted this as "straight talk."[5] Nothing was decided until Secretary of War John C. Calhoun on 7 April 1823 appointed a commission to negotiate a treaty with the Florida Indians, the objective of which would be to move them "south of Charlotte Harbor" in Florida. Jackson, tiring of the governorship, had sent in his resignation on 14 November 1821, and his successor William P. DuVal, a Virginian by way of Kentucky, did not arrive in Pensacola until June 1822. DuVal was named chairman of the commission. Other members were Bernard Segui of St. Augustine and Colonel James Gadsden of Charleston, South Carolina.[6]

Indians were summoned from different parts of Florida, and seventy of them, with Neamathla the acknowledged chief, began a meeting with the commissioners on 6 September 1823 at an encampment on Moultrie Creek four miles from St. Augustine. The Indians were informed that the president, their father, "wishes you to go south," where there would be no conflict with white men who were soon to settle this part of northern Florida. Sufficient good land would be provided for crops, and the Indians would be given plows and other farm implements as well as cattle. Neamathla immediately objected to a move south of Charlotte Harbor "where neither the hickorynut, the acorn nor the persimmon grows." The commissioners were ready to concede the point. As the treaty was drawn their reservation of 4 million acres extended from a line drawn across the peninsula at Tampa Bay to a line drawn across the peninsula just to the north of present Ocala, the eastern and western boundaries nowhere coming closer than fifteen miles of the coast. The commissioners made concessions to "six influential chiefs whose assent to the treaty would not have been obtained without extensive provision for them and their connexion." Instead of moving to central Florida, Neamathla and his thirty warriors and their families would be assigned to a four-square-mile reservation in the middle of Gadsden County, incorporating the old village of Taphulga, while five other chiefs would be assigned to reservations (where some already lived) on the west side of the Chattahoochee and Apalachicola: Econchattimicco and his thirty-eight men four square miles just above the forks; Emathlochee and his twenty-eight and Mulatto King and his thirty just below the forks; John Blount and his forty-three between present Blountstown and the river; and Tuski Hajo or Cochrane and his forty-five just below Blount. The treaty was signed by thirty-three chiefs on 18 September 1823, and these included Neamathla.[7]

Spanish Florida became an American Territory in 1821 but Jackson, in organizing the
territory as governor, soon faced Neamathla, who had in fact touched off the Seminole
War by an "ils ne passerant pas" stand at Fowltown, Georgia, and who became head
man of one of the "fowl towns" near present Tallahassee. (Portrait by Charles Bird
King, from Thomas L. McKenney and James Hall, *History of the Indian Tribes of North
America*, 3 vols. [Philadelphia: J. T. Bowen, 1848], vol. 1, p. 80, courtesy of Florida State
Archives)

The ink was hardly dry on the Treaty of Moultrie Creek when, on 26 September, Dr. W. H. Simmons set out from St. Augustine with instructions to meet John Lee Williams of Pensacola at St. Marks so that they could jointly explore the territory to the north and select a new seat of government for the territory. Governor DuVal was determined to plant this capital somewhere in the area of the Fowltowns, and there was strong sentiment within the Territorial Council for placing a capital midway between the existing capitals because of the difficulty some members had in attending meetings at Pensacola or St. Augustine. There was therefore much support for a resolution adopted on 18 June 1823, instructing the governor to appoint one commissioner from East Florida and one from West Florida who would examine prospective sites between the Ochlockonee and Suwannee rivers for "the quality of the soil, the local situation and the streams by which it was watered" and select "the most eligible and convenient situation" for a capital and its government buildings. The commissioners met at the house of William Ellis just west of the Ochlockonee, and on 26 October 1823 set out, as Simmons observed in his journal, "to take a view of the situation about [the Indian town of] Tallahassee, which had been represented as high and healthy and well watered."[8]

En route, Simmons left his companion to explore the country to the north, and so it was Williams who was the first to reach the Fowltowns. "Seeing a fine stout Indian in a nut patch I left my horse and accosted him, asking for information where the chief of the village might be found," Williams reported. "He very strongly demanded what I wanted and said he was Neamathla. I told him we were sent him by Governor DuVal to inform him that he wished to build a house in which he might meet his council; that the distance to St. Augustine was so great, that he wished to select a spot near the center of the territory." Neamathla asked several questions, then indicated he would consider the matter overnight. Williams meanwhile was treated to special entertainment, a ball game between young men and young women. The women won the game, after which the men "were sentenced to bring lightwood for the council fire, which having procured, they brought it into the great square singing all the while." Simmons having arrived at Cahallahatchee by nightfall, the guests were housed overnight under the shed of the council house.[9]

In the morning Neamathla asked more about the purpose of the Simmons and Williams visit. After being told for a second time, the old chief "said that he was much annoyed by people from Georgia, who endeavored to get his land from him. But at length he told us to go and do as we pleased, but not to tell anybody . . . , that he had given us permission to select a site for the seat of government." Williams observed: "Neamathla is a shrewd, penetrating man; he evidently feels no affection for the white man. His interest restrained him at this time, so that he wished not to obstruct our progress, but he feared that his lenity would render him unpopular with his people." Three miles away on Lake Lafayette, Chief Chefixico expressed himself more strongly to the other commissioner. Said Simmons: "He angrily caught up a handful of dirt, and presenting it asked if that was not his land; he then mounted his horse and rode off to Neamathla's, to enquire further into the objects of our visit. From the behavior of this chief and other Indians we met, I am convinced that these people will not be removed without difficulty."[10]

It was a foregone conclusion that the commissioners would select a site at or near present Tallahassee, which they did less than a week after they met. The site was described as being about a mile from the old fields of the abandoned town of Tallahassa Taloofa and at a place "where the old Spanish Road is intersected by a small trail running southwardly." Simmons's East Florida constituents were not enthusiastic about a site so far from St. Augustine; it was almost halfway between Pensacola and St. Augustine. Consequently, not until 20 November did Williams, having obtained Simmons's final consent, send in a report of the commissioners, one copy to DuVal and one to congressional delegate Richard K. Call.[11] DuVal made it clear that the territorial capital was here because the place was at the center of the largest body of rich land in Florida. He added that this must "forever remain the center of our population." He issued a proclamation in March 1824 calling the Legislative Council together here for its next meeting, to be held in the fall.[12]

On 9 April 1824 the first wagonload of settlers arrived, two white men, two white women and two white children, and a mulatto man. One of the two white men was evidently John McIver, who brought his household from Fayetteville, North Carolina. They pitched their tent on the southern slope of the hill which was to hold the original town of Tallahassee and at its highest point the capitol. The correspondent of a Pensacola newspaper who told of this event a year and a half later said the land about the camping site might be called "the land of the Fairies." At the eastern base of the hill on which the capitol would be built, "a beautiful rivulet meandered its course through a rich hammock"—this was later called "the St. Augustine Branch" but is today a drainage ditch in the center of Franklin Boulevard—that bent toward the west around the southeastern corner of the original town. Several springs on the southern slope, where the Duncan U. Fletcher Building now stands, formed branches of Spring Creek, now a drainage ditch north of Canal Street.[13] Looking out from the McIver encampment to the south and west, the country "opened to their view like a magnificent park." To the southeast "the view was more confined by the thick foliage of the undergrowth, which served to screen the view, though not the sound, of a beautiful cascade, which was formed by the rivulet above described, falling over a ledge of rocks into a deep glen, which forms almost a circle of seventy yards in diameter, and disappears at the bottom of the same ledge of rocks, very near the cascade. . . . The same day in the evening Judge Robinson and S. McCall Esq arrived with hands and put up three buildings to accommodate the Legislative Council . . . , and in a few days a small store was erected." By November 1824, when the Legislative Council met, Tallahassee was still only "a woods town," according to the Pensacola newspaper, but there were "well roofed houses, all with chimneys—more or less—great plenty of fuel, as old Boon required it, two lengths of a tree from the doorsill—good beds and blankets plenty, some chairs and an occasional table," as well as plenty of food "and all the variety of Bar Comfits and comforts—all good and plenty."[14]

In addition, presumably, the Legislative Council members could stay, as they did in many future sessions, at the Planters Hotel, long a landmark across Pensacola Street from the capitol square near the corner of Adams. The builder and innkeeper, William Wyatt, described as "a self-made man" from Maryland, seems to have been in the fledgling town as early as June 1824. The sloop *Hector*, at any rate, sailed from Pensacola on 23 June with a Mrs. Wyatt and family aboard, bound for St. Marks. A month later the same sloop brought a cargo to St. Marks that included fifteen hundred feet of lumber; this must have begun a change from the prevailing log cabin architecture. This shipment was followed a week later by the schooner *Tice* with thirteen thousand feet, perhaps for Wyatt's hotel.[15] Although more of a favorite with legislators, the Planters was immediately followed by Hall's, also on Capitol Square and just to the east of the Planters. This was the hotel of a former Virginian, Major William Hall, who had arrived by way of Pulaski and Irwin counties in Georgia.[16]

While the Legislative Council was in session, a press, type, and other materials for a printing plant and newspaper arrived from Pensacola via St. Marks. The principal proprietor, Ambrose Crane, did not start the Tallahassee *Florida Intelligencer* until 1825, but he had arrived with his wife and family on the same sloop that had brought the Wyatt family the previous June. His partner in the publishing business was a lawyer named Adam Gordon. Like some others, Crane preferred a suburban home and by December 1824 was living in a house on 160 acres southwest of town.[17]

Governor DuVal also liked suburban living and shortly obtained a quarter section (160 acres) whose northwestern corner was at the southeastern corner of Tallahassee. He built his house where the tennis courts and softball field are now located in Myers Park, overlooking the beautiful cascade. This sixteen-foot waterfall was the most conspicuous landmark found in the vicinity by Commissioner John Lee Williams. He and Simmons designated the prospective capitol site as about one-half mile north-northwest of this spot. The fact that DuVal had obtained his valuable property under the preemption law, which enabled him to claim residence and cultivation and buy it for $1.25 an acre, led a political enemy, congressional delegate Joseph M. White (who succeeded Call), to accuse the governor of having virtually appropriated the waterfall for his front yard. This hilltop, covered with majestic live oaks and overlooking the valley through which the St. Augustine Branch curved around the town, was indeed a splendid residential area, much later to be called Country Club Estates. And the hill must have been what in August 1824, before the town was even laid off, was called "Mount Aventine," for the southernmost hill of Rome.[18]

From this location the governor had an easy buggy ride to the capitol. He had only to follow the general route of Myers Park Drive and Pensacola Street across a watery ravine and up another steep hill, his workplace being only seven-tenths of a mile from his residence. Earlier, in 1824, though, according to an early nineteenth-century source, DuVal had a log cabin about fifty paces south of the log cabin capitol used for sessions of the Legislative Council (and probably one of the three structures erected by Robinson and McCall). Here the Florida governor caught the eye of Washington Irving, who assigned him the name Ralph Ringwood, told of his adventurous boyhood in Virginia and Kentucky, and continued with his residence at this "log cabin palace" where he lived on "hunters' fare" while coming to grips with the Indian problem. Previously, however, even at the time the first settler, McIver, was arriving and Robinson and McCall were building the first capitol, DuVal was informing the *Pensacola Gazette and West Florida Advertiser* of his aims for Tallahassee and "his intention to proceed shortly to that place and have a town laid off, which will enable those who intend making establishments there to place their buildings in the situation in which they will remain permanently." In June he and Colonel George Walton, the territorial secretary for West Florida, were in Tallahassee.[19]

Perhaps Governor DuVal's greatest contribution as chief executive was the city plan for Tallahassee. One cannot help suspecting, although there is no evidence, that Judge Augustus Brevoort Woodward had a share in designing it. Arriving in the "woods town" in the autumn of 1824, Woodward took his oath as judge of Superior Court for the Middle District of Florida on 4 October and began to preside over this court.[20] A philosopher-scientist as well as judge, he had lived for a time in Washington and counted Jefferson and Pierre Charles L'Enfant, the planner of the nation's capital, among his acquaintances. With a nascent but keen interest in city planning, Woodward proved ready to apply some of his ideas when he was assigned in 1805 to a judgeship at Detroit. Detroit, a new town, had burned to the ground, and Woodward formulated a plan for its rebuilding. His plan featured a triangular arrangement of thoroughfares 200 feet wide combined with a grid of narrower streets, being distinguished particularly by the numerous open spaces, reserved for public use, at the intersections of the major boulevards and within the triangles. Woodward was a cranky and eccentric bachelor, and his abrasive manner made as many enemies as friends for the plan. Although it was put into use, it was then largely abandoned by Detroit. Woodward lost ground politically until in 1824 he was demoted to the judgeship in Florida.[21]

DuVal had been accumulating suggested plans for Tallahassee. On 10 November 1824 he submitted to the Legislative Council three separate plans laying out streets and blocks of the original quarter-square-mile town. The plan agreed upon meshed perfectly with DuVal's ambition of having a Richmond, Lexington, or Philadelphia in this Florida wilderness. In fact it was modeled on William Penn's original plan for Philadelphia. According to the historian of American town planning John W. Reps, the Philadelphia plan of a grid with one or more central squares was widely copied through the Midwest and South, but Raleigh, North Carolina, and Tallahassee, Florida, enjoy the distinction among state capitals of having started with five such central public squares, so that there was an abundance of open public meeting places. Four of these squares in the Tallahassee plan were near the corners of a larger square that was reserved for the capitol building. Most streets were sixty feet wide, but some were eighty and two others one hundred feet. Monroe and Adams formed two sides of Capitol Square. Although no streets were provided along the border of the square of hilltop that became Tallahassee, space was left at the four sides for 200-foot-wide boulevards that could be extended as the town expanded.[22]

But after the selection of Tallahassee for the capital in November 1823, DuVal was busier with the Indians than with city planning. Troops that had been stationed at St. Marks had been removed, and some Indians under Neamathla now killed the cattle of settlers. As DuVal wrote from Pensacola on 12 January 1824, he was confident that the Indians "will not remove into the boundary given to them by the late treaty, unless there is a military force in the vicinity to overawe them." Around Tallahassee the rapidly increasing presence of white skins created in the leader Neamathla a feeling that the whites' sole objective was to kick the redskins out of this fertile land and give them only a swamp or sandy plain to live in. And even though Neamathla had agreed to removal in the Treaty of Moultrie Creek, he now adopted a distinctly warlike stance. Washington Irving called his plan of action "The Conspiracy of Neamathla," but it might as well have been called "The Complaint of Neamathla." While he was in Pensacola, DuVal received on 18 June 1824 an express letter from the Indian agent at St. Marks, telling about a turn for the worse.[23]

An infantry company was finally stationed at St. Marks, and Governor DuVal summoned sixty or seventy militiamen to be present also for talks with the Indians. The armed militiamen assembled at Tallahassee. Before a meeting at St. Marks on 26 July 1824, DuVal enlisted the aid of Blount and the other Apalachicola chiefs, who sent a force of warriors to aid the militia. DuVal wrote the secretary of war from St. Marks after they arrived: "This sudden movement so surprised the Tallahassee and Mickasuky Indians, that they hurried to meet me, and promised to obey my orders and to respect my authority."[24]

DuVal first met Neamathla in his own town. The confrontation has often been pictured as a physical encounter, a kind of David-and-Goliath match between a governor who was five feet seven inches tall and an Indian chief who was six feet tall. Neamathla, however, was seventy-two years old and DuVal only forty. As DuVal later wrote, "I took the interpreter with me, and went to Neamathla's town. I found there about 300 warriors, and I saw many of them armed. I immediately went into their square yard (which is their forum) and gave them a talk, and ordered them to meet me on the 26th instant at St. Marks; and assured them that their ruin and destruction was certain, unless they obeyed my orders." Six hundred Indians attended the St. Marks meeting, and DuVal, as he put it, "appointed John Hicks head chief to lead them south to their land. . . . I have directed

Succeeding Jackson as governor (1822–34), William P. DuVal, a native Virginian, humbled and replaced Neamathla as the principal Seminole chief in Florida, this chief having resisted the hundreds of American settlers now coming to the Red Hills, and the Seminoles were confined to a reservation in central Florida. (Courtesy of Florida State Archives)

the Indians to prepare to move, and to be on hand by the first day of October next."[25]

October 1824 came, and there was now indeed a considerable movement of Indians to their central Florida reservation. By May 1825, though, 120 Indians remained west of the Suwannee River. The situation had worsened by fall 1825, and in August of that year there were, according to the 1825 census, some 900 settlers between the Ochlockonee and Suwannee rivers. Nearly all of these were in or near the new town of Tallahassee. The danger of incidents between reds and whites increased with a new development reported by Acting Governor Walton from Tallahassee on 6 October: he had received information "that most, if not all, of those [Indians] who formerly resided between the rivers Suwannee and Apalachicola are on their return hither." The explanation, he added, was that the Indians simply had no means of subsistence, the country beyond the Suwannee being less productive than the Red Hills [26]

Finally all of the Indians left the Red Hills. Neamathla had spurned the Gadsden County reservation assigned to him and his people and had even spurned the offer of a white school for the Seminoles, saying, "We wish our children to remain as the Great Spirit made them, and as their fathers are, Indians."[27] Now, however, he returned to the Creek Nation after being humbled and replaced by DuVal. He became the chief of Hitchiti Town on the Hutchechubbee River.[28] Always an implacable enemy of the white man although soft-spoken and cooperative on occasion, Neamathla in pursuing this course of action was only taking a suggestion that had been made in 1821 by Andrew Jackson. In a few years, though, Jackson himself had become the Great White Father in Washington and was committed to sending all of the eastern tribes, friends like Blount and foes like Neamathla, to the Indian Territory assigned to all in the West.

And so it was that this noble Hitchiti chief ended his long career of resistance with one last hurrah in 1836, at the age of eighty-four leading several hundred of his followers in Alabama in a Creek rebellion. The rebellion occurred after the Creeks had been ordered to dispose of their lands, ceded in a treaty of 24 March 1832, and make ready to be removed to Oklahoma. It was common knowledge among both Indians and the whites who had now heavily settled Alabama, that a group of white speculators centered in Columbus, Georgia, were engaged in defrauding the Indians of the individual tracts they had been given under this treaty. There was a suspicion also that these same speculators fomented the rebellion itself. When the uprising occurred, an armed force of ten thousand regulars and citizen soldiers was assembled to repress it. Neamathla, who is credited with leading the Lower Creeks in this revolt, was arrested and put in irons. He and sixteen hundred Indian men, women, and children were held at nearby Fort Mitchell. Then in the heat of July 1836 they were marched to Montgomery. An observer of this march said in the *Army and Navy Chronicle* that despite the chief's eighty-four years, Neamathla's eyes "indicate intelligence and fire and his countenance would give the impression that he was a brave and distinguished man. . . . They were all handcuffed and chained together; and in this way they marched to Montgomery, on the Alabama, ninety miles. Old Eneah Mathla marched all the way, handcuffed and chained like the others, and I was informed by Captain Page, the agent for moving the Indians, that he never uttered a complaint."[29]

The journey continued by boat to Mobile, then to New Orleans and up the Mississippi, Arkansas, and White rivers to Rock Row, Arkansas, where an overland journey began to the Indian Territory. The ragged party finally reached Fort Gibson on 3 September 1836, but there they were met by an angry group of Creeks, members of the McIntosh faction, which had opposed the Red Sticks in 1813–1814, had sided with Jackson in the 1818 campaign, and in 1829 had compliantly agreed, the first of all the Creeks, to removal. Only when Neamathla agreed to submit to the existing government of this faction were he and his followers accepted on the Creek lands in the West. This magnificent chieftain and hero of the Red Hills now disappears from view.[30]

8

Tallahassee and
the "Old Dominion"

Between 1825 and 1835 the Red Hills increasingly attracted settlers from the Carolinas, Virginia, and Maryland and even from New York and New England, most of the newcomers settling in or around Tallahassee. That this community at the start had an appealing urbanity and style is shown by an account of a celebration on 8 January 1825, marking the tenth anniversary of General Jackson's victory over the British at New Orleans. "The dinner was sumptuous, the wine excellent and the ladies of our infant metropolis graced the table with their presence," said a newspaper, while outside Wyatt's Hotel an old six-pound cannon found at San Luis "performed its functions in the celebration of the day."[1]

Judge Woodward presided at the dinner and was a prominent figure at other celebrations of Washington's birthday and Independence Day. Woodward himself was honored by a dinner before making a trip to Washington.[2] At a ball on 22 February 1826, ladies and gentlemen present represented more than half of the twenty-four states. A cosmopolitan flavor was added by Achille Murat, nephew of Napoleon and son of one of his marshals. After Bonaparte's downfall Murat had come to pursue his fortune in Florida and had a plantation in what became Jefferson County.[3]

The most elaborate of all the early celebrations was that on 4 July 1826, when Tallahassee observed the fiftieth anniversary of American independence. Men of the community gathered at the Capitol Square, where a new brick capitol was nearing completion. Built by John W. Levinus, a New Yorker who was one of the first settlers in Tallahassee, the structure was no thing of beauty, but it established the classic revival style that became the rule for public buildings and for some private ones as well.[4] Women of the community gathered at the "meetinghouse," evidently the Methodist Church that had been erected in 1825 at the northwestern corner of the original town, on the south side of present Park Avenue. This very plain wooden structure was described as "neither ceiled nor plastered, with no glass in the windows which were closed by solid shutters, not blinds."[5]

At the firing of a "national salute," Governor DuVal led a march of men to the meetinghouse. The Reverend Joseph Smith greeted the assemblage of 150 there, and after the ceremony there was a procession to "the arbor"—perhaps a "brush arbor" that had preceded construction of the church. The cooks had prepared "one ox, one sheep, two shoats, three dozen fowls, ten hams, fish and vegetables in the greatest variety." After the feast there were many, many toasts.[6]

Some of this style wore off rapidly as the town filled with officeholders, speculators, and tradesmen: there were 500 persons in 1826,[7] 932 in 1830,[8] and 1,300 to 1,600 in 1835. The traveler Charles Joseph Latrobe, who visited in 1833, voiced the impression that here was "an adventuring, speculating and money-making race."[9] There was an immediate need for mills to grind corn, and not surprisingly, Robert Butler was operating a millhouse just to the north of the cascade by 1827.[10] Although the mill was evidently not successful, it was shortly joined by a lime quarry on the other side of the waterfall.[11] A decade later Tallahassee leased twenty-five acres, including the waterfall, to Thomas Brown. Although the principal purpose was to place this beautiful area at the edge of town in the hands of someone who would take care of it, a provision allowed two acres where several springs flowed out of the slope south of the capitol to be used for a tanyard. If a tannery was erected here the stench must have tempered the welcome that townspeople gave a cooling Gulf breeze.[12] The waterfall itself was finally obliterated by railroad building in the 1850s, leaving the "gulf" into which it flowed a nauseous pool. All of John McIver's "land of fairies" persisted as a semiindustrial wasteland well into the twentieth century.[13]

Such noisy, dirty operations as sawmills, however, were from the start of settlement placed well outside the community. The first sawmill was located beside a stream (now only a drainage ditch along the east side of the Mabry Heights subdivision). The land here falls off from an elevation of one hundred feet to thirty-two feet at Black Swamp, the water from this flowing through Munson Slough to Lake Munson. The owner of the sawmill, Brazil R. Bradford, said it was capable of earning a profit of four thousand dollars a year. Bradford built his house on "a handsome elevation near the saw mill" that looked out to the south on a beautiful lake, which was named after the pioneer lumberman. He shortly went to other enterprises in Alabama and left the mill and 160 acres around it in the hands of a brother,

Thomas Madison Bradford. The mill seems to have prospered, for in March 1829 Bradford's Sawmill advertised forty-seven thousand board feet of lumber for sale, including "weatherboarding and flooring from the most beautiful yellow pine."[14]

The original town of Tallahassee, one-quarter of a mile square, was divided into 322 lots that, offered for sale in the spring of 1825, brought $45,000.[15] Many were bought by speculators, who turned a pretty penny in their resale. By 1828 the population explosion required an expansion to the north, into a quarter-mile square extending from the present Park Avenue to Brevard Street.[16] Some speculators, such as Isham G. Searcy, dreamed of much more growth. He and a partner owned eighty acres at the southwest corner of original Tallahassee, and in about 1829 he published a "Plan of the City of Tallahassee" showing a "city two miles long and one and a half broad" laid out in streets and blocks that never came into existence.[17]

Searcy's dream of a populous Tallahassee did not materialize. After its population reached about 1,500 in 1835, the town quit growing. However, by 1830, DuVal's prediction that the area near Tallahassee would become the most populous part of Florida had been fulfilled; the five Red Hills counties had a population of 19,133, or 55 percent of the territorial population of 34,730. The Red Hills were increasingly a rural region, Tallahassee then having 932 persons, Quincy 212, and Marianna and Monticello a smaller population, while the town of Madison did not exist.[18]

Far more realistic than Searcy's conception of Tallahassee was the description of a visitor in the 1830s: a little town "built round a knoll and surrounded by dense hammocks through which diverged roads like the spokes of a wheel." These, today's "canopy roads," are Old Bainbridge, Meridian, Centerville, Miccosukee, and Old St. Augustine.[19] During the 1830s short-staple cotton moved in large wagons over them from the northern part of Leon County and neighboring Georgia to Tallahassee. After being weighed in Tallahassee, the cotton traveled the old Spanish road to St. Marks. In 1825 John and Nathaniel Hamlin, formerly of Augusta, Maine, were at St. Marks to load the cotton aboard schooners and brigs and sell in exchange the merchandise in their store. By 1828 the Hamlins had established the town of Magnolia, six miles upriver, which for a brief time shipped cotton from planters in Jefferson County, and from some in Leon and a few in Madison County, who could bypass Tallahassee and wagon their cotton here. Magnolia flourished for a while and was the second largest town in Middle Florida in 1830, with a population of 276. The town declined and disappeared, though, after the completion of a railroad from Tallahassee to St. Marks in 1837.[20]

Meanwhile Tallahassee, becoming more a market town for cotton than a territorial capital, further declined in style and increased in shabbiness. The town shocked Judge Robert Raymond Reid, who recorded in his diary a couple of stays during 1833 and 1835. A brooding intellectual, native South Carolinian, and former resident of Augusta, Georgia, Reid had gone to St. Augustine in 1832 as judge of the East Florida Division of Superior Court. Periodically he and the judges for Middle and West Florida met in the capital as the Florida Court of Appeals. "How far preferable is St. Augustine to Tallahassee. The latter place is full of filth—*of all genders*," he confided to his diary.[21]

Reid always liked to escape from the Tallahassee hotel where he sometimes stayed to the plantation Blackwood, six miles northwest of town. Here his son-in-law Charles Black had bought eight hundred acres in 1828 but had died at the age of twenty-two on 28 August 1830. His widow inscribed on the tombstone the comment that this South Carolinian "came to Florida in pursuit of happiness and wealth. He found THIS GRAVE." Reid sometimes wept at the grave, but he relished the time away from "a noisy, senseless crowd; a legislative council with little wisdom, a fashionable circle with little taste" and away from "the public house where noise and dirt prevail to a disgusting degree." He could even withstand extreme cold in a log house not built for it: the thermometer fell to four degrees above zero on 8 February 1835. Here at Blackwood, Reid walked in the gloomy woods, read, and sought in his devotionals (as regular as breakfast) the balm for doubts that crept into a mind of the Enlightenment about some passages of the Holy Scriptures. He was always ready at the end of the appeals court meetings to ride in his Stanhope on the long road to St. Augustine, his faithful driver John at the reins. John, said Reid, "is worth of his single self half the white men in the country."[22]

As the style and appearance of Tallahassee declined during these early years, the plantations increased in splendor. The plantations also exceeded the town in many industrial activities. In addition to the many field hands who did the plowing, hoeing, and cotton picking, skilled black mechanics kept the cotton gins, cotton presses, and lumber mills running on plantations, and there were also carpenters, brick masons, and plasterers. The plantations sometimes even had "day care centers for working mothers" in the form of a "nursery" run by a stern black mistress of cleanliness whose services allowed mothers only a few hours after childbirth to join men in the cotton fields.[23]

So many Virginians settled in Jefferson and neighboring Leon counties that their combined domain became known as the "Old Dominion." They included William B. Nuttall, an early settler at El Destino on Burnt Mill Creek and, south of him, Edmund B. Vass on Sweetwater Branch.[24] Near Vass was Lipona, the plantation of "Prince Murat," as he was called, for Achille was the son of Joachim Murat, the King of Naples, who had married Napoleon's sister Caroline. In 1826, the same year Murat showed up at the ball in Tallahassee, he married Catharine Willis, a Virginia beauty. A great-grandniece of George Washington, Catharine had accompanied her father, Byrd Willis, and his family to Tallahassee. Like other big plantations, those of the Old Dominion usually oversaw agricultural and industrial operations as efficient as those of a medieval fiefdom. But this little bit of Virginia was fondly remembered particularly for the "hospitality" of the masters and mistresses, evident in the many parties, some of which lasted for days as planters and guests played charades and danced or picnicked on Lake Catharine. None of the places was more popular with the party-going gentry than Lipona, and a contemporary said the second story of the Murat house was "fitted up with small compartments, like the berths of a ship, in order to entertain the greatest number of guests."[25]

James Gadsden on nearby Wacissa was no Virginian but had a pedigree as distinguished as any in the the Old Dominion, having come from one of the old families in Charleston, South Carolina.[26] The largest family connection of all was that of the brothers John G. and Robert Gamble, who came to Florida in midcareer from Richmond, Virginia. John's plantation house, Waukeenah, gave its name to the present-day community; Robert owned Welaunee several miles to the southeast.[27] Six miles northeast of Waukeenah, where an interchange connects U.S. Highway 19 with Interstate 10, was Dulce Domum, the place of the Cabell family of Richmond, which was closely connected with the Gambles.[28] Three miles north of Dulce Domum was one of the grandest of the houses in the Red Hills, a three-story frame mansion, Casa Bianca. The owners of this and three thousand surrounding acres were Joseph M. White, who for twelve years was Florida delegate in Congress, and his wife Ellen, called Florida to distinguish her from the wife of another congressional White in Washington. Both were from Kentucky.[29] Casa Bianca and a house still standing on the southern edge of Monticello that was the home of a Virginian, Martin Palmer, lay at the northeastern corner of the Old Dominion.[30]

Wirtland, a two-thousand-acre plantation some three miles west of Monticello, was owned by William Wirt, the Maryland-born and orphaned son of a German mother and a tavern keeper father of Swiss

Casa Bianca, the Jefferson County frame plantation home of Congressional Delegate Joseph M. White and his wife "Florida," burned to the ground in 1905. (Courtesy of Florida State Archives)

origin. A self-made man, Wirt wrote early in life *The Letters of a British Spy* (1803), celebrating the virtues of a "natural aristocrat," and later in life a biography of Patrick Henry (1817) that went into twenty-five editions. He was equally well known as a lawyer, having helped prosecute Aaron Burr for treason and served several years as U.S. attorney general. All of his life Wirt wanted to be a planter, but he died in 1834 without achieving this goal and without ever having visited Wirtland. However, several of his family, including his wife, Elizabeth, a sister of the Gamble brothers, lived there.[31] Wirt gave his daughter Laura one thousand acres of land at the southern edge of Waukeenah and near the western edge of Welaunee in 1827 when she married a Virginia lawyer, Thomas Randall. Randall paid two thousand dollars to have a frame house built immediately, and this move was controversial because the Gambles, along with many others, had started out in log cabins.[32]

Like the Gambles, four Virginia families that settled along Black Creek in northeastern Leon County at first erected very modest homes. Francis Eppes, a grandson of Thomas Jefferson whose early education was supervised by the Sage of Monticello, settled about two miles east of Pisgah Methodist Church.[33] Below him on Black Creek was Thomas Eston Randolph, his father-in-law. South of Randolph were two brothers from Richmond, natives of Ireland, Samuel and John Parkhill. But although the log-pen houses of these pioneers admitted rivers of water and cold blasts of air through their many chinks, they wore the proud names L'eau Noir, Ethelmere, Springwood, and Tuscawilla. Eppes was a lawyer just getting his career well under way and twenty-eight when he made the move in 1829. Randolph, sixty-two, hoped to improve his financial condition. Settled in their log houses, the families suffered several jolting experiences: Mrs. Randolph, an invalid for twenty years, died in 1832; her daughter Harriet, who married the young physician Dr. Lewis Willis, died in childbirth the same year. Mary Elizabeth, the wife of Francis Eppes, wrote from L'eau Noir on 20 March 1835 that the log pen leaked badly, the lower rooms were uncomfortable, and the upstairs uninhabitable, "but these are little grievances and do not distress me much for in May we shall move into the kitchen of our future abode, and hope to get the great house completed by December." Within a month she too was dead.[34]

Harriet Randolph was fond of the Randolphs' neighbor, Samuel Parkhill, "a very charming fellow." He was, moreover, "a pushing man," and indeed in the decade of the 1830s he prospered more than anyone in the Black Creek settlements, coming to own not only an enlarged Springwood but "Lake Jackson and Orchard Pond," 5,404 acres in all, along with 210 slaves. He was, after John G. Gamble, the president of the Union Bank of Florida, the largest stockholder in this enterprise, with 1,612 shares. His borrowing was also extensive. When he died in 1841, he left a debt of $143,782 to the bank that wiped out his large estate.[35]

West of the Parkhills was a full township (thirty-six sections) of land that pressed against the eastern boundary of Tallahassee. This was granted by Congress in 1825 to the Marquis de Lafayette. Two Virginians, William B. Nuttall and Hector Braden, and a Marylander, Dr. John A. Craig, eventually bought this great domain, but Nuttall died, and Braden moved away. Only the Marylander Craig stayed, his plantation along the Thomasville Road and extending to Lake Hall remaining intact as Andalusia.[36] Some five miles east of Tallahassee, off the Old St. Augustine Road, was Southwood Plantation. A stone in the cemetery proclaims: "Sacred to the memory of George W. Ward, born Feb. 22, 1781, in the state of Virginia, died Aug. 22, 1835." Ward had held one of the two principal jobs in the Land Office as receiver of lands.[37]

Another Virginian, Richard K. Call, was receiver of monies in the Land Office. A protégé and aide-de-camp of Andrew Jackson in the Creek and Florida wars, Call served a term as Florida delegate in Congress and then settled on the edge of Tallahassee. Although a planter and investor, his principal interest was politics. As the head of what was called "the Nucleus" or land office faction, he built his house at the foot of North Adams Street. From the front porch it had a view ten blocks away of the City Hotel and of the capitol across the street, the center of political activity for all of Florida. The house still stands today, its warm red brick and wide white steps, two-story portico, and four massive columns and pediment asserting the favorite architectural style of old Tallahassee from the midst of an eleven-acre grove of oaks and magnolias.[38]

Still another Virginian, Thomas Brown, lost a big investment in an ambitious sugarcane farm on Lake Jackson in an 1829 freeze and thereafter moved to Tallahassee. He speculated in town real estate and became the principal hotel owner, first having the Planters, then the City Hotel.[39] Sugarcane had almost the appeal of cotton at first, and Isaac Fort of Jackson County claimed to have made a clear profit of $6,900, or $139 a hand, on only a small part of his 1,200 acres north of Marianna in 1831–1832. He produced 125 hogsheads (125,000 pounds) of sugar and 14,000 gallons of molasses. The conversion of sugarcane into sugar required an enormous investment in buildings and machinery, though; his farm had a 250-foot-long row of buildings that included a grinding room; a boiling room; a cooling room, or purgery, made of brick; and a distillery. By 1834, with cotton prices high and with many failures in sugarcane, planters were shifting from sugar to cotton.[40]

The wealthiest planter in early Leon County was Benjamin Chaires, but he had many other enterprises. A native of Onslow County, North Carolina, he came to Florida after several years in Milledgeville, Georgia, and in 1822 pioneered the laying out of Jacksonville. Moving to Tallahassee, Chaires led in early efforts to establish a bank and also a railroad. But Ben Chaires was primarily a planter. Spurning a log cabin, he built the most elegant house in all of the Red Hills, Verdura, his thirteen-room, three-story brick seat on nine thousand acres of land some seven miles east of Tallahassee. Although the structure was destroyed by fire in 1885, five majestic columns still reach high into a jungle of hardwoods in a remote field, continuing to flaunt the style of this palace's builder.[41]

It was quite the thing to become a "planter." David Macomb, a Detroiter (and nephew of Alexander Macomb, soon to become the ranking general of the U.S. Army) aspired to be one. He had hardly settled in Tallahassee in 1825 when he began to invest in five hundred acres at the edge of Southwood Plantation, about four miles southeast of Tallahassee. One can look out from Capital Circle across a misty lake of thirteen acres and a nearby hill that appear to have inspired the name Macomb gave to this plantation, slightly misspelled from Sir Walter Scott's *Lady of the Lake*, "Ben Venue on Loch Acray."[42]

Macomb was largely engaged in other enterprises: he practiced law, held a contract to carry the mails, made various surveys of harbors and rivers, and served as county judge. He appears to have benefited from both the patronage of friends of Andrew Jackson in the Nucleus and friends of the Monroe administration and delegate White. David Macomb adhered mainly to the latter, however, and threw caution to the winds while proposing a toast during the Independence Day celebration in 1826. Macomb raised his glass to Henry Clay, "whose republicanism was strikingly manifested in preferring the civilian to the military chieftain" (in the U.S. House, he had delivered Kentucky's vote for president to John Quincy Adams rather than to Jackson in the 1824 election).[43]

Prince Murat, reacting to this toast or something very like it at a political rally, shouted "Turncoat!" from the fringe of a crowd, and then "Liar!" when Macomb sought to explain his actions. In a few days they were on the dueling field on the border of Lake Lafayette. By this time the mercurial Murat regretted the confrontation. According to the account given half a century later by a physician who called himself Murat's friend and medical adviser, the Prince "took his place with perfect *sang-froid*, a cigar between his lips, and a smile on his face." When the signal was given to fire he made only a flourish with his uncocked pistol. Macomb, of a different mind, fired, and the bullet cut off part of the little finger of Murat's right hand. "In an instant, smarting from the wound, Murat cocked his pistol, took deliberate aim and fired, the ball passing so near Colonel McComb as to leave a mark around a part of his body." As Murat put it, the bullet "went through his shirt and scared out the lice."[44]

Macomb's hostility to the Nucleus may have accounted in part for his downfall and the tragedy that soon engulfed his family. However, most of his troubles stemmed from an extravagant lifestyle and growing indebtedness. A long line of creditors soon had all but a small part of his estate up for sale, one exception being a pianoforte that Macomb was able to prove at a jury trial was the particular possession of his oldest child, Eleanor.[45] Finally Macomb gave up in Florida, traveling in 1835 to Harris County, Texas, where he joined the war for Texas independence in the army of Stephen F. Austin. Mary and family joined him in 1836, but she barely survived the trip across the Gulf. She died 19 October and four months later David, in a fit of despondency, slit his own throat and died, leaving five hostages to fortune, the oldest, Eleanor, being only seventeen.[46]

Half a dozen or more duels occurred in the early days. The bad aim of the duelists saved several lives. Tallahassee took the blame for much of the violence of the time; a South Carolina newspaper complained of "half a dozen duels and street fights with pistols, dirks, &c" and *Niles' Register* of "several horrid assassinations and duels" here.[47] This characterization was unfair, however; although there was much "disorderly conduct" in and around the shabby taverns and dives near Capitol Square, Tallahassee saw no murders during its first twelve years.[48] Outside town, though, there was considerable violence. When Thomas Randall succeeded Woodward as superior court judge in October 1827, following Woodward's death, he had to handle two murders that occurred in Leon County during the hot July of that year.[49]

One of the accused was Ben, a slave on the plantation of Dr. Isaac Mitchell, which lay for two miles along the south shore of Lake Iamonia. At the end of a workday the overseer, Irvin Kent, accused Ben of having been idle and promised to whip him unless he completed his task. Ben went to the overseer's house and clubbed Kent to death. When confronted by the other blacks and accused of having killed the overseer, according to the newspaper account, Ben said he did not care whether he had. An attorney appointed by his master, as required by custom and law, defended Ben, but he was convicted on "very satisfactory circumstantial evidence" and the confession of Ben, "made to white persons including an officer of the court," again according to the newspaper. Although the conviction was first reversed because of a defect in the indictment, Ben was convicted again on retrial and was hanged on 23 May 1828.[50]

The same grand jury that charged Ben with murder brought an indictment at the same time, 3 October 1827, charging John R. Watkins with the murder of Jesse Butler in July 1827. Watkins lived on a small acreage near the present interchange of U.S. 27 and Interstate 10. In a community called Milltown, he had shot Butler in the arm during an argument, and the victim lingered several days before he died. The incident created something of a stir around Tallahassee, one account in verse suggesting that he had intended to shoot a second victim, Mahalah: "She may be thankful she did run. / The other load 'twas in the gun." Watkins was convicted on 17 April 1828 and was sentenced to be hanged, but then the judicial machinery moved in a way that suggests that the equal protection of the law was somewhat more equal in the case of a free, white "yeoman" than in that of a defendant who, although a black slave, was supposed under the law to enjoy the same right to life, if not to liberty. Watkins's counsel filed a motion to quash the indictment, it not having been signed by the foreman of the grand jury, and this motion was granted. After another indictment but before another scheduled trial, counsel pleaded that the defendant, having once been convicted of a crime, could not be placed in second jeopardy ("autrefois convict"). Judge Randall agreed and allowed Watkins to go free. Evidently badly frightened, he left Florida.[51]

Most political arguments of the day were settled not by violence but by words and finally by a decision at the ballot box. The bitterest of all political contests were the territorywide elections for delegate to Congress. Every other year James Gadsden and Joseph M. White emerged from Wacissa and Casa Bianca like boxers from their corners in the Old Dominion, as champions of the Nucleus and anti-Nucleus factions. White, with a masterful appeal to squatters rather than to speculators, always won. But in 1831 the vote was close enough to tempt Governor DuVal into making one of his worst mistakes. He asserted that irregularities had occurred in some precincts, such as Sadbury in Gadsden County, declared the election a "tie," and decreed that there would be another election. This was clearly beyond the governor's powers, and there was a storm of disapproval.[52] The battle's outcome was presumably assured by a ditty sung to the tune of *Yankee Doodle*:

In Tallahassee's famous town,
   The Nucleus was frisky
And marv'lous wise have lately grown,
   By drinking of much whiskey.
     Yankee Doodle, doodle do
     Yankee Doodle dandy
   With the Nucleus let us go,
     And for their work be handy.

The capitol they say is crack'd,
  And eke the skull of Billy
By counting votes his brains were rack'd
  And he is craz'd and silly. . . .
A new election then we'll have,
For James to try again, Sir. . . . [53]

DuVal's mistake in 1831 appears to have been the beginning of the end of his tenure as governor, an office he took in 1822. But in the summer of 1832 he returned from one of his many long trips out of the territory and committed another blunder. While he was gone one David S. Rogers was convicted of the murder of John Farmer by a Leon County jury that, while sending him to the gallows, "recommended the prisoner to the mercy of the executive." James D. Westcott, the territorial secretary and acting governor in DuVal's absence, stayed Rogers's execution, allowing time for DuVal to return. But when the governor had returned to Florida, he refused to interfere with the execution, now set for 27 July 1832, and being ill went to the coast for a rest. Meanwhile Rogers's parents had come from South Carolina to plead for clemency. Rogers's attorney argued that the governor had acted in too peremptory a manner, without a hearing, and pursued DuVal to his coastal retreat. Rather than act on the question, DuVal wrote out his resignation as governor and sent this to Westcott by way of the attorney, asking that his resigned commission be sent to Washington. The resignation was accompanied by a note asking Westcott to step into the governorship himself. With the hour of execution approaching, the lawyer carried these documents to the capitol in Tallahassee. But Westcott had no more stomach for handling the Rogers case than DuVal. Hearing that the attorney intended to visit him, he ducked across Pensacola Street to the Planters Hotel and from there, according to the lawyer, "made his way through a back window, to an outhouse on the adjoining lot," where he was finally cornered with the help of some boys who had discovered that Westcott had exchanged his executive office for these unseemly chambers. Westcott refused to act on DuVal's request, however, and afterward returned DuVal's commission and letters. According to the lawyer, who recounted the events in a letter to the Floridian signed "Florida," "during the time this farce or rather mockery was going on, poor Rogers was launched into eternity, there to await another but more awful trial, before a Governor who will not resign." A detachment of militia stood by to prevent any interference with the execution, and Rogers "met his fate with great firmness," according to the Floridian.[54]

DuVal finished a term ending in 1834. President Jackson replaced him with John H. Eaton, who with his wife, the controversial Peggy, arrived in Tallahassee in December of that year. The marriage of Peggy, a barmaid, with Jackson's secretary of war, had created a furor that had split the presidential cabinet. But Peggy said there were "no ugly passages" in Tallahassee. She was much impressed by the greeting when they arrived, for an old cannon from "the fort"—perhaps the same one that had celebrated the victory at New Orleans—was brought out to sound thirteen salutes, one for each of the original states, outside the Eatons' hotel. The loading and firing of this venerable Spanish piece took so long that the firing, which began near dusk of one day, lasted until seven o'clock the next morning. The intervals were so great between firings, said Peggy, "that we forgot about it, until suddenly would come a little short surly boom!"[55]

Despite political antagonism and occasional violence, a state of euphoria settled over Leon County and the Red Hills in 1835. Cotton prices and cotton crops were good, shipments from the port of St. Marks having increased from 328 bales in 1827 to 15,917 in 1834–1835. The Union Bank of Florida opened for business in Tallahassee in January 1835. With the bank pouring money into the economy in the form of loans to planters, in addition to cotton prosperity, the *Floridian* said: "The countenance of every one seems lit up with joy." Leon County planters particularly had cause for joy. More than one hundred of them became the beneficiaries of a large part of the $3 million subscribed principally by unsuspecting Dutch and English capitalists for Florida "faith bonds"—which in a few years would be repudiated and in the meantime provided money the bank would lend for practically any purpose, including "pleasure carriages."[56] Much of the prosperity of the planters trickled down to tradesmen and others in Tallahassee, including builders, who began to improve the appearance of this town of about fifteen hundred persons. The products of the prosperous late 1830s included the handsome columned St. Johns Episcopal Church at Monroe and Call; the equally beautiful Presbyterian Church, still standing at Adams and Park; and the suburban home of Bryan Croom, Goodwood, the finest of all of the Leon plantation houses still standing.

9

Those Seminoles
Again

A treaty to remove the Seminoles from central Florida was signed in 1832. Regular army troops had arrived by 1835 to enforce it and take the Seminoles across the Mississippi River. Growing rage against this plan broke out like a forest fire in the fall and early winter of 1835 in the wilderness around the army encampments. In the bloodiest act of all, 180 warriors lay in wait for and attacked Major Francis Dade and 106 officers and men on 28 December as they marched from Fort Brooke on Tampa Bay to Fort Drane to strengthen the American force there. A lone survivor spread the news.[1]

Neither Brigadier General Duncan L. Clinch, in command of 250 regular troops, nor Major General Richard K. Call, in command of 500 Florida Volunteers, had heard about the Dade Massacre when they encamped three miles from the Withlacoochee River two days later. But Seminole violence had already led to an order by President Jackson to inflict "just punishment," and Clinch and Call planned to attack the Indians within their stronghold in a great bend of this river that flows northward and then into the Gulf south of the Suwannee. Any secrecy the expedition might have had vanished on the morning of an expected engagement, 31 December 1835, when a militia bugler filled the piney woods with the sound of reveille. Clinch took his regulars across the Withlacoochee, but only between thirty and sixty of the militia could be coaxed across; the next day, New Year's Day of 1836, marked the end of their four-week enlistment, and they had been promised that they could return home. The American force lost four (all regulars) killed and fifty-nine (fifty-two regulars) wounded.[2] Even though Call crossed the river himself and made it possible for the regulars to return after their defeat, the Withlacoochee became this general's Rubicon, a river that had to be crossed.

Call retained his command of the Volunteers and on 4 April 1836

Richard K. Call (governor 1836–40 and 1841–44) was a protégé and aide-de-camp of Jackson. He led the Florida Volunteers as a general when in 1835 the Seminoles violently resisted a second move, to the Indian Territory, and he continued as governor for most of the Second Seminole War, 1835–42. (Courtesy of Florida State Archives)

became the third governor of the Florida Territory as well. President Jackson also gave him temporary command of both volunteer and federal troops and then approved a campaign that Call had proposed. This necessitated another crossing of the Withlacoochee, and Call got up from a sickbed on 12 September 1836 to lead several hundred volunteers eastward. He was joined by some regulars and tried for an entire day, 13 October, to cross the Withlacoochee, then at high water, without success. Food being low, he then retreated to Fort Drane and Black Creek. When the news reached Washington, the angry Jackson relieved Call of his command. However, the militia general did not learn of Jackson's action for more than a month and after the first try did cross the river and engage the Indians in three days of fighting.[3]

After this campaign by Call the Second Seminole War became increasingly a job for the regulars, commanded by a succession of generals. Like the Viet Nam War much later, the Seminole War of 1835–1842 troubled the American conscience, was extremely costly in American lives and wealth, and ended inconclusively. The wily Seminoles dictated the terms of battle, guerrilla warfare in the swamps and hammocks of central Florida that were familiar to them. The 1,400 Seminole warriors made the U.S. Army pay with 1,466 lives at a dollar cost of $30 million to $40 million. At the end of the fighting, the objective of the Jackson administration, removal to the Indian Territory, had still not been completely achieved. A remnant remained— and their descendants still remain—in southern Florida.[4]

For Floridians west of the Suwannee, the war was now almost altogether on the home front. There were far more civilian than military casualties. Hit-and-run raids by the Seminoles continued throughout the war in remote settlements, frequently on the edge of the Cody Scarp, by Indians who then retreated into the swamps of the lowlands south of the Red Hills. Tallahassee continued with business as usual, as did most of the Red Hills. Despite the war, the population of the five Red Hills counties increased between 1838 and 1845 from 26,959 to 33,173. The area still held half the population of Florida. Madison, the county most exposed to Indian attack, grew the fastest, from 1,695 to 3,762. Leon and Gadsden still led in population, with 9,612 and 7,645 persons, respectively, while Jefferson County had 6,525 and Jackson County 5,629 in 1845. Blacks now outnumbered whites 19,618 to 13,445.[5]

Cotton growers added to their own and the region's prosperity. The year 1836 was a banner one for cotton. The prosperity enabled Tallahassee to complete in 1837 a railroad to St. Marks that became the principal mover of Red Hills cotton. A depot placed at the foot of a hill sloping from North Adams Street made it possible to reach an elevation of only eighty feet above sea level, creating an easy grade to St. Marks at near sea level. At first a steam locomotive was tried, but it proved impractical. General Call, who continued as governor until 1839, became the principal owner of the railroad that must have been called "General Call's trot line," for it depended on a team of

four to six mules, which pulled the cars.[6] The railroad proved a surprisingly efficient mover of cotton. Shipments from the port reached
28,055 bales in 1838 and more than 30,000 in 1839, about three-fourths
passing through the hands of Tallahassee merchants and handlers.[7]

The merchant R. H. Berry sought to supplement the prevailing
coastal trade with New York and short-circuit Yankee middlemen by
shipping directly to Liverpool. Tallahasseans in the winter of 1838–
1839 excitedly watched the building in New York of a vessel for this
trade, the *General Samuel Parkhill*, named for the Black Creek planter
and militia officer; Benjamin Chaires had joined Parkhill in financing
the enterprise. Tallahasseans glowed with pride as the big vessel, of
600 tons burthen, 131 feet long, 13 feet in beam, and 21 feet deep in
the hold, arrived in February 1839 and anchored well offshore in
Apalachee Bay. Loaded with 1,923 bales, it sailed on 12 March. This
vessel and two others carried 5,000 bales of cotton to English mills in
a year's time. Merchants along Monroe and a cross-street, Clinton,
prepared for this trade. Berry himself built "an elegant fireproof store"
in the midst of a district of frame buildings. "Berry's Row" on Clinton
Street (now College) soon filled with tenants. Dennis Shea advertised
an assortment of "superfine broadcloths" just arrived from Liverpool.
Other Berry Row tenants were James E. Broome & Company and
Ward & May. The partnership of Kerr & Kirksey erected on Monroe
Street during the winter of 1838–1839, according to the *Floridian*, "a
three-storied fireproof brick store, granite front, which will a little
surpass, we think, any similar one in the city."[8]

In addition to cotton and the largesse of public funds that was
spread around through the Union Bank, the Red Hills and particularly
Tallahassee prospered from the presence of thirteen thousand "volunteers" who came from half a dozen states during the seven-year
war to help fight the Seminoles. Often they spent some time in Tallahassee going to and coming from the front, as did the Tennessee
Volunteers in 1836. This unit crossed the Florida line on 9 September
1836. One of its officers, First Lieutenant Henry Hollingsworth, discovered that Florida, far from being "a universal swamp inhabited by
alligators," as he had heard, was a place of prosperous farms and
nice homes. At Marianna, which he described as a "beautiful little
town," the people hung out flags and fired a cannon to greet the
soldiers. Quincy was "a most delightful town" where the people
looked healthy and prosperous, and between Quincy and Tallahassee
he discovered "the most beautiful country thus far I have ever seen."
In the vicinity of what today is called Midway but was then Salubrity,
his unit encamped on the plantation of Joseph McBride, a lawyer,

judge, and planter, at whose table officers dined for thirty-seven and one-half cents a person. Mrs. Julia McBride, a "friendly and social woman," particularly impressed him. He was also pleased with Tallahassee. The Tennesseans paraded in full dress through the capital. Although it was "emphatically annihilating" that the pretty girls scarcely noticed them, Hollingsworth drowned his disappointment at the Planters Hotel bar and registered at City Hotel for a pleasant stay of one week before marching (actually riding) to the Withlacoochee with General Call.[9]

Brigadier General Zachary Taylor, one in the parade of generals who managed the war, complained that some Floridians wished the war to go on so that government money would keep flowing into Florida. The northern press echoed the theme, declaring that the war went on because Floridians sought to profit from it.[10] Horse racing, so popular that a North Carolina newspaper said, "A good Virginia race horse is in more demand in Florida than ministers of any denomination,"[11] continued without abatement through the 1830s and early 1840s. Tracks were opened at Quincy in 1830, then in Marianna and Tallahassee in 1832. The biggest racing enthusiast was a transplanted North Carolinian, James J. Pittman of Jackson County, whose Virginia stallion, John Henry, standing at stud in his Marianna stables, left progeny all over the Red Hills.[12]

The prosperity flowing from war expenditures, good prices for cotton and the flow of money to planters through the Union Bank is partly evident today in the building that was erected in 1841 to house the bank itself. By this time, however, the bank had come upon bad times, and angry farmers spoke as if they intended to come in and rip up its "marble floor."[13] Controversy over the bank indeed split the entire territory into political factions, called "the bankites" and the "antibankites," the former principally Whigs and the latter Democrats. The Bank's troubles began in 1837 when some banks in the northeastern United States failed, sending much of the nation into a depression. This "panic" led the Union Bank, like its northern counterparts, to stop paying in specie, a development that distressed farmers and planters. Some, particularly in a broad area in the vicinity of Pisgah Methodist Church that was called Centerville, held angry meetings.[14]

In the territory at large, particularly East Florida, there were complaints against the bank for another reason, namely the extension of Florida's credit for the benefit of a few already well-to-do planters in the Red Hills. It was noted that the interest alone on nearly $4 million in territorial bonds that were floated on behalf of the Union and two

smaller banks amounted to $260,000 a year, or about $5 for every
man, woman, and child, black and white, in the territory—five times
the annual territorial revenue from taxes.[15]

The controversy between bankites and antibankites was hottest in
Leon County. The Second Seminole War during its first two years
had produced a "war hero" to lead the latter group. Leigh Read, a
native Tennessean, came to Tallahassee early in the 1830s, studied
law under Call, and became as much a favorite and protégé of Call
as Call had been of Andrew Jackson. Read's military skill and daring
became apparent on the first Withlacoochee campaign. Not long afterward he took a force of eighty men twelve miles up the Withlacoochee
River from the mouth and without firing a shot rescued fifty men in
a lonely blockhouse, where they had virtually been hostages of the
Seminoles for forty-eight days. Read immediately became a widely
acclaimed war hero, and although he continued in the militia, where
he soon became a brigadier general, he began to invest his military
capital in territorial politics.[16]

In 1838 a surge of antibank sentiment fed on the action of Governor
Call in approving $2 million additional faith bond money for the bank
in addition to the original $1 million. Planters with the most property
were favored for loans. Some who were excluded joined in the complaints about tight money. In this same year Read was elected a delegate to a convention in December that wrote a constitution to be used
when Florida became a state. The bank dominated discussion, and
Read helped East Florida antibank delegates elect Judge Robert Raymond Reid as president over former Governor DuVal. The same group
wrote into the constitution a provision forbidding the state to collect
taxes in support of a bank or any other corporation.[17]

Antibank people took their battle to the next session of the Legislative Council, but this body, still controlled by probank Whigs,
turned a deaf ear. In 1839 Read ran for representative in the house
of the newly bicameral legislature and was elected. It soon became
apparent that the antibank Democrats would control the House and
would elect him Speaker. The Whig party, formed a few years earlier,
had controlled Leon County and was now little disposed to accept
the success of this upstart antibank politician. The "political violence"
that ensued led the historian Arthur W. Thompson in writing about
this period to suggest that violence had become an "opposition tech-
nique" by which the Whigs sought to put down the "levelers."[18]

Read was the leader of Democrats in Leon County. His counterpart
among Whigs was Colonel Augustus Alston, a planter on Lake Miccosukee. As colonel of a regiment of Volunteers in 1836, Alston had

Robert Raymond Reid (governor 1840–41) became head of the Democratic party and of an "antibank" faction, while Call was a leader of what came to be known as The Nucleus, or land office party, and later a Whig. Shortly after leaving office, Reid died along with several members of his family in the yellow fever epidemic that struck the Tallahassee area in the summer of 1841. (Courtesy of Florida State Archives)

dueled with George T. Ward over the killing, by Alston's order, of Ward's brother, a drillmaster in the regiment. Read had also been in a duel, in 1833, in defense of Call's honor. Since then Read had come to oppose dueling, and when a challenge reached him from the Whig camp during the 1839 legislative canvass, he ignored it until, challenged again and publicly criticized, he agreed to meet Alston. Too anxious for a shot, Alston swung his rifle around awkwardly when the signal was given and his shot went wild. Read then took careful aim and killed his opponent.[19]

Whigs and friends of the fallen leader did not let the matter rest here. A brother of Augustus, Willis Alston, undertook to avenge the planter's death. He had moved to Texas but returned. On a Sunday evening as one hundred Democrats celebrated their legislative victory just before the meeting of the legislature in January 1840, Willis Alston appeared at the door of the dining room at the City Hotel. Alston shot Read as he was about to sit down, fled in the confusion, and then returned to plant a knife in Read's abdomen. The wounds were not critical but prevented Read from accepting the speakership of the House that he was scheduled to receive. Alston escaped to Texas.[20]

Meanwhile President Van Buren had removed Call as governor in December 1839, replacing him with the Democrat Robert Raymond Reid. With the executive office and House now in the hands of Democrats, antibank men raised the question of whether the Union Bank bonds had been issued illegally. Shortly thereafter the faith bonds were repudiated. Whigs and bankites fought back savagely. Tallahassee had a summer of violence in 1840 unlike anything seen before as the bank issue was fought out again.[21]

Willis Alston returned a second time to Tallahassee and on the morning of 26 April 1841 had his revenge. Hiding in the house of Michael Ledwith on Monroe Street just off the corner of the two-hundred-foot-street, he waited until Leigh Read had passed the doorway and then at short range fired two barrels of a shotgun filled with slugs and small pistol bullets into Read's body. Read lingered in great pain and died within a few hours.[22] His assailant, although arrested and bound over for willful murder, made bail a month later on a lawyer's trick instigated in the law office of David S. Walker, his brother-in-law and an attorney. A justice of the peace who had refused to admit Alston to bail was voted down by two others whose commissions had expired. Superior Court Judge R. C. Allen issued a warrant for Alston's arrest after discovering the error, but Alston was now on his way to Texas, where he soon died a violent death.[23]

The Read murder shocked the Red Hills into abandoning dueling, and there was less violence of other kinds. However, the 1840s saw a number of overwhelmingly sad events. A year before the decade began, news of the sinking of the steamboat *Home* with Hardy Bryan Croom and all members of his family filled the Red Hills with gloom. During the 1820s and 1830s Croom and his brother Bryan had had plantations in Gadsden County, but Hardy's favorite avocation had been botanizing in the forests just to the east of the Apalachicola River, where he had discovered a new species, the Torreya tree. Alvan Wentworth Chapman, who became the foremost plant taxonomist in the nation, credited Croom with starting him on his own career; "a mere tyro at botany," Chapman had met the planter in October 1835. Chapman was living at Quincy when Croom's coach-and-four "drew up before my office, and a gentleman of middle age, spare habit, and blue eyes, came forth and introduced himself as Mr. Croom of North Carolina." Croom remained at New Bern, North Carolina, but in the fall of 1837 was in the process of moving to Charleston, South Carolina. He planned after landing there to go on to Leon County, Florida, where he and his brother Bryan now had four square miles of land on Lake Lafayette. A winter cottage Hardy was having built there would also be the base for exploring the Florida peninsula—that "terra australis incognita."[24]

The violence that troubled Tallahassee hardly matched the violence around remote homesteads of the Red Hills, the frequent targets of Seminole attacks during seven years of warfare. The Indians were despised as aggressors against whom settlers could retaliate in good conscience, for they were protecting their homes. Small war parties often came from bases across the Suwannee River and took a heavy toll in sparsely settled Madison County and along the edge of the Cody Scarp in Jefferson. After a lightning attack, killing and burning, the Indians were usually deep within a coastal forest by the time the home guard reached the field. In May 1836, Indians attacked the plantation Waukeenah and killed a slave on nearby Belmont.[25] Shortly afterward a Jefferson countian named Carter was shot and scalped,[26] and nearby a fifteen-year-old boy was killed within hearing of his mother.[27] In the spring of 1837 a large war party attacked the house of a Mr. Wallace who operated a ferry on the Aucilla. The ferryman escaped but his wife and two daughters died.[28] In 1838 Seminoles attacked with particular ferocity. The wife of the Reverend D. Purifoy escaped from their home in the Springfield community of Jefferson County during an attack while her husband was away on an appointment. Two children lost their lives when the house was burned, and three black servants were also killed.[29]

Creeks who had left Alabama and Georgia were responsible for some of the raids. In midsummer of 1838, they spread terror in Gadsden County. A farmer named Laslie on the Ochlockonee, about fifteen or twenty miles from Tallahassee, was found dead with his daughter, their bodies "dreadfully mangled, particularly the old gentleman, who had his throat cut."[30] But most of the violence was east of Tallahassee. On the evening of 13 July 1838, just after the Laslie murder, four Indians and one black struck the Singletary home in Jefferson County, leaving Mr. and Mrs. Singletary and two children dead. Only a five-year-old girl survived to tell of the raid. Heretofore killings had been with guns and knives; in this one, three-foot-long arrows, tipped with metal points, had been used. One small girl had two in her breast.[31] Some three weeks later the Baker family in Madison County, about fifteen miles east of Monticello, was attacked at the supper table. Mrs. Baker was killed by the first shot. Mr. Baker seized two grandchildren, one in each arm, and ran outside, but a bullet passing through one of the children also killed the grandfather. These victims were found next day with the other child asleep between their bodies.[32]

In Leon County attacks seldom occurred nearer Tallahassee than a community on the St. Augustine Road that at the time was known as Chaires Cross Roads, about ten miles from the capital. Leon County had an organization of "Minute Men" that bumbled as much as most other home guards in retaliating against attacks. In July 1839 on the north side of Lake Lafayette, a Seminole band attacked the home of a brother of Ben Chaires, Green H. Chaires, and his wife and one or two children died. The Minute Men lost one of their own number when, as they pursued a wisp of smoke believed to have come from the enemy, one of the men accidentally discharged his gun into the back of another.[33] The Indian attacks continued, but with most of the Seminoles now west of the Mississippi, including John Blount and the "friendly" Indians on the Apalachicola,[34] the war finally ended in 1842.

Personal tragedy had begun to dog Robert Raymond Reid before he was appointed governor. His daughter Janet, the widow of Charles Black, died at Blackwood on 28 October 1839.[35] As Reid entered upon the office of governor in 1840 and struggled with the problems of the bank, violence, and the Second Seminole War, word came that his son, James, had been lost off Cape Horn aboard the vessel *Sea Gull* that he had been commanding in a scientific expedition to the Antarctic. Reid continued to lose sleep months afterward. In his diary he wrote: "Dear Son! when night comes I think of you more intensely.

I con over every feature, remember the lustre of your eyes, the laugh of your lips: even the moles on your neck and brow are visible to me. I shall never be happy again."[36]

The old warrior President William Henry Harrison had hardly taken his oath on 4 March 1841 when he replaced Reid as governor of Florida with a newfound Whig supporter, Richard K. Call. Reid was therefore a private citizen again at the time that Leigh Read was murdered. The funeral was held on 28 April 1841 at Live Oak, the plantation of Read's father-in-law John Branch. Reid and his wife Martha missed the funeral; by the time of their arrival the cortege had already moved to the cemetery at Pine Hill, the plantation of another Branch son-in-law, Edward Bradford.[37]

On the very same day Reid received news of the death of President Harrison. He noted sardonically, "The remover is removed." Now fifty-one, Reid had every reason for believing that a bright future lay ahead of him as leader of the increasingly strong Democratic party in a territory soon to become a state. He had another ambition: "I will strive to be an author, and place my chief dependence on that." After hanging up his shingle as a lawyer, Reid moved to Blackwood plantation from the house he had been occupying in Tallahassee. But in midsummer, just two months after commenting on the removal of "The Remover" Harrison, he himself left the earth, struck down on 1 July by one of "the fevers" that hit Tallahassee and the surrounding area with unprecedented force. He was buried in the family cemetery, where his daughter Janet and son-in-law Charles Black lay. One reaches this burial ground today by walking half a mile through the forest where Reid liked to stroll alone by the light of the moon— although in winter "the gloom of the forest and sighing of the winds make me sad." Today the tiny cemetery on a hilltop where the Black house evidently stood also holds the remains of Millard F. Caldwell, a Florida governor who served one hundred years after Reid and died in October 1984.[38] Six days after her father, twenty-two-year-old Rosalie Raymond Reid died. She had nursed him during his illness. She was followed on 17 July by Rebecca, Reid's granddaughter and the only daughter of Charles and Janet Black. Finally on 20 July John Graham, the second husband of Janet Black, died of the yellow fever that was now raging more fiercely than ever in and near Tallahassee and that struck also at the port towns of Apalachicola, St. Joseph, and Port Leon.[39] Former Governor DuVal wrote from Tallahassee on 13 November: "There has been buried here the last season up to this time 400—out of a population of about 1,600." This estimate must have included deaths, for example those in the Reid family, in subur-

ban and rural areas of Leon County; an estimate by the bookseller
William Wilson may have reflected the period of greatest virulence
in Tallahassee alone: one-tenth of the population in two months.[40]

In the meantime a depression, lagging four years behind the Panic
of 1837, gripped the Red Hills from 1841 to 1847.[41] As though death
and depression were not enough, along with political troubles and
violence, to convince Tallahassee that it was being subjected to some
awful retribution, there was a disastrous fire on Thursday, 25 May
1843. Of unknown origin, the blaze started at 5:00 P.M. east of the
capitol, the wind pushing it northward across Lafayette, Jefferson,
and Clinton streets and westward between Monroe and Adams. The
entire mercantile district was destroyed in three hours.[42] The bookseller William Wilson said his losses from the fire were fifteen thousand dollars "and as much more by the failure of banks and
individuals."[43]

Tallahassee celebrated statehood with some restraint when a bill
signed on 3 March 1845 admitted Florida to the Union. In another
political overturn, Call, the Whig, had given way to John Branch, the
Democrat, who served as interim governor of the territory until an
elected governor of the state could take over. When news of statehood
reached Tallahassee, Governor Branch invited the public to Live Oak.
His daughter wrote a friend: "Bonfires blazed on the edge of the grove
and lanterns were hung in the shrubbery. The house was brilliantly
lighted and from top to bottom was thrown open to the public. Across
the front entrance in large letters of greenery on a white banner were
the words STATE OF FLORIDA and inside the house all was music and
jollity and congratulations."[44]

10

King Cotton
Takes Control,
1845–1850

Having suffered violence, political bitterness and economic depression, the Second Seminole War, a yellow fever epidemic, and a disastrous fire, Tallahassee needed something to boost its spirits. This something was, in the words of the local newspaper, the "newly finished and elegant capitol." Untouched by the fire of 1843 that started to the east and burned to the north of it, the capitol, six years in building, became the pride of all of Florida. It was exhibited to legislators who assembled on Wednesday, 25 June 1845, for the inauguration on its east portico of the first elected governor of the new state, William D. Moseley. On this occasion "a goodly number" of other visitors also viewed the building, which was described as "spotless white within and without."[1]

The inaugural ceremony was dull, and the eyes of most spectators must have been on the building. It must have appeared much as it does today when the restored structure is viewed from Apalachee Parkway. Today the capitol is off white instead of "spotless white," but the front wall is that of the capitol of 1845, a thick wall of brick covered by a layer of cement plaster. The fenestration is that of the original capitol, while on both the east and the west sides the porch with six large columns and pediment in the restoration completed in the 1980s match those of the original. Here, though, the similarity ends, for the restoration incorporates additions made in 1902, principally a flimsy dome of the sort found on courthouses of the period. The length was also slightly extended, a hip roof substituted for the simple gabled roof of slate and a showy balustrade added at the cornice.[2] The most controversial additions in the restoration are the red and pink canvas awnings on the windows.

The new capitol took command of Tallahassee's skyline, its handsome gabled roof becoming the first sight to greet the traveler's eye.

William D. Moseley (governor 1845–49), a North Carolinian who had barely missed becoming a governor of the Old North State, became a planter in Jefferson County, Florida. He was elected the first governor of the new state in 1845. (Courtesy of Florida State Archives)

The 1845 capitol shown in this old engraving looked like this to Sidney Lanier in 1875 and indeed presented this appearance until a dome was added in 1902. (From Sidney Lanier, *Florida: Its Scenery, Climate & History,* 1865)

If the newcomer traveled by stage he got off at the stage stop on Washington Square a block north of Capitol Square. If he traveled by sea, he landed at St. Marks, journeyed by "the cars" to the Tallahassee depot, then took a hack up the steep hill to one of the hotels along Adams, Pensacola, or Monroe, all near the capitol. Tallahassee should now have become a "state capital" if it was ever to be one, but it simply accepted the handsome gift of a capitol as its own while becoming more of a cotton town. Professional men rented the empty first-floor offices, while the handsome third-floor Hall of Representatives became Tallahassee's "civic center" for lectures, performances by traveling players and the annual May Party. More than ever during the late 1840s, Tallahassee devoted itself to the handling of cotton.[3]

The care of visitors was of secondary concern. Accommodations were third rate at the shabby hotels. The best in food and entertainment was to be found at a seedy enterprise, the Florida Exchange, at Monroe and Pensacola, that advertised a restaurant, a bar, an oyster room, and a billiard room "open all night" with "hot coffee always

on hand."[4] Lucky were visitors such as the correspondent of the
Boston Post, who signed his dispatches "Communipaw" and while in
Tallahassee in January 1847 was an invited guest at the beautiful home
of General Call. Here he found himself "tilting through a quadrille,"
enjoying the unaffected hospitality of Call's daughter, the hostess
Ellen Call Long, and laughing at the stories of former governor DuVal,
who had an "inimitable talent at spinning a yarn."[5]

As a part of the inaugural program in 1845, legislators, other visitors, and townspeople participated in a "civic procession" down Monroe Street preceding the noontime ceremony. Already, on the west
side of the street, red brick stores had begun to replace the shabby
frame structures destroyed by the fire. There were wide walkways in
front under wooden or metal awnings, and newly planted trees. Soon
the street had two dozen or more stores, on both sides of the street.
The business community here was hardly interested in visitors at all
except for the planters who came in to exchange their cotton for merchandise.[6]

This store row continued northward from Capitol Square for only
three blocks to McCarty Street, usually called "the 200-foot street."
Beyond this the North Addition was mainly residential. McCarty
might well have been called "Church Street." On the north side the
Methodist Episcopal Church stood at the present location of Trinity
Methodist, at Park and Duval, the Presbyterian in a building, completed in 1838 and still used by the First Presbyterian, at Park and
Adams.[7] The Protestant Methodist Church also chose a location
north of Park, on the east side of Monroe Street half a block from the
two-hundred-foot street.[8] The St. Johns Episcopal Church, like the
Presbyterian and Methodist Episcopal churches a white, columned
building but a frame one, stood on Monroe at Call.[9] Catholics had
the only other church building near midcentury, constructed in 1846
on the north side of McCarty between Gadsden Street and the city
limits.[10] Thus until a new congregation of Baptists built in 1858 across
Clinton (College) Street from the present First Baptist Church,[11] the
two-hundred-foot street separated sacred from secular activities as
well as, generally speaking, residential from business.

But this was "Church Street" only on Sundays; during the remainder of the week it was a street of mules and wagons. In fact, during
the fall and winter following the cotton harvest, the mule team and
wagon "took possession" of most streets, according to the *Floridian*.[12]
McCarty had become a bobtailed boulevard after the City Cemetery
halted its westward advance, and its two-hundred-foot width, now
little needed for vehicular traffic, was used principally for parking.

On the north side, between Monroe and Adams, was the courthouse[13] and in the street space itself the City Market.[14]

Large wagons heavily loaded with cotton bales, traveling principally along what are called the "canopy roads" today, appear to have aimed at the intersection of the two-hundred-foot street and Adams, but their first stop was at the vacant lots on the east side of Adams, behind the Monroe Street stores, where the bales were unloaded and weighed. Sometimes they were stored at a warehouse where the Hilton Hotel now stands,[15] but as frequently the cotton was immediately wagoned downhill to the depot to be put aboard the cars for St. Marks and shipped to New York. After unloading, the wagons might be parked on the two-hundred-foot street to take care of courthouse business or on Monroe Street to be loaded with supplies from the stores. For a time John R. Lloyd operated, over Barnard's Drug Store at Monroe and Clinton, the "Daguerrean Room and Skylight Gallery," the studio of Tallahassee's lone portraitist, but the booming cotton economy led him to move to Adams Street, where he became an auctioneer, commission merchant, and cotton broker.[16]

Having lost population during the 1840s, Tallahassee found itself with 1,391 persons in 1850.[17] But the city was growing again and had tasted enough prosperity in 1847 to contribute $929.59 for famine relief in Ireland.[18] Quincy had several hundred fewer persons, Marianna 377, Monticello 329, and Madison a smaller population; these five county seat towns provided only a small urban part of the overwhelmingly rural Red Hills whose five counties contained 15,732 white persons, 24,243 slaves, and 98 free blacks.[19]

The Red Hills were rural and agricultural. Tallahassee, sometimes called "the metropolis," was really just a small country town. Cotton planters were principally in command in the increasingly large domain of King Cotton. Although crime and violence were on the decrease, the planter community, big and small, became particularly sensitive to the crime of Negro stealing, which was made a capital offense in 1845. In Jefferson County it was discovered that one Stephen P. Yeomans was the leader of a gang of ruffians along the Georgia-Florida border that had been engaged in this pursuit. It was announced at a mass meeting held on 19 November 1845 that Yeomans "has been indicted for stealing negroes, and running them into Alabama under false names." The group voted to offer a reward for his arrest and delivery to the sheriff of Jefferson County "so that he may be dealt with according to the law." This notice was relayed to the public by William Bailey, the chairman of the meeting.[20]

Yeomans was arrested and jailed in Baker County, Georgia, and was then released under a writ of habeas corpus there. He was no sooner free than he was seized by men named Moloney, Brinson, and Adams and taken to Florida. The purpose was clear to Yeomans, and he offered one thousand dollars for his freedom. Instead of freeing him, the captors delivered Yeomans to an assemblage of Jefferson County residents who on a vote of 67 to 23 decided to hang him without benefit of a court trial. Yeomans was strung up at a noontime execution on 2 January 1846. Before he died he revealed that he and several accomplices, dressed like Indians, had simulated Indian attacks during the Second Seminole War, killing and robbing their victims. The killings and robberies continued without disguises after the end of the war. Yeomans named several names.[21]

The Jefferson County group now closed in on one of Yeomans's accomplices, Jackson Jewell, who, after an informal "trial," was hanged on 28 April 1846. Until this time, there had been no account of this regulator activity in the Florida press, although the *Savannah Republican* had condemned the proceedings. Joseph Clisby, editor of the *Florida Sentinel*, now told the whole story and observed regarding the lynch party that had dispatched Yeomans: "There were ministers of the gospel there—had they forgotten the Divine injunction, 'Thou shalt not kill' or the instruction of an inspired apostle 'let us not do evil that good may come'?"[22]

Clisby's exposure of the incidents ended the reign of lynch law in Jefferson County, but late in the summer of 1846 a tense situation developed in the western part of the Red Hills. In Gadsden County, suspicion of slave stealing and other crimes focused on Alvin Flowers, who drove the stage between Quincy and Chattahoochee and was believed to have robbed it on occasion. A net closed around some of his associates, who were lodged in the Quincy jail. Flowers fled westward and was soon suspected of continuing his thievery on the boat between New Orleans and Mobile. A group organized in Quincy went after Flowers, found him on the New Orleans boat as it arrived at Mobile, and placed him in the Quincy jail with his companions.[23]

Then late on the night of 12 August 1846, as the stage from Chattahoochee crossed a small creek within half a mile of Quincy, the driver, named Fish, was shot and killed by someone concealed in a thicket. Fish was an incriminating witness in the forthcoming prosecutions of those in jail. Citizens promptly blocked roads and caught a man named Holloman, who was jailed with the others. The town of Quincy, according to the *Floridian*, was now filled with "the greatest excitement." A citizens' group volunteered to stand watch at the jail to prevent an escape or any violence against the prisoners. The citizens asked Superior Judge Thomas Baltzell to call a special term of court lest there be "a popular outbreak, and the summary punishment of the offenders." Baltzell complied, and four men were quickly indicted, tried, and sentenced to death. Holloman, the first offender to be condemned, went to the gallows on Friday, 2 October, and the other three were hanged on 9 October 1846. Flowers, the principal offender, almost escaped this fate. On the night before the execution, he opened a vein in his arm with a sherd of glass and had nearly bled to death when he was found in the morning. Revived with stimulants, he went to the scaffold seated in a chair.[24]

The Quincy trials, a victory for courts and the rule of law, appear to have pacified the Red Hills. Tendencies toward violence found expression in the Mexican War, which also provided an opportunity for patriotic fervor. The Independence Day 1846 celebration was marked by big parades and a military display.[25] Several Revolutionary War veterans were in the Red Hills at this time. When Ansel Ferrell, a veteran of Guilford Courthouse and other battles, died on 8 November 1846, his family erected a stone and gave the newspaper an obituary that sparkled with the patriotic rhetoric with which the South responded to "Mr. Polk's war" against a weak neighboring country: "He lived through the gloomiest days of the Republic, and poured out his blood that his posterity might be free. He survived long enough to see star after star appear upon the banner of the glorious old Thirteen . . . , and he could say with old Simeon, 'Lord, let thy servant now depart in peace.' "[26]

But although the Red Hills boiled with anger against Mexico, direct participation in the war was minimal although costly in lives. Volunteer companies were organized, but enlistments lagged. A company was about to be broken up for lack of men when John W. Levinus, a middle-aged carpenter who had been in Tallahassee since 1825, volunteered for service. Levinus had built the first permanent capitol in 1826, and $1,673.46 still was owed on his contract to do all of the carpentry on the 1845 capitol. The company was mustered into service at the capitol on 13 August 1847. Sixty-five members then marched to Newport and boarded the schooner *Tallahassee*, which picked up fifteen other recruits who had traveled to St. Marks by train. The men arrived in Mexico too late for any important military engagements, but their ranks were decimated by illness. Twenty-eight men died in Mexico, including Levinus.[27]

Restlessness and a spirit of adventure took some away in the California Gold Rush. Thomas Hayward, the Tallahassee merchant, returned to Tallahassee near the end of 1849, bringing news of the death in California of T. Bezeau, operator of a Tallahassee meeting place called Captain Bezeau's Long Room. Florida friends visited Bezeau during his illness and buried his remains in Sutter's Burying Ground at Sacramento.[28]

Just as Tallahassee had prospered during the Second Seminole War on government expenditures, faith bond bank loans, and cotton, it began to thrive—especially the merchants—on cotton alone after the end of the 1841–1847 depression. Leon County produced 16,107 bales in 1850, far more than any other Florida county and more than every county but three in Georgia—Stewart, Houston, and Burke near the fall line. Another 9,468 bales were packed in Jefferson County; the production on these old fields of Apalachee totaled 25,575 bales.[29] Pressed into bales on the plantation, the Leon County cotton was loaded into schooners, brigs, and barks at St. Marks and was sent to New York, where it was shipped to American or English mills. Cotton quotations in the local market advanced from five or six and one-half cents a pound in the spring of 1846 to twelve and three-quarters or thirteen and one-half cents in November 1850.[30]

The account books of a young Virginia-born merchant, James Madison Williams, at what he called 110 Monroe Street, across from the present courthouse, along with Williams's advertisements in the newspapers, show the close connection of cotton and the mercantile trade.[31] Williams advertised a "cash advance on cotton and tobacco shipped to his friends in New York" and ordered $28,491 worth of merchandise in New York.[32] In November 1850 the ebullient storekeeper addressed a rhyming message "To the Public":

> Ladies and Gentlemen, call and behold
> As varied a stock as in town e'er was sold. . . .
> Tis true that my store, tho' large, is too small
> To contain all the goods I have purchased this fall:
> But the old Rail Road Depot can hold a few more,
> And there, for a few days, the remainder I'll store. . . .
> A thirteen to a half our best cottons now sell,
> Which pleases our Planters remarkably well:
> I invite you again to call at 110
> For once having been there, you'll call there again.[33]

Williams's purchases in cotton during the year 1850–1851 totaled 2,666 bales, for which $143,914.23, or $54 a bale, was paid. Although a decline in the cotton market caused Williams's business to collapse and he died in 1854,[34] a store a few doors to the north, that of another

Virginian, David C. Wilson, who went in business in 1839, survived until 1971. A block beyond, near the corner of the two-hundred-foot street, the department store of a former Pennsylvanian, George Washington Scott, soon filled the *Floridian* and *Sentinel* every week with small advertisements sprinkled over the page. One that appeared near Christmas of 1852, entitled "Piquancies and Delicacies," offered sweets just received aboard the schooner *Elizabeth*.[35]

During the fall of 1849, one thousand or more bales of cotton per week passed through Tallahassee; the figure for one week reached 1,278.[36] The hauling of this much cotton taxed the capacity of the rickety little Tallahassee Railroad Company, which advertised at about this time for more "fuel" to feed forty mules that pulled the freight and passenger cars. The railroad needed five hundred bushels of corn.[37] The cotton of Jefferson and Madison counties now came by wagon to Newport, which was founded in 1843 by Daniel Ladd on the west side of the St. Marks River about four miles upriver from St. Marks. Newport had a population of 132 whites and St. Marks 126 in 1850, each with a somewhat smaller floating population of blacks.[38] Together these made up St. Marks Port, which during the 1848–1849 season handled 33,720 bales of cotton, increasing to 41,155 in 1850–1851.[39]

Loading this cotton aboard vessels small enough to negotiate the nine miles of the shallow St. Marks River below St. Marks was a constant problem. Fairly large transoceanic ships could anchor off the sandbar beyond the mouth where the water was three or four fathoms. Some vessels of less draft could cross the bar into water three fathoms deep at Spanish Hole. The principal difficulty for still smaller vessels, barks, brigs, and schooners was at Devil's Elbow on the St. Marks, where little more than eight feet of water flowed above some of the rocky obstructions in the channel and ten thousand dollars' worth of dredging by the federal government a few years earlier had failed to solve the problem.[40]

Vessels anchoring offshore had to lighter cargoes aboard, and even brigs, schooners, and barks often found it difficult to reach Newport. Steam locomotion would help. The resourceful Mr. Ladd and some associates were having built for them in New Albany, Indiana, at midcentury a one-hundred-foot-long steam towboat, *The Spray*, that was designed to tow sailing vessels in and out of Newport.[41] Despite these limitations, St. Marks Port and Apalachee Bay sometimes resembled a little Hampton Roads. During the last week of December 1849, the ship *Elisha Dennison*, a survivor in the transatlantic trade, lay in deep water off the bar, loading for Antwerp. Smaller vessels were docked at St. Marks or Newport—there were eight barks, three brigs, and two schooners either loading for New York or waiting for clearance. Several larger vessels sailed during the week, the bark *R. H. Gamble*, pride of Coe, Anderson and Company, and the *J. G. Anderson*, named for the Tallahassee partner in this firm, on Christmas Day.[42]

The town builder Mr. Ladd turned Newport into a far more attractive town than St. Marks and even promoted Newport Mineral Springs as a spa that competed with the Upper and Lower Mineral Springs on the Suwannee.[43] Health resorts became popular after "the fevers" of 1841, and planters on the west side of the Red Hills built vacation cottages on St. Andrews Bay,[44] while some visited the heights of Orange Hill in Washington County that had relieved the tedious journey of Bishop Portier in 1827.[45] The most puzzling of all selections for a summer vacation community was that of Bel Air four miles south of Tallahassee, where the tracks of the mule-drawn railroad ran through what today is an unattractive stretch of pinelands, sand, and turkey oaks. However, the "difficult circumstances" in which many found themselves following the bank crisis and depression made this summer resort where an occasional Gulf breeze could be savored in congenial company an acceptable alternative to White Sulphur Springs, Saratoga Springs, or Newport, Rhode Island.[46]

In addition to being a port and a resort, though, Newport, Florida, became a center for naval stores, a new and unfamiliar industry that began to stir much interest in the pinelands south of Tallahassee. N. P. Bemis, a native of Massachusetts, began experimenting with naval stores and set up a turpentine distillery at Newport in the spring of 1848. During the following winter half a dozen turpentiners entered the business in southern Leon and Wakulla counties.[47]

Ladd promoted Newport primarily as a shipping point for cotton, though, and he was one of the region's strongest advocates of plank roads. Little came of the plank road movement, but it did show the value of providing an all-weather surface through the "watery wilderness" hereabouts. After six miles of sawed logs had been installed out of Newport, a wagon belonging to James L. Tompkins and pulled by four mules carried a load of nineteen bales of cotton from the plantation of J. Butler Chaires in Leon County to Newport.[48]

The strangest plan for the development of Newport sprang from the fertile brain of a former Virginian, Benjamin G. Thornton, who had supervised many of the harbor improvements at St. Marks but who now, at sixty-three, lived in Jefferson County. Thornton proposed to turn Newport into a Lowell, Massachusetts, even exceeding

Lowell in textile milling, by diverting the immense flow, "a greater volume of water than the Potomac or James River," from the head-springs of the Wacissa River in Jefferson County and taking it by a five-foot-deep canal to the St. Marks River thirteen or fifteen miles away. This, he claimed, would turn Newport into a mill town "in the midst of a rich cotton-growing region, and on a navigable stream which will afford, with slight improvements, thirteen feet of water in the Gulf."[49]

John G. Gamble, by this time living near Tallahassee on his plan-tation, Neamathla, advocated a cotton factory in every county in the South. It is strange to find him, especially at the age of seventy-one, participating in mid-December 1849 in a four-day expedition through the jungle between the Wacissa and St. Marks rivers to determine the difference in elevation between the Wacissa's headwaters and the St. Marks at Newport. It is also surprising to find that Thomas Brown, who had just embarked on his duties as governor, could spare the four days needed for this journey designed to further the Thornton plan. No stranger to the spirit level, having engineered some of the canal work on the James River many years earlier, Gamble became "the leveler" of the party and sighted through an instrument bor-rowed from the Tallahassee Railroad. Governor Brown was one of three "staff bearers."[50] The seven members of the expedition met on 12 December 1849 and encamped on the most northerly of a group of Indian mounds known as Callico Hills, the next day going a short distance to a place where the Wacissa, having accumulated water from all of the headsprings, flows one hundred yards wide and six to eight feet deep. This would be the start of the canal. During the next three days the party traveled, camping overnight, to the St. Marks at New-port. They found the headwaters thirty-two feet higher than high tide at Newport bridge.[51] Nothing came of the plan, and the *Florida Sentinel* scoffed at it. According to the newspaper, Thornton's claim that "with slight improvements" there would be thirteen feet of water at New-port was "desperately at war" with the reports of pilots who said that only vessels of no more than eight and one-half feet of draft could be brought to Newport.[52] One wonders today whether the Thornton plan had really been designed by the wily Newport promoter, Mr. Ladd, to steal the Wacissa River for his harbor.

With all of its infirmities, St. Marks Harbor continued in use, and people of the Red Hills had an affection for this port. At St. Marks on 7 December 1849, several members of the bar bade former Gov-ernor DuVal good-bye after his unsuccessful race for Congress in 1848 and before he sailed for his new home in Texas. The farewell turned out to be final, for he died on 19 March 1854.[53] Six months later, Tallahasseans prepared to welcome back William Wyatt, now sixty-three, another pioneer. Wyatt had served up at his hotel, the Planters, the dinner on 8 January 1825 marking the tenth anniversary of the Battle of New Orleans, Tallahassee's first big celebration. A "self-made man" from Maryland, Wyatt entered politics, served in the territorial Legislative Council, and seemed likely at one time to become Florida's delegate to Congress. After 1840 ill health forced him to leave politics and pursue sugar planting in the "Manatee settlements" in South Florida. Finally, in 1850, his worsening health took him to New Orleans for expert medical assistance. In the absence of relief, according to the *Tallahassee Floridian*, he "determined to return to Tallahassee to die among his friends." Some of the friends went to St. Marks to meet his boat, which was scheduled to arrive on 9 May 1850. It arrived on time, but Wyatt had died aboard it the day before. He was buried from the hotel he had built, and the body was "followed to the grave by nearly every one of his fellow citizens who remained among the living."[54]

11

The Florida
Cotton Kingdom, 1850:
Jackson and
Gadsden Counties

The five Red Hills counties produced 40,952 of the 45,131 bales of Florida cotton grown during the 1849–1850 season. The westernmost county, Jackson, accounted for a tenth of this crop.[1] A young physician, Dr. Charles Hentz, came to Jackson in 1848 and noted in his memoirs that the plantation country along the Apalachicola River was particularly attractive to doctors. Planters had sizable slave forces, which "were sure to have their attacks of sickness attended to," and the physicians would see their bills paid.[2]

Hentz replaced the lone doctor at Port Jackson, a cotton port on the Chattahoochee a few miles above the forks. Here he found himself well outside the plantation country and indeed in "one of the worst, whiskey drinking, fighting, horse racing, gambling communities to be found this side of Texas."[3] Hentz did find a planter living several miles south of Port Jackson with whom he loved to visit. The scion of a prominent North Carolina family, J. McG. Hunter was a graduate of the University of North Carolina but had failed at farming and affected an odd lifestyle. Wearing "a round about jacket and an immense shirt collar that lay like a cape over his shoulders," with "an immense broad brimmed straw hat, with a bright red ribbon around it," he rode into Port Jackson occasionally on an Indian pony so small that his feet almost trailed the ground, a "little fice dog trailing behind him."[4]

A mile or so south of Hunter, though, was the thirty-two-hundred-acre plantation of Jesse Coe, which extended for five miles along the Apalachicola to the Calhoun County line. Coe, with a 250-bale crop on the Toney and Mount Pleasant places, was the largest cotton grower in Jackson County.[5] Now sixty-eight, Coe was a native of Maryland, who, as a Methodist minister, had served churches in Virginia and North Carolina. The minister-planter traveled in the 1820s to Limestone County, Alabama, and by 1830 had 114 slaves. He shortly moved south, buying among other tracts 960 acres on the Apalachicola owned by John Yellowhair, chief of one of the "Apalachicola" tribes that were being transported to the West. His modest two-story house was a mile and a half north of Ocheesee Landing. Dr. Hentz moved downstream, practiced medicine up and down the river, and married a Coe granddaughter. Two sons, Jesse and Will by a second Coe marriage, who had both just reached manhood in 1850 were the only members of the family still at home. Jesse had gone off to college in Virginia and Kentucky and had acquired a habit of eating opium. This, in combination with drink, destroyed his health, and he died at the end of the decade. To the discomfort of the household, Jesse seduced the Coes' well-regarded housemaid, Celia, who bore him two children.[6]

Although Calhoun County lay outside the Red Hills, the cotton lands of 1850 extended southward to some extent along the natural levees and rolling lands to the east and west of the Apalachicola. There was a distinct advantage in growing cotton on the Apalachicola: it could travel by steamboat to the Port of Apalachicola. This port between 1849 and 1853 received for reshipment 108,000 to 150,000 bales a year of cotton that came principally from Georgia and Alabama.[7] But Calhoun County had only two cotton planters at this time, and the combined production of Jason Gregory and William B. Wynn was only 137 bales.[8] Just below the Jackson County line, at Ocheesee Landing, was the fine house of Gregory. Here Hentz stayed for three years. A kind of tolerant fatalism about Jason Gregory eased his misfortunes. A hurricane struck on 23 August 1851, and rain poured down for twenty-four hours, followed by heavy winds that made the big Gregory house shake and groan and pinched the doors shut. The winds blew a warehouse on the riverside off its blocks and scattered fifteen hundred dollars' worth of tobacco that was being cured under the ginhouse. The storm also ruined a splendid crop of cotton and corn. Hentz said this planter always spoke of the Creator as "Uncle Billy." As he witnessed the great work of destruction in progress, he would laugh and say: "Uncle Billy always did everything right."[9] Some ten miles south of Gregory was the plantation of Wynn, a native of Gates County, North Carolina, who was a member of the legislature and a probate judge.[10]

Jackson County to the north had no large planters except Coe in this eastern one-third of the county. Practically all of the cotton production took place within a Y-shaped region, the stem starting two and a half miles southeast of Marianna, one branch of the wishbone

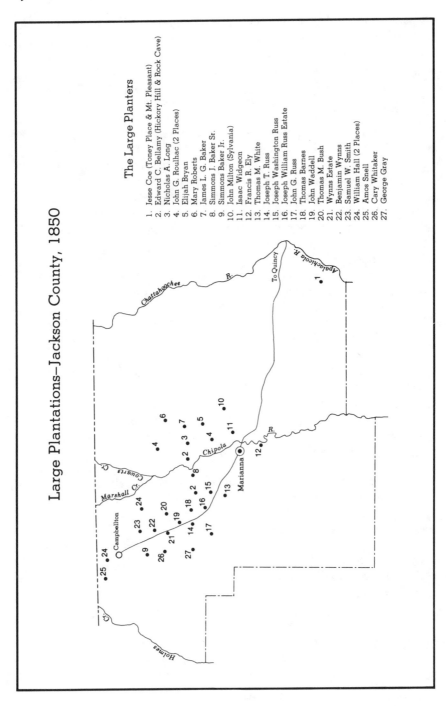

Large Plantations–Jackson County, 1850

The Large Planters

1. Jesse Coe (Toney Place & Mt. Pleasant)
2. Edward C. Bellamy (Hickory Hill & Rock Cave)
3. Nicholas A. Long
4. John G. Roulhac (2 Places)
5. Elijah Bryan
6. Mary Roberts
7. James L. G. Baker
8. Simmons J. Baker Sr.
9. Simmons Baker Jr.
10. John Milton (Sylvania)
11. Isaac Widgeon
12. Francis R. Ely
13. Thomas M. White
14. Joseph T. Russ
15. Joseph Washington Russ
16. Joseph William Russ Estate
17. John G. Russ
18. Thomas Barnes
19. John Waddell
20. Thomas M. Bush
21. Wynns Estate
22. Benjamin Wynns
23. Samuel W. Smith
24. William Hall (2 Places)
25. Amos Snell
26. Cary Whitaker
27. George Gray

traveling northwestward to Campbellton and the Alabama line, and the other branch northward to and somewhat past the present-day community of Greenwood.

After Coe, the largest cotton planter in 1850 was Edward C. Bellamy, who had 2,240 acres along the east side of the Chipola River north of today's Florida Caverns State Park, the old sugar farm of Isaac Fort.[11] The romantic novelist Caroline Hentz, mother of Charles Hentz, described the place in a novel with a local setting in 1852. The house on Hickory Hill became a kind of beacon for travelers at night "when its myriad windows reflected the hospitable radiance glowing within, and the pine torches blazed from the tall posts without." Mrs. Hentz held up the master of the 168 Bellamy slaves as the South's answer to Simon Legree, who had just flashed upon the horizon in the serial form of *Uncle Tom's Cabin*. Ned Bellamy treated his "people" with kindness, never separating families—"no sable Rachel, 'weeping for her children,' would rise up in judgment against him."[12]

But although Ned Bellamy doubtless had all the noblesse oblige attributed to him, he and a brother, Samuel, were engaged in a bitter dispute at this time that would shortly end the careers of both as Jackson County planters. The Bellamy brothers had both been influenced to come to Florida by Hardy Bryan Croom. Sam, the first to arrive, had a plantation, Rock Cave, along Baker Creek. At one time it was said to have the most productive cotton crops in the county at 250 to 300 bales. But Sam's career was one of continuing tragedy. Both Bellamys were physicians, and both had married sisters of Croom, the older brother marrying Ann and Sam marrying Elizabeth Jane. The latter died in 1837, followed in a few days by their only child, eighteen months old. In the 1840s, mounting debt led Sam to turn over Rock Cave and his slaves to his brother, but an argument ensued over the terms of the transfer, and the year 1850 found Sam trying to repossess the properties. The plantation and slaves in 1850 were in the hands of Edward Bellamy, and Rock Cave was evidently responsible for a large part of Ned Bellamy's 230-bale cotton crop. By this time Sam had begun to drink heavily. In December 1853 his body was found at the Chattahoochee ferry station, the throat slit with a razor. His death was thought to have been self-inflicted during an attack of delirium tremens. Not long afterward Ned Bellamy sold Hickory Hill and moved away.[13]

Simmons J. Baker typified the gentry from a section of long established plantation wealth in North Carolina who were numerous among the large planters of Jackson County. His oldest son, James L. G. Baker, had a plantation at the community of Greenwood. Simmons J. Baker, Sr., born in 1775 at Scotland Neck, North Carolina, now lived in Raleigh. He had come to Jackson County much earlier and remained for a time. Although an absentee planter in 1850, he was the largest property owner among the three members of the family with lands in Jackson County and with a crop of two hundred bales had the third largest cotton crop in the county. His principal holding, in the rich lands west of the Chipola, encompassed a mile and a half of the course of Baker Creek. The acreage adjoined Rock Cave to the west and was a mile and a half from Hickory Hill on the east. Simmons J. Baker, Jr., farmed land farther to the west, on the southern border of Campbellton.[14]

Some twenty-eight hundred acres of land around Blue Springs about six miles east of Marianna belonged to John Milton, but he had not yet built his fine house, Sylvania. A Georgian with roots in Halifax County, North Carolina, Milton studied law and left Louisville, Georgia, to practice in the rapidly growing city of Columbus. He left Columbus to practice in Mobile, then in New Orleans, and after a brief stay in Texas hung out his shingle in Marianna in 1845. He prospered in law, planting, and politics and became the Civil War governor of Florida.[15]

The largest merchant in Marianna, Thomas M. White, also decided in 1847 to take a fling at planting and acquired several hundred acres in the Tanner Springs area about six miles northwest of Marianna, then two plantations five miles north of Marianna, at one time the farms of Peter W. Gautier and James J. Pittman. White seems to have found planting intoxicating, for by 1860 he had expanded his improved acreage from four hundred to three thousand and had produced by far the largest cotton crop in Jackson County at 375 bales.[16]

West of White, the Simmons Baker, Sr., place, and Rock Cave plantation were the farms of four members of the Russ family and north of them, along the road from Marianna to Campbellton, were two tracts of the Wynns family from Hertford County, North Carolina. William B. Wynns had bought land in the 1830s that was now in his estate, while a brother, Benjamin Wynns, in 1850 farmed a plantation just to the north. Benjamin was the father of William B. Wynn, the Calhoun County planter, who had dropped the "s" in the name and who during the 1850s moved to Jackson County to plant.[17]

The thirty-one producers of fifty or more bales dominated cotton production, accounting for 3,177, or 67 percent, of Jackson County's 4,744-bale crop. Two-thirds of these big planters were North Carolinians, the Bakers, Roulhacs, and others forming the nucleus of the Whig party in Jackson County, which at this time was known as "the

Gibraltar of Whiggery" in the Red Hills. Yet there were 287 farms altogether, many of these lacking slaves and most with small acreages, their production principally subsistence crops. Yeoman farmers were on the increase. Between 1850 and 1860, Jackson County almost doubled in population, growing from 6,639 to 10,209, becoming the second most populous county of the Red Hills. The increase was mainly in small yeoman farmers, and the number of farms increased from 287 to 581, while the county's racial balance changed from a slightly black majority to a slightly white one, with 5,263 white persons, 4,903 slaves, and 43 free blacks. Cotton production also doubled, from 4,744 to 8,635 bales, and although forty-eight large planters produced 5,093 bales, or 59 percent of this cotton, a large share was evidently produced by yeomen on the 147 farms with one hundred to five hundred acres.[18]

In Gadsden County, the large cotton planters in 1850 chose to grow somewhat less cotton and to rely on tobacco for about one-third of their cash income. Nothing better illustrates the success story of this cotton-tobacco mixture than the experience of two Scottish-born brothers, Thomas and William Munroe. Thomas accompanied his father to America as a young man, going to Madison County, Alabama. In 1832 his rise to wealth was assisted by his marriage to Sarah Elizabeth Fitzgerald, from a well-to-do family in Nottoway County, Virginia.[19] A physician, Munroe chose to live in the town of Quincy, but Thomas Munroe's heart was in the highlands of Gadsden County, rich with Orangeburg sandy loam soils, that rise from the left bank of the Little River. Munroe's magnificent twenty-two-hundred-acre farm, starting seven miles east of Quincy, extended for about five miles along the course of Hurricane Creek and along two miles of Little River, into which it flows. Munroe produced the largest cotton crop in the county at 230 bales and 8,200 pounds of tobacco.[20]

Thomas's brother William farmed an acreage as large. William followed his brother's lead in marrying a Fitzgerald daughter, Mary Cornelia, and although Thomas and Sarah Elizabeth remained childless, the family of William Munroe increased at a pace matching the expanding spread of his vine and fig tree. "Corny begins to look like a young hogshead," Sarah Munroe wrote her kin in Virginia during one of her sister's pregnancies. Then, in December 1856, following the birth and death of a sixth child and of Cornelia herself, she wrote about the Christmas of five motherless children.[21] Not long afterward William married Julia E. Welch of Norfolk, Virginia, who bore sixteen children. Like his brother, William lived in Quincy.[22] William's cotton production was only one hundred bales, but he was much more suc-

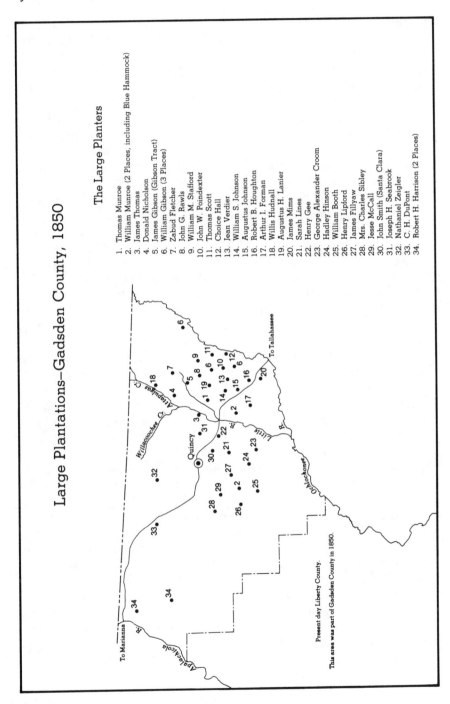

Large Plantations–Gadsden County, 1850

The Large Planters

1. Thomas Munroe
2. William Munroe (2 Places, including Blue Hammock)
3. James Thomas
4. Donald Nicholson
5. James Gibson (Gibson Tract)
6. William Gibson (3 Places)
7. Zabud Fletcher
8. John G. Rawls
9. William M. Stafford
10. John W. Poindexter
11. Thomas Scott
12. Choice Hall
13. Jean Verdier
14. William S. Johnson
15. Augustus Johnson
16. Robert B. Houghton
17. Arthur I. Forman
18. Willis Hudnall
19. Augustus H. Lanier
20. James Mims
21. Sarah Lines
22. Henry Gee
23. George Alexander Croom
24. Hadley Hinson
25. William Booth
26. Henry Lipford
27. James Fillyaw
28. Mrs. Charles Sibley
29. Jesse McCall
30. John Smith (Santa Clara)
31. Joseph H. Seabrook
32. Nathaniel Zeigler
33. C. H. DuPont
34. Robert H. Harrison (2 Places)

Present day Liberty County.

This area was part of Gadsden County in 1850.

cessful in tobacco, with a production of fifteen thousand pounds. One secret of this success appears to have been a plantation that he called Blue Hammock, a tract lying north of what was called Maner and became Munroe or Monroe Creek. In addition to Blue Hammock his plantation holdings included 750 acres in the Forbes Purchase north of Sweetwater Creek.[23]

But the Munroes were primarily cotton planters and were among twenty-one large planters who farmed an area east of the Little River that comprises about one-tenth of the county as it presently exists and who produced nearly one-third of the county's cotton crop of 5,609 bales. North of Munroe was the big Malcolm Nicholson tract. Donald Nicholson, twenty-seven, a nephew, farmed on this place.[24] Joining the Thomas Munroe land at Lake Tallavana was the "Gibson tract," extending three miles up Hurricane Creek to the edge of present day Havana, the farm of James Gibson, seventy-five, a native of Ireland.[25] A son, William H. Gibson, born in South Carolina, was as large a planter, two of his farms being south of the community that is today called Scotland.[26] Adjoining the lower Gibson tract on the west was the plantation of the largest planter in the area, Jean Verdier, a physician who, however, soon returned to his native Beaufort, South Carolina.[27]

North of Verdier on Lanier Road was the plantation of Augustus H. Lanier, a Georgian who, next to Thomas Munroe, was the largest cotton grower in this east Gadsden County cotton belt. His house, built in 1837, stood until the 1970s. When Lanier died in 1855 he owned another 1,610 acres on Patterson Hammock in Madison County.[28] Many of the twenty-one planters in the cotton belt traded with James Madison Williams, the Monroe Street merchant in Tallahassee. Some of them went heavily into debt when cotton prices fell or crops failed. At Williams's death in 1854, Augustus Lanier owed his store $3,792.55. [29]

Forbes Purchase takes in the southernmost one-third of present Gadsden County, which in 1850 also enclosed all of present Liberty County. Most of the Forbes Purchase was spurned by farmers. The big plantation of Jonathan Robinson west of Little River was partly on "the Purchase," but for the most part it was in the red hills to the north and was now in the hands of his daughter, Sarah Ann Lines, a widow.[30] George Alexander Croom, a brother of Hardy B., favored this part of the Forbes Purchase, the Little River Survey, and produced one of the largest cotton crops in the county, 146 bales, much of it Sea Island, on sixteen hundred acres bought from Bryan Croom just

Typical of the houses of the large planters was this home of Augustus H. Lanier, one of the largest cotton planters in Gadsden County in 1850. The sketch was made from snapshots just before the building was torn down in the 1970s. (Drawing by Mrs. Cornelia Stout, courtesy of J. Armand Lanier)

to the south of the Lines Place and extending along Magnolia Farms Road.[31] Although Sea Island cotton was grown here, Upland Short Staple cotton was preferred on the richer soils above the Forbes line. In a bend of Rocky Comfort Creek as it turns from south to east to form the northern boundary of the Purchase was the Fillyaw Place, where James Fillyaw produced the second largest cotton crop in the county at 175 bales.[32]

Several members of the extensive Gregory family farmed west and southwest of Quincy. Jason Gregory, Jr., farmed across the Apalachicola River at Ocheesee Landing. In 1849 his brother, Charles Raymond, then twenty-six, bought 740 acres from him at Rock Bluff, on the east bank of the Apalachicola, cleared 100 acres, and produced sixteen thousand pounds of tobacco.[33] Charles committed himself to the Apalachicola River valley and, after selling his Rock Bluff place to Samuel Caldwell in 1858, moved to Calhoun County where, on a farm valued at twenty-seven thousand dollars in 1860, he produced the largest cotton crop on this river, 154 bales, but no tobacco.[34]

South of the community called Sawdust was one of several plantations owned by William E. Kilcrease, a thirty-year-old native of South Carolina. Kilcrease was the largest slave owner in the county with 148 hands and had 5,240 acres of land, but his 1850 cotton production appears to have been assigned to overseers or agents. By

1860, Kilcrease's three big plantations produced the largest cotton crop in the county, 250 bales, along with a tobacco crop of twenty thousand pounds.[35]

"He was a queer character," said Charles Hentz, "a large, portly man, with very little education, dressed in broadcloth—he undertook to be an ornament to society & made a prodigious ass of himself—he courted many ladies." Unsuccessful in his Florida courtships, Kilcrease returned to South Carolina in 1853 to marry Rhoda E. Waller of Greenwood, taking care to inform the *Tallahassee Floridian* of this triumph.[36] Back in Florida, he was active politically, became a member of the legislature, and seemed to be ambitious to become governor, for he was always running for the position of general in the militia, usually a stepping-stone to this office. His last race for general was unsuccessful, and the returns were hardly in during May 1860 when he died.[37] His only surviving child, Albert W., following his father's wishes and assuming the surname Gilchrist, became a bachelor governor of Florida in 1909.[38]

Dr. David L. White was never classified as a "large" planter, but at sixty-nine he continued a modest production on nine hundred acres along State Road 267 south of Quincy. He conducted a one-man experiment station here, getting a yield of twelve to twenty bushels an acre with bearded wheat, although wheat had never been found to grow in the Red Hills. Dr. White won an award for his bearded wheat at the agricultural fair held in Tallahassee in November 1852 and another prize for his "Haitian yams," which the editor of the *Floridian* could attest were "in flavor and richness . . . not to be surpassed."[39]

At midcentury, though, the practical planters of Gadsden County were reaping the benefits of a diversification of crops dating from experiments about ten years earlier in growing a kind of tobacco that was in demand for cigar wrappers. Gadsden County had a production of 776,177 pounds of tobacco in 1850; all of the other four counties of the Red Hills had a total of 55,082. Only Decatur County, Georgia, just across the line, among nearby counties, was a rival with 157,937 pounds.[40]

Tobacco growing got its start in Gadsden County during the late 1820s with the simultaneous appearance in the county of seed from Cuba and planters who were used to growing tobacco in Virginia, among them John (who became known as "Virginia") Smith, and members of the Gunn, Hagood, and Wyatt families.[41] What we know about early tobacco growing in Gadsden County comes almost entirely from an address by Arthur I. Forman, a Gadsden planter and businessman, before a southern planters convention in South Carolina in 1853. Forman said that a leaf that was attractive for cigar wrappers had been developed by experimentation, and in 1842 a chance shipment was sent to Bremen, Germany, home of the principal cigar makers of the world. Foreign buyers descended on Gadsden County the next season. In 1845 the county produced a crop of 1,200,000 pounds, which glutted the market. Production settled down to about half of this amount and produced an income of $100,000 or more a year. The leaf grown in the county, silky, thin and attractively spotted, was used exclusively for wrapping, not filling, cigars. It could be grown to advantage only on freshly cleared hammock land, and the hard work and care necessary to bring the crop to maturity made it too demanding for many farmers. Forman said, "Twenty-five cents per lb. may be considered the intrinsic value of the Florida wrapper tobacco."[42]

Cotton nevertheless remained king in 1850, even in Gadsden County. "Virginia" Smith, the father of the tobacco industry here, although planting tobacco, also produced 120 bales of cotton. His tobacco production, twenty-two thousand pounds on his Santa Clara Plantation bordering the Gee lands southeast of Quincy, was the second largest tobacco crop in the county.

Eight miles northwest of Quincy stands a great dome of largely flat and rolling lands in the vicinity of Mount Pleasant, some of this land three hundred feet above sea level. By 1850 tobacco had become the main cash crop of planters large and small here and the only cash crop of others such as Joshua Davis, Sr., sixty-two, and his son, Henry Jefferson Davis, thirty-four, each of whom grew ten thousand pounds of tobacco but no cotton.[43] The large plantation of Charles H. DuPont, a Supreme Court judge, on the headwaters of South Mosquito Creek where U.S. 90 and County Road 379 cross, was an exception to the rule of tobacco primacy here, for no tobacco was grown on his twenty-five hundred acres, which had a 130-bale cotton crop.[44]

In the same community as the Davises, Jesse Wood, twenty-seven, produced seven thousand pounds of tobacco on a small acreage and attracted considerable attention outside Florida for an experiment, along with other Mt. Pleasant farmers, in controlling the tobacco worm. In its fly stage this pest was known to visit the blossoms of the jimsonweed in the evenings to drink the sweet syrup. Jesse Wood and his associates concocted a suspension of honey and cobalt in water and placed it in a bottle with a quill through the cork. One drop was left in each of the blossoms of the jimsonweeds in an infected area. It was found that the fly died before being able to deposit its eggs. Wood expressed hope that this discovery would also be valuable in attacking the cotton caterpillar. "Very true," the entomologist Townsend Glover commented in reporting Wood's experiment to the U.S. Agricultural Society.[45]

An increasing emphasis on tobacco was found west of Mt. Pleasant. Four miles southeast of Chattahoochee, William Rodgers produced 23,000 pounds of tobacco, the largest crop in Gadsden County in 1850, but no cotton.[46] Arthur I. Forman estimated that between 1831 and 1853 tobacco brought Gadsden County farmers $1,149,000 and in 1850 alone $120,000.[47] At a price of ten cents a pound, cotton must have brought $224,360 in 1850. At twenty-five cents a pound, 8,000 pounds of tobacco were therefore equal to fifty 400-pound bales of cotton, and a big tobacco farmer like Rodgers was the equal of a cotton planter producing 150 bales. The thirty-seven producers of 50 or more bales of cotton dominated cotton production, just as they did in Jackson County. Their total crop of 3,422 bales was 61 percent of the Gadsden County production of 5,609 bales. They also dominated tobacco but not to the same extent; their 210,540 pounds composed 27 percent of the total.

The number of "large" planters must be expanded by twenty-one, now totaling fifty-eight, to include those growing tobacco alone or tobacco and cotton and making the two thousand dollars produced by 50 bales of cotton. Some were substantial planters with thirty or more slaves and hundreds of acres of land. Roderick K. Shaw and Jesse Gregory each had thirty-two slaves, the former 1,150 acres and the latter 964 acres, while Daniel Bradwell had fifty-two slaves and 1,600 acres of land. These twenty-one farmers added 653 bales to the cotton production, giving the fifty-eight large planters 4,075 bales, or 73 percent of the cotton production. The twenty-one produced 145,100 pounds of tobacco, and the fifty-eight large planters 355,640, or 46 percent of the total production of 776,177 pounds.

The diversification of crops was clearly profitable for the large planters, who also had numerous slaves to do the backbreaking work. And for nonslaveholding farmers, usually called "yeomen," tobacco was also important. After the Civil War, Judge C. H. DuPont, who did not grow one leaf of tobacco on his Mt. Pleasant plantation in 1850, credited the "cash surplus" from tobacco with having elevated the income primarily of small planters and farmers and "the moral and intellectual status" of the people of Gadsden County.[48] There may have been some truth in this assertion for the agricultural census shows that 324 of the 482 farms in Gadsden County grew some tobacco in 1850, while 259 grew some cotton, and the smaller farms grew at least half of the tobacco.

12

The Florida
Cotton Kingdom, 1850:
Leon County

One of Tallahassee's few "tourist attractions" during the late nine-teenth century was a modest suburban cottage where Catharine Murat, having refused the offer of a French château, had come to live in the 1850s and entertain her friends in a style made possible by an upturn in the fortunes of the Bonapartes, her late husband's family. The cottage, sitting on a 560-acre plantation, was called Bellevue by "Princess" Murat, but in 1850 she still lived on Lipona in Jefferson County, and this Leon County place was the property of Maryland-born Richard Hayward, who had two other plantations and was one of the ninety-one large cotton planters in Leon County.[1]

Hayward held Bellevue in trust for his daughter Anna Maria, who appears to have lived here in 1850. Her late husband, Dr. William Tradewell, had been one of the most violent of the Whig zealots in the political confrontations of 1839–1841, and, seeming to crave even more violence, left to die in the Mexican War. Bellevue was on a shady hilltop half a mile west of Lake Bradford Road on Jackson Bluff Road as this strikes out to become State Road 20. The house remained there until 1967, when the Junior League and others rescued it from bull-dozers, moved it, and restored it at the gateway to the Tallahassee Junior Museum.[2]

Adjoining Bellevue on the south was a plantation twice its size that was bought in 1852 by William Bloxham, a Virginian, who shortly deeded it to his son, William D., much later a governor of Florida. Known as Buena Vista, the twelve hundred acres became the farm of Florida State University, which later built Alumni Village and the broadcasting center there, using part of the land for a golf course. In 1850 this was part of the agricultural enterprise of Noah L. Thompson, one of the nabobs of the cotton fields with a crop of 480 bales. However, the richest part of Thompson's cotton lands lay in the eastern part of the county.[3]

Only a few other planters farmed west of Tallahassee. Far richer lands lay north of town, along the thirty-mile shore of Lake Jackson. Planters loved the rich lands along its borders, and they loved equally well the high hills rimming the lake. From their houses they enjoyed an almost aerial view of this, the most beautiful of four large lakes in Leon County. The first of the Lake Jackson places was Whitehall, a square mile of land covering the hilltop site of Tallahassa Taloofa. It extended from Meridian Road to present-day Monticello Drive, with Tharpe Street forming the southern boundary. The land was bought in 1849 by James E. Broome, a merchant and judge of probate court. This South Carolinian, strongly grounded in "southern rights," was an attractive candidate for Democrats who were anxious to retrieve the governorship of Florida from the Whigs. Perhaps to add "planter" to his political image, Broome launched an agricultural career. He lived on Whitehall as governor from 1853 to 1857.[4]

After driving today for a mile across Whitehall on U.S. 27, one reaches at Lake Shore Drive a plantation that was called The Grove, celebrated for its "never failing springs of good water." The Grove belonged to William H. Burroughs, formerly of Savannah.[5] Beyond, Crowder Road to the east leads in one mile to the hilltop site of the onetime plantation home of Robert Butler. A native Pennsylvanian, Colonel Butler had been in "fifteen or sixteen engagements," mainly in the War of 1812. He accompanied Jackson as adjutant general at New Orleans and afterward served in the Florida campaign. He left the army and in 1824 was appointed surveyor general of Florida. Not surprisingly, as a Democrat Butler supported Lewis Cass of Michigan for president and his cousin W. O. Butler of Kentucky for vice-president in the 1848 campaign. He was incensed, though, when the winner, Whig President Zachary Taylor, unceremoniously replaced him as surveyor general in mid-1849.[6]

After his forced retirement, Butler had more time for his plantation and the activities for which he is most remembered today. Ellen Call Long said the portly old soldier presided in a baronial manner here, singing Scottish songs and reciting his own poetry. The many guests at his annual "Feasts of Roses" stopped first at "the office" near his house. Here they quaffed a big tankard of punch or apple toddy dipped out of tubs, then danced in a hall of the house that opened on a rose garden and orange grove. At midnight all sat down to a dinner.[7]

The plantation house Casa de Lago, scarcely a quarter of a mile away from Butler's on Alpine Way, stood 120 feet above Lake Jackson. The resident here in 1850 was Benjamin F. Whitner. Wealthy, cultivated, and a participant in Democratic party politics but no officeholder, this South Carolina patrician built the house and planted an immense floral garden, then in 1850 virtually exchanged his 1,127 acres here for George Alexander Croom's 1,600 acres in Gadsden County. Croom soon doubled Whitner's ninety-bale cotton crop. Moreover, while his neighbor Robert Butler clung to a dying technology with a waterwheel, Croom changed to steam; a ten-horse-power steam engine drove his cotton gin and gristmill.[8]

Just west of Butler's place, the Reverend George C. S. Johnson had only 320 acres of land but a remarkable cotton crop—150 bales—more than the combined production of Whitner and Butler. His house on the Old Bainbridge Road, recently moved, is the last surviving house of the ten large Lake Jackson planters.[9] It is nine miles from this site to Orchard Pond, owned by Richard K. Call. Having retired from officeholding, Call at midcentury deeded his house and lands at the foot of Adams Street to his daughter, Ellen, and lived in a lakeside house where Mrs. John H. Phipps's house stands on present Ayavalla Plantation. With more than 3,000 acres he was both the largest landowner and, as owner or agent, the largest slaveholder on Lake Jackson, with 137 hands. He also had the largest cotton crop at 381 bales.[10]

Call's plantation extended to the fence of William Carr near the intersection of Orchard Pond and Meridian roads.[11] Carr had only a two-hundred-bale cotton crop, but the lands to the south of him on the west side of Meridian were some of the richest in the county, with a production of three hundred or more bales per farm. South of Gardner Road were the 2,121 acres of "Harris Hammock," long tied up in an estate and lawsuit but soon to be purchased by William Bailey, a Jefferson County planter who was entering Leon County agriculture on a big scale,[12] while John S. Shepard, a scientific farmer, owned the lake shore from Rollins and Brill points to the Call plantation,[13] and two wealthy Georgians, John and James Whitehead, held four miles of land along the west side of Meridian, extending to Broome's Whitehall plantation.[14]

Gentleman farmers were plentiful in the Red Hills community. The agricultural writer Solon Robinson noted after a visit to the Tallahassee area in 1851 that the country hereabouts had been settled by "a high-bred class of inhabitants, which makes society there very agreeable." And although they were "land destroyers, they are money makers."[15] George Whitfield, just to the east of Broome, between Meridian and Thomasville roads, sold the northern part of his place in the 1850s to

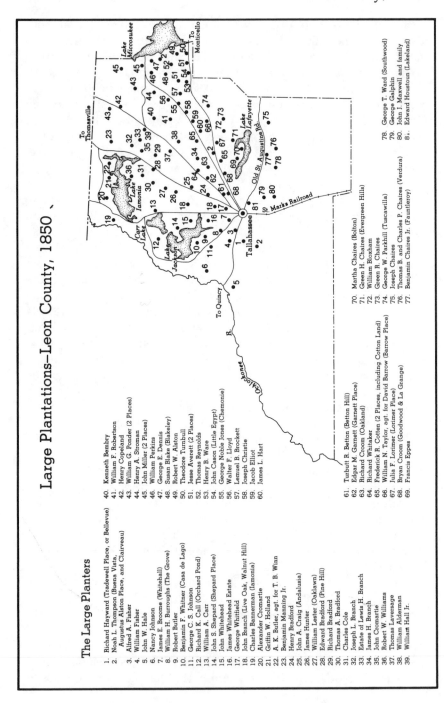

Large Plantations–Leon County, 1850

The Large Planters

1. Richard Hayward (Tradewell Place, or Bellevue)
2. Noah L. Thompson (Buena Vista,
   Augustus Alston Place, and Clairveau)
3. Alfred A. Fisher
4. William Fisher
5. John W. Hale
6. Nancy Johnson
7. James E. Broome (Whitehall)
8. William H. Burroughs (The Grove)
9. Robert Butler
10. Benjamin F. Whitner (Casa de Lago)
11. George C. S. Johnson
12. Richard K. Call (Orchard Pond)
13. William A. Carr
14. John S. Shepard (Shepard Place)
15. John Whitehead
16. James Whitehead Estate
17. George Whitfield
18. John Branch (Live Oak, Walnut Hill)
19. Charles Bannerman (Iamonia)
20. Alexander Cromartie
21. Griffin W. Holland
22. A. K. Butler, agt. for T. B. Winn
23. Benjamin Manning Jr.
24. Henry Bradford
25. John A. Craig (Andalusia)
26. James Hunter
27. William Lester (Oaklawn)
28. Edward Bradford (Pine Hill)
29. Richard Bradford
30. Thomas A. Bradford
31. Charles Cole
32. Joseph L. Branch
33. Estate of Lewis H. Branch
34. James H. Branch
35. John Cromartie
36. Robert W. Williams
37. Thomas Laversage
38. William Alderman
39. William Hall Jr.

40. Kenneth Bembry
41. William F. Robertson
42. Henry Copeland
43. William G. Ponder (2 Places)
44. Henry A. Stroman
45. John Miller (2 Places)
46. William Perkins
47. George E. Dennis
48. Susan Blake (Blakeley)
49. Robert W. Alston
50. Theodore Turnbull
51. Jesse Averett (2 Places)
52. Thomas Reynolds
53. Henry B. Ware
54. John Cason (Little Egypt)
55. George Noble Jones (Chemonie)
56. Walter F. Lloyd
57. Lemuel B. Brockett
58. Joseph Christie
59. Jacob Eliot
60. James L. Hart

61. Turbutt R. Betton (Betton Hill)
62. Edgar M. Garnett (Garnett Place)
63. Richard Croom (Oakland)
64. Richard Whitaker
65. Frederick R. Cotten (2 Places, including Cotton Land)
66. William N. Taylor, agt. for David Barrow (Barrow Place)
67. Julia F. Lorimer (Lorimer Place)
68. Bryan Croom (Goodwood & La Grange)
69. Francis Eppes

70. Martha Chaires (Bolton)
71. Green H. Chaires (Evergreen Hills)
72. William Bloxham
73. Green R. Chaires
74. George W. Parkhill (Tuscawilla)
75. Joseph Chaires
76. Thomas B. and Charles P. Chaires (Verdura)
77. Benjamin Chaires Jr. (Fauntleroy)
78. George T. Ward (Southwood)
79. George Galphin
80. John J. Maxwell and family
81. Edward Houstoun (Lakeland)

John Branch, and this became Waverly plantation. Branch's main place, Live Oak, extended for another mile and a half along Meridian. He had a third place, Walnut Hill, to the north on Lake Elizabeth.[16] Born, it was said, with wealth enough to make it unnecessary for him to practice his profession, law, Branch spent a lifetime in politics, mainly in North Carolina, becoming governor, U.S. senator, and in 1829 Andrew Jackson's secretary of the navy. He bought land in Leon County beginning in the 1830s. Four of his daughters married Floridians, and he served briefly as the last territorial governor of Florida. But at midcentury the Tallahassee *Floridian* called Live Oak his "winter residence." A flock of grandchildren eagerly awaited the caravan of vehicles, animals, and servants that he brought south from Enfield, North Carolina, on his winter visits, the governor himself sometimes astride a Spanish mule.[17]

Just to the north of Live Oak, with his house near the interchange of I-10 and the Thomasville Road, was Henry B. Bradford, first of four Bradford brothers from Enfield, North Carolina, to enter farming in Leon County, all in the 1830s.[18] Some six miles to the north on Thomasville Road was the home of Dr. Edward Bradford, the largest planter among the brothers. His frame residence, "white and green, as a country house should be," was the focal point of Pine Hill plantation and of his daughter Susan Bradford Eppes's memories of "the aristocracy" that once lived and visited here. Nothing remains of the place but a few crumbling bricks among the leggy crape myrtles that reach up into the forest and a large cemetery that served the Branch and Bradford families (Mrs. Edward Bradford was a daughter of John Branch).[19] Richard and Thomas Bradford farmed nearby.[20]

While Robert White Williams, a former Tennessean, was a member of the same gentlemanly class, Solon Robinson praised him as a farmer and said Williams's use of "sidehill ditching" and manures did full justice to what he called "the finest red land in America." Williams, another connection of the Branch family, having married a daughter of John Branch, had five thousand acres extending for several miles along the south shore of Lake Iamonia. It is not surprising to find that he produced 488 bales of cotton and the largest corn crop in the county at 12,710 bushels.[21]

A score of large planters farmed in the northeastern corner of the county. Fast becoming the largest landowner among these was William G. Ponder, a South Carolinian.[22] Mostly North Carolinians formed a tightly knit community of prosperous planters along the west shore of Lake Miccosukee, among them Susan, the widow of Miles Blake, whose house, Blakely, still stands on a shady hilltop off

Rococco Road, a lane leading up to it from the yard of one of Blake's descendants, the late Jack Cromartie.[23]

Four miles southwest of the community of Miccosukee, along the road to Tallahassee, one reaches Chemonie plantation in four miles and drives for two more across its sixteen hundred acres. This, along with El Destino in Jefferson County, was acquired in 1840 by George Noble Jones of Savannah, Georgia, scion of a family that owned the old plantation Wormsloe. Jones continued to live in Savannah and required his two Florida overseers to report on alternate weeks about every detail of the management of these properties. The reports, along with plantation journals and other papers, were discovered at the old El Destino plantation house in 1924 by James O. Knauss, a historian at Florida State College for Women. Before they could become lost to "collectors," they were rescued by the Missouri Historical Society. Published in 1927, they provide a classic record of plantation management and slavery.[24]

Productive as were the planters around Lakes Jackson, Iamonia, and Miccosukee, a region just to the east of Tallahassee and midway between these lakes, the heartland also of Apalachee's "corn and beans" kingdom, was the principal cotton belt of Leon County in 1850. Near the intersection of Miccosukee and Crump roads were the plantations of Joseph Christie,[25] Dr. Jacob Elliot,[26] and James L. Hart,[27] and although these planters produced only a little over 50 bales each, their lands marked the northeastern corner of a rectangle comprising this fertile district. The rectangle extended from Roberts Road on the north to Lake Lafayette on the south, and from a mile or so east of Crump Road and Chaires Crossroad to a western border marked by Bryan Croom's plantation house Goodwood and Betton Hill plantation. Twenty-two large planters farming primarily in this seven-by-ten-mile rectangle produced 4,792 bales, or 30 percent of the 16,107 bales of Leon County cotton.

A large plantation south of Roberts and west of Crump Road had gained a reputation in the early days as one of the best in Leon County and was appropriately called Cotton Land. The owner, originally of Edgecombe County, North Carolina, had been John Cotten, who was wealthy enough, according to Ellen Call Long, to decorate the harness and carriage of the coach-and-four in which he attended the races in Tallahassee with "the real ore"—she did not say whether gold or silver. However, in 1844 we would have found him in distress, for Isaac Mitchell of Thomas County, Georgia, had pressed Cotten for payment of a $15,555 note he had cosigned. Cotten solved this problem by directing attention to the principal signer, a neighbor living three miles to the east, Henry Doggett, who he said was far richer than he and produced six hundred bales of cotton.[28]

If we had visited Doggett, whose Home Place extended northward from present I-10 along the east side of Chaires Crossroad, at the north widening and extending to Black Creek, we would have found a planter whose troubles were several times as great as Cotten's. Doggett had debts of sixty thousand to seventy thousand dollars. He finally solved his problems by offering the Leon County place and one in Jefferson County, along with 178 slaves, to his brother-in-law, David Barrow of West Feliciana Parish, Louisiana, at a bargain price of forty-five thousand dollars. All he wanted out of the deal was five hundred dollars a year from Barrow to support him in his old age, along with a manservant to wait upon him. Barrow now came into possession of what became the Barrow Place, and Doggett returned to North Carolina. In 1850, managed by W. N. Taylor, the Barrow Place was responsible for 305 bales of cotton.[29]

Miccosukee Road running from the northeast to the southwest corner of the fertile rectangle was the busiest of the cotton roads in 1850. When one travels it today, the journey passes through forests that shade the way as a canopy. After crossing the southeastern corner of Cotton Land, the motorist in another mile is at the corner of a sixteen-hundred-acre plantation enclosing the interchange of I-10 and U.S. 90 that had been owned by State Senator James H. T. Lorimer but soon became part of the growing estate of Noah Thompson.[30] Following the death of Augustus Alston in 1839, Thompson had bought his seven hundred acres on Lake Miccosukee. A dedicated Whig and friend of the famiy, Noah in the spring of 1841 loaned Willis Alston sixty-five dollars in New Orleans, it is to be hoped without knowing of his bloody plan of murdering Leigh Read in Tallahassee a few weeks later. Thompson's principal place, producing most of his 480-bale cotton crop, was just to the west of the Lorimer tract. One drives for a mile across it as Miccosukee Road underpasses I-10. The plantation extended from this vicinity for two and a half miles to the south along both sides of a stream forming Alford Arm of Lake Lafayette. Thompson died in 1854, as a gossipy overseer noted, "in the New Yourk asylum."[31]

Thompson's neighbor to the west was Frederick R. Cotten, a brother of John. His plantation extended south for two miles and, south of Thompson, took in a mile of the Alford Arm stream valley. He produced 381 bales of cotton. John Cotten now being dead, Fred as the executor of his brother's will had control of Cotton Land, with a 305-bale crop, making a total production of 686 bales.[32]

Goodwood, built around 1840 near the edge of (and now within) Tallahassee, was the home of the land-rich planter Bryan Croom, one of the cotton barons of 1850. The home still stands on a considerable acreage, the most handsome of the few plantation houses remaining in the Red Hills. (Courtesy of Florida State Archives)

After crossing Fred Cotten's land on our westward journey, we drive into the heart of present-day Tallahassee through the land of the Crooms and stay there except to cross the plantation Clifford Hill. Finally at Medical Drive is the entranceway of Goodwood. Bryan Croom and his brother Hardy acquired the section of land here and three to the east of it, running along the border of Lake Lafayette, in 1836. Bryan Croom later extended this ownership northward from the easternmost section by purchase of the fine plantation La Grange. La Grange's fifteen hundred acres turned the Croom ownership into an L, his land joining his brother Richard Croom's Oakland at the Miccosukee Road. The wealthiest of the Leon County landowners, Bryan Croom had real estate valued on the tax rolls at $105,000, and he owned 195 slaves. His cotton production was 486 bales. Bryan extended his estate during the decade but had to dispose of all of it, even his house Goodwood, after losing "the steamboat Home case" in 1857.[33]

Of the four largest planters in 1850, Bryan Croom left the state during the decade, Thompson died, Robert W. Williams virtually withdrew from Leon County planting, and only Frederick R. Cotten remained among the mighty in 1860 with a production on his own farms, now along Lakes Jackson and Iamonia, and on Cotton Land, totaling 1,000 bales. A young newcomer in this decade, Joseph John Williams, now took over the richest lands of the fertile rectangle. The son-in-law of Noah Thompson, Williams inherited some of his lands and bought from Fred Cotten the seventeen hundred acres just to the west and south of Thompson, acquiring also the fifteen-hundred-acre La Grange plantation from Bryan Croom. At one time he owned La Grange, Clairvaux, Shiloh, and two other places. Barely twenty-eight at the end of the 1859–1860 planting season, he reported a production on his seven thousand acres, with 245 slaves, of 1,113 bales, the largest cotton crop in Leon County and in Florida.[34]

In 1850 the fertile rectangle continued eastward from Bryan Croom's Lake Lafayette lands with Francis Eppes's place;[35] the plantation Bolton, which had been left by Benjamin Chaires to his daughter Martha;[36] and the plantation of her uncle Green H. Chaires, the only survivor among three Chaires brothers.[37] Just to the east of the Barrow Place was Tuscawilla, the old plantation of John Parkhill and now that of his son, Dr. George W. Parkhill.[38]

South of Lake Lafayette, along the course of the Old St. Augustine Road, the plantation community consisted largely of Ben Chaires's heirs. His two youngest sons, Charles Powell, twenty, and Thomas Butler, twenty-two, controlled Verdura, the old homestead just to the west of Williams Road, and had the largest share of his land at twenty-seven hundred acres. The thirteen-room brick house, Verdura, stood here in addition to a cluster of brick outbuildings that were built, it was said, "in the most substantial manner."[39] Of all the Chaires connection, George T. Ward, who had married Sarah Jane, daughter of Ben Chaires, had the most productive farm. His Southwood plantation had a crop of 372 bales.[40] On Paul Russell Road south of Old St. Augustine Road were farms of the Maxwell family, John J. Maxwell having bought 1,641 acres here in 1839.[41] To the northwest was Lakeland, the plantation of Edward Houstoun. His house stood near the intersection of Magnolia Drive and Apalachee Parkway and close to the site of De Soto's winter encampment of 1539–1540.[42]

There were 356 farms in all in Leon County,[43] many of them tiny acreages with a subsistence production. The ninety-one planters with fifty or more bales dominated cotton production more than in any other Red Hills county. Their 1850 production of 13,753 bales amounted to eighty-five percent of the 16,107 total. Cotton seems to have reached its peak at about this time in Leon, for in 1860 it was only 16,686. The large planters still produced all but a tiny fraction.[44]

Benjamin Chaires was the richest of the Red Hills planters in the early days, and in the 1830s he built this brick palace, Verdura, here shown as envisioned by an artist, in Leon County. The home burned in 1885, and only five of the tall columns remain in a remote field. (Courtesy of Mrs. G. Lester Patterson)

13

The Florida Cotton Kingdom, 1850: Jefferson and Madison Counties

The plan of Benjamin G. Thornton to capture the Wacissa River and turn Newport, Florida, into a city of spindles and bobbins drew some opponents from the start. Jefferson County planters had planned a canal of their own since the 1830s, this one connecting the Wacissa and Aucilla rivers.[1] After Leon County, Jefferson in 1850 had the largest cotton crop in the Red Hills at 9,468 bales, but planters had never found a better way of sending the cotton to market than wagoning it to Magnolia and later to Newport. Yet Jefferson was favored with a seacoast, if only of six miles, together with two sizable rivers flowing to the coast. The Aucilla, forming most of the eastern boundary, could be used for transportation to the sea only in the last few miles, for a dozen miles from the mouth, it dips below the ground surface to emerge at Nuttall Rise.[2]

The Wacissa runs wide and deep for eight or ten miles—the most popular place in the region for canoe races today. The river then begins to twist and turn, form many small channels, and lose itself in the swampy wilderness. One channel finds its way to the Aucilla below Nuttall Rise, and during the winter of 1849–1850, the Jefferson planters found that by removing a few hundred feet of limestone obstructions from this channel to form a canal, boats and barges of less than three-foot draft could be coaxed into the Aucilla and floated to the mouth.[3] There still remained a problem, for Apalachee Bay in this area was too shallow and too distant from shipping lanes to attract more than an occasional schooner. And so the planters continued to send their cotton by mule team to Newport. There was no demand for speed, after all, in transporting their imperishable commodity, and the great six-mule-team wagons had one distinct appeal: they used during the winter off season the same hardworking animals that had "made" the crop in the spring.

The cotton plantations were all north of the Scarp, one-third of the forty-five large ones being within a four-mile-wide strip of rolling country in the middle of the county that extended northward for sixteen miles from the Scarp. Monticello, a town of three hundred, lay near the northern extremity of this fertile rectangle. South of this county seat, Nakoosa, the one-time plantation of Abram Bellamy, extended for four miles to the southeast and was now in the hands of a Bellamy connection, Daniel Bird.[4] West of Nakoosa were the thirty-five hundred acres in Casa Bianca. Standing on a knoll here that separates the drainage basins of Lake Miccosukee and the Aucilla River, the house of Casa Bianca, which burned down in 1905, was known as one of the finest plantation houses in the Red Hills. It was built by Joseph M. White, who was Florida's delegate to Congress during half of the territorial period.[5] He and his wife Ellen (Florida) White were rarely there. In Washington, Florida's charm and beauty captivated everyone. On several tours of Europe she hobnobbed with celebrities. Sir Edward Bulwer-Lytton wrote after one of her departures from England:

> You have gone from us, lady, to shine
> In the throng of the gay and the fair,
> If you're happy, we will not repine,
> But say, can you think of us there?[6]

White died in 1839. In 1850, after being widowed a second time, Mrs. Theophilus Beatty, forty-nine, was alone at Casa Bianca. Yet her travels still took her far away: at the time of the 1850 census she was on a year-long tour of Europe with her niece, Etta.[7] To the north of the big plantation was the somewhat smaller Wirtland, now in the hands of Elizabeth Wirt, the widow of William and sister of John and Robert Gamble, but Mrs. Wirt now lived in Anne Arundel County, Maryland.[8]

John G. Gamble and his brother Robert of the "Old Dominion" community hereabouts now lived on the edge of Tallahassee, although their Jefferson County plantations were intact. Prominent Whigs both, the Gambles must have felt uncomfortable in a county that had become the Democratic stronghold in the Red Hills. Jefferson had voted Democratic in every important election from 1839 to 1845, while the vote elsewhere was often Whig.[9]

However, a nephew of the Gambles, Edward Carrington Cabell, who was thirty-six in 1850, had used Jefferson County as his base and had become the most successful Whig politician in Florida. He

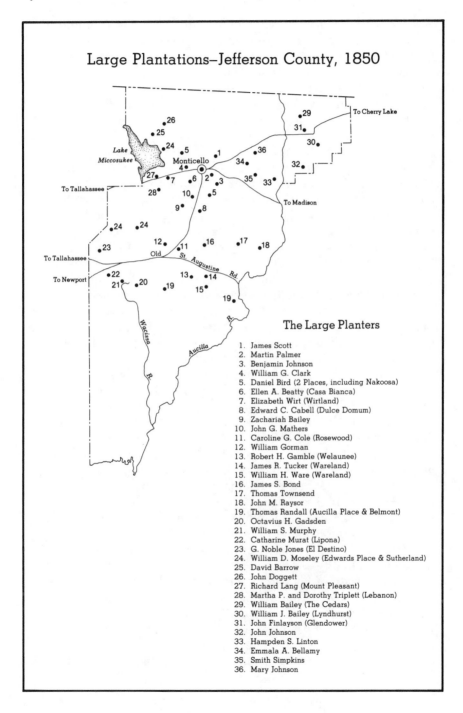

Large Plantations–Jefferson County, 1850

The Large Planters

1. James Scott
2. Martin Palmer
3. Benjamin Johnson
4. William G. Clark
5. Daniel Bird (2 Places, including Nakoosa)
6. Ellen A. Beatty (Casa Bianca)
7. Elizabeth Wirt (Wirtland)
8. Edward C. Cabell (Dulce Domum)
9. Zachariah Bailey
10. John G. Mathers
11. Caroline G. Cole (Rosewood)
12. William Gorman
13. Robert H. Gamble (Welaunee)
14. James R. Tucker (Wareland)
15. William H. Ware (Wareland)
16. James S. Bond
17. Thomas Townsend
18. John M. Raysor
19. Thomas Randall (Aucilla Place & Belmont)
20. Octavius H. Gadsden
21. William S. Murphy
22. Catharine Murat (Lipona)
23. G. Noble Jones (El Destino)
24. William D. Moseley (Edwards Place & Sutherland)
25. David Barrow
26. John Doggett
27. Richard Lang (Mount Pleasant)
28. Martha P. and Dorothy Triplett (Lebanon)
29. William Bailey (The Cedars)
30. William J. Bailey (Lyndhurst)
31. John Finlayson (Glendower)
32. John Johnson
33. Hampden S. Linton
34. Emmala A. Bellamy
35. Smith Simpkins
36. Mary Johnson

was the son of William H. Cabell of Richmond, a governor and Virginia Court of Appeals judge who bought land five miles south of Monticello in the 1820s. A son, Abraham, was sent to manage the plantation, called Dulce Domum, but died in 1831, and Edward, after completing a degree at the University of Virginia, replaced him. This brilliant and restless young Virginian was not to be tied down to mere planting, though. When he was not quite twenty-three, he was elected delegate to a convention that in 1838 wrote the constitution Florida would use when it became a state. This taste of politics was attractive enough for Cabell to jump in again after returning to Richmond and studying law. After statehood in 1845, Cabell ran as the Whig candidate to become Florida's lone representative in the House, won, and held the congressional post until a rising tide of Democratic votes retired him in 1852.[10] Cabell was absent from his "sweet home" most of the time during the 1840s and 1850s, either in Tallahassee or in Washington. However, in 1850 he still had ninety-eight slaves and a big acreage in Jefferson County and produced 202 bales of cotton.

South of Dulce Domum there was a gap in the cotton belt until one reaches the present community of Capps. Here, living in a house called Rosewood, Caroline G. Cole farmed a considerable acreage; her father, Burwell McBride of South Carolina, had left her this land.[11] Adjoining Mrs. Cole on the east and south and extending southward to the Cody Scarp was Welaunee, the most productive cotton plantation in the county, with a 599-bale crop in 1850. Long the plantation of Robert Gamble, these 6,319 acres were now in the hands of his son, Robert H. Gamble, who also managed other plantations of the Gamble-Wirt-Cabell-Randall connection.[12] A visitor to Iamonia Lake on this plantation today retreats in his imagination through three or four centuries of time, for here at the town of Ivitachuco on Iamonia Lake De Soto encamped on his march toward Iniahica in 1539 and Father Prieto witnessed a peace pact between the Utina and Apalachee Indians in 1608. This acreage retained the name Welaunee as a "quail plantation" in the twentieth century until in 1985 it was bought by Ted Turner of Atlanta, owner of the Cable News Network, who renamed it Avalon.[13]

After the death of his wife, Laura, Thomas Randall lived in Tallahassee but still owned and farmed Belmont, a section and a half adjoining the western boundary of Welaunee.[14] In 1827, staying on Welaunee while a house was being built on Belmont, Laura Randall rode the countryside and discovered the site, a mile north of the Randall house site on the plantation of her Uncle John Gamble, of the mission Nuestra Señora de Purissima Concepción de Ayubale, where a bloodbath in January 1704 had spelled the end of Apalachee. She described only the ruins of a Spanish "fort or some large public building." However, 113 years later, J. Clarence Simpson, a curious young employee of the Florida Geological Survey, discovered that Scott Miller, a black farmer, had dug up five whole Spanish olive jars here. He told historian Mark Boyd. In 1947 a dig by Hale G. Smith and John W. Griffin uncovered the foundation of two large mission structures and a quantity of Spanish and Indian artifacts.[15]

In 1850 the 5,460 acres of land in Waukeenah, where the Ayubale ruins were found, were still under the name of John G. Gamble on the tax books, but Gamble had no slaves in Jefferson County. Southwest of the John Gamble place, at the community of Wacissa, Octavius H. Gadsden, the youngest brother of James, had his own farm and as agent handled the forty-eight hundred acres and 205 slaves of his brother, James having left for his old home Charleston to become a railroad president and then to serve a brief career as a diplomat (he negotiated the Gadsden Purchase).[16] To the northwest of Octavius Gadsden on Moore Branch was Catharine Murat,[17] and northwest of her on Burnt Mill Creek was El Destino, now owned by George Noble Jones of Savannah.[18]

To the north of El Destino and lying in parcels to the southwest and southeast of present-day Lloyd was land that before 1846 had been in the hands of John D. Edwards, who had come to Leon County in 1825. Litigious, confrontational, and occasionally violent in his early years, Edwards served several terms in the territorial legislature. Moving to Jefferson he saw his political career come to an abrupt end in 1840 when, running as a "Conservative," he was overwhelmed in a Democratic landslide that brought one of Florida's newcomers, William D. Moseley, into the Legislative Council. Edwards also began to suffer from debts incurred in the wildcat banking of the 1830s. His 3,280 acres of land—2,200 in Jefferson and 1,080 in Leon—were sold by court order to satisfy judgments of $13,630 and $15,343.[19] Although he had earlier been a large planter, Edwards is shown to have had only a forty-five-bale cotton crop in 1850. The most notable member of John Edwards's family was his daughter, Mary, born in 1844 at Fonda—perhaps the name of the Edwards's Jefferson County plantation house. Later, as Mary Edwards Bryan, she became a popular novelist and magazine editor.[20] Mary remembered from her childhood her father's admiration for Florida White. He had visited her and dined with her, dressed in his finest clothes, and returning home at nightfall told her mother he had been visiting "the most beautiful woman I ever saw." Mrs. Edwards showed "a little natural pique to hear another woman so extravagantly praised."[21]

The purchaser of Edwards's debt-burdened lands was the politician William D. Moseley, who already had six-hundred-acre Sutherland on Lake Miccosukee.[22] In 1850, having completed a term as governor, he lived in Tallahassee. North of Sutherland and extending for six more miles along the lake, taking in the present community of Festus and Mays Pond, was a plantation reputed to be "the most fertile and productive in the state." This, the second of two plantations that had been acquired from Henry Doggett of Leon County by David Barrow of Bayou Sara, Louisiana, produced 505 bales of cotton and ten thousand bushels of corn, the largest corn crop in Jefferson County.[23]

William D. Moseley, more politician than planter, had been unusually successful in North Carolina politics. Born in Lenoir County in 1795, he graduated in the University of North Carolina class of 1818. James K. Polk was one of his classmates. In 1829 he succeeded Hardy Bryan Croom as state senator and was reelected through 1836. In 1833 he became Speaker of the Senate and in 1834 was defeated for governor of North Carolina by only a few votes in legislative balloting. An upsurge of Whig power finally ended his North Carolina political career in 1837, and he came to Florida.[24]

Moseley entered Florida politics almost immediately. Jefferson County sent him to the House in 1840, then the Senate. Soon he clashed head-on with William Bailey, another Jefferson County resident of his own party, who hoped to become governor. A native of Camden County, Georgia, Bailey had been one of the earliest settlers in Jefferson County. He married a member of the rich Bellamy family and amassed considerable wealth by lending money. He eventually entered into more formal banking as president of the State Bank of Florida. In 1850 at sixty he was probably the largest slaveholder in the Red Hills, having 269 slaves in Jefferson County alone, and he was now beginning to buy plantations in Leon County.[25]

With all of his wealth, Bailey should have been a Whig, but when Whigs approached him in 1845 to be their candidate for governor he refused, saying he would like their support if he became the candidate of the Democrats. This he expected to be. Friends pushed his candidacy at a convention that, however, turned to the more experienced Moseley, who then defeated Richard K. Call to become the first governor of the state of Florida. Again in 1848 Bailey stood for governor, this time as the Democratic candidate, but he was buried in an avalanche of votes that elected the Whig Thomas Brown.[26]

But if Bailey was not as good a politician as Moseley, he was by far the superior farmer. *De Bow's Review* took notice of his cotton production on 320 acres, a phenomenal 364 full-sized bales.[27] His largest place, called The Cedars, was a rectangle two miles wide and three miles deep on the Georgia line just to the east of the Aucilla River. Here Bailey produced 550 bales of cotton, second only to the crop of Welaunee, and a corn crop of eight thousand bushels.[28] To the south of Bailey, John Finlayson, a South Carolinian by way of Georgia, had a 330-bale cotton production on Glendower.[29]

The forty-five producers of 50 or more bales accounted for 7,007, or 74 percent, of Jefferson County's 9,468 bales of cotton. Jefferson County had the smallest white population in the Red Hills in 1850 at 2,775, with about twice as many slaves, and there were 377 farms in all.[30]

The number of South Carolinians who had settled in Madison County led it to be called "the Palmetto County." Carolinians dominated cotton plantation agriculture in 1850, two-thirds of the thirty-three large planters being natives of the Palmetto State. But in one of the principal cotton-growing regions, around, to the south of, and for six miles to the west of six-hundred-acre Cherry Lake just below the Georgia line, the planters were mostly Georgians. The largest among them, with two thousand acres on the lake, was Lucius Church, now fifty, a native of New Hampshire who before coming to Florida in the 1830s had been a merchant in Georgia.[31]

The "Cherry Lake community" lay mainly to the west of Church, stretching across beautifully rolling land along both sides of State Road 150. William L. Tooke, fifty-five, a native of North Carolina but more recently of Telfair County, Georgia, was rapidly becoming the largest of the planters here. During the 1850s Tooke's landholdings quadrupled to 4,520 acres and included the so-called Wardlaw Place of 2,160 acres south of his farm.[32] But Tooke's life came to a distressing end on Monday, 8 October 1860, during a dispute with his overseer, Thomas F. Drew, who, according to the *Tallahassee Floridian*, drew a knife and stabbed Tooke in the abdomen, then knocked him down, mounted a horse and rode away.[33]

The sixteen hundred acres adjoining Tooke on the west were in one of the several plantations of Reddin W. Parramore, fifty years old, who had come to Florida in the same migration stream as Tooke. Parramore's father had come from Onslow County, North Carolina; the son had grown up in Telfair County, Georgia. Although his cotton production is now unknown because the folded edge of a page in the manuscript census was cut off during binding, Parramore is shown

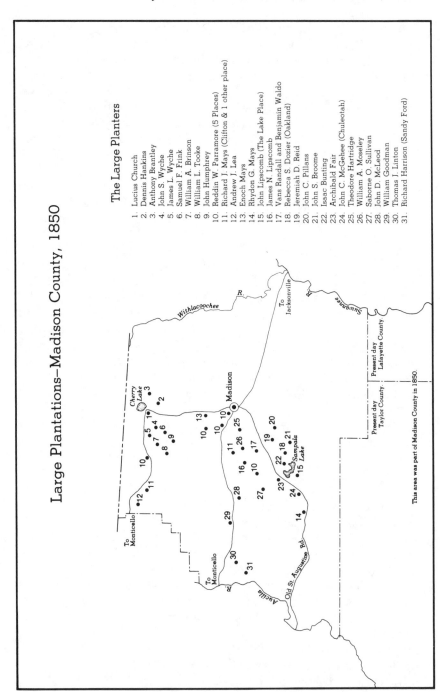

Large Plantations–Madison County, 1850

The Large Planters

1. Lucius Church
2. Dennis Hankins
3. Anthony Brantley
4. John S. Wyche
5. James L. Wyche
6. Samuel F. Frink
7. William A. Brinson
8. William L. Tooke
9. John Humphrey
10. Reddin W. Parramore (5 Places)
11. Richard J. Mays (Clifton & 1 other place)
12. Andrew J. Lea
13. Enoch Mays
14. Rhydon G. Mays
15. John Lipscomb (The Lake Place)
16. James N. Lipscomb
17. Vans Randall and Benjamin Waldo
18. Rebecca S. Dozier (Oakland)
19. Jeremiah D. Reid
20. John C. Pillans
21. John S. Broome
22. Isaac Bunting
23. Archibald Fair
24. John C. McGehee (Chuleotah)
25. Theodore Hartridge
26. William A. Moseley
27. Saborne O. Sullivan
28. John D. McLeod
29. William Goodman
30. Thomas J. Linton
31. Richard Harrison (Sandy Ford)

to have had livestock valued at $20,000, three times that of his nearest rival among the large cotton planters, and this was his specialty. Following his death in 1851 the estate showed his stock cattle herds had grown to 3,692 head valued at $14,768. Of his personal estate of $89,672.85, $26,169.23 consisted of promissory notes—and the tax rolls of 1854 show that the estate had $20,000 on loan and his widow, Mary Ann, $15,000.[34] Parramore's purchases of real estate were largely in partnership with his brother-in-law, Simeon Alexander Smith of Thomas County, Georgia. The first purchase, in 1842, included the western one-third of the present town of Madison, and Parramore's house was built here.[35]

Most of the twenty or more large Madison County planters from the Palmetto State farmed within an area in central Madison County that was shaped like a football on its tee, ready for the kickoff. The eastern boundary of this football was a sweeping curve that began four miles north of Madison. This boundary traveled through the town of Madison and along State Roads 14 and 360 and westward to the community of Moseley Hall. The middle of the football extended from just to the east of Sampala Lake to 10,000-acre Hixtown Swamp, seven miles west of Madison.

South Carolinians came to Madison County by the scores beginning in the late 1820s and 1830s to farm this land. Much of it was in "hardwood hammock," good for Upland Short Staple cotton, which according to one observer in 1853 constituted four-fifths of the cotton grown in Madison County. The same observer forecast, however, that Sea Island, comprising the remainder of the production, would become the favored crop.[36] Sea Island had begun by the 1840s to take over the pinelands of inland southeastern Georgia as well as some counties in northeastern Florida. It prevailed east of the Suwannee River in Florida. According to a correspondent of the *Southern Agriculturalist* in 1844, Sea Island had been almost the exclusive cotton crop in Hamilton and Columbia counties for eight or ten years. It was tempting for farmers in Madison to grow Sea Island where it would do well, for the price usually was twice that for Upland.[37]

Besides this fertile football in the center of Madison County, an extension of it in the vicinity of Greenville and on the Aucilla River to the west of Greenville, and the Cherry Lake plantation region, the only land farmed by the thirty-three large planters lay in the northwestern corner of the county. Here, near the present-day community of Lovett, Richard J. Mays, forty-five, one of several brothers who had come to Florida from the Edgefield District of South Carolina, built Clifton, his fine plantation house. Mays's memory still survives in the county. A Baptist minister as well as planter, he founded Concord Baptist Church in 1841, and the charter of the Florida Baptist Association was drawn up in 1854 at a round table in his house, the table becoming the proud possession of Mays's grandson, Parkhill Mays of Monticello, and then of his widow.[38]

Mays had only one other large planter as a neighbor in 1850. This was Andrew J. Lea, thirty-five, a North Carolinian. In February 1855, the New York commission merchants Smallwood, Anderson & Company complimented "the industry, enterprise and management" of this planter after selling twenty-eight bales of his Upland cotton handled through the port of St. Marks for eleven and one-quarter cents a pound—"the highest price for Florida cotton that will be realized this season."[39]

Richard Mays had chosen the fertile central Madison County farmlands for planting when he first came to Florida. So had his older brother James, who bought land on all sides of Sampala Lake in 1834 but after service in the Second Seminole War died of pleurisy in 1836. Richard is said to have accompanied James to Florida and to have farmed in the same area until the death of a child, Elizabeth, led him to move to what he thought was a healthier part of the county.[40] Another brother, Rhydon G. Mays, forty-nine, was the largest cotton grower in the Mays family in 1850. Rhydon had eighteen hundred acres at the southern tip of the football-shaped area, his land extending from the vicinity of the Wigginsville Church on State Road 360 (then the St. Augustine Road) to Sundown Creek four miles to the north. This Mays moved to Putnam County, Florida, to grow oranges, in 1852, selling his Madison County acreage to Owen E. Sullivan and Nancy DeLaughter.[41]

Evidently the largest of all the cotton planters in Madison County in 1850—although his cotton production, like Parramore's, is unknown because of the marred page of the agricultural census—was a Mays connection, John Lipscomb, sixty, a native of Edgefield, South Carolina. Lipscomb prospered in the mercantile business and for many years had a plantation and fine house at a place in South Carolina called White Hall.[42] In the 1830s he began acquiring Madison County land, first buying some of the Mays property along the west side of Lake Sampala, his land extending well to the south of the lake.[43] Lipscomb seems never to have committed himself to living in Florida, although the 1850 census shows him to be a resident. Late in life he decided to leave each member of a considerable family twelve thousand dollars in land, slaves, cash, or other properties of his estate.[44] An advertisement in 1859, following Lipscomb's death, offered

John McGehee, who is said by his newspaper obituary to have entered the service of his country as a teen-ager during the American Revolution, came to Madison County, Florida, in the 1830s. His death occurred during the heyday of the South's Cotton Kingdom, and this fine marble slab, though broken in two, records in great style his reputation as an "honest man." (Photo by Clifton Paisley)

6,180 acres of his land for sale, including the "Lake Place," 3,000 acres of oak and hickory lands on Lake Sampala.[45] Although it does not show Lipscomb's cotton production, the 1850 agricultural census indicates that his was the most valuable farmland in the county, worth forty-nine thousand dollars.

Typical of the Carolina upcountry settlers was John McGehee (1763–1834), who, according to his newspaper obituary, "entered the services of his country at sixteen" during the Revolutionary War and sometime after the war left Louisa County, Virginia, and settled in what became Greenwood, South Carolina. He taught school there and then, evidently in company with his son John C. McGehee, came to Madison County.[46] Here, on the St. Augustine–Tallahassee road, Superior Court Judge Robert Raymond Reid found the older Mr. McGehee and his wife in 1833 conducting the best "public house" along the two-hundred-mile road. Reid said he offered Mrs. McGehee half a box of snuff, and she produced a silver snuff box that had been in the family almost one hundred years. Its top "was composed of one center stone—I looked through it at the sun—he was as red as blood. The old man told me 'the box was in request in Carolina at the time of the spots on the sun and more spots had been discovered through this stone than by the best telescopes.' "[47]

After practicing law for a time in Cambridge, South Carolina, the younger McGehee decided to move to Florida in 1831.[48] Soon he was active in this easternmost county of the Red Hills as a lawyer, circuit court judge, planter, scientific farmer, industrialist, buyer and seller of land, Presbyterian elder and advocate of states' rights and secession. So active was he as a secessionist, in fact, that as a measure of caution following the Civil War he left for a brief sojourn in Mexico.[49]

At the southwestern end of the fertile football of cotton lands, the unpaved road from Moseley Hall to Madison leaves State Road 360. On a beautiful wind-swept hilltop here a fine marble stone, now broken into pieces, marks the grave of John McGehee.[50] This was also the principal plantation of his son John C., who built a fine house, Chuleotah, on this hilltop, but on the very day that it was completed, 2 August 1858, his wife, Charlotte, died.[51] McGehee also owned Oakland, about four miles to the northeast, where Charlotte was buried in what is today called Old Oakland Cemetery.[52] Her beautiful gravestone, carved during the height of the prosperity of the Carolina upcountry planters hereabouts, contrasts starkly with the modest stone of her husband, who died in 1882. The inscription even misspells his name, although he was prominent enough to be president of Florida's secession convention. The Old Oakland Cemetery record encapsulates the experience of the planter society here and in the South generally for the twenty years preceding and following the Civil War. John C. McGehee was buried beside a cedar tree. Around the McGehees are the graves of Wallers, Buntings, Reids, Sullivans, Doziers, and Mayses from the Carolina upcountry. Nature has been kinder than the times to these secessionists, for the cedar, a very large one, has entrapped a sweetgum within its trunk, and the two now hoist a banner of stars and needles, if not stars and bars, to shade the rebel band.

Two South Carolina families, the Lintons and the Harrisons, farmed initially in this central Madison County region but by 1850 had other places farther to the west, near or on the Aucilla River. Thomas J. Linton had a cotton production of 250 bales on his 3,380 acres, but his dairy enterprises were the most impressive part of his diversified farming. He had the largest dairy production of the big planters, six thousand pounds of butter and four hundred pounds of cheese, while his livestock was second in value only to Parramore's at seven thousand dollars.[53]

McGehee's gravestone is on a hilltop beside the onetime St. Augustine Road that was the site also of the plantation house Chuleotah of his son, John C. McGehee. When the second McGehee, the president of Florida's Secession Convention, died in 1882 the onetime affluence of the cotton South had "gone with the wind," and his grave in Old Oakland Cemetery is marked by a modest stone that even misspells his name. A giant cedar tree beside the grave has entrapped within its trunk a tall sweetgum, and the two cast a shade of stars and needles on the headstone of this second rebel in the McGehee family. (Photo by Clifton Paisley)

From the Greenville District of South Carolina, Richard Harrison also had land in the central Madison County area, but his main farm lay along the west and south sides of Linton's west Madison County farm. The Harrison land here extended to a crossing of the Aucilla River known as Sandy Ford.[54] In 1850 Richard Harrison had a cotton production of 220 bales, but his farm operation was rapidly growing, and the agricultural census understates his importance as a planter. From forty-four in 1847 his slave force grew to 145 in 1854, as shown by the tax rolls, while his entire personal estate was valued at this latter time at $133,490.56. Cotton production from the Harrison acres now totaled 318 normal-sized bales, probably as many as 375 bales of the four-hundred-pound size used in the agricultural census.[55]

Harrison's debts were also accumulating. On Wednesday, 3 January 1855, the young planter took on $20,000 in additional debt and at the same time expanded his landholdings in a big way. On that day in Tallahassee he signed a mortgage and agreed to pay $6,666.67 a year for three years to David Barrow, the planter in West Feliciana Parish, Louisiana, for his fine plantation, the Barrow Place, in Leon County, Florida.[56] The ink was hardly dry on this document when Harrison, in a confrontation in the Planters Hotel in Tallahassee, was stabbed to death by Cade Godbold, the proprietor of City Hotel. There was a quick trial on 23 March, with some of the best legal talent in the state on hand. The case went to the jury at 12:30 A.M. and the jury presented Judge J. Wayles Baker with a verdict thirty minutes later: "Not guilty."[57]

The outcome of the case gave Tallahassee some of the worst press it had experienced for years. The *New York Police Gazette* headline read: "Life in Tallahassee—The Bowie Knife the Ruler." "Horrible as this case is, a correspondent from Tallahassee represents that such scenes are not uncommon in that place and that they never pretend to carry out the law against these murderers and man butchers."[58] Tallahasseans were still talking about the case two years later when a Massachusetts businessman visited the Florida capital, took lodging at the City Hotel, and commented regarding the innkeeper Godbold: "The fact of his being a *mason* is said to have affected his acquittal."[59] "B," in Godbold's obituary following the hotel man's death in April 1858, noted that the innkeeper was "the victim of a violent and ungovernable temper." The writer charitably added, "As the grave now covers his mortal remains, so should his many noble and disinterested charities cover his foibles."[60]

Harrison's widow, Margaret Isabella Bradley Harrison, meanwhile returned her husband's body to Greenville, South Carolina, for burial and started to work on debts that began to eat into the considerable estate. Sandy Ford plantation, with its 1,500 acres and quarters for 150 slaves, went on sale on 15 November 1856 to pay some of these debts, and the widow transferred another tract for five dollars to a prosecution lawyer, Waddy Thompson, a few days after the trial.[61] In March 1856 the 2,123-acre Barrow Place in Leon County, "purporting to belong to the estate of Richard Harrison, deceased," was levied on by the tax collector to satisfy state, county, and railroad taxes for 1855. This plantation returned to its Louisiana owner and was sold in 1857 to Bryan Croom.[62]

Just as in Jefferson County, practically the only way to get cotton to market from Madison County was by a long wagon trip to Newport on the St. Marks River. Taking a load of cotton from Madison County, someone complained in 1855, took "a prime six-mule team a whole week to carry and return."[63] The beautiful Suwannee River was of little assistance, providing only a marginal avenue of transportation. The head of navigation for steamboats was at the old town of Columbus, where a railroad crossing was later made, and steamboats could normally go this far for only about half of the year or during very high water.[64]

Just as in the other Red Hills counties, the thirty-three large cotton growers of Madison County dominated production, accounting for 3,652, or 73 percent, of the 5,024 bales produced in 1850. Unlike all of the other Red Hills counties, Madison now had a majority—although only a slight majority—of whites in the population: 2,802 whites and 2,688 black slaves, with no free blacks. A measure of diversification was evident in the emphasis on livestock and dairying. Madison County had more milch cows at 5,536 than any other county in Florida with the exception of Columbia and was fifth in the state in the number of cattle other than milch cows or work oxen, with 14,086. Madison County was the largest producer of butter in the state. Its production of 102,970 pounds accounted for nearly one-third of the Florida total, while the 11,304 pounds of cheese produced in Madison accounted for nearly two-thirds of the statewide production.[65]

14

The Railroad-Building Boom

The only railroad in Florida in 1850 was the mule-drawn line that ran twenty-one miles from Tallahassee to the wharf at St. Marks. Richard K. Call, the owner, proposed to rebuild this line to accommodate locomotives and extend it northward to connect with the impressive rail system of Georgia. Georgia had the best rail system in the South; tracks connected Savannah with Macon and Augusta and those towns with the growing rail center of Atlanta, where a state-built line to the border of Tennessee near Chattanooga would soon begin bringing grains, meats, and other provisions into the Georgia and South Carolina cotton belts. Lines were also being extended to the Chattahoochee River to gather cotton from nearby Alabama and to Albany and the plantation belt along the Flint River.[1] These connections would shortly cause the cotton grown in these areas to flow by rail to Savannah rather than by way of the Chattahoochee-Flint river system to the port of Apalachicola. This port, which loaded 130,256 bales in the 1859–1860 season, would soon be turned into a lumber port and finally a fishing village.[2] Both Savannah and Brunswick, Georgia—soon connected by rail in Ware County—planned a "main trunk" to Pensacola running through a row of Georgia counties along the Florida line. In proposing a connection of the Tallahassee Railroad with the main trunk some twenty or thirty miles away, Call suggested—although no one believed him—that St. Marks would serve even better than Pensacola as the Gulf port of a rail-steamer system that would cross the Tehuantepec peninsula of Mexico, tying California with the American East Coast, a plan of much interest in Savannah at the time.[3]

Red Hills planters welcomed a connection with Savannah, a deepwater port from which their cotton could be shipped to New York. But the Call plan immediately encountered opposition from backers of two other Florida railroads. These were the Florida Railroad, which planned to build from Fernandina to the unknown Gulf port of Cedar Key just south of the Suwannee, and the Atlantic & Gulf Central. The latter, based in the rapidly growing town of Jacksonville, which was anxious to become the Atlantic port for all of Florida, planned to build westward toward a Gulf connection. The two lines would run through or near most of a cluster of thirteen counties composing the northeastern corner of Florida that by the end of the decade of the 1850s would have a third of Florida's population, the Red Hills counties accounting for another third in 1860. These primarily white, mostly nonplantation counties would shortly replace the Red Hills in the political power structure of Florida.[4]

The Florida Railroad, moreover, belonged to the astute politician U.S. Senator David L. Yulee, who had replaced the late Robert Raymond Reid as the chieftain in the Democratic party and who claimed the backing of northern financiers for his road. However, it was A. D. Baldwin of Jacksonville, the headman of Atlantic & Gulf Central, who spoke out against the plan of Call, an erstwhile backer of his road who was now in favor of "directing the trade of our state into Georgia."[5]

Even as Call expressed his views in January 1853, another railroad plan was being formulated in Tallahassee, this one more in keeping with the Fernandina and Jacksonville plans of linking the Atlantic and Gulf altogether within Florida. Although this railroad was called the Pensacola and Georgia, a Pensacola connection lay far in its future. It would start in Tallahassee and build eastward through Jefferson and Madison counties to Alligator (Lake City). Although "Georgia" was in its name, the P&G answered critics of a Georgia connection by proposing to connect with Georgia only in Hamilton County "east of the Alapaha River." Governor James E. Broome, a Democrat, was a backer and campaigned to raise $800,000 in stock subscriptions from people in Middle Florida. These, he said, would give the section a majority of the $1,500,000 in authorized stock and would enable Middle Florida to control the place of the Georgia connection. David S. Walker, a Whig and the register of state lands, backed the plan and warned Floridians that Savannah would shortly have a line running across southernmost Georgia. Unless Florida went in for railroad building in a serious way, it was "a gone fawn skin forever, an outside row of corn for the coons and squirrels to devour." The subscription campaign, though, was a failure.[6]

Call now stepped out of the railroad picture. The president of Pensacola & Georgia Railroad was Edward Carrington Cabell, now thirty-seven, who had demonstrated his familiarity with Florida's railroad needs in a widely circulated history of transportation in Florida that he wrote in 1852.[7] All three Florida railroads began to build under revised charters with the passage of the Internal Improvements Act of 6 January 1855, which provided liberal state aid in the form of land grants. The act also allowed the railroads to call upon counties through which the roads passed to pay for half of the cost of the construction by official county subscriptions of stock; taxpayer approval was needed to issue bonds and to levy a tax to retire them.[8] Using this law, the Pensacola and Georgia was able to collect $375,000 in stock subscriptions from the counties of Leon, Jefferson, and Madison to go with $149,000 in private subscriptions. The Florida Railroad meanwhile built from Fernandina toward Cedar Key; the Central from Jacksonville toward Alligator, present Lake City, where it agreed to meet the P&G from Tallahassee. Still without a Georgia connection, the P&G was authorized to acquire control of the St. Marks line. As its first action it replaced the mule cars with locomotives.[9]

The question of a Georgia connection was sidelined for a time. Sixty hands were at work by May 1855, improving the roadbed between St. Marks and Tallahassee under the direction of R. A. Shine, the perennial public works contractor. During the next month Governor Broome returned from New York with a contract for rails, and the first load of these arrived in October. Unlike the flimsy strips of iron on wood that had been used since 1837, the new rails were of a T pattern and weighed sixty pounds a yard. Track laying began in January 1856 and was completed in time for one of the two new sixteen-ton engines acquired from W. W. Baldwin Company of Philadelphia, the *H. L. Rutgers*, to begin steam travel between Tallahassee and St. Marks in October 1856. The trains had eight or ten freight cars and one passenger car. Goods were transferred directly from the hold of a vessel and were delivered to Tallahassee the same day. Cotton in turn was loaded directly onto vessels. The railroad at the same time offered its forty mules for sale.[10] All of Tallahassee was caught up in the big enterprise, along with the plantation community and Monticello and Madison, other towns along the route. Cabell used every little milestone for a celebration, to which legislators from other parts of the state, in Tallahassee for the sessions, were often invited. Therefore, on 13 December 1856, Governor Broome, members of the General Assembly, other officials, and several Tallahassee citizens made an excursion to St. Marks on the rebuilt line. Before returning, the company of eighty sat down to a dinner served at the St. Marks Hotel.[11]

By this time 370 hands were at work preparing the roadbed on the main line which, since the rails could be shipped to St. Marks and carried by rail to the end of the line, was built eastward from Talla-hassee. Months of grading, ditching, culvert building, bridge build-ing, and tie laying had to be done before the tracks were laid down. Contracts were let, a mile at a time, for the clearing and grading, and planters along the way—John Lipscomb of Edgefield, South Carolina, a wealthy Madison County planter, director of the railroad, and "lib-eral subscriber" among them—used their slave forces to clear the right-of-way and mound up a roadbed.[12] From the Tallahassee depot, crews under the direction of Captain Shine took the construction east-ward across Adams Street and just south of the cascade, destroying the beautiful waterfall in the process.[13] The right-of-way followed the curving St. Augustine Branch northward, then turned eastward through a ridge of high ground where a cut was made for one thou-sand feet, forty-five feet at the deepest, the biggest ditch that had ever been dug in Florida. Completion of this "herculean task" was celebrated by the one hundred black workers with a barbecue on 4 July 1857.[14]

By 9 October 1857, track laying on the main line had been completed eight miles east of Tallahassee. The railroad picked up its first load of cotton; forty-five bales from the Lake Lafayette plantation of Francis Eppes had a free ride to St. Marks. On 28 November 1857, the railroad announced that it was receiving cotton and passengers at Station No. 1 (Chaires). By 1 January 1858, the line had opened to Station No. 2 in the vicinity of Bailey's Mills in Jefferson County.[15]

There were various excursions, one with five hundred men, women, and children aboard, unhappily ending at Chaires Station when the train ran off the track (only the fireman was injured). The public needed to be reminded from time to time that the Pensacola & Georgia (which still had no assurance that it would ever reach either Pensacola or Georgia) was part of a greater enterprise. President Cab-ell told stockholders that the road would eventually become an ex-tension of the Southern Pacific, and a visitor to Tallahassee foresaw that the road and its connections would extend from Jacksonville through Pensacola, Mobile, Baton Rouge, and Austin and through the El Paso Gap to California. When it was complete, travelers "will be able to take the short cut across the cotton fields to California."[16]

Cabell reported after a year's trial of the rebuilt St. Marks line that it "is now one of the best paying roads in the country."[17] As the main line proceeded through Jefferson and Madison counties and then over a Suwannee River bridge—this being at the head of navigation to avoid the expense of a drawbridge—arrangements were made with stagecoach lines to load and unload passengers near the end of the track. A trip from Tallahassee to Savannah by rail and stage through Valdosta now required only twenty-two hours.[18] Surveys were meanwhile made westward in Gadsden County, and clearing began there—even though Gadsden County voters had turned down, 239 to 234, a proposal to tax themselves for stock in the railroad company.[19]

Other railroads had not been idle. In June 1860 the Florida Railroad became the first to unite the Atlantic and Gulf coasts of Florida, only one and a half miles of track on a trestle remaining to be laid before Way Key and its planned depot. Fernandina began receiving cotton from Alachua and Marion counties, which now rivaled Red Hills counties in population, number of slaves, and cotton production.[20] Central meanwhile built westward to what became Lake City, and P&G completed its line to the same place and announced schedules between Tallahassee and Lake City on 8 December 1860.[21] Nor had Georgia railroad builders been idle. From Savannah the "main trunk" was completed to Thomasville and was put into service by mid-April 1861.[22]

Yet the Pensacola and Georgia still did not have a Georgia connection when the trains began to run. Cars bearing Red Hills cotton could continue on the Central to the port of Jacksonville or (if permitted by Central to do so) could be transferred to the Florida Railroad at Baldwin, the transfer point twenty miles from Jacksonville, and from there could proceed to the port of Fernandina. However, these two ports had little appeal for Red Hills planters who had hoped to send their cotton to Savannah, the largest port in the Southeast. Cabell, who had directed the P&G railroad building since the start, resigned as president in 1859. His successor, the Leon County planter Edward Houstoun, originally from Savannah, was particularly sensitive to the loss of the Georgia tie-in and bemoaned the "fatal blunder" of an agreement to join the roads that permitted Central "to prevent the produce and freights from passing through Fernandina and compel them to pass through Jacksonville."[23]

Builders of the Pensacola & Georgia had boasted from the start that its road tapped the principal cotton belt to be found either in extreme south Georgia or Florida. The *Floridian* cited the *Seventh Census*, published in 1853, to show that the five Georgia counties along the "main trunk" of the Savannah line, from Ware to Decatur, produced a crop of 16,389 bales in 1850, while six Florida counties on the line of P&G, from Columbia to Gadsden, produced 37,570.[24] That Central counted on gaining the bulk of the Red Hills cotton going to St. Marks and even much of the cotton going to the port of Apalachicola is shown in the report of J. P. Sanderson, president, to directors of Central on

6 July 1859. He said that the total would amount to at least 100,000 bales, providing revenues of seventy-five thousand dollars at seventy-five cents a bale.[25]

However, as the P&G built eastward, it continued to carry cotton westward to St. Marks. Even before the main line was in operation, the port of St. Marks shipped 53,277 bales of cotton worth $2,530,285 in 1856. As the main line progressed, Newport's share of the cotton shrank from about one-half to one-fourth. The town suffered an economic collapse from loss of the cotton business.[26] The enterprising Daniel Ladd handily survived the depression. He opened a store at Walker's south of Monticello to take advantage of the railroad, kept the Wakulla Iron Works going, and devoted the spare time of the steam towboat *Spray* to passenger excursions to Cedar Key, charging $10 a passenger.[27]

St. Marks boomed for a time. Two Tallahassee bankers with railroad investments had locomotives named for them. When the *H. L. Rutgers* and *General Bailey* steamed to the wharf, they met the fine new brig, *General Bailey*, owned by Smallwood, Earle and Company, and the bark, *Henry L. Rutgers* of six hundred tons' burthen, owned by Brodie & Pettes. Both plied the waters between New York and St. Marks carrying cotton north and merchandise south, as well as passengers in both directions. On the *Rutgers'* maiden voyage she was welcomed by a Tallahassee group that went down to St. Marks to celebrate the occasion. The space between decks was converted into a ballroom, and two hundred persons boarded the vessel to entertain themselves with quadrilles, waltzes, and promenades followed by a grand "march to the dining room." The *Rutgers* soon surpassed all expectations by sailing from St. Marks to New York in eleven days, discharging cargo, taking on freight, and returning to St. Marks in another eleven days.[28]

St. Marks even demonstrated more than ever before that it was able to accommodate heavy transatlantic ships, although they could anchor only far offshore. The ship *Hartley* from England arrived with 625 tons of rails that caused it to draw sixteen feet eight inches. She was at anchor in September 1860 "with nineteen feet under her at low water and twenty-three feet at high, in good and safe anchorage, harbor well protected within twelve miles of the wharf at St. Marks and within four miles of the lighthouse," a correspondent wrote in the *Floridian*.[29]

The *Floridian* was nevertheless already of the opinion that St. Marks was unlikely "to remain a terminus of any railroad," and predicted that an "extension of this road [the P&G] to White Bluff will soon become, in our judgment, a necessity."[30] The newspaper's enthusiasm for a new Gulf port at White Bluff can be traced to the appearance of a new edition of James R. Butts's Map of Georgia (which recorded in some detail the Gulf shoreline of adjacent Florida). It showed a land feature near present Carrabelle, where the New and Crooked rivers come together, called "White Bluff" and offshore from the entrance of Alligator Harbor to the east, "Duer Channel discovered by U.S. Coast Survey 1858. 30 feet Water."[31]

The enthusiasm nearly led the P&G into a fatal mistake. Duer Channel is still to be found on ocean charts of the area; fishermen there sometimes call it "Dewey Channel." Starting east of Dog Island Reef, Duer Channel runs toward the spit of land that is called Alligator Point, but there are no thirty-foot depths nearer than about five miles offshore.[32] George K. Walker was the principal advocate of a rail terminus and port town on Alligator Harbor, on the north shore opposite Alligator Point. Now nearing sixty, Walker and his brother David S. Walker had come to Florida in the 1830s from Logan County, Kentucky. After a brief career in public life George Walker settled down to land speculation and, in partnership with Benjamin L. Curtis, a New Yorker interested in Florida yellow pines for lumber, purchased 70,461 acres of Forbes Purchase lands that included much of twenty-mile-long St. James Island.[33] Walker's house was on top of the hill in present Tallahassee that is now occupied by Florida A&M University, a place called Highwood,[34] and when the engines *General Bailey* and *Henry L. Rutgers* pulled passenger and freight cars to and from St. Marks they were in view in the valley below Highwood, while Walker also had a sweeping view to the southwest across the pinelands of Forbes Purchase and toward his land on St. James Island.

At a meeting that heard a report of a committee chaired by Walker, the stockholders of P&G in July 1859 tentatively favored "immediate construction" of a branch line to follow somewhat the route of today's Crawfordville Road toward the proposed port town. The plan was fortunately abandoned, but the attention drawn to St. James Island led to increasing use of the seacoast here, called St. Theresa, for summer homes and fishing.[35]

Tallahassee came alive during the railroad building of the 1850s. The population increased from 1,391 in 1850 to 1,932 in 1860. There was even an unfamiliar hum of industry; the new plants included I. W. Bowen's steam sash and blinds factory at the depot and the foundry of John Cardy. Leading the parade was railroad car building in the shops of the P&G. Eight freight cars were under construction in January 1857, to be followed by several passenger cars.[36] "Car building" became the principal industry of Leon County. The 1860 census of manufactures shows that one hundred freight cars and eight passenger cars, valued at eighty thousand dollars, were built in one year by an industry employing 62 persons. With twenty-six industrial establishments, 246 employees, and a production of $261,000, Leon became the third largest manufacturing county in the state, behind only Santa Rosa and Duval counties, with their many sawmills.[37]

Elsewhere in the Red Hills, Madison and Jefferson counties had the only plants manufacturing cotton yarn. N. P. Willard constructed the first such factory in 1851 on the edge of the town of Madison, beside a lake. Said to have cost thirty thousand dollars, it employed thirty males and females between the ages of ten and eighteen who were paid between eight and fifteen dollars a month. The factory used 330 bales of cotton a year, and turned out cheap cotton yarn, principally for the local market. But the plant was destroyed by fire in 1857.[38]

The showiest cotton mill was that of William Bailey, the Jefferson County planter and Tallahassee banker. It made a display of "southern independence." A mile and a quarter east of Monticello on the Madison road, the building was seventy-five feet long, forty-eight feet wide, and three stories high. Its bricks were made from local clay, and the roof and interior framing had come from local pine trees. The mill made its principal statement in a brick smokestack that was ten feet square at its independent base but tapered to four feet square at the top, fifty-six feet above ground, an undersized Bunker Hill monument, while the mill company was organized under the resounding name of Jefferson Southern Rights Manufacturing Company.

But although this creation drew on southern independence, patriotism, and protest, its backers were not averse to going to the industrial North for the machinery and skill to operate it. Moreover, Bailey seems, like Willard, to have approached the New England Yankees for the labor plan, its sixty-five "operatives"—forty of them male and twenty-five female—earning an average of ten dollars a month. In addition to fifteen hundred spindles, the plant had fifty looms to weave osnaburgs and other cheap cloths. It was designed to consume 400,000 pounds (nearly 1,000 bales) of cotton annually. The plant continued in operation during the Civil War but in 1860 used only 200,000 pounds of cotton, together with a small quantity of wool.[39]

In general, however, Tallahassee and all of the Red Hills preferred to continue to enjoy the products of the North's industrial plants without trying to match them. Monticello, like Tallahassee, had a boom in population, reaching 1,083 persons in 1860, while Quincy had about the same population, and Marianna and Madison had about 400 persons apiece. Even the planter society became more urban.

This 1885 photograph shows Tallahassee's Academy Building, which was built in 1855 on the hilltop now occupied by Florida State University's Westcott Building. (Courtesy of Florida State Archives)

Joseph John Williams moved his family to a Tallahassee town house in 1860. This planter now chose to be known as a devotee of animal husbandry. He bought a two-year-old bull, Defender, in England,

The home of Richard K. Call was an impressive structure at the northern edge of antebellum Tallahassee and is as impressive today. Although the state capital, Tallahassee was only a tiny little cotton town in 1850, but Leon County produced a third of all the cotton grown in Florida. During the 1850s, Tallahassee suddenly came alive in the midst of the building of a railroad toward Jacksonville, called the Pensacola & Georgia. There was considerable construction, and the town favored (as it had all along) the classic revival style. A great "tricorn crown" of columned buildings joined Call's already built home at one corner of the tricorn, the 1845 capitol at another and the new Academy at the third corner. (Courtesy of Florida State Archives)

and the arrival of this animal of "elephantine proportions" aboard the bark *R. H. Gamble* in December 1857 was a notable event.[40] Considerably larger and more impressive than Defender, though, was the "Broadway omnibus" that Peres B. Brokaw, the Tallahassee liveryman, bought in New York for seven hundred dollars and used to taxi passengers between uptown hotels and the railroad station.[41] People who had known Tallahassee commented on improvements. "She has aroused from her slumber, gone to work, and ere many years she will rank among the most beautiful and desirable cities of the South," said a visitor from Quincy.[42]

The building of the Pensacola & Georgia was the most ambitious enterprise ever undertaken by Tallahassee, and a surge of civic pride, accompanied by prosperity, led to the construction of several fine new residences and one beautiful public building. Some of these even survived a march of the bulldozers accompanying the population boom following World War II. The finest building of all during the 1850s was the result of Florida's nod to "free public schools"; it was no more than a nod, however. Free schools were vigorously debated in the legislature just after statehood, and thanks to the efforts of David S. Walker, the Whig register of state lands and ex officio superintendent of public instruction, a Florida system of public schools was established.[43] Unfortunately there was no tax base to support it. Taxpayers, and least of all Middle Florida's prosperous planters and merchants, would not tolerate a tax beyond their ad valorem tax, especially after a "railroad tax" had been added.

In Tallahassee, nevertheless, a free school opened in 1850 under Principal Jesse P. Smith, a graduate of the University of North Carolina and the brother of the discoverer of the Wakulla Springs mastodon.[44] Thanks to the efforts of H. L. Rutgers and others, the City Council in 1856 was allocating $2,442 of its annual budget of $8,512 for teachers' salaries.[45] The city had just erected a schoolhouse for its "academy" on the hilltop today occupied by the Westcott Building of Florida State University, with a circular drive around it much like the present one that joined the Quincy road on the west. There was method in this "monumental" approach to education, for the city's offer of a ten-thousand-dollar "package," including this fine building, induced the state to locate one of two "seminaries of learning" in Tallahassee. The Seminary West of the Suwannee, which eventually became a college and was renamed Florida State University, opened on 1 October 1857. The masonry building, however, succumbed to underlying "pipe clay" in the 1890s, as did a successor building and an auditorium addition to the present Westcott.[46]

The building was indeed impressive. The *Floridian* called it "the handsomest edifice in the city." It was really a Greek temple, built of brick covered by concrete plaster, a two-story structure measuring sixty by forty feet, with a wide porch supporting four tall columns, also of brick, which in turn supported a pediment and simple gabled roof. Newel posts, banisters, and the rails on interior stairways were of cherry, and there were venetian blinds.[47] At the same time that this building was erected, Edward Carrington Cabell, president of the Pensacola & Georgia, built himself a residence four long blocks to the east, facing Clinton (College) at Duval. It was very much like the academy building, another Greek temple, exact in proportions but built of wood and like the capitol and academy building a "spotless white." The Cabell house dominated the neighborhood until, in 1948,

In 1855, four blocks away from the masonry Academy, Edward Carrington Cabell, the president of the Pensacola & Georgia, built a "Greek temple" befitting the head of Tallahassee's biggest enterprise. This building joined several other handsome structures within the tricorn, some even standing today. (Courtesy of Florida State Archives)

it was torn down to make way for a furniture store, the pieces being saved by the Avant family and reassembled as the chapel of East Hill Baptist Church.[48]

Fenton Garnett Davis Avant (1889–1980) recalled from a turn-of-the-century girlhood that the interior exhibited the same elegance, including mantels of white marble, high ceilings "frescoed by Italian artists," doors of mahogany, and doorknobs, door hinges, and locks of silver. When it was completed in 1855, the academy building, the capitol, and General Call's house at the foot of Adams Street became three jewels at the points of a tricorn crown of classic revival architecture. Within this great triangle the Greek temple of Cabell was another gem, while "Sister Fenton" Avant recalled another residence known as a "temple house." This was the Harrison house, on the northwest corner of Monroe and Carolina streets. These and several other buildings remained for most of the nineteenth century to celebrate Tallahassee's love affair with broad steps, wide porches, high columns, and simple pediments and roofs, which continued even while a railroad was under construction. In the middle of the triangle "The Columns," the oldest remaining residence from early Tallahassee, and the First Presbyterian Church, completed in 1838, still remain, as well as Call's house at the foot of Adams. The Harrison "temple" survives after a second move; builders have told preservationists to "get it on wheels."[49]

Architecture of a different kind had guided the rebuilders of fire-ravaged Monroe Street. Most of the street had rather plain storefronts. One thirty-foot front called "110" was used by James M. Williams and afterward became William Slusser's hardware store. Opening late in the 1850s, this establishment continued until Slusser's death in 1892. The store supplied Tallahassee and the plantation community at midcentury with fine stoves and such luxuries as bathtubs and even "washing machines," along with a variety of other items of northern manufacture. Near Christmas time its shelves and counters filled with hobby horses, toys on wheels, boxes of alphabet letters, rabbit drummers, April butterflies, and grace hoops.[50]

But at 1:30 A.M. on the weekend night of 22 November 1859, when an alarm went out, everyone feared a repetition of the disastrous fire of May 1843. The first to respond to the alarm was Richard Hayward, who soon had a bucket brigade carrying water from nearby wells and cisterns to the roof of a shed beside the "ten pin alley and drinking saloon" of Hill and Groner, where the blaze had started. Governor Perry soon arrived, but Secretary of State F. L. Villepigue and a few others, operating two "garden fire engines" from this shed, were credited with limiting losses to water damage. The fire engines had been borrowed from the stores of Slusser and George Meginniss. The *Floridian* called for prompt purchase by the city of two engines "capable of throwing a liquid stream thirty feet high." Shortly afterward a volunteer fire company, long advocated by the newspaper, had formed and succeeded in controlling a fire that broke out in the barber shop of City Hotel.[51]

15

The Blacks

"Every morning at daybreak Bob, the wagoner, stood outside his cabin and blew his bugle to wake up the hands on the plantation. Then he would come and knock on father's window, and wake him and get orders for the day." So wrote the daughter of Virginia-born Kidder Meade Moore, the master of Pine Tucky plantation on one of the southernmost of the red hills of Jefferson County. Mrs. Helen Moore Edwards treasured fond memories from a childhood in the "big house," a two-story place looking out across twenty miles of flatwoods to the Gulf. Christmas dinners were spread under the giant oaks between this house and the "quarters," and there were gifts for the slaves; another big dinner for the blacks was held in the same place on Independence Day; and often weddings among Negroes took place in the yard.[1]

The picture of slavery left by white narrators was often rosy, peopled with happy-go-lucky blacks who readily tolerated the status quo. A somewhat different story appears in the "slave narratives" compiled in the 1930s, but some of the memories that they record are as mellow as those of Helen Moore Edwards. The parents of Louis Napoleon, a black boy who was only eight when Emancipation came in 1865, enjoyed a privileged status among the slaves on Dr. Arthur Randolph's San Luis at the edge of Tallahassee. The plantation of eight hundred acres lay among high hills and steep valleys along two miles of present-day Mission Road. The ruins of an old blockhouse, a mission compound, and a large Indian village enhanced its romantic interest as the site of the seventeenth-century San Luis de Talimali.[2] Louis's father was a wagoner. His mother was assigned light household duties. Louis himself was free from all but a few duties, such as looking for hens' nests and gathering eggs. He spent much of his time romping, hunting, and fishing with the master's three young sons.

At seventy-nine, Louis Napoleon recalled, however, that for field hands the workday was sunup to sundown. A little time remained at night for either religious singing and shouting or dancing to fife, banjo, or fiddle in front of the cabin door. It was a benevolent regime; the master, who was the son of parents from two branches of the Randolph family in Virginia, and his wife, Laura, the daughter of Governor William P. DuVal, were both kind.[3]

The boyhood of Willis Williams at the town house of Thomas Hayward in Tallahassee was also a pleasant one. Hayward, a well-to-do Marylander, was a merchant and planter. Willis's father was a carpenter and did light work around the few acres of garden and poultry sheds at this Adams Street house. There were quantities of vegetables, as well as chickens, ducks, and geese, together with groceries sent home from the Monroe Street store, all made available to family and slaves alike. Willis's mother as the cook saw to it that her children were well fed. Their food came from the master's own table, where biscuits appeared twice a day, and cornbread was always present. Willis looked after his brothers and sister while his mother managed the kitchen.[4]

The slave population of the five counties of the Red Hills numbered 24,243 in 1850, more than a fourth of the entire white and black population of Florida, which was 87,445, and 60 percent of the entire population of the Red Hills.[5] The vast majority of the slaves lived on plantations. Except for the privileged house servants and skilled artisans, the slaves labored largely in the fields and, as at San Luis plantation, from dawn to dusk. Picking eight two-hundred-foot rows of cotton was sometimes a full day's work.[6]

Almost always there was insistence on "putting in a good day's work," but the routine differed from plantation to plantation, as did the degree of punishment for malingering. A mild regime prevailed on the Jefferson County plantation of James Parish. He seldom punished his slaves and never allowed his overseer to do so. If the slaves failed to do their work, they were reported to him, and he would warn them and show his black whip. Usually a glimpse of it was sufficient to set them to working.[7] On San Luis plantation Dr. Randolph had a white "driver," but Randolph neither whipped the slaves nor allowed his driver to do so. Any slave who had been whipped could report the incident to the master, and the driver would be fired.[8]

Memories of quite a different kind fill the interview of Margrett Nickerson, who grew to maturity on the big Leon County plantation of William Carr, which extended from Carr Lake and Mallard Pond on the northeastern edge of Lake Jackson to Lake Overstreet. Recorded by the interviewer in a dialect that is almost unintelligible today, Mrs. Nickerson said: "Ole Marse Carr fed us, but he did not care what an' whar, jes so you made dat money and when yo' made five and six bales o' cotton, said: 'Yo' ain don' nuthin'.' " Her bitterest memories were about sweet potato planting time in May or June when her job was carrying the vines to be planted. She could never deliver the plants fast enough to the planting crews, and an overseer beat her with strops and sticks. "At night my pa would try to fix me up cose I had to go back to work next day. I never walked straight from dat day to dis."[9]

The easygoing nature of the young masters relieved tensions in the master-slave relationship on the Jefferson County plantation of the brothers Tom and Bryant Folsom. Cruelty to the hands was unheard of, according to Acie Thomas, who grew up there. Although there was a busy work schedule, time off was given for frolics (dances), and Marse Bryant played the fiddle while the servants were "cutting the pigeon wing." Weddings, far from the traditional ceremony of jumping over the broom, became richly costumed galas in which master and mistress often participated.[10] On another Jefferson County place, Douglas Parish, who was fifteen when the war ended, recalled gaining favor with his master by learning to be a good runner. The master, James Parish, was a sports fan who loved nothing more than to match his "nigger" against those of other planters in Independence Day races where the prize ranged from a pair of fighting cocks to a slave. If Parish did not win the prize, he was bad tempered for several days, but Douglas, well trained by running from the boundary of the plantation and back, seldom let him down. Douglas also elicited the envy of other young blacks by becoming stable boy for the plantation.[11]

Housing, food, and medical attention for the slaves appear in quality to have matched and probably exceeded those for a considerable part of the white population. The number of skilled doctors whose practice was mainly on the plantations is evidence enough that planters, whether feeling kindly toward their "people" or not, found it necessary to preserve them as able-bodied members of the labor force. In September 1851 when young Demps Russ cut his arm badly in a cotton gin, the Chemonie plantation journal shows that he was provided with a black nurse for several days after Dr. Cary B. Gamble came from Tallahassee to amputate the arm. The doctor then cared for Demps at his own house. He was treated so well that he resisted coming back to the plantation. The overseer, John Evans, had to go after him three weeks later.[12]

Even on plantations where the whip was not a constant persuader against malingering or rebellious activities, some attention was paid to "thought control" as a means of preventing slaves from dwelling on a future better than slavery. Bolden Hall, who grew up on the Thomas Linton place near Waukeenah, Jefferson County, recalled that Linton provided enough food and clothing and saw to it that the cabins were livable but was careful to see that the slaves received no education. Linton permitted slaves to attend church with the master and to hear a white minister, and he even sometimes provided an itinerant colored minister. Still, Hall retained the impression that the visiting minister's message emphasized obedience to the master.[13]

A master named Wilkerson in Madison County—so cruel, according to Charlotte Mitchell Martin, who spent her first years there, that the slaves remained in constant fear of him—permitted no meetings of any kind. Sometimes religious services were held secretly, but if their instigators became known or suspected, they were severely flogged. Charlotte said that her oldest brother was whipped to death for taking part in such a meeting. After his death the meetings at the plantation at Sixteen, Madison County, came to an end.[14]

The master of the Carr plantation "never 'lowed us to have a piece uf paper in our hands," said Margrett Nickerson. But the plantation management went much further than that, she said, in controlling "trouble-makers": "Dere wuz Uncle George Bull, he could read and write and, chile, de white folks didn't lak no nigger whut could read and write. . . . So dey useter jes take Uncle George Bull and beat him fur nothin; dey would beat him and take him to de lake and put him on a log and shev him in de lake, but he always swimmed out." As for white ministers she related: "We had church wid de white preachers and dey tole us to mind our masters and missus and we would be saved; if not, dey said we wouldn'."[15]

White ministers did not question the institution of slavery. On the contrary, many were outspoken advocates of slavery. In 1854 the most influential minister in the region, the Reverend Simon Peter Richardson, was an author of a resolution approved by the Florida Conference of the Methodist Episcopal Church South asking that the General Conference expunge from the Book of Discipline all of the discussion of slavery starting with the question: "What shall be done for the extirpation of the evil of slavery?"[16] Early in the history of this church in America, many clergymen adopted the views of John Wesley and Francis Asbury, both bitter opponents of slavery. However, the ownership of slaves by the clergy split the Methodists into northern and southern branches in 1845.[17] Richardson himself owned several slaves during the 1850s,[18] and other Methodist ministers who owned slaves included the Reverend Jesse Coe, Jackson County planter, with more than one hundred,[19] and Adam Wyrick of Jefferson County, with $11,600 worth of slave property.[20] In the Baptist Church the Reverend Richard G. Mays and H. Z. Ardis, both Madison County planters as well as ministers, owned $57,000 and $13,500 in slave property, respectively.[21] In the Episcopal Church the Right Reverend Francis Rutledge, rector of St. Johns Church in Tallahassee and bishop of the Florida diocese, owned $32,000 in slave property in 1860. The Presbyterian minister, the Reverend Duncan McNeil Turner, who was also the president of West Florida Seminary, owned ten slaves valued at $10,000, while another Presbyterian, the Reverend John E. DuBose, owned one slave.[22]

Although they were friendly to slavery, all of the denominations conducted missionary work among the blacks, who also attended services in the larger city churches, usually occupying the gallery. The Methodists and Baptists were more active in black missionary work than the other churches, and in 1860 the Florida Conference of the Methodist Church counted 7,798 blacks among 17,557 members.[23] Some white ministers, such as the Reverend Alexander Moseley, were said to be quite effective with blacks. Moseley came to Madison County, Florida, from Lenoir County, North Carolina, in 1840. Although he was ill much of the time until his death in 1846, it was said of him: "His ministry was directed chiefly to the colored population, and he possessed a strong hold upon their confidence and affection."[24] Few other white ministers appeared to be as influential. When the white Presbyterian minister, the Reverend Edwin T. Williams, traveled to Bel Air and heard the preaching of the colored Baptist minister the Reverend James Page, he asked him about white Presbyterian ministers' missionary work among the slaves and summarized Page's reply: "Some ministers at first seemed very affectionate and kind, but his people waited to see if this would continue year in and year out and if so, they believed in and loved them."[25]

In the all-black congregations, permitted on only some of the Red Hills plantations, slaves found balm for their emotional wounds, hope for improvement of their lot, at least after death, and sometimes visions of the goal that the Children of Israel had been able to achieve: freedom from their bondage. Some masters like Reddin Parramore or his young widow, who inherited many of his extensive properties in Madison County after his death in 1851, not only treated their slaves with kindness but allowed them to have a black minister who could hold services any time he chose as long as they did not interfere with the plantation routine. The minister was freed from menial labors and went about the plantation, as a former slave Amanda McGray recalled, all dressed up in a frock coat and store-bought shoes, enough in themselves to awe his listeners. He often also visited neighboring plantations to hold services. From this minister Parramore slaves first heard of the Civil War, and among his congregations they whispered prayers for the success of the Union armies. There was a praying ground where Mrs. McGray said "the grass never had a chancet ter grow fer the troubled knees that kept it crushed down."[26] Pine Tucky was another plantation with a freedom-to-preach rule for black ministers. In Helen Edwards's memoirs, she relates after telling about the dances in the yard of the big house: "But after a while they all got religion and quit dancing. Father then let them preach in our school house."[27]

"Father James Page," as the minister at Bel Air was called, was the most successful among the black ministers, just as the Reverend Simon Peter Richardson was among the whites. Page was a slave of the Parkhill family, which moved from Richmond, Virginia, to Leon County, Florida. He appears to have followed his master, John Parkhill, in that move and from Tuscawilla, the Parkhill plantation, to the resort community Bel Air, where Parkhill lived in his last years. Page was ordained as a minister of the Baptist church at Newport in 1851. At that time he presented letters of recommendation not only from Parkhill but also from Probate Judge James E. Broome of Tallahassee, soon to be elected governor, and from Benjamin F. Whitner, a Leon County planter and banker.[28]

Not long afterward Page began to attract widespread attention among blacks and whites. Whites often came to hear him preach. Page traveled about the county and conducted services. One meeting that he held at El Destino plantation on the edge of Jefferson County resulted in forty-one baptisms.[29] Page is said to have visited each of several plantations around Tallahassee once a month. At San Luis, the Randolph slaves gathered at one of the cabins to hear Page read from the Bible, preach, and sing. On the day of baptism, candidates attired in flowing white robes walked to the pond between two lines of believers.[30] Page's ministry continued after the war. In about 1870 he founded Bethel Missionary Baptist Church in Tallahassee and served as pastor there until his death in 1883.[31]

Although the master and mistress of Pine Hill plantation, Dr. and Mrs. Edward Bradford, employed a white minister to preach every other Sunday to the slaves, a black minister, Ellick, served them on alternate Sundays. Ellick had been assigned the job of driving a log cart to the Bradford mill, but when he was told in a vision to stop work and preach, he obeyed. The Bradfords indulged him in his determination to do so, though they had scant regard for him as a spiritual leader.[32]

Other masters were less tolerant of black ministers. When twenty-seven-year-old Sandy of the Lake Jackson plantation of Robert Butler ran away in October 1858, he was described as having such good qualities as being "an experienced body servant" who also "plays the fiddle and dances well," but Butler noted in an advertisement asking for his capture that Sandy "latterly has been engaged among the blacks as an exhorter." Butler offered a ten-dollar reward if the slave was captured in the state and twenty dollars if he was caught outside.[33] Sandy was still missing on 20 November, and Butler now asked also for the return of another valued slave, Julius Cezar, a thirty-year-old blacksmith and cooper. "The community are requested to look out for Abolitionists as I have strong reasons for believing their interference with these servants," said Butler. It was possible, though, that Julius Cezar might be found around the neighboring plantation, called The Grove, of Dr. Burroughs, where Julius's wife lived. Possibly, too, Sandy was on the nearby Orchard Pond Plantation of Governor Call, where *he* had a wife.[34] By 4 December Julius Cezar had apparently been recovered, but Sandy was still gone and had been seen "a few days since near Governor Call's plantation." Meanwhile Butler was advertising for a new overseer. And as for Sandy, who was still missing on 18 December, Butler's description indicated a somewhat flashy person "of low stature, good looking, with whiskers and mustache, and perhaps a geodery." Butler still valued him as "a good carriage driver, fiddler and dancer" but about his exhorting now said only that Sandy "pretends to be religious."[35]

Running away was the extreme to which slaves in the Red Hills usually carried their resentment against ill treatment. Never once was there a revolt, although the *Tallahassee Floridian* reported the threat of an uprising scheduled to occur between Christmas Day and 1 January 1857. The *Floridian*'s anonymous informant, "evidently a man of sense" from Quincy, wrote the newspaper a letter. The report immediately created a panic in Gadsden County, whose leading citizens nevertheless condemned it as "a sheer fabrication and an unfounded slander upon the character of our slave population."[36] There nevertheless was not the slightest sign of trouble. After this experience the *Floridian* discounted a report in the *Thomasville Enterprise* of an "extensive plot among the Negroes of Leon County" two years later in the Lake Iamonia section. A threat against the ginhouse of Charles Bannerman was reported—and indeed there had been a series of mysterious fires in ginhouses—but the *Floridian* labeled the arrest of Dr. H. Fairbanks in connection with the purported plot a "gross outrage on Dr. Fairbanks."[37]

Although group violence by blacks was unheard of, there were occasional instances of extreme violence by and against individuals. The *Madison Messenger* recorded a "horrible tragedy" near Madison on Thursday night, 30 October 1856. William Pierce, while eating supper, told a slave that when he had finished he would give the slave a flogging. As the punishment was about to be inflicted the servant manifested submission, then "drew an axe, which he had concealed, and split in twain the head of his master, scattering the brains in every direction." The slave then ran away and had not been caught a week later.[38]

What appeared to be violence was sometimes excused as accidental, or as acts in self-defense, for example when a black woman, accused of the murder of Christopher C. Bryant, overseer for Charles Bannerman in Leon County, was acquitted, as the *Floridian* reported in April 1849, "because of the belief that the blow which caused his death was . . . inflicted by throwing up a hoe she held in her hand to ward off the whip with which he was chastising her." When the slave Aberdeen went after the overseer on El Destino plantation with an axe, the overseer (uninjured) was blamed for the severity of the flogging he had given Aberdeen.[39]

At other times, violence appeared to result from an affront to the dignity of the servitor of an important master. The Tallahassee bookkeeper Frank Hatheway entered in his diary for Sunday, 25 January 1846: "The Marshal, Wilson, whipped by one of Branch's Negroes this morning, while attempting to arrest him. Negro caught afterward by dogs."[40] Some blacks among the servants of John Branch were, in fact, noted for their assertion of status in their dealings with both whites and blacks. On Dr. Edward Bradford's plantation, Uncle Davie, whose commands were said to be second only to those of the master himself, was in fact a snob, according to Susan Bradford Eppes. He talked by the hour about trips to Europe or the "winters I spent up Washin'tun City, along o' ole Marster de Gubberner [John Branch, his former master] an' his lady." Davie dressed up in a fine broadcloth suit with velvet vest and high beaver hat to perform his chores as sexton of Mt. Zion Church in the Bradford neighborhood, but when a low-class white neighbor of the Bradfords died, he embarrassed the family by showing up at the funeral in ordinary clothes.[41]

Fugitives usually kept the newspapers filled with advertisements from the first settlement of the Red Hills to the Civil War. Margrett Nickerson told an interviewer seventy years after freedom that "when de big gun fiahed [ending the Civil War], de runerway slaves comed out de woods from all directions."[42]

Kidder M. Moore, the master of Pine Tucky, reported that four blacks had run away on the night of 28 February 1847, Sam, twenty-five; Joe, forty; Bob, twenty; and Bryant, twenty-eight. He had offered three hundred dollars in rewards for them and for two others who had previously run away as well as "any information of any white man who may have assisted them." Rachel, thirty, had run away at Christmas "but I presume will get with the others." Moore's advertisement devoted particular attention, however, to a much earlier runaway, Tom: "This fellow run away from me about three years ago, and I presume from information I have lately received, intended to make his way to Augusta, Ga., as in that section I purchased him from Mr. Henry B. Ware.—Tom is, I suppose, 48 years old, low, thick set, and tolerable stout, has a bald head, on which he generally wears a cloth cap under his hat. I think that some white scoundrel is at the head of it, and has induced them off."[43]

Augustus H. Lanier, a planter with a large place in Gadsden county and another in Madison, lost two valuable hands, both with a record of violence, who ran away in 1851 and 1852. After Adam, thirty-four years old, a "good field hand and a rough carpenter," left the Gadsden place on 28 October 1851, Lanier offered twenty dollars for lodging him "in a safe jail so that I get him." He added that "if harbored in the possession of any white man or negro with proof to convict, I will give $100 more." Lanier said Adam wore many scars "with other marks by the whip for fighting." He had been bought in 1835 at Savannah.[44] Adam was in fact returned and, placed on his Madison County plantation, ran away again on 14 December 1852. Lanier advertised for him on 22 January 1853 and now offered a reward also for George, thirty-two, who had run away from the same Madison County plantation on 10 December 1852. George, said the advertisement, "is a smart, sensible fellow, and ran off after an attempt to murder my manager and one or two of my negroes. George may say he belongs to some other person beside the subscriber. He has played the game once. George was shot some years back while on a runaway trip and received eight or nine shot in (I think) his left leg and thigh and has some small marks of the whip on his back."[45]

Few runaways from the Red Hills appeared to be headed for free territory. To reach Indiana, Illinois, or Ohio, they would have to travel the length of Georgia or Alabama and cross Tennessee or North Caro-

lina as well as Kentucky or Virginia. Most appeared to be looking for
a more acceptable home within the slave states, a familiar place where
they had lived before, a place where their friends or relatives (sometimes a wife or husband) lived, a more indulgent master, or even a
few weeks of freedom in the wilds. Some nevertheless undertook
ambitious journeys. In newly settled Marion County in central Florida
lived Dick, thirty-two, his wife Margaret, twenty, and their son
Charles, five, the property of Lloyd Hill. In the summer of 1848 the
three undertook to reach New Orleans and, after crossing the Florida
peninsula to Cedar Key, set out in a canoe. However, a St. Marks
pilot spotted the small craft a few miles away from St. Marks light
and the family was lodged in a jail until their owner could come for
them.[46]

Cornelius Devane, the owner of a family of five that left Leon
County on 19 May 1833, said he thought they "are trying to get back
to North Carolina where they were raised." Loveless, a thirty-five-
year-old mulatto, was accompanied on the trip by his wife, Pink, and
their children Isac, five, Ellen, three, and Jane, five months. "Pink
will try to pass for a free woman," said Devane. "She has obtained
a pass for that purpose."[47] Peter, who ran away from Dr. A. M. R.
Sessions of Leon County on 13 December 1851, was probably headed
toward Richmond, Virginia, where he had previously lived.[48]

Many escapees sought refuge in another part of the same county
or in another county of the Red Hills. Richard A. Whitfield advertised
in November 1860 that Abner, thirty, who had left his Centerville
Road plantation, had formerly been owned by George A. Croom of
Casa de Lago only a few miles away "and is probably lurking about
Lake Jackson or the Ochlockonee River."[49] Often slaves were looking
for a wife or husband on another plantation. Thus James Ormond,
the Newport merchant, said in 1856 of the runaway West, twenty-
five or twenty-six years old: "He was raised in Gadsden County where
he has a wife at Mr. W. H. Gibson's, and relatives all over the
county."[50] V. V. Skreine of Leon County asked in October 1849 "delivery to William Johnson, on Lake Jackson," of the slave Sylvia, who
had run away the previous February. "She is supposed to be lurking
around Tallahassee, and is no doubt often in the city of evenings
among the free negroes," said Skreine. "Her husband, when she left,
was R. Hayward's boy Henry, on the Tradewell place [later Bellevue],
and it is supposed that she has got him yet."[51]

The youthfulness of some runaways and their distance from home
indicate in a shocking way the distance that some young members of
a family were taken from their parents. It was rare for a runaway to

go south, but when a boy of about thirteen was jailed in Monticello on 2 November 1855, he said he belonged to Nat Berry of the Sumter District in South Carolina. "Very pert spoken; of a dark complexion, and about four feet ten inches high," Sheriff William H. Andrews described this independent youngster, who "has a scar on his right arm which he says was caused by a mule running away with him."[52] J. H. Rhodes of Leon County advertised on 20 May 1854 for the return of "a negro boy named Lee, or Lawrence, about 14 years old . . . , originally brought from Griffin or Atlanta to Columbus, Ga., and from thence to Marianna, Fla, where he was sold to Thomas F. Clark, and brought here by Mr. Clark. I suppose he will endeavor to make his way to Marianna, Columbus, Griffin or Atlanta, at one of the latter of which places his mother is supposed to be."[53]

Age appeared to be no barrier to slaves dissatisfied enough to make a break, but it may have hindered their progress toward a destination. Cook, seventy-five, ran away from a plantation in Madison County but was captured and jailed in Tallahassee before his disappearance was advertised.[54] Peter, who ran away from Asa Munson of Leon County in December 1836, had not been caught by 11 March 1837. He was fifty-five but had a more distinguishing characteristic than age: he "speaks Spanish very well," while "his English is broken."[55] The Negro Christmas, "a very shrewd, artful fellow, and a pretty good carpenter," who ran away from N. M. Vaught's Cherry Lake place in Madison County in January 1854, would be easy to recognize in a crowd: "Said boy is between six and seven feet high, very black, thin built, speaks quick when spoken to, and has his forefinger on one of his hands cut off at the first joint."[56]

Slaves abhorred being hired out, especially for distasteful work. Edenborough, twenty-two, had been rented by Thomas H. Triplett of Jefferson County for one year to a Mr. Hodgson of Wakulla County. He ran away in 1851 but within a few days was in the Jefferson County jail.[57] Even the fear of anticipated duties away from the familiar plantation caused some to run away, as it did Laurance on Pine Hill plantation. "I was skeered you mought sen' me ter St. Marks," he said when he was caught. The Bradfords, the plantation owners, were surprised that Laurance had run away. The owner of a pack of bloodhounds on a nearby plantation caught him, and two horsemen arrived one summer afternoon with the runaway, accompanied by the dogs. The master, Dr. Bradford, far from grateful, chased the captors off his land. "How dare you set those dogs on one of my people!" said Bradford as he personally attended to Laurance's wounds. The only habitual runaway on the Bradford place was Affie, an old conjure

woman without husband or family, whose absences went almost un-
noticed. Within a few months she would be back from the woods and
fields with a sack full of herbs and roots from which she concocted
remedies.[58]

There were patrols to round up runaways, but their laxity was
proverbial. Most of the clamor for tightening patrol service came from
nonslaveholders who also demanded tighter controls on the plantations, for example asking that a white master or overseer always be
present. Runaway notices often offered additional rewards of one
hundred or two hundred dollars for the arrest of Negro stealers, and
patrols were on the lookout for these also. Slaves feared these "nigger
stealers" more than patrols, and free blacks also feared them. Florida
Clayton, a free black who spent her childhood in Tallahassee with
her mother, Charlotte Norris, a free mulatto, recalled a fear of both
"nigger stealers" and "nigger hunters" with their dogs. Her great-
grandfather was a white man who came to Tallahassee in the early
days from Washington, D.C., with children he had begot by one of
his slaves. She recalled in the presence of an interviewer in 1936 that
a "Mr. Nimrod and Mr. Shehee" were "nigger hunters" who spe-
cialized in catching runaways with their trained bloodhounds, and
her parents warned her to find refuge in someone's yard if she encountered them lest the animals tear her to pieces. As for "nigger
stealers," she said a covered wagon used to come to town occasionally
with the purpose of stealing children. She was admonished to stay
away from it because it was occupied by a ghost, "Dry Head and
Bloody Bones," that did not like children.[59]

In an advertisement in November 1850, W. H. G. Sanders, who
said he was guardian of Matilda—perhaps a free black, since free
blacks were required to have a guardian—said that five men came to
the house of Matilda at the mouth of Black Creek and stole two of
her children. "I hereby offer a reward of $100 for the recovery of the
children and the conviction of the thieves," he said.[60]

Slave owners chose to reward favored old servants within the
framework of slavery without resorting to manumission. Thus the
will of Jonathan Robinson, the Gadsden County planter who died in
1838, directed: "My will and desire is, that my boy George, the carpenter, shall be allowed to choose his own employer, annually, during
his lifetime, such employer paying the sum of one dollar to my exe-
cutors."[61]

Florida law was severe for both slaves and free Negroes, but the
law was often softened by practice. In addition, the courts themselves
sometimes came to the aid of blacks who had run afoul of the law

through no fault of their own. However, the courts were always more comfortable when their rulings could be made within the framework of slavery. Thus Ann, who had told her Leon County master, Simon Partridge, on his deathbed whom she wished to have for a future master, was allowed to remain with this master, Dr. Thomas K. Leonard, who bought her.[62]

The supreme court overturned the death sentence imposed in Jackson County against Cato, a slave of the Ely family in Marianna, who had been convicted of raping a white woman. In an opinion by Justice Charles H. DuPont, the court noted that the complainant and the only other witness were "common prostitutes" and that both identity and use of force were poorly established.[63] Sometimes the courts even ruled in favor of a black's right to freedom instead of slavery, as in the case of Maria. Maria and her four children found themselves still in bondage in 1847 although freed by a will probated in South Carolina in 1828. William Oliphant, her South Carolina owner, had directed in his will that she should be "permitted to enjoy the privileges of a free person" in the household of a nephew, W. H. Hollingsworth, to whom he willed some property. Oliphant had suggested that Maria be taken to the free state of Ohio, funds having been provided to start her in a life of freedom. Instead, Maria came eventually to Florida, and in 1847, finding herself and family the slaves of Samuel S. Sibley, she sued for freedom. Both the lower court and the Florida Supreme Court held that she was entitled to it.[64]

Ten years later, though, the supreme court was less ready to award freedom in a borderline case. On petition of Thomas N. Gautier in behalf of Dick, a Jackson County mulatto, the Jackson County Circuit Court awarded Dick freedom on a writ of habeas corpus, ruling that he was being unlawfully held as a slave. Said to be the son of a black man and a white woman, Dick had nevertheless been held in slavery since early infancy and now, at the age of about twenty-five years, was claimed by William Clark. The supreme court overturned the lower court and an opinion by Justice Baltzell cited the new *Dred Scott* decision in holding that whatever rights Dick had "are accorded to him, not by right, but permission and grant of the state in which he is" and that the burden of showing he was not a slave rested on him and could not be decided on a writ of habeas corpus.[65]

In contrast with the slave population of the Red Hills, the population of free blacks was only ninety-eight in 1850. Forty-six were in Leon County, and of these thirty-one lived in Tallahassee. Madison County listed no free blacks at all, and Jefferson County only five, all in one family of mulattoes. Seven free blacks lived in the households of six white families in Gadsden County, and thirty free blacks were scattered, principally in all-black families, as in Leon County, across Jackson County.[66]

Despite an almost absolute prohibition on the migration of free blacks to Florida and legislation that increasingly restricted the freedom of those already present, a general tolerance enabled some to survive and a very few to prosper to a small degree. The most interesting of all the free blacks in 1850 was the centenarian Antonio Proctor, a native of Jamaica who boasted that, as a body servant of a British officer, he had witnessed the battle between Wolfe and Montcalm on the Plains of Abraham before Quebec in 1759. Subsequent service of the same sort as a slave took him to the site of the Battle of Lexington, which triggered the American Revolution. Afterward, still a slave, he had come to St. Augustine and had remained there after Florida became American territory. He made himself useful to American forces as an interpreter during the Second Seminole War. Having acquired his freedom, he came to settle in Tallahassee. When he died in 1855, reportedly at the age of 112, he was making his home on the place of Henry L. Rutgers, a banker, whose house still stands on Calhoun Street in Tallahassee.[67]

Described by the press at the time as "a remarkable Negro," Proctor was no more remarkable than his son George Proctor, a free black who established himself in the building trades in Tallahassee in the 1830s. He built the Rutgers house and, across the street, a house for the lawyer and former superior court judge Thomas Randall, also still standing. In fact, George Proctor is credited with the construction of at least a dozen houses during a contracting career that reached its peak about 1841, when a depression began. In 1839, George Proctor purchased the freedom of Nancy, a house servant, at an unusually high price of thirteen hundred dollars, much of it in notes at unspecified interest. He then married her. The depression, accompanied by other problems, made it impossible for him to pay out his notes, while several other debts, lawsuits, and court judgments whittled away his estate. Finally in 1849 George Proctor left for California and the goldfields to try his luck as a builder there. In 1850 the manuscript census shows that Nancy, the five children, and his aged father, Tony, were living on a small rural plot near Tallahassee. Because of George's unpaid debts, meanwhile, Nancy and the children returned to slavery and were eventually sold to George W. Scott.[68]

For years after the first settlement of the Red Hills, public opinion, as in the South generally, frowned on the African slave trade. In fact it had been outlawed by the United States in 1808. In February 1837 the schooner *Emperor* appeared at St. Joseph's Bay with what was supposed to be a cargo of oranges but was actually a small cargo of slaves. The *Floridian* applauded an effort to bring the slave dealers to justice.[69]

Slave trading, usually associated with bringing blacks from Virginia, the principal source of supply, had greater respectability. One of the slave traders supplying the Red Hills was Ephraim Ponder of Thomasville, brother of William G. Ponder, who had plantations in Leon County. In the fall of 1849 a twenty-six-year-old member of the family, John G. Ponder, was killed by highwaymen at a camp near Hawkinsville, Georgia, while he was bringing a drove of blacks from Virginia. Sixty-five blacks reached their destination, however, and were duly offered for sale at Ephraim Ponder's plantation on Forshala Lake in Leon County.[70] Ephraim sometimes advertised his commodities through another brother, James, of Duncansville, Georgia, who had a sideline, "negro shoes" at one dollar a pair. The "forty likely Negroes" offered in June 1851 included some to fill the demand for black concubines: "two likely semstresses, one of them a No. 1 fancy girl, about sixteen years old."[71]

Slave auctioning was also respectable, although visitors found the slave auctions only slightly less shocking than the rough treatment accorded runaways. The more gentlemanly planters avoided them when possible, but sometimes these were the only means of disposing of slaves. As the decade of the fifties wore on, auctioneers in Quincy and Tallahassee began to boast of the high prices received. Colonel Berry in February 1859 had sold a thirty-five-year-old blacksmith for $1,505; a slave named Abram, twenty-four, for $1,500; and Henry, twenty-nine, for $1,520. The *Tallahassee Floridian*, which had followed with approbation the diligence of the U.S. marshal Samuel H. DuVal in prosecuting the schooner *Emperor* case, in 1859 commented about the African slave trade: "Advocates for the reopening of the trade in 'wool' are increasing. An investment in a ship load to be landed on the coast of Florida would be profitable. Who'll take stock?"[72]

16

"A Slight Touch of
Ashby de la Zouche"
and Secession

The Mexican War and prospective addition of California and other new territories had raised the slavery question anew. In 1846 northern politicians proposed in the Wilmot Proviso to prohibit slavery in these new territories. This proposal created a storm of protest in the South, including Florida, where Whigs were as loud as Democrats in denouncing it. In Florida a bipartisan convention in the Whig county of Madison complained about an "infamous war" that was being conducted by "northern Whigs and northern Democrats" against "southern institutions." Samuel S. Sibley, the senior editor of the Democratic newspaper the *Floridian*, misread this protest as "Whiggery in disguise"[1] but was soon to regret the label, for it was noised around that Sibley had claimed he would "vote for a Wilmot Proviso man in preference to a Whig." The angry editor traced this rumor to W. G. Burgess, who protested that he had not said just that and at any rate had not intended for his remarks to travel beyond the St. James Island vacation house of Joseph Chaires, where he had spoken with fellow Whigs R. J. Floyd and Captain Joshua Byrd.[2]

It was subsequently mainly the Democrats who trumpeted "southern rights," and Representative Elias E. Blackburn from strongly Democratic Jefferson County introduced a resolution, adopted by the General Assembly in January 1849, declaring that "under no circumstances will the people of this state be willing to recognize as binding any enactment of the Federal Government which has for its object the prohibition of slavery in any territory south of the line of the Missouri Compromise." The resolution spoke darkly of taking measures "for the defense of our rights."[3]

Thomas Brown, newly embarked on a four-year term as the Whig governor of Florida, condemned the resolution in his inaugural address, saying that it would set a course ending in "the inevitable dissolution of the confederacy." Such rhetoric, said the blunt Talla-hassean, was "empty vaporing" of the sort being heard too often from "southern demagogues," who, he declared, had done as much to weaken the Union as "northern fanatics." It used to be, he com-plained, that a politician could not "calculate the value of the Union without bringing down upon his head the indignation of the people."[4]

This forthright Unionist also rejected the notion that the state gov-ernment should bear the expense of sending delegates to a southwide convention at Nashville to assert "southern rights." The move to send delegates started in Gadsden County, which like Madison was a Whig county. Here again there was a bipartisan effort led by the Democrat Charles H. DuPont and the Whig Arthur I. Forman.[5] Brown could have stopped by saying, as he did, that the state constitution did not authorize paying the expenses of these delegates, but he went further: "I consider such a convention as revolutionary in spirit and directly against the spirit if not the letter of the Constitution of the United States."[6] Some other Whigs joined Brown in criticizing the Nashville convention, but county after county adopted the "Gadsden resolu-tions" supporting it. In Leon County, one of the Whig strongholds, Whig opponents managed only a flank attack against the plan at a county convention on the question.[7]

The Nashville convention proved futile anyway; by the time it met in June 1850, Senator Clay had come forward with his famous com-promise, which gained support in the North and the South and de-fused the slavery issue for a few years.[8] Not everyone in the Red Hills was happy with the compromise, however. On 31 May 1851, with DuPont again taking a lead, a Gadsden County Southern Rights As-sociation was formed, modeled on one recently organized at Charles-ton, South Carolina.[9] The Southern Rights Association movement caught on particularly in Madison County, where a Southern Rights Association staged a colorful celebration on a bluff near the margin of Lake Sampala on Independence Day 1851. Said a correspondent of the *Floridian*: "About 10 a.m. people began to pour in—a long line of carriages, buggies, &c from the courthouse preceded by the omni-bus filled with ladies, their banners with appropriate mottoes and streaming to the breeze, followed by a large road wagon, crowded with staunch Southern Rights men, who were *determined to be there*—presented a spectacle well calculated to gladden the heart of every friend of *the cause*."[10]

Banners proclaimed "State Sovereignty," "We will never submit," "Equality in the Union, or independence out of it." At 11:30 A.M. an invocation was offered by the Reverend Mr. H. Z. Ardis, a Baptist minister and planter. Former governor W. D. Moseley then read the

Declaration of Independence. The oration of the day, delivered by the attorney Dannitte H. Mays, "riveted the attention of the large crowd," said the correspondent, and twenty or more toasts were offered along the lines of that by Archibald Fair, a planter: "A seceder in 1832—the same in 1851."[11]

The Madison association set up a "Council on Vigilance and Safety," whose business it was "to detect, prosecute and report all attempts to corrupt our slave population, disseminate abolition doctrine, produce insubordination, or otherwise impair the value or disturb the peaceful employment and benefit of these our domestic relations."[12]

John C. McGehee was president of the Madison County association, whose membership soon numbered 199. McGehee ran the organization with an iron hand. He was an elder in the Presbyterian Church in Madison, where a young graduate of Princeton Theological Seminary, the Reverend William Henry Crane, was "stated supply" minister. Crane had recently transferred from Marianna. During 1850 his efforts had added thirty converts to the faith. But when the Southern Rights Association was formed, he refused to attend its meetings. This brought him into conflict with the session of the church of which McGehee was the secretary and his fellow South Carolinian Fair, the seceder since 1832, a member. The session dismissed Crane but, failing to have this move ratified by the Presbytery, declared the church unable to provide adequate support for the pastor. Crane left to pursue a successful ministry of forty-eight years elsewhere in Florida, while the church now engaged a "safe" South Carolinian, the Reverend Donald John Auld, to replace him.[13]

Local Southern Rights associations were organized in a few other places in the Red Hills, but the movement toward secession cooled considerably in most of the region. When the issue of southern rights came up at all, Democrats used it to whittle away Whig majorities that had permitted Brown to be elected governor in 1848; Edward C. Cabell to be elected Florida's lone representative in the U.S. House of Representatives from 1846 to 1852; and Whigs such as David S. Walker to continue in high office. The Whigs, who typically carried Jackson County by a vote of 3 to 1 and Gadsden, Leon, and Madison counties by as much as 2 to 1, now lost ground. Many prominent Whigs, such as George W. Parkhill, became Democrats.[14]

It is difficult to understand the movement toward secession and the bloodiest war in American history without devoting attention to causes beyond slavery, with its economic and social importance, which was as stoutly defended by nonslaveholders as by slave owners. The Italian historian Raimondo Luraghi viewed the Civil War as a contest between the agricultural "seigneurial society" of the South and the industrial "Puritan" society of the North. While Puritan New England and the North generally prospered with industry, the pre-capitalist agricultural South pursued its own ideals of honor before profit, careers in the military, classical studies, and office holding as a civic duty.[15]

Tallahassee's May Party to some extent fits into Luraghi's ideas about the seigneurial society at play. Beginning in the 1840s, the event continued into the seventh decade of the twentieth century. The formal part of the May Party was as uninteresting as a Sunday school pageant. A girl of thirteen or fifteen was queen, "her lovely eyes beaming with the pleasure and excitement of the occasion." But always, at least in the early days when the May Party was an evening event in the Hall of Representatives, there was dancing for everybody, and dancing was the favorite social activity of the Red Hills, or at least of Tallahassee.[16]

After the coronation ceremony the May Party suddenly came to life. Everyone ate dinner at long tables. After the dinner a black fiddler struck up a tune. "The older 'young folks' did not let the evening pass without some fun of their own making," said an account of the 1847 May Party. "The music waked the spirit of dancing and they formed numerous sets, which, having got in motion, did not cease till two or three o'clock [A.M.]."[17] Sometimes the merrymaking must have gotten out of hand. After the 1849 party, correspondents in Madison and Monticello poked fun at Tallahassee's May Party by describing alleged "May parties" held in these places. At Madison the "grown people concluded to have a little jollification," said a correspondent, and a musician named Truss was summoned to the stand by his friend to "give 'em 'Shoe Morocco' or 'Honey on the Mountains,' " after which the fiddler "turned loose in one of the real scamper-down piney-woods reels," accompanied by the clapping of his friend, who observed afterward: "I never seed the like of it in my life and I never heared of it 'till just before dark." The polite assembly soon melted.[18] At Monticello in the same year, the May Party was held on the fourth instead of the first. That would have been all right, said a correspondent, except that some "mistook the fourth of May for the fourth of July." Independence Day celebrations with their barbecues had become known for their multitudes of toasts, each followed by a sip from the wineglass, and these occasions had become so rowdy that the ladies often stayed away. According to the Monti-cello correspondent, toasts began after the ladies left the May Party.

In the round of toasts the correspondent himself passed out. He finally awakened in alarm at what sounded like a pistol shot. Instead he found "one of the boys standing with a champagne bottle just uncorked . . . , a glass in hand."[19]

In 1851 the Tallahassee May Party was moved outdoors, with a Maypole ceremony in the afternoon and a party and dinner at night.[20] This plan was followed in 1854 when the Maypole ceremony, at 5:00 P.M., appears to have been somewhere in the greensward of present Park Avenue where the "May Oak" long stood. The *Floridian's* account of the party reported the site as "a grove near the Catholic Church, where they erected a throne and May pole." The narrator of this event, identified only as "B"—could this have been former Governor Brown?—took occasion to blast opponents of dancing, who were numerous at the time, invoking "Puritan" and "Cavalier" traditions: "The Queen and her court commenced a dance around the Maypole such as would have set old Oliver Cromwell and his Puritanical contemporaries almost crazy." After the outdoor ceremony the Queen and Court were joined at Brown's Saloon [the ballroom of City Hotel] by young ladies and gentlemen who danced "and from the appearance enjoyed themselves as much as their younger brothers and sisters."[21] By 1860 the May Party had been turned over to the decorous custody of the Female Department of the Seminary West of the Suwannee, but here again a royal banquet was spread and "grown-up people mingled with the smaller fry in the dancing."[22]

More than the May Party, the "ring tournaments," borrowed from the pages of *Ivanhoe*, appealed to the romantic seigneurial community of the Red Hills. The first of these "passages of arms"—having what the newspaper called "a slight touch of Ashby de la Zouche"—was scheduled for Thursday, 18 December 1851.[23] The day proved to be an unlucky one, for rain, followed by a north wind and severe freeze, produced the first ice storm Tallahassee had ever experienced, and "trees about town resembled coral, being covered from head to foot with frozen rain drops." Even though the event was postponed for one day, when it was held in the valley that is today crossed by Colonial Drive as it proceeds from East Sixth Avenue to the Thomasville Road, ice still clung to trees and shrubs, and the turf was a "boundless carpet of frost work." The *Florida Sentinel* described the proceedings:

> At the northern end of a valley, from which the ground rose by gentle acclivity to the sparkling woods surrounding it, was suspended a small

ivory ring, the object at which the knights, who enrolled themselves in the conflict, were to direct their lances. About 200 yards distant, the southern extremity of the lists, was the point from which they were to run their course. A large concourse of ladies and gentlemen from the adjoining counties as well as from our city and the country round about, were assembled on the rising ground surrounding the lists. At 11 A.M. a distant sound of the bugle announced the advance of the knights, and now they may be seen approaching in order from their bivouac in the neighboring woods.[24]

One after the other, at a signal from the marshal, the knights charged at a fast gallop across the valley, the object being to "take the ring" as often as possible in three tries. It now became apparent that the tournament should have been postponed for a longer time. For young Dr. George W. Parkhill, a favorite to win the tournament and now riding a wild and restless bay as the "Knight of Tuscawilla," spurred his horse to a fast charge but just at the moment of reaching the ring his horse became frightened, and performed "such lofty evolutions" that the gallant knight was "forced to throw down his lance in order to give him undivided attention. He missed the ring." Because the failure was through no fault of his own, the other knights awarded him a new trial. But this opportunity he refused and this "elicited a short round of applause from one end of the list to the other."[25]

Parkhill's bad luck, however, did not match that of William G. Moseley, son of the former governor and now in charge of Moseley's plantation holdings in Jefferson County. As "El Caballero de Esperanza" and seated on a magnificent roan, he moved slowly to the post, and the crowd admired his rich costume of dark blue set off by a scarf of light blue silk and black chapeau with light plume, also blue. Perfectly motionless at the starting line, rider and steed suggested an equestrian statue that, however, was awakened into life by the bugle. Moseley's charge was admired as that of "a perfect specimen of the dragoon officer"; he had been in a regiment, the Third Dragoons, during the Mexican War. However, his horse shied, and he missed the ring. Then, in descending the hill just beyond, slippery with ice, "his steed fell and turned a complete somerset, which would probably have killed his rider but for the remarkable agility in extracting himself—still, he was somewhat bruised."[26] The experience must have been one of even more painful embarrassment for Lieutenant Moseley, one of three candidates to become a major general in the militia.

Soon thereafter he left the Red Hills so abruptly that he forgot to pay a hundred-dollar subscription toward building a brick schoolhouse that still stands in Monticello.[27]

Despite this distressing accident, the tournament proceeded through a fourth trial between four knights who were tied. The winner, the "Knight of the Lake," Robert H. Hall, from a place on Lake Hall noted more for its horses than for its cotton crops, was entitled to pick the "Queen of Love and Beauty." He placed a crown on the brow of Dora Triplett, the daughter of Mrs. Martha P. Triplett of Lebanon Plantation in Jefferson County. The final events of the day were a banquet and ball in the Senate Chamber and Hall of Representatives, respectively.[28]

At the ball held in 1854 ladies were dressed to represent Night, Evening Stars, Gypsies, "La Belle France . . . , with tricolor floating around her stately form," Highland Lassies, and Swiss Peasants. But this brightly candlelighted affair sent a chill through the heart of C. H. Austin, the state treasurer, who was responsible for taking care of the capitol. He expressed the hope there would be no more applications to hold "amusements"of the sort in the capitol, for there was no fire insurance on the building, no local fire company, and "no adequate supply of water is convenient, except perhaps when the two capitol cisterns are full."[29]

The Red Hills renewed its interest in military activities during the 1850s and, as often in the past, these concerned "Indian unrest." Brushes between settlers southeast of Tampa Bay and a remnant of the Seminoles in the Everglades became violent enough in the late 1850s to be called the Third Seminole War. Governor Broome, returning from Washington in June 1857, reported that the new administration of President James Buchanan seemed "determined to close the war as speedily as possible" and said he was "authorized by the war department to raise an entire regiment of Mounted Volunteers." Being federal troops, they would be paid with an appropriation of $413,000. Most of the companies were from eastern and central Florida, but there was one from Madison County captained by N. P. Willard and a sixty-five-member company from Leon captained by John Bull Parkhill, son of Samuel.[30]

Less of a horseman than his cousin George, who had won the 1854 ring tournament, John B., wearing green as the Knight of Erin, missed the ring on his first try.[31] But John Bull Parkhill was drawn by some compulsion to risky adventure and led a scouting party to destroy Indian lodges near Palm Hammock in the Big Cypress Swamp and followed an Indian trail for three miles to a river twenty yards wide.

At the front of his unit, Parkhill was beginning to wade into the water when a brisk fire from the opposite bank mortally wounded him and also injured five others. The war was soon over, and Parkhill was memorialized in a tall monument in front of the old capitol that was to be joined nearly 130 years later, across Monroe Street, by a memorial inscribed with the names of 1,952 Florida dead or missing in the Viet Nam War.[32]

In politics Democratic incursions into Whig strength were aided in the elections of 1852 by the unpopularity of the Whig standard-bearer for president, General Winfield Scott. Floridians still fumed at Scott's General Order No. 48 during the Second Seminole War, in which he seemed to be calling Floridians cowards—they "could see nothing but an Indian in every bush." A Jefferson County veteran of the war when asked to vote for Scott replied: "When I do so, may my tongue cleave to the roof of my mouth, and my arm fall palsied to my side." The Florida vote in the 1852 presidential election therefore was 4,308 votes for Democrat Franklin Pierce and 2,853 for Scott. The Whig Edward C. Cabell was a casualty of the election, losing by twenty-two votes to Augustus E. Maxwell, the Democratic candidate for Congress. In the governor's race, James E. Broome, the Democrat, won over his fellow Leon Countian, the popular George T. Ward, 4,457 to 4,346.[33]

Whig losses in Jackson County were particularly conspicuous, for in this "Gibraltar of Whiggery" where 100 Democratic votes were a rarity, there was a tie vote for president, 260 for Scott and 260 for Pierce. Cabell won a majority of 121, and Ward a majority of 113. These returns hardly seemed to justify a celebration by Democrats, but celebrate they did with a nighttime march through Marianna streets, the celebrants holding a torch in one hand and an old field broom (for Broome) in the other. Forming a semicircle around the courthouse, the crowd then heard rousing talks among others by the aging party regular Jesse Coe, who admonished his hearers against too much jubilation. "Take no such course toward our Whig friends, for they are already sufficiently distressed by their misfortunes," said Coe.[34]

"Southern rights" was hardly an issue at all, but as Whig strength declined, party members joined the strange new "Know-Nothing" Party, which was anti-Catholic, anti–foreign born, and anti-immigration. Even General Call was discovered, to his embarrassment, campaigning for a politician friend in Tennessee in 1855 and using language of "the Dark Lantern." "I will not vote for a man . . . who owes an allegiance to the Pope of Rome or any other prince or earthly power, higher than the allegiance he owes to the Constitution and government of the United States," said Call. "The foreign emigrant is hostile to one of the institutions of your country. He is from want, ignorance and necessity opposed to African slavery."[35]

Even with the election of Madison Perry of Alachua County as governor in 1856—a Democratic politician far more of a secessionist than Broome—the issue of separation from the Union remained a remote one. His opponent, the Whig David S. Walker, was a supporter of the compromise and also mildly Know-Nothing, but he was widely respected and won 5,894 votes to 6,214 for Perry.[36]

The secession issue did not, in fact, flare up again until, on 22 October 1859, the *Floridian* came out with a large headline, "Terrible Insurrection," reporting a rumor reaching Baltimore about "whites and blacks, supposed to be led by an abolitionist," having taken the town, armory, and arsenal at Harpers Ferry, Virginia. Now even Governor Call, a stout defender of "the glorious Union," talked like a secessionist. Writing a northern friend who was soliciting his support for William Henry Seward for president, Call said that, while he had once believed the Union "could not be destroyed," it needed to be known in the North "that William Seward will never preside over the southern states of the Confederacy."[37]

The first opportunity to nominate a candidate acceptable to the entire South occurred at the Democratic National Convention in Charleston, South Carolina, in April 1860. Call later said he would have supported any candidate nominated there, even "if he had been but a little man of straw."[38] This convention, with the partisans of Stephen A. Douglas in control, broke up when southern delegations walked out. In the end the only candidacy to the liking of the Deep South was that of John C. Breckinridge of Kentucky, who was the overwhelming choice of Florida, including the Red Hills plantation belt. Whigs like Call and Ward, along with some Democrats, supported the Constitutional Union candidacy of John Bell of Tennessee, while the candidacies of Abraham Lincoln, the Republican, and Stephen A. Douglas, the Democrat, were ignored. Within the Red Hills, only in Jackson and Gadsden counties was the voting close. Breckinridge carried Gadsden by eight votes and Jackson by fifty-eight, while secessionists won by a 3 to 1 margin in Jefferson County, by 2 to 1 in Madison, and by a vote of 482 to 282 in Leon.[39]

Meeting only a few days after newspapers reported the victory of Abraham Lincoln, the "black Republican" (he was not even on Florida ballots), a Madison County convention called on the General Assembly, which was scheduled to meet within a few days "to proceed immediately after convening to call a convention of the people to take such action as the convention may determine proper in the present crisis."[40] About a similar convention in Leon County, the *Floridian* reported on 1 December:

> The spacious hall of the House of Representatives was filled to utmost capacity. The meeting resolved, with united voice, in favor of a state convention, to consider a course to be pursued by Florida in the emergency now existing. Before the question was taken on the adoption of the resolutions, the 2nd Battalion of the Eighth Regiment of militia, under the command of Maj. H. T. Blocker, numbering several hundred men, marched into the Hall with trailed arms and thundered forth one unanimous Aye in their favor.[41]

One marvels today at the structural security of the 1845 capitol that was able to withstand this tumultuous demonstration on its third floor. And yet an inspector for the architect in charge of restoring the 1902 capitol (with the 1845 capitol entombed within it) said in 1981 that the heart pine trusses and joists, the oldest of them dating to their installation in 1842, "are as sturdy as when they went up." In all, he said, only 5 percent of the floor and ceiling joists had to be replaced, while the thick brick walls of the 1845 capitol were also in good condition.[42] The appearance of the "noble yeomanry" of Leon in Captain Blocker's command, according to the *Floridian*, "produced great excitement in the meeting" and on motion of Major General Parkhill, the militia unit was "welcomed by three cheers."[43]

One Leon Countian manifestly did not sway to the rhythm of the trembling Hall of Representatives but showed instead a determination as strong as the sturdy heart pine girders. This was the aging Whig politician Richard K. Call. When Lincoln had been named the candidate of the new Republican party, Call let it be known that he was more acceptable than Seward. After the election of Lincoln, Call emerged from retirement and directed all of his energies to a speech- and letter-writing campaign, begging his old political friends and enemies alike not to take Florida out of the Union. Call must have worked far into the night, writing his messages. Anticipating his needs, even before the election, his daughter Ellen on 30 October bought for him at Slusser's hardware store a $5.38 kerosene lamp. But under the leadership of secessionist Governor Perry, the General Assembly had set a convention date, 3 January 1861, and an election on 22 December 1860 to select delegates. So on 1 December, the very day that the *Floridian* informed its readers of the Hall of Representatives meeting,

Call issued a pamphlet saying secession would be treason. "Wait then, I pray you, wait!"[44]

Assembling on 3 January 1861, the convention elected John C. McGehee president and assigned a special seat in the Hall of Representatives to Edmund Ruffin of Virginia, the foremost advocate of secession in the entire South, who had arrived to observe the proceedings. Before getting down to serious discussions the assemblage recessed for a day of "fasting and humiliation" that President Buchanan had asked be held nationwide. Ruffin expressed irritation at the delay but satisfaction upon hearing that, at a service held in St. John's Episcopal Church, the minister warmly favored secession. Speaking with Bishop Francis H. Rutledge afterward—Rutledge, like him, had not attended the service—Ruffin learned that the bishop "had himself already seceded, with his native state," South Carolina.[45]

But even though it was apparent that most of the delegates favored immediate secession, there were some, particularly among former Whigs, who questioned the wisdom of secession, at least so early and without having a clear mandate from the electorate. Alabama and Mississippi were expected to secede momentarily, but neither they nor Georgia had done so. The foremost proponent of delay was the Leon County planter and Whig politician, George Ward. Before the delegates were elected, Ward expressed the opinion that a secession ordinance should be submitted to a popular vote. He also mentioned the practical consideration of whether Florida, with its long and vulnerable coastline, dared secede in advance of Alabama and Georgia.[46]

Even though the Red Hills and the rest of Florida favored secession, a majority of the Red Hills delegates now supported a delay. They backed a motion to await secession in Alabama and Georgia and, if these states refused to secede, submitting the question of Florida secession to voters. This was voted down by the convention 42–27. However, the four delegates from Gadsden County (Thomas Y. Henry, Abraham K. Allison, E. C. Love, and Samuel B. Stephens); the entire delegation from Jackson County (S. S. Alderman, Joseph A. Collier, Adam McNealy, and James L. G. Baker), and four of the five delegates from Leon County (John Beard, James Kirksey, George T. Ward, and William G. M. Davis) voted for the delay, a majority of 12 to 9 among the Red Hills delegates favoring delay. Only George W. Parkhill among Leon County delegates joined all of the Jefferson County delegation (Thompson B. Lamar, J. Patton Anderson, Thomas M. Palmer, and William S. Dilworth) and the four-man delegation representing Madison, Taylor, and Lafayette counties (John C. McGehee, A. J. Lea, W. H. Sever, and E. P. Barrington) in opposing delay. The Red Hills majority held together 11–10 on three other delaying moves, while the vote for delay was 8 for and 12 against on two other motions. A vote was set on Thursday, 10 January, on the final Ordinance of Secession, and this was approved 62 to 7. Only James L. G. Baker of Greenwood, Jackson County, among the Red Hills delegates, now voted no.[47]

Ruffin stayed to the end of the voting, then left for home. At Charleston on 12 April 1861, he was given the honor of pulling the lanyard when the first shot was fired at Fort Sumter.[48] Word reached delegates that Mississippi had seceded on the day before, and now Florida became the third state to leave the Union. Delegates reassembled on the east portico of the capitol on Friday, 11 January 1861, to sign the enrolled Ordinance of Secession. But Major Ward said before signing the ordinance, "When I die I want it inscribed upon my tombstone that I was the last man to give up the ship."[49]

17

The Civil War

Although less enthusiastic about immediate secession than much of Florida, the Red Hills rushed into the approaching Civil War with more men in uniform than any other section of the state. The counties of Jackson, Gadsden, Leon, Jefferson, and Madison provided at least 320 of the 480 on duty in the First Infantry Regiment of Florida Volunteers three months after secession.[1] Their first assignment was Pensacola, with its deep harbor, Federal navy yard, and three forts. Fort Pickens on the western extremity of Santa Rosa Island controlled the sea approaches to Pensacola with its big guns, and this fort soon had a force of Federal regulars under the command of Captain Harvey Brown, supported by a militia regiment from New York City. The land-side installations were in Confederate hands, the government at Montgomery, Alabama, having requisitioned five thousand troops from the now Confederate states of Georgia, Alabama, Mississippi, Louisiana, and Florida, all to be sent to Pensacola. The 480 in the First Florida were under the command of Colonel James Patton Anderson, a Jefferson County planter and veteran of the Mexican War. This entered Confederate service on 5 April and reached Pensacola on 12 April to join "the Provisional Army of the Confederate States" being assembled there by Brigadier General Braxton Bragg of Louisiana. As they arrived, word came that Fort Sumter had been fired upon. When the Floridians heard the news, a veteran later said, "there was cheering."[2]

There was a summer-long standoff between the Federal and Confederate forces, but in September 1861, the Federals made land-side raids in which there were a few casualties—the first bloodshed in Florida. Bragg then countered with an expedition of 1,050 picked men who were transported by barges on the night of 8 October, 100 of these being Floridians under Colonel Anderson. Landing on the north shore of Santa Rosa Island after midnight, the Confederates advanced westward, overrunning the sleeping encampment of the Sixth New York Volunteers. Soon, however, regulars from Fort Pickens drove the Confederate force back to its landing place, inflicting heavy casualties. In all, eighteen of the Confederates were killed, thirty-nine wounded, and thirty missing, as compared with fourteen Federals killed, twenty-nine wounded, and twenty-four missing. One-third of the Confederate losses were among the Floridians, who composed one-tenth of the force. In addition to six Floridians killed, eight were wounded and twelve taken prisoner.[3] At least two of the dead soldiers were from the vicinity of Tallahassee. Susan Bradford wrote in her diary on 10 October 1861: "War has come to the Bradford neighborhood! . . . Last night, October 9th, Captain Richard J. Bradford was shot in the breast and instantly killed. . . . Mr. William Routh was killed also, he was engaged to be married to Cousin Sallie." There were complaints that the Battle of Santa Rosa Island was unnecessary.[4]

But much bigger and bloodier battles in Tennessee awaited the Red Hills volunteers. In March of 1862, General Bragg's Gulf Coast command, now in southern Alabama, was summoned to reinforce the Confederate Army of General Albert Sidney Johnston at Corinth, Mississippi. A Federal general in the west, Ulysses S. Grant, had taken Fort Henry on the Tennessee River on 6 February and Fort Donelson on the Cumberland River on 16 February, causing Confederate troops in Upper Tennessee to pull back.[5] En route to Corinth, the Florida regiment had reached Montgomery, Alabama, when, on 4 April 1862, the twelve-month enlistment of all the men expired. This was a typical farm-boy regiment during planting season, and only 250, or about half of the men, reenlisted.[6] Organized into four companies, they now became a battalion in a brigade commanded by Anderson, and he became the first of four brigadier generals from the Red Hills. Forty years old, Anderson had commanded units of Mississippians in the Mexican War. Recently he had come to Florida to manage, and then for a time own, the plantation Casa Bianca of his aunt, Florida White Beatty. Before his return to military service he had devoted much of his time to agitating for secession.[7]

The 250 men remaining from the First Florida were barely organized into a battalion when they found themselves in Shiloh, one of the bloodiest battles of the Civil War, where casualties cost the two sides more than twenty thousand men. The Florida battalion lost sixteen killed and fifty-eight wounded. After Shiloh, the battalion was joined by six companies fresh from Florida in a reorganized First Regiment commanded by Colonel William Miller of Pensacola. As such it participated in the Battle of Perryville, Kentucky, as did the Third Florida, with two Jefferson County companies and one from Madison County, and these units were now combined into one unit under the command of Colonel Miller. By this time James Patton Anderson had advanced to major general in command of a division that included these units. The Fourth Florida, with one company each from Madison and Gadsden counties and two from Jackson County, fought alongside the First and Third in another bloody contest, at Murfreesboro, Tennessee, on 31 December 1862, where the Floridians suffered 332 additional casualties.[8]

Three other Florida regiments were in the East Tennessee command of General Edmund Kirby-Smith, who was from St. Augustine, Florida. These were the Sixth and Seventh Florida Infantry and the First Florida Cavalry, a unit that went into battle dismounted for lack of horses.[9] The First Cavalry, dismounted, was commanded by Colonel William G. M. Davis, a Tallahassee lawyer who had become rich in the cotton business. He was one of the four Leon County delegates voting to delay secession but afterward contributed fifty thousand dollars toward outfitting a regiment. Shortly he advanced to brigadier general but served only until mid-1863, when he resigned to engage in blockade running at Wilmington, North Carolina.[10] The Sixth Infantry, with companies from Gadsden and Jackson counties, was commanded by Colonel Jesse John Finley, a Marianna judge and lawyer and one-time mayor of Memphis, Tennessee, who like Davis soon became a brigadier general.[11]

John Milton, the Jackson County lawyer and planter, succeeded Perry as governor in October 1861. Milton expected the principal role of Florida troops to be defending the twelve hundred miles of Florida coast that were exposed to Federal attack. But the war was scarcely a year old, in the spring of 1862, when four regiments of Floridians were in Tennessee. With some now also being sent to Virginia, there was considerable worry about the defense of Florida itself.[12] Captain George W. Parkhill wrote his wife from a remote post in Virginia: "I would like to be in Florida to help defend it & why I am not ordered there I know not." Parkhill's company of Leon County residents, called the Howell Guards, had been one of the first units to leave Florida. In August 1861 it traveled by train from Tallahassee to Monticello, then marched to Boston, Georgia, where the men took a train to Richmond. A physician and the owner of Tuscawilla Plantation, Parkhill installed his wife, Lizzie, and their children, Charlie, aged two, and Em, one, in Richmond. But the company did not remain there long; by September 20 it was encamped on the banks of the

Like practically all of the other governors of territorial Florida and early governors of the state, John Milton, the Civil War governor, was from the Red Hills. He was an attorney and had a fine plantation and home, Sylvania, in Jackson County. (Courtesy of Florida State Archives)

Potomac a few miles south of Washington. For the next seven months Parkhill saw his family little, if at all. Every three days when he could do so he wrote Lizzie a letter. Forty of these letters survive.[13] The company was reassigned to the Fredericksburg area for a time and then early in May 1862 encamped at the first of several locations near

Richmond. But although the Federal army of General George B. McClellan was now advancing toward Richmond from the east, the nearest thing to an encounter with the enemy for a time came when Parkhill and a fellow officer rode on a reconnaissance, encountered three suspicious-looking riflemen, and disarmed and captured two. They then found that the men were Confederate pickets from a North Carolina company who in turn had taken Parkhill and his colleague for Yankee cavalrymen.[14]

A month before the Howell Guards reached Virginia, the Second Regiment of Florida Volunteers arrived in Richmond. The regiment's colonel, George T. Ward, had fought hard to delay secession but after the die was cast served in the Provisional Confederate Congress, then resigned, and, suggesting to the Secretary of War that Florida be represented in the defense of Virginia, joined the army. His was the first Florida unit to go to Virginia. While Ward was stationed at York-town, Virginia, in April 1862, General McClellan threatened the base. Ward was commended for "coolness and gallantry" in the defense of two redoubts when his unit charged and drove back the Federals. Like the First, the Second Florida had many men from the Red Hills, among them the Leon County Rifles, the Gulf State Guards of Jackson County, and the Madison County Rangers.[15]

Orders then came to give up Yorktown, which was virtually under the guns of a Federal fleet, and the Confederates retreated to Williamsburg, twelve miles away. The last troops to leave bore the brunt of a brisk Federal pursuit. Ward's unit, sent back to engage the enemy, traveled double-quick through mud that was knee-deep. The unit was in little condition to go into an engagement, according to Private David E. Maxwell of the Leon Rifles, who wrote home afterward: "But *our gallant* and *brave colonel* ordered a charge and we followed him, but not long was he allowed to lead us . . . for at an evil hour (and when we needed him most) a ball struck him under the left shoulder and came out on the right breast—killing him instantly—he never spoke." Captain Theodore W. Brevard of the company and some others took the body to Williamsburg, where Ward was buried.[16] Parkhill's Howell Guards were finally assigned to the same Second Florida Regiment which continued to defend Richmond against McClellan. Captain Parkhill wrote his wife from a "Camp of the 2nd Florida Regiment" on 25 June 1862 that his company was marching at 6:00 P.M. and headed for a battle. Said the captain in a postscript: "Remember me at the throne of God."[17] Private Francis P. Fleming of the St. Augustine Rifles wrote about "the storming of the batteries on Gaines farm": "Our regiment . . . lost sixty five men, killed & wounded, among the former the lamented Capt. Parkhill, his loss is greatly felt by the regt."[18]

Additional fighting in the Seven Days' Battle around Richmond further decimated the ranks of the Second Infantry. In the fall of 1862, Governor Milton, hearing the unit "does not number fifty effective men," suggested to the secretary of war that it be combined with two other Florida regiments that had arrived in Virginia during the summer. The Fifth got there in July and the Eighth in August and, in line with Milton's suggestion, the three were formed into the Florida Brigade of the Army of Northern Virginia with Edward A. Perry of Pensacola, who had replaced Ward as colonel of the Second, in command as brigadier general. The entire brigade numbered 717 when in July 1863 it went into action at Gettysburg. On 3 July it was assigned to support the right wing of General Pickett's famous charge. In this battle the unit suffered 455 casualties—33 killed, 217 wounded, and 205 missing.[19]

Richard Parkhill took command of the Howell Guards after his cousin was killed but was then dangerously wounded and returned to Florida. Elliot L. Hampton, who succeeded to the captaincy, was killed at Gettysburg. His place was taken during the battle by a nineteen-year-old first lieutenant, John Day Perkins, the son of a Tallahassee cotton merchant. Perkins fell in the same battle with a wound in the leg and, left on the battlefield for two days without food or water, plastered his leg with mud and muck to stem the flow of blood. Federal surgeons who amputated the leg predicted he would not live. Perkins became a curiosity at the prison hospital at Fort McHenry and a visiting woman from the North, asking to see "that little Johnnie Reb captain," exclaimed after he popped up in bed: "Oh—he is nothing but a boy!" But Perkins survived the wound and nine months of imprisonment to perform limited service in Florida and, until his death in 1904, related his experiences at Confederate reunions.[20]

Others lived to record their imprisonment in half a dozen Federal prison camps. Wilbur Gramling, a Leon Countian in Company K of the Fifth Florida, told in a vest pocket diary of his experiences after 2:00 P.M. on 6 May 1864 when he went into battle in the Wilderness campaign. Wounded in the right arm, he was imprisoned in Washington, D.C., and then spent more than a year in Elmira Prison Camp in New York. His homesickness and despair were renewed almost as surely as Sunday came around: "Sunday, July 21, 1864. I cant help thinking about home & about Pisgah Church every Sunday and wishing I was there to go to meeting." In the little more than one year of their imprisonment, 2,963 prisoners among the 12,123 Confederates confined there died at Elmira Prison. Gramling survived and returned home, but pneumonia had broken his health, and he collapsed and died on 31 December 1870 at age twenty-six following a service at his beloved Pisgah Church.[21]

Florida units in the west were badly cut up at Chickamauga and particularly at Missionary Ridge in Tennessee. When the surrender came, the Fourth Regiment gave up only twenty-three men. In Virginia the Second Florida surrendered sixty-eight, the Fifth fifty-three, and the Eighth thirty-three.[22] Additional troops had arrived from Florida during the final year of fighting around Richmond, among them the Eleventh Florida, headed by Theodore W. Brevard of Tallahassee. Brevard, who had been captain of Company D of the Second Florida, had run for colonel of the regiment in May 1862 and returned to Florida when he was defeated. There he raised a battalion and in 1864 brought it to Virginia, where his and other units were intended to bolster the weakening forces of General Robert E. Lee. In March, Brevard was appointed brigadier general—the fourth from the Red Hills—but his commission reached him only after the capture of Brevard and his regiment on 6 April 1865, three days before the surrender at Appomattox.[23]

Cotton was the lifeblood of the Red Hills economy as the war began. One week after Fort Sumter, President Lincoln proclaimed a Federal blockade of the southern coast, the purpose being to shut down the exchange of cotton for foreign-made goods. One vessel was sent to stand guard off Apalachicola and another off St. Marks. The *Mohawk*'s arrival at the latter port had been sped along by a message from Lincoln to his secretary of the navy, Gideon Welles: would he mind having the blockade vessel rescue Elizabeth Smith, a lady friend of a friend of his in Chicago, who was stranded at Newport, Florida, behind Confederate lines?[24] After Miss Smith was sped along to safety, Lieutenant J. H. Strong of the blockade fleet took his first Confederate prize on 5 July 1861, the sloop *George B. Sloat* trying to make a run out of the mouth of the St. Marks River. It was customary to seize the flag of a captured ship, but Mrs. Holland, "the lady . . . of Adjutant General Holland of Florida," who was aboard with three children and two servants, "claimed the flag to be her private property, and secured it to her person." Continued Strong: "As I could not possess it without using violence to a lady, and she is in a very delicate situation, I determined to let it go."[25]

Governor Milton championed an embargo on cotton, especially keeping it out of the hands of the North. As for blockade running, he considered this a "villainous traffic" conducted by speculators. He reported in August 1862 that some vessels had left Florida ports with cotton and returned with coffee, salt, and various kinds of merchandise, the latter bearing American labels over which "the names of English manufacturers were stamped."[26] Far off in a Virginia camp, Captain Parkhill expressed irritation at a report reaching his company: "Amos Whitehead read a letter from his wife in which she mentions that the vessel in which J. J. Williams, Hawkins and others shipped cotton has been found beyond a doubt to be a Yankee vessel. . . . Williams & Co. exchanges cotton for cargo, which consisted principally of coffee."[27] The principal beneficiaries of blockade runners were the rich, and some people now prospered in the spendthrift wartime economy of the Confederate and state governments. Susan Bradford Eppes remembered long after the war the "new uniforms, just from Paris, via Zeigler's Blockade Runner," that were worn by high-ranking officers of the Florida Military District when they attended parties at Goodwood.[28] Others in Tallahassee, though, were hard-pressed to get bare necessities: J. T. Bernard, running the blockade, had given the mother of Nettie Clare Bowen "enough taffeta for a dress," but she "had to swap it for a peck of salt."[29]

During much of the war, salt making along the coast was a substitute for cotton in the economy, but the farms and plantations of the Red Hills turned also to food crops and livestock. In 1860 the five counties of the Red Hills already grew 1,602,212 bushels, or 57 percent of the corn produced in Florida. Leon County farms alone had $503,626 worth of livestock, leading all the state, while the value of livestock in the Red Hills counties was $2,011,595, or 71 percent of the state total.[30] Little seems to have gone to the army, and for beef the Confederacy looked to the pine and grass rangeland along the Caloosahatchie, Peace, and Kissimmee rivers in southern Florida. The absence of the very Georgia rail connection from Live Oak that the Pensacola and Georgia had sought but had never been able to obtain now hindered the movement of Florida cattle to the troops. For a time Baldwin, with its commissary depot, was an objective of Florida cattle drives, but after March 1862 when Federal forces landed at Jacksonville, seizing also Fernandina, some drives were made from the rangelands directly to Savannah.[31]

During the first year of the war, the building of the twenty-two miles of railroad to Georgia was advocated as a military necessity, the Savannah, Albany & Gulf having graded a roadbed and promised tracks to the Florida line. After Federal forces took Fernandina in advance of Jacksonville, Brigadier General J. H. Trapier of the Florida

Military District ordered tracks of the Florida Railroad west of Fernandina stripped and taken to Lake City for use in making the connection. A storm of opposition met the order, Trapier was replaced, and former senator David Yulee, the major stockholder of the Florida Railroad living in the Confederate states and president of the line, obtained an injunction that prevented the line from being built until the last year of the war.[32]

Cutting off the supply of beef to the Confederacy was one of the Federal objectives in fighting the Battle of Olustee on 20 February 1864. The lack of a Georgia connection delayed the arrival of Georgia and South Carolina troops for the battle, for two days were required for a march from the Georgia line. This battle, with about 5,000 troops on each side, was nevertheless a resounding victory for the Confederates. Federal losses were 203 killed, 1,152 wounded, and 506 captured or missing, Confederate losses 93 dead, 846 wounded, and 6 missing. Florida cattle now, it appeared, could resume their march through Georgia.[33]

Olustee was as near as the fighting had come to the Red Hills, but Governor Milton had concerns of other kinds to worry him. As in other wars, much of the white population regarded the conflict as a rich man's war and a poor man's fight. While the well-to-do could evade military service by paying one thousand to three thousand dollars and sometimes as much as five thousand dollars, for a substitute, a poor man with a family to support had no choice but to dodge conscription by "laying out" or, if he was already in the service, deserting. Desertion and draft dodging were so frequent that much of the cavalry duty in Florida involved tracking down deserters.[34] Occasionally the people of Tallahassee, unless they turned their eyes away, saw an execution. Susan Bradford wished she had not looked once when, after turning the corner by Fisher's Green, she saw "two poor fellows . . . , and, while we were looking, the squad fired and the deserters fell dead."[35]

Some dissidents became Unionists. Governor Milton noted near the end of the year 1863 that his own section, West Florida, was in a "bad condition" where "the disloyal were in touch with the enemy." The sheriff of Washington County, he said, was among these, and a "large proportion if not a majority of the citizens of West Florida are represented as disloyal; at all events advocate reconstruction and have threatened to raise the United State flag, even in Marianna."[36] Capitalizing on the dissidence in West Florida, Brigadier General Alexander Asboth, earlier a partisan of Kossuth in Hungary but in 1864 commanding Federal troops at Fort Barrancas, set out on 18 September

1864 across the Florida Panhandle with seven hundred troops. The destination of his raid was Marianna, but when the vanguard of his force, a battalion of Maine cavalry, rode down Lafayette Street on 27 September, the reception was surprisingly hostile: a burst of musket fire killed Captain Mahlon M. Young at the head of the units, he falling "at Mrs. Ely's gate," and wounded one other soldier.[37]

Marianna was the headquarters of Confederate troops in West Florida, but the forces there, perhaps three hundred men under the command of Colonel A. B. Montgomery, were dispersed. One company had sighted the Federal force near "the old Scotch settlement" at Euchee Anna on 23 September and brought back news of the raid. Time enough remained for a force of about one hundred "minute men" to be organized, fighters armed with old shotguns, flintlocks, and pistols. This company, because of its age spread (the men ranged from thirteen to seventy-six) became known as "the cradle and grave company." Jesse Norwood of Marianna captained the group, but a recent historian of the battle, Charlotte Corley Farley, suggests that he may not have signaled resistance to the vastly superior Federal force and that one of the men became "trigger-happy." "On July 5, 1954, as Miss Lossie Holden and I were standing on the Holdens' front porch and looking across at St. Luke's [Episcopal Church] she said to me: 'There wouldn't have been any Battle of Marianna if old man Bill Wynn hadn't been trigger-happy!' "[38]

The cradle and grave company was badly cut up by the combined weight of Federal cavalry and infantry with Enfield rifles. Confederate sharpshooters along the north side of Lafayette Street were nevertheless able to pick off a number of Maine cavalrymen, while Asboth himself had to leave the battle with a crushed cheekbone and an arm broken in two places. Nine—some said ten—of the Rebel band were killed and sixteen wounded, while Asboth claimed eighty-one prisoners, ten of whom (including William B. Wynn, now a Jackson County lawyer and planter) died before reaching Elmira Prison Camp and twenty-five afterward.[39] Colonel Montgomery's part in the contest has been controversial: he retreated to the Chipola bridge in the face of the Federal counterattack; historian Mark Boyd thinks Montgomery must have ordered a retreat of all the force, including the cradle and grave company, in the face of overwhelming Federal strength. Whether or not the small band's defense of Marianna was justified, Asboth quickly returned to Pensacola, and the cradle and grave company won fame for a display of bravery equaled by no other unit serving in Florida during the war.[40]

William Miller, the Pensacola lumberman and Mexican War veteran, was wounded at Murfreesboro, Tennessee, as commander of the First and Third Florida Infantry, and in 1864 was assigned to the Florida Military District as brigadier general of reserves.[41] With headquarters at Lake City, this battle-hardened veteran, also skilled in logistics, devoted himself to making Florida's railroad network more a part of the defense of Florida. He was a champion of the Georgia connection from Live Oak, which was finally made early in 1865, while he considered the V-shaped rail system reaching westward from Baldwin to Quincy and southwestward from Baldwin to Cedar Key an ideal one for the defense of Florida. At the time he took command, there was a gap of ten miles between Baldwin and Lake City where the Federals had taken up the track. To repair it Miller mobilized a labor force, assembled four flatcars east of the gap, and with twelve hundred troops and a borrowed locomotive steamed to White House, within five miles of Jacksonville, and, almost under the eyes of Federal soldiers, ripped up the track from there to Baldwin, hauled the rails westward, and repaired the gap.[42]

Miller's lone superior in the Florida command in February 1865 was Major General Sam Jones, in command of the Florida District, now headquartered in Tallahassee. The Red Hills and Tallahassee, having been threatened from the east and the west, were now threatened from the south by Brigadier General J. H. Newton of Key West, who with a force of nine hundred Federal soldiers sailed up the west coast of Florida. At daybreak on Tuesday, 28 February, during a dense fog, their three transports dropped anchor off the Ochlockonee Buoy thirteen miles from land. A naval force of thirteen vessels from the blockade fleet soon joined them, with some five hundred sailors. One of the sailors' objectives was to proceed upriver and take old Fort St. Marks, now defended by the Confederates; however, their vessels ran aground. Fourteen vessels landed Newton and his command at the lighthouse, however, and some sailors traveled inland near here, reaching the East River Bridge at 4:00 A.M. on Saturday, 4 March.[43]

Until this time neither Tallahassee nor St. Marks had been aware of the Federal threat. Fortunately a force of about one hundred in "Scott's Cavalry" were stationed at Newport. Pickets from this unit encountered the Federals at East River. A stronger force then tried without effect to prevent a Federal crossing.[44] George Washington Scott, the Tallahassee storekeeper, had volunteered before secession and with the aid of *Benn's Tactics* had become one of the ablest cavalry commanders in Florida. On 19 March 1864, while on duty in East Florida, he wrote his wife Bettie, living on his plantation at the southern edge of Tallahassee, with directions for taking the family and some of the servants to Albany, Georgia, should Federals threaten Tallahassee.[45]

Now Scott, having learned of the heavy Federal force of Newton near the St. Marks lighthouse, sped the news to Tallahassee by a train arriving there at 9:00 P.M. Saturday: the Yankees, fourteen hundred strong, had landed. The news traveled by telegraph eastward to Lake City and westward to Quincy, while Georgia was asked to transfer rolling stock to Florida over the just completed Live Oak–Lawton connector. At 8:00 A.M. Sunday, 5 March, Newton began moving several hundred men of his force, black companies with white officers, together with a few Navy artillerymen, toward the Newport bridge spanning the St. Marks River. Scott's men tore the bridge apart and burned some of it and, with a few other Confederates, prevented a crossing of the river. As everyone around Tallahassee knew and the Federal commander now learned, the next available dry crossing was at the Natural Bridge eight miles to the north. Newton now took his army in a night march over "an old and unfrequented road" to this crossing.[46]

The Confederates also knew what Newton learned during the battle, that this crossing "could have been defended by 200 resolute soldiers, with a few pieces of artillery," against five times that number. The river disappears here in a broad and deep sink. After a land bridge scarcely one hundred feet wide, there are several other sinks and rises, as well as swamps, before the river rises again in "the basin," where after passing a ledge of rock it begins to run unimpeded. On the western approach to the natural bridge, the land rises steeply and is fairly open. The open area allowed defenders of the crossing to form a semicircle of entrenched infantrymen, supported by seven cannon. These blocked all Federal attempts to advance beyond the crossing from the east. General Miller, on assuming field command the night of 4 March, wired Colonel J. J. Daniels, commanding the First Regiment of Reserves, "to be ready to move on the arrival of a train at Madison." On the following night this unit with seven companies and three hundred men arrived at "the oil still" on the St. Marks line and at 10:00 P.M. marched to the battlefield, arriving there at 4:30 A.M. on Monday, 6 March. This force was soon joined by Colonel Scott and his experienced cavalry and Miller himself, his force including eighty militia.[47]

After two bold charges were turned back, a desultory fire was kept up by skirmishers until 11:00 A.M. Then the Federals made four more efforts to cross the natural bridge, with heavy losses. Additional Confederate units arrived during the battle, among them a battalion of the Second Cavalry, dismounted, under Colonel Carraway Smith. Federal losses were heavy, particularly among the officers, two of whom were killed and nine wounded. Nineteen Federal enlisted men were killed and eighty wounded, while the Confederate losses were only three killed and twenty-four wounded. Newton hurried back to the lighthouse near the end of the day, leaving some dead and wounded on the field. A force sent by Colonel Scott to harass the retreating enemy rounded up thirty-five captives, bringing Federal casualties to 148.[48]

In addition to active participants in the fighting, a host of Confederate volunteers, some of them unarmed, were present on the field or nearby. The Confederates probably far outnumbered the several hundred Federals who were engaged. A cannon had begun firing at the courthouse in Quincy at 4:00 A.M. Sunday, 5 March, summoning volunteers, and these, including Judge DuPont in an over-age group, boarded a train for Tallahassee at 9:00 A.M. Then, shortly after dark, they took a train that traveled to the oil station, this also carrying Colonel Daniels's reserves.[49] The Male Department of the Seminary West of the Suwannee had taken on light military duties during the war, but mothers of the youngest among the thirteen- to seventeen-year-old cadets there were alarmed when a dozen or more of these also went to Natural Bridge. "We were placed just to the left of Houstoun's battery as an artillery guard and told not to fire a gun unless there was a charge made on the battery, so we had nothing to do but sit there and wait," said one of the cadets long afterward.[50] After the battle, as a train returned to Tallahassee with veterans of the battle aboard, including the cadets, along with the body of Captain Henry K. Simmons, the lone Tallahassean killed, the cadets were projected into long-lasting fame as heroes of the battle. Flagging down the train in the darkness at Bel Air, a company of little girls sang to the tune of *Dixie*:

> The young cadets were the first to go
> To meet and drive away the foe
> Look away!

The din of the battle just nine miles away had made families of the cadets living at Bel Air uneasy. Sue Archer and some other young ladies boarded the train there and placed wreaths made of wild olive, in bloom at that time, on the caps of the teenage corps.[51]

Dr. Charles Hentz, who had accompanied the Quincy group, traveled to the Confederate encampment at Newport the day after the battle just in time to witness a darker side of the military victory. Adjudged "deserters" by a drumhead court, two young soldiers were tied to posts. One was defiant and asserted he "didn't give a damn." The other was as pale as ashes, "his lips quivering convulsively." The first was killed instantly by a volley of shots but the firing squad botched the job with the next victim, who "fell with an awful struggle . . . , uttered a fearful, bloodcurdling, bubbling wail . . . , and struggled for several moments dreadfully." Afterward, to the disgust of Hentz, there was a rush from all sides as soldiers stripped the bodies of their Federal-issue clothing.[52]

Tallahassee still boasts occasionally of being the only Confederate capital east of the Mississippi that remained out of Federal hands to the end of the war. But in Virginia the military machine of General Grant was rapidly bringing the war to a close. As the end drew near, Governor Milton, an able and conscientious wartime governor, was worn out and depressed. Dr. Hentz saw him at the Tallahassee depot on the night troops were boarding for Natural Bridge, "walking up and down the depot platform with the air of the most profound abstraction and dejection—I think he must have been suffering from some disease of the brain." Milton returned to his home, Sylvania, and on 1 April, while the family was seated downstairs, he went to a bedroom upstairs. A shot was heard, and his body was found with a shotgun sprawled across his legs.[53]

Tallahassee was still savoring the victory at Natural Bridge on 9 April 1865, although events in Virginia somewhat dampened an evening of song that was held in the Hall of Representatives. Roses were profusely in bloom, and vases of the flowers perfumed the hall. Some of the old gaiety emerged as the crowd joined in the chorus of *Dixie* and applauded singers of old favorites before a piano above which hung the Confederate flag. A quartet was singing "The Southern Marseillaise" when a man entered the hall with a telegram and advanced rapidly up the aisle. Twice he tried to read it but his voice failed him. Then in a loud voice he read: "General Lee surrendered the Army of Northern Virginia today, at Appomatox." There was silence at first and then, according to Susan Eppes, "men, women and children wept aloud as they realized the calamity which had befallen us. Few slept that night and the sun rose upon a miserable, broken-hearted people—far too miserable even to talk it over with each other."[54]

Epilogue

There were 30,000 black slaves, three-fifths of the entire population of the Red Hills. These, unlike Susan Bradford Eppes, welcomed the appearance of the Union army. The Stars and Stripes went up in Tallahassee on 20 May 1865, and this became Emancipation Day in Florida. Freedmen celebrated thereafter with a picnic on Bull's Pond (Lake Ella), where speakers with northern accents urged upon their two thousand listeners the exercise of such new-won rights as voting. Doing so, blacks ran up against a determined white minority that through the Young Men's Democratic Clubs (YMDC) discouraged them from voting. The dispute between black and white was a comparatively polite one in Leon County; blacks there outnumbered whites three to one. In the midst of the discussion, a colored hook-and-ladder company was the first to arrive in the middle of the night of 9 May 1869 to save from fire the house of Peres B. Brokaw, president of the Tallahassee YMDC. This fine residence much later became the headquarters of the Historic Tallahassee Preservation Board. In Jackson County, where the races were equally divided, there were from 153 to 175 deaths, while in Madison County there were more than 20.[1]

Agriculture, the principal activity of the Red Hills since the native Apalachee farmers, revived briefly with paid labor instead of slaves, but this revival hardly outlived lingering high prices for cotton. Afterward freedmen found themselves on thirty- and forty-acre tracts on a plantation, rented on shares, their share sometimes amounting to nothing when there were debts to pay. In Leon where the black population increased to six blacks for every white, travel books illustrated the proverbial poverty of a typical rural black by showing a stooped farmer behind a plow pulled by a single ox or by showing the same ox pulling his two-wheeled cart to town on market day. The old cotton lands had worn out by the turn of the twentieth century. Northern industrialists bought the best of these and turned them into vast hunting preserves, becoming at the same time the landlords of the tenants. Since quail became the main crop on these "quail plantations" extending over 100,000 Leon County acres, agriculture suffered still further.[2]

The quail kingdom that succeeded the cotton kingdom spread also across Grady, Thomas, and Brooks counties in Georgia and into Jefferson County in Florida. It never, however, touched Jackson or Gadsden counties to the west of Tallahassee or Madison County east of Jefferson. Jackson County agriculture flourished in the hands of yeoman farmers who produced cotton crops surpassing the record one of Leon County in 1860. When the boll weevil ended the reign of cotton in 1916, Jackson found as good a crop in peanuts. Gadsden County farmers, with the help of paid black labor, built a prosperous shade tobacco industry matching its antebellum counterpart and supplied cigar factories with wrappers. This industry lasted until the 1970s. In Madison County a big "cotton factory" built after the Civil War enabled agriculture to survive. Called "the largest Sea Island cotton gin in the world," its machinery made possible for the first time the rapid ginning of large amounts of "long cotton." Madison County farmers thrived growing it. When the boll weevil obliterated this crop, they adapted to others.[3]

In 1984 only Jefferson among the Red Hills counties derived as much as one-fourth of its personal income from the farm. The amount, $12,188,000, was about the same as in more diversified Madison County. In Gadsden, the only Red Hills County still with a black majority, farm income was $14,799,000; in Jackson it was $19,685,000. Nowhere in northern Florida have the frosty winters allowed orange growing and winter vegetables to succeed as they have in central and southern Florida. Jackson's farm income was therefore exceeded by eleven counties in southern Florida and by eight in central Florida, although only by one, Suwannee, in northern Florida. In populous Palm Beach County in the same year, 1984, personal income from the farm totaled $178,054,000, nearly ten times that of Jackson. Leon County, the most important farm county in the state in 1860, was far behind all other Red Hills counties in 1984, with a farm income of only $2,362,000, less than anywhere in Florida except eight coastal or lowland counties. Farming was not missed at all here, for government (principally state government) now provided $616,032,000, or 42 percent of total personal income, $1,457,632,000.[4]

Florida, the thirty-second state in population in 1900 with 528,542, had 10,881,000 persons in 1984 and appears likely in a decade or two to become the third most populous state, behind only California and Texas. Only Leon among the Red Hills counties has participated in this population explosion. Most of the growth has occurred in Tallahassee and the suburbs. Leon changed from a rural county to an urban one in 1940 when the population of the lone town, Tallahassee, passed that of the remainder of the county. By 1982 Tallahassee was a city of 102,000. Rapid growth created something of a dilemma for the old cotton town, which had a population of only 2,981 in 1900. Building after World War II was particularly destructive as the capitol center spread and businesses covered the original one-square-mile town of the nineteenth century. Thirty-nine antebellum houses were described in 1933; fewer than half of them remain.[5]

Now a capital indeed, Tallahassee with its governmental center and two state universities has become a city of newcomers. Curious about the past but knowing little about it, the public nevertheless responded enthusiastically to archaeologists' discovery in 1985 of the ruins of a large council house on the hilltop site of seventeenth-century San Luis de Talimali. This council house, two miles west of today's skyscraper capitol, was the "civic center" of the community of San Luis. The response was even more enthusiastic with the discovery in the spring of 1987, on a hill one mile east of the capitol, of artifacts showing that in the winter of 1539–1540, this had been the stopping place of Hernando De Soto and his army, in the midst of the Nation of Apalachee, which had its main town here.

The birdwatching New Englander Bradford Torrey, walking between the lichen-covered banks of the road here and across "Captain Houstoun's plantation" in April 1893, never dreamed that De Soto had been here. What impressed him particularly during ten days in Tallahassee were the mockingbirds. Torrey said "there were never many consecutive five minutes of daylight in which, if I stopped to listen, I could not hear at least one mocker."[6] Although many of the old houses are gone, the present-day generation of environmentalists will now perhaps save almost the last remaining heritage from the cotton planters of 1850–1860, namely the canopy roads that stretch to the north and east from Tallahassee. It is tempting for city and county officials to use these for rapid transportation between Tallahassee and the people and businesses that have flown to distant suburbs. However, young residents of the Miccosukee Land Co-op stormed into a county commission hearing in the spring of 1985 with

A visitor to the tiny town of Tallahassee in the 1830s noted that roads ran out like spokes of a broken wagon wheel into the hammocks around the town. These were the cotton roads along which six-mule-team wagons hauled heavy bales to market, carving deep vertical walls of red clay along the sides. Today these pleasantly shaded roadways, such as Meridian Road here, are the principal physical heritage remaining of Leon County's conspicuous part in the Cotton Kingdom. (Photo by Clifton Paisley)

a petition bearing five thousand names, including those of many Tallahasseans, that halted a move to widen the pavement of Miccosukee Road by only two feet at the cost of several prized live oak trees. This victory, however, was only momentary, for several "improvement plans" have been advanced for other canopy roads.

Appendix 1

Jackson County Planters Producing Fifty or More Bales of Cotton in 1850

Name	Census Schedules, Population		Tax Rolls, 1850		U.S. Agriculture Census Schedules, 1850				
	Age	Native State	Slaves	Acres of Land	Improved Acres	Farm Value (dollars)	Value of Livestock (dollars)	Corn (bushels)	Cotton (400 lb. bales)
James L. G. Baker	51	NC	70	960	470	8,000	1,900	2,600	100
Simmons J. Baker, Sr.	75	NC	84	2,242	800	12,500	2,000	5,000	200
Simmons Baker, Jr.			55	1,277	500	8,000	1,600	2,000	95
Thomas Barnes	46	NC	55	1,110	570	5,700	1,600	2,690	100
Edward C. Bellamy	49	SC	168	4,000	2,000	30,000	5,000	8,000	230
J. H. Brett	38	NC			400	2,500	1,000	2,000	75
Elijah Bryan	55	GA	48	2,500	400	18,000	2,600	3,600	60
Thomas M. Bush	59	GA	72	5,674	1,000	5,500	4,000	4,500	165
Jesse Coe	68	MD	125	3,233	1,000	10,000	2,000	3,000	250
Francis R. Ely	38	NC	70	536	650	9,156	2,700	3,000	55
George Gray			38		500	6,000	1,600	3,000	102
William Hall	38	NC	16	400	260	3,000	1,350	1,500	50
N. A. Long	37	GA	61	2,160	720	16,000	3,000	6,000	160
John Milton	43	GA	33	2,860	320	3,200	2,000	3,600	63
William Nickels	50	ME	25	880	240	7,000	1,200	2,000	70
Mary Roberts	54	NC	54[a]	2,480[a]	250	12,400	2,200	2,000	75
John G. Roulhac	52	NC	86	1,840	850	15,000	5,482	7,000	170
John G. Russ	43	NC	31	540	350	6,000	1,500	1,500	94
Joseph W. Russ	46		26	420	300	6,000	1,600	3,000	54
Joseph T. Russ					400	3,000	1,700	2,000	90

Estate, Joseph W. Russ			60	480	500	4,000	1,400	1,500	82
S. W. Smith	34	NC	19	740	375	3,000	1,400	1,900	75
Amos Snell	46	GA	4	800	100	4,500	1,300	1,500	50
Hugh Spears			28	1,500	300	6,000	1,000	2,000	57
John Waddell			33	640	350	14,000	1,400	2,000	125
Cary Whitaker		NC			300	4,000	1,300	2,500	50
Thomas M. White	39	NC	88	400	500	5,000	2,000	4,000	130
Isaac Widgeon	40	VA	28		350	5,000	2,500	2,500	60
Benjamin Wynns	60	Bermuda	42[b]	1,720[b]	800	10,000	2,500	4,000	90
Wynns Estate			33	650	500	5,000	1,400	2,000	100
Robert A. Young	44	SC	17	800	400	4,500	1,250	2,000	100

[a] Including property owned by Hiram Roberts.

[b] Including property owned by his wife, Caroline.

Source: Seventh Census, Manuscript Schedules; taxroll information.

Appendix 2

Gadsden County Planters Producing Fifty or More Bales of Cotton in 1850

Name	Census Schedules, Population		Tax Rolls, 1850		U.S. Agriculture Census Schedules 1850				
	Age	Native State	Slaves	Acres of Land	Improved Acres	Farm Value (dollars)	Value of Livestock	Corn (bushels)	Cotton (400lb. bales)
William Booth	51	VA	69	1,200	800	6,000	2,100	2,500	128
Harriet F. Carnochan	60	GA	35	990	400	5,000	1,900	3,500	100
George Alexander Croom	28	NC	59	1,680	800	10,000	3,000	3,000	146
C. H. DuPont	45	SC	70	2,146	700	15,000	3,000	2,500	130
James Fillyaw	32	NC	105	960	700	18,000	240	5,500	175
Zabud Fletcher	47				200	3,500	3,000	4,000	50
Arthur I. Forman	42	MD	38	1,600	900	18,000	3,000	3,000	115
Henry Gee	68	NC	75	1,300	400	15,000	3,500	2,400	52
James Gibson	75	Ireland	73	2,445	800	15,000	2,800	4,000	90
William Gibson	33	SC	38	1,240	600	8,000	1,700	2,000	100
Choice Hall	43	GA	66	1,060	400	6,000	1,900	1,500	75
Robert H. Harrison	43	VA	66	2,093	300	17,000	1,460	1,500	50
Hadley Hinson	42	NC	19	1,000	175	2,000	800	1,500	58
Robert B. Houghton	21	GA			450	7,500	2,400	2,000	114
Willis Hudnall	54	SC	32	500	300	5,000	1,100	2,000	50
Augustus Johnson	27	GA	17	80	500	8,500	1,100	2,000	80
William Johnson	53	GA	24	750	500	5,000	1,600	2,000	80
Augustus H. Lanier	45	GA	84	1,260	800	10,000	3,500	4,000	161
Sarah Lines			86	1,600	800	15,000	3,000	5,000	86
Henry Lipford	37	SC	30	930	400	8,000	1,500	4,000	50
John Luton	18	SC			175	5,000	950	1,500	125

Jesse McCall	44	GA	42	750	400	10,000	1,400	2,000	70
James Mims	51	SC	53	800	350	4,000	1,700	1,200	70
Thomas Munroe	47	Scotland	72	1,680	1,200	15,000	2,980	4,000	230
William Munroe	31	Scotland	79	2,155	900	12,000	1,900	2,500	100
Donald Nicholson	27	NC	5		500	4,500	1,700	2,000	75
J. W. Poindexter	33	VA	16	800	350	7,000	1,500	1,500	72
J. G. Rawls		GA			250	5,000	1,400	2,500	50
Thomas Scott	22	SC	14		160	3,000	750	500	60
Joseph Seabrook			32	560	300	4,500	1,200	1,500	50
Mrs. Charles Sibley			49	1,814	600	25,000	2,500	2,500	78
John Smith	63	VA	45	920	250	8,000	1,650	2,000	120
William M. Stafford	58	SC	44	1,120	250	4,000	1,400	1,500	80
James Thomas	47	GA	26	1,520	350	10,000	2,000	2,000	60
Jean Verdier	30	SC	64	1,200	800	6,000	2,900	2,000	155
Catharine Woodburn	52	SC	22	550	350	5,000	1,160	1,200	75
Nathaniel Zeigler	43	SC	44	1,040	500	12,000	3,000	4,000	62

Source: Seventh Census, Manuscript Schedules; taxroll information.

Appendix 3

Leon County Planters Producing Fifty or More Bales of Cotton in 1850

Name	Age	Native State	Slaves	Acres of Land	Improved Acres	Farm Value (dollars)	Value of Livestock (dollars)	Corn (bushels)	Cotton (400 lb. bales)
David Alderman	48	NC			700	10,000	1,355	4,200	140
William Alderman	35	GA	7		400	4,000	1,750	2,800	50
Robert W. Alston	69	NC	20	800	305	7,000	1,600	2,000	112
Jesse Averett	54	NC	87	1,680	1,180	19,680	3,275	1,000	192
Charles Bannerman	43	NC	37	1,114	700	10,000	2,000	2,000	80
Joseph W. Bannerman	49	NC	15	360	600	4,000	1,700	3,000	120
Kenneth Bembry	49	NC	38	1,120	450	10,000	1,900	2,500	107
Turbutt R. Betton	55	MD	55	900	600	10,000	2,000	2,000	200
Susan Blake	41	NC	51	880	425	9,000	2,000	2,300	81
William Bloxham	45	VA	41	680	400	6,000	1,955	1,800	84
Edward Bradford	52	NC	105	3,003	1,200	30,000	3,430	5,000	280
Henry Bradford	59	NC	70	1,525	700	20,000	3,700	3,000	130
Richard Bradford	49	NC	50	1,835	700	12,000	2,300	3,000	200
Thomas A. Bradford	60	NC	52	1,120	1,000	12,000	2,500	200	140
James H. Branch	25	NC	34	720	350	7,200	2,080	1,500	84
John Branch	68	NC	104	2,320	700	12,500	3,000	5,000	235
Joseph L. Branch	33	NC	7		400	10,000	1,530	2,000	95
L. H. Branch Estate			32	860	350	8,000	3,200	1,000	80
Lemuel B. Brockett	45	NC	19	199	160	1,000	1,200	2,000	73

Name	Age	State							
James E. Broome	41	SC	31	660	310	3,960	1,800	1,600	90
William H. Burroughs	44	GA	35	634	325	9,600	2,957	2,000	74
A. K. Butler, Agent for T. B. Winn	26	VA			270	2,920	710	1,000	103
Robert Butler	63	PA	52	1,069	400	75,000	3,000	3,000	55
Richard K. Call	57	VA	137	4,254	(1) 600 (2) 700 (3) 65	22,000 25,000 2,500	1,415 3,705 2,400	3,500 4,000 500	178 203
William A. Carr		VA	52	1,880	600	20,000	2,000	3,000	200
Abraham Cason	23	GA			150	2,600	1,020	800	60
John Cason	50	GA	39	1,000	700	15,200	2,500	1,500	100
N. W. Cason					400	10,000	1,500	2,250	75
Benjamin Chaires, Jr.	29	GA	63	1,000	600	12,000	2,300	3,600	126
Green R. Chaires	34	GA	70	920	600	11,000	2,740	2,500	75
Green H. Chaires	59	GA	72	5,440	1,800	32,000	5,400	3,500	215
Joseph Chaires	38	GA	70	1,055	800	24,800	4,500	5,000	175
Martha Chaires	21	FL			650	10,000	2,887	2,000	200
Thomas B. and Charles P. Chaires	22 20	FL FL	118	2,720	1,400	84,810	3,700	5,000	220
Joseph Christie	37	GA			150	3,000	578	900	65
Charles Cole	60	NC	16	760	260	5,000	1,000	800	50
Henry Copeland	24	SC	22	460	250	1,500	1,200	2,000	50
Frederick R. Cotten	30	NC	120	3,653	(1) 1,000 (2) 700	25,000 20,000	3,350 2,530	3,000 3,000	127 254
Frederick R. Cotten, Executor, John W. Cotten Estate			77	1,520	1,150	16,500	3,000	5,000	305
John A. Craig		MD	50	1,540	800	30,560	1,200	700	180
Alexander Cromartie	44	NC	28	1,021	450	10,000	1,770	3,000	72
John Cromartie	41	NC	33	500	250	4,000	1,724	700	50
Bryan Croom	47	NC	195	4,400	(1) 780 (2) 800	19,000 16,000	1,310 5,750	4,000 6,000	236 250
Richard Croom	45	NC	65		600	10,000	1,666	4,500	200

Name	Age	State							
Edmund Davis	26	GA			100	1,000	1,050	1,080	60
George E. Dennis	45	NC	45	548	200	4,064	1,310	3,000	64
Jacob Elliot	44	NC	8		120	8,000	1,125	1,500	52
Francis Eppes	49	VA	69	1,920	700	28,800	3,325	3,500	230
Alfred A. Fisher	39	NC	35	370	115	5,400	3,925	1,400	85
William Fisher	59	VA	24	320	280	3,000	700	1,000	50
George Galphin	39	GA	27	400	240	4,000	1,810	1,200	50
Edgar M. Garnett	29	VA	47	640	500	10,000	2,000	2,000	100
John W. Hale	50	NC	30	700	250	4,000	1,900	1,200	52
William Hall	38	GA	20	960	400	5,000	940	1,000	75
James L. Hart	46	GA	21	720	220	2,000	1,212	1,600	56
Richard Hayward	49	MD	63	1,398	(1) 400	7,000	1,500	400	200
					(2) 700	20,000	3,000	5,000	100
Griffin W. Holland	44	VA	63	1,870	700	14,000	4,000	4,000	170
Edward Houstoun	40	NC	41	1,291	600	15,000	2,000	2,500	140
James Hunter	40	NC	13	560	400	10,000	2,617	1,400	84
George C. S. Johnson	44	MD			100	3,200	380	1,360	150
Nancy Johnson	65	NC	1	400	150	1,000	440	700	200
George Noble Jones		GA	85	1,600	841	19,000	2,690	4,500	289
Thomas Laversage	52	NC	41	960	500	10,000	250	1,000	110
William Lester	53	GA	110	3,462	1,200	25,000	6,400	5,000	200
Walter F. Lloyd	32	NY	33	480	350	4,800	2,200	2,000	80
Julia F. Lorimer			100	1,660	800	40,000	4,280	7,000	192
Benjamin Manning, Jr.	25	AL	26	1,320	350	4,500	1,870	2,000	50
John J. Maxwell	66	GA	88	920	600	9,200	1,620	2,000	100
John P. Maxwell	39	GA	31	320	300	3,200	1,098	1,500	51
John S. Maxwell	38	GA	48				1,000	1,000	83
William M. Maxwell	42	GA	23	440	400	3,200	1,360	1,200	50

Name	Age	State							
John Miller	50	NC	56	1,540	970	16,500	2,700	2,000	200
John C. Montford	52	NC	20	300	360	8,600	1,150	1,500	60
George W. Parkhill	26	VA	69	1,517	700	10,000	2,850	4,000	240
William Perkins	32	NC	21	720	350	7,200	1,200	1,000	70
William G. Ponder	47	SC	85	3,400	500	15,000	2,000	3,500	125
Thomas Reynolds	71	MD			259	4,800	1,425	3,000	66
William F. Robertson	36	VA	58	1,100	650	9,600	2,100	3,000	125
John S. Shepard	52	NC	109	2,899	1,850	18,500	5,000	6,000	310
Henry A. Stroman	29	SC	29	373	100	3,200	500	1,000	58
William N. Taylor, Agent for David Barrow	25	NC	81	2,320	1,100	15,000	3,600	6,000	317
Noah L. Thompson	37	NC	122	2,682	(1) 700 (2)1,600	5,200 40,000	1,325 5,000	3,000 6,000	180 300
Theodore Turnbull	39	SC	27	640	300	16,600	1,068	2,000	100
George T. Ward	40	KY	114	2,000	1,450	25,000	7,000	5,000	372
Henry B. Ware	44	GA	26	720	235	5,000	1,545	1,500	65
Richard Whitaker	49	NC	83	1,320	700	20,000	3,000	3,500	220
John Whitehead			82	1,036	900	12,000	4,030	5,000	301
James Whitehead Estate			101	225	1,200	22,050	3,230	4,000	326
George Whitfield	46	NC			720	8,000	3,750	2,000	146
Benjamin F. Whitner	60	SC	56	1,127	500	13,000	3,500	2,500	90
Robert W. Williams	40	TN	196	5,100	(1) 1,850 (2) 400	46,000 4,000	4,500 2,540	9,200 3,510	438 50

Source: Seventh Census, Manuscript Schedules; taxroll information.

Appendix 4

Jefferson County Planters Producing Fifty or More Bales of Cotton in 1850

Name	Census Schedules, Population		Tax Rolls, 1850		U.S. Agriculture Census Schedules, 1850				
	Age	Native State	Slaves	Acres of Land	Improved Acres	Farm Value (dollars)	Value of Livestock (dollars)	Corn (bushels)	Cotton (400 lb. bales)
William Bailey	60	GA	269	3,960	1,600	8,000	10,020	8,000	550
William J. Bailey	42	GA	73	4,760	1,250	12,000	4,450	5,000	156
Zachariah Bailey	57	FL			200	3,000	2,100	1,200	60
Ellen A. Beatty	49	KY	93	3,560	1,000	4,000	2,700	4,000	281
Emmala A. Bellamy		SC	209	3,760	400	4,000	1,600	3,000	121
Daniel Bird	66	SC	43	1,856	750	11,250	2,050	3,000	240
James S. Bond	52	GA	24		200	200	890	1,500	60
William G. Clark	54	GA	32	320	200	2,000	1,700	1,300	88
Caroline G. Cole	33	SC	65	2,556	350	5,250	2,030	1,500	150
Joseph Dawkins, Agent for David Barrow	27	SC	128	1,800	1,000	2,000	2,800	10,000	505
John Doggett	31	NC	43	224	550	3,500	2,950	2,000	135
James B. Edwards	38	FL	25	400	40	400	1,000	1,400	112
John Finlayson	41	SC	99	1,960	1,000	10,000	3,750	5,000	330
Washington Floyd, overseer for E. C. Cabell	37	SC	98	3,700	800	6,400	2,450	3,000	202
Octavius H. Gadsden	41	SC	39	840	500	5,000	1,700	2,000	115
Octavius H. Gadsden, agent			205	4,800	800	12,500	2,600	3,500	200
Octavius H. Gadsden agent					700	10,700	1,940	2,500	112
Robert H. Gamble	38	VA	165	6,319	1,541	14,000	4,500	7,000	599

Appendix

William Gorman	57	GA	28	800	350	8,000	1,500	1,800	55
Oliver Hearn, overseer for Thomas Randall	30	SC	65	4,400	750	6,750	1,990	3,000	173
William S. Hill	60	NC	28		200		700	1,000	53
Benjamin Johnson	52	VA	37	720	300	3,000	1,570	2,000	90
John Johnson					240	1,920	1,240	1,000	50
Mary Johnson					200	1,500	1,445	2,200	56
G. Noble Jones			131	3,814	1,400	21,600	4,200	4,000	277
Richard Lang	57	GA	31	840	275	2,500	1,170	1,300	64
Hampden S. Linton	44	SC	26	400	350	3,000	1,200	1,250	74
John G. Mathers	60	GA	14	760	285	2,800	1,200	1,500	75
Newton Mathers	24	GA			150	2,050	665	800	50
William D. Moseley			80	2,400	850	8,500	2,652	7,000	200
William S. Murphy			19	720	300	6,500	1,000	900	55
Martin Palmer	62	VA	56	2,000	700	10,000	3,285	5,000	92
John G. Plant, overseer for John G. Anderson	37	SC	96	1,600	700	8,400	3,000	6,000	348
William H. Prudal					270	2,500	915	750	75
John M. Raysor	38	SC	19	600	170	4,000	1,080	1,400	50
James Scott	55	GA	53	1,480	410	3,000	1,620	2,000	65
Smith Simpkins	30	SC	27	720	250	3,000	910	2,000	59
Noah H. Teat	35	SC	14	400	230	2,500	1,850	1,300	57
Thomas Townsend					1,000	10,000	3,960	5,000	183
Dorothy Triplett	20	GA	15	160	160	960	320		112
Martha P. Triplett	47	GA	26	440	160	2,400	1,210	1,200	108
James R. Tucker	46	SC	64	117	500	7,500	3,000	1,500	91
William H. Ware	41	SC	41	857	348	8,000	2,350	2,100	90

R. W. White, agent for C. Murat	28	NC			500	12,200	1,620	2,000	100
Elizabeth Wirt			102	3,400	1,000	6,000	2,570	4,000	289

Source: Seventh Census, Manuscript Schedules; taxroll information.

Madison County Planters Producing Fifty or More Bales of Cotton in 1850

Name	Census Schedules, Population		Tax Rolls, 1847[a]		U.S. Agriculture Census Schedules, 1850				
	Age	Native State	Slaves	Acres of Land	Improved Acres	Farm Value (dollars)	Value of Livestock (dollars)	Corn (bushels)	Cotton (400 lb. bales)
John Bradley	24	SC			400	7,000	1,200	1,600	90
Anthony Brantley	52	SC	32	480	250	4,000	1,200	800	70
William A. Brinson	30	GA	25	700	250	1,200	1,400	1,500	60
John S. Broome	39	SC	26	480	275	5,000	1,500	2,000	80
Isaac Bunting	51	SC	69	640	885	1,100	3,000	3,500	150[b]
Lucius Church	50	NH	37	2,000	600	12,000	2,600	2,000	200
Rebecca S. Dozier	36	SC	37	560	300	10,000	1,400	1,200	90
Archibald Fair	51	SC	30	400	300	6,000	1,200	1,600	75
Samuel F. Frink	30	NC	21	80	300	3,000	1,000	1,400	60
William W. Goodman	38	GA	30	900	230	5,000	1,000	1,400	50
Dennis Hankins	58	SC	33	1,080	450	10,000	2,600	1,500	100
Richard Harrison	32	SC	44	920	550	10,000	2,400	2,100	220
Dr. Theodore Hartridge	31	GA	25	680	500	12,000	1,800	2,000	100
John Humphrey	31	GA	4		208	1,000	800	1,000	60
Andrew J. Lea	35	NC	30	240	130	7,000	1,000	2,000	60
Thomas J. Linton	52	SC	47	1,360	690	20,000	7,000	3,000	250
James Lipscomb	23	SC			467	10,000	2,000	1,400	50[b]
John Lipscomb	60	SC	100	3,000	1,350	49,000	6,000	7,000	300[b]
John C. McGehee	49	SC	41	1,520	600	25,000	3,000	4,000	200
John D. McLeod	32	NC	65	1,360	120	6,000	1,200	600	76
Enoch G. Mays	34	SC	21	1,000	400	9,000	1,600	70	70

Name								
Rhydon G. Mays	49	SC	82	1,516	750	15,000	3,900	4,000	240
Richard J. Mays	45	SC	77	3,360	700	15,000	4,000	2,000	200
William A. Moseley	36	SC	28	880	400	6,000	1,000	1,000	62
Reddin W. Parramore	50	GA	73	4,455	1,400	35,000	20,000	4,000	160[b]
John C. Pillans	62	SC	20	320	200	2,500	1,500	750	65
Vans Randall	30	SC	41	1,330	260	5,520	1,400	1,200	50[b]
Jeremiah D. Reid			32	1,360	400	10,000	1,400	1,000	70
Seaborne O. Sullivan	46	SC	22	480	190	10,000	1,000	1,200	70
William L. Tooke	55	NC	32	1,000	400	5,000	2,000	1,200	80
Benjamin Waldo	34	SC			300	6,000	2,500	2,000	84
James L. Wyche	22	GA	45	1,800	250	4,000	1,300	1,500	60
John S. Wyche	39	GA	24	1,000	300	1,000	1,800	1,000	100

[a]The Madison County taxrolls for the period 1848-53 are lost. Number of slaves and acres of land are from taxroll of 1847.

[b]Cotton production is an estimate, the reported production having been lost on a marred page of the agricultural census.

Source: Seventh Census, Manuscript Schedules; taxroll information.

Abbreviations

ASP, Indian Affairs	*American State Papers, Indian Affairs*
ASP, Military Affairs	*American State Papers, Military Affairs*
ASP, Public Lands	*American State Papers, Public Lands*
DAB	*Dictionary of American Biography*
DDR	Dorothy Dodd Room of Florida History, State Library of Florida, Gray Building, Tallahassee
DOCS	Documents, Maps and Micromaterials Department, Robert M. Strozier Library, Florida State University, Tallahassee
FGS	Florida Geological Survey
FHQ	*Florida Historical Quarterly*
Floridian	*Tallahassee Floridian*
GPO	Government Printing Office, Washington
PKY	P. K. Yonge Library of Florida History, University of Florida, Gainesville
Sentinel	Tallahassee *Florida Sentinel*
SPC	Special Collections Department, Robert M. Strozier Library, Florida State University, Tallahassee
USDA	U.S. Department of Agriculture
USGS	U.S. Geological Survey
WL	Woodbury Lowery Manuscripts, transcribed from the Archivo General de Indias, microfilm, Documents, Maps and Micromaterials Department, Robert M. Strozier Library, Florida State University, Tallahassee

Manuscript records in the Office of Circuit Court Clerk in Gadsden County (Quincy), Jackson County (Marianna), Jefferson County (Monticello), Leon County (Tallahassee), and Madison County (Madison) are cited by the name of the county, followed by Deed Book, Probate Court, or Superior Court and a further description of the document.

Notes

1. Piedmont Florida

1. Sidney Lanier, *Florida: Its Scenery, Climate, and History* (1875; repr., Gainesville: University of Florida Press, 1973), pp. 103–105.

2. Bradford Torrey, *A Florida Sketch-Book* (Boston: Houghton Mifflin, 1894), pp. 207–208.

3. "From Pensacola to St. Augustine in 1827: A Journey of the Rt. Rev. Michael Portier," *FHQ* 26 (October 1947):150.

4. Maurice Thompson, *A Tallahassee Girl* (Boston: Houghton Mifflin, 1881), pp. 5–6, 40–51.

5. Section 2, 2N1W, on the Lake Jackson, Fla., Quadrangle, USGS topographical map.

6. Roland M. Harper, "The Geography and Vegetation of Northern Florida," *Sixth Annual Report* (Tallahassee: FGS, 1914), pp. 266–67, 270.

7. *Seventh Census*, 1850 (Washington, D.C.: Robert Armstrong, 1853), 1:408.

8. Lanier, *Florida: Its Scenery, Climate*, pp. 106–108.

9. Robert O. Vernon, director, Florida Bureau of Geology, interview, 5 July 1973.

10. John Lee Williams, *A View of West Florida* (1827; repr., Gainesville: University Presses of Florida, 1976), p. 79.

11. Clifton Paisley, *From Cotton to Quail: An Agricultural Chronicle of Leon County, Florida, 1860–1967* (Gainesville: University of Florida Press, 1968), pp. 20–22 and note pp. 21–22.

12. Mrs. Colin English, interview, 4 June 1973.

13. Williams, *View of West Florida*, p. 33; B. Calvin Jones, archaeologist, Florida Division of Archives, History, and Records Management, interview, 1 December 1978.

14. From Betty Watts, *The Watery Wilderness of Apalach, Florida* (Tallahassee: Apalach Books, 1975).

15. Charles W. Hendry, Jr., director, Florida Bureau of Geology, interview, 14 May 1973; Hendry and Charles R. Sproul, *Geology and Ground-Water Resour-*

ces of Leon County, Florida, Bulletin no. 47 (Tallahassee: FGS, 1966).

16. E. H. Sellards, early state geologist, in "Some Florida Lakes and Lake Basins," *Third Annual Report* (Tallahassee: FGS, 1910), pp. 43–76.

17. Sellards, "Geology between the Ochlockonee and Aucilla Rivers in Florida," *Ninth Annual Report* (Tallahassee: FGS, 1917), pp. 85–139, and "Geology between the Apalachicola River and Ochlockonee River," *Tenth Annual Report* (Tallahassee: FGS, 1918), pp. 11–55.

18. Wayne E. Moore, *Geology of Jackson County, Florida*, Bulletin no. 37 (Tallahassee: FGS, 1955), pp. 7–8, 14–16.

19. Harper, "Vegetation of Northern Florida," pp. 163–437.

20. Ibid., pp. 193–200.

21. Ibid., pp. 201–209.

22. Ibid., pp. 210–11.

23. Ibid., pp. 229–41.

24. Ibid., pp. 254–65.

25. Ibid., pp. 266, 270, 278.

26. Ibid., pp. 254–65.

27. See Paul Murray, "Agriculture in the Interior of Georgia, 1830–1860," *Georgia Historical Quarterly* 19 (December 1935):293; Kenneth K. Krakow, *Georgia Place Names* (Macon: Winship Press, 1975), p. 189.

28. Kathleen T. Iseri and W. B. Langbein, *Large Rivers of the United States*, USGS Circular 686 (Washington, D.C.: GPO, 1974), p. 9.

29. Allen Morris, *The Florida Handbook, 1981–1982* (Tallahassee: Peninsular Publishing, 1981), p. 434.

30. *Florida Lakes, Part III, Gazetteer* (Tallahassee: Florida Division of Water Resources, 1969), pp. 31–40.

31. Elmer O. Fippin and Aldert S. Root, "Soil Survey of Gadsden County," USDA Bureau of Soils, *Field Operations of the Bureau of Soils, 1903* (Washington, D.C.: GPO, 1904), pp. 331–53; Henry J. Wilder et al., "Soil Survey of Leon County," USDA Bureau of Soils, *Field Operations of the Bureau of Soils, 1905* (Washington, D.C.: GPO, 1907), pp. 363–88.

2. The Nation of Apalachee, Narváez, and De Soto

1. Lanier, *Florida: Its Scenery, Climate*, p. 115; *Tallahassee Floridian and Journal*, 25 May 1850.

2. Herman Gunter, "Once Roamed Land of Sunshine," *Florida Highways*, August 1941, pp. 13, 35–36.

3. C. Vance Haynes, "Elephant Hunting in North America," *Scientific American*, June 1966, pp. 104–12; Albert Ernest Jenks in collaboration with Mrs. H. H. Simpson, Sr., "Beveled Artifacts in Florida of the Same Type as Artifacts Found near Clovis, New Mexico," *American Antiquity* 6 (April 1941):314–19.

4. Wilfred T. Neill, "A Stratified Site at Silver Springs, Florida," *Florida Anthropologist* 11 (June 1958):33–52.

5. Wilfred T. Neill, "The Association of Suwannee Points and Extinct Animals in Florida," *Florida Anthropologist* 17 (March 1964):17–32.

6. Stanley J. Olsen, "The Wakulla Cave," *Natural History*, August 1958, pp. 396–98, 401–403.

7. Wally Jenkins, interview, Wakulla Springs, 14 December 1974; memorandum, Jenkins, Panama City, Fla., to the author, 13 November 1974.

8. C. J. Clausen et al., "Little Salt Spring, Florida: A Unique Underwater Site," *Science*, 16 February 1979, pp. 609–14.

9. Wayne T. Grissett, amateur archaeologist, interview, 13 July 1974.

10. Louis Daniel Tesar, *The Leon County Bicentennial Survey Report: An Archaeological Survey of Selected Portions of Leon County, Florida*, Florida Bureau of Historic Sites and Properties Miscellaneous Project Report Series, no. 49, rev. ed. (Tallahassee: Florida Division of Archives, History, and Records Management, 1980), pp. 33, 575–76 (hereafter cited as *Archaeological Survey*).

11. Ibid., pp. 34–35, 794–95, 840.

12. Gordon R. Willey and Richard B. Woodbury, "A Chronological Outline for the Northwest Florida Gulf Coast," *American Antiquity* 7 (January 1942):232–54; Willey, *Archeology of the Florida Gulf Coast*, Smithsonian Miscellaneous Collections, vol. 113 (Washington, D.C.: GPO, 1949).

13. Jerald T. Milanich, "Life in a Ninth Century Indian Household: A Weeden Island Fall-Winter Site on the Upper Apalachicola River, Florida," Florida Bureau of Historic Sites and Properties, *Bulletin* no. 4 (Tallahassee: Florida Division of Archives, History, and Records Management, 1974), pp. 1–44.

14. John F. Scarry, "Subsistence Costs and Information: A Preliminary Model of Fort Walton Development" (paper presented at the Thirty-seventh Annual Southeastern Archaeological Conference, New Orleans, 1980), pp. 9–18.

15. James B. Griffin, "Culture Periods in Eastern United States Archeology," in *Archeology of the Eastern United States*, ed. James B. Griffin (Chicago: University of Chicago Press, 1952), pp. 352–64; John W. Griffin, "The Historic Archaeology of Florida," in *The Florida Indian and His Neighbors*, ed. John W. Griffin (Winter Park: Inter-American Center, 1949), pp. 45–47.

16. Willey, *Archeology of the Florida Gulf Coast*, pp. 95–97, 284–85, 452–69; Scarry, "Fort Walton Culture: A Redefinition" (paper delivered at the Thirty-seventh Annual Southeastern Archaeological Conference, New Orleans, 1980), pp. 10–25, map, fig. 2, p. 28; Larry Letchworth, interview, 10 February 1974.

17. John W. Griffin, "Test Excavations at the Lake Jackson Site," *American Antiquity* 16 (October 1950):99–112.

18. B. Calvin Jones, interview, 6 November 1975; talk (the author's notes), First Regional Convention and Symposium, Archaeological Institute of America, Tallahassee, 7 May 1976; Jerald T. Milanich and Charles H. Fairbanks, *Florida Archaeology* (New York: Academic Press, 1980), pp. 198–99.

19. See Tesar, *Archaeological Survey*, pp. 199–200, 244, on the change from Mississippian to Apalachee and some possible explanations for the disappearance of the former.

20. John R. Swanton, *Early History of the Creek Indians and Their Neighbors*, Smithsonian Institution Bureau of American Ethnology Bulletin no. 73 (Washington, D.C.: GPO, 1922), pp. 109–10. Both the mound builders and the Apalachee are included in the culture called Fort Walton.

21. Tesar, *Archaeological Survey*, pp. 617–18.

22. *A Seventeenth Century Letter of Gabriel Díaz Vara Calderón, Bishop of Cuba, Describing the Indian Missions of Florida*, trans. Lucy L. Wenhold, with an introduction by John R. Swanton, Smithsonian Miscellaneous Collections, vol. 95, no. 16 (Washington, D.C.: Smithsonian Institution, 1936), p. 13 (hereafter cited as *Calderón*).

23. Milanich and Fairbanks, *Florida Archaeology*, p. 230.

24. *Calderón*, pp. 12–13.

25. Gary Shapiro, *Archaeology at San Luis*, vol. 2: *The Apalachee Council House*, Florida Archaeology Series, Bureau of Archaeological Research (Tallahassee: Florida Department of State [forthcoming]).

26. *Calderón*, p. 12; S. H. Katz, M. L. Hediger, and L. A. Valleroy, "Traditional Maize Processing Techniques in the New World," *Science*, 12 May 1974, pp. 765–73.

27. *Calderón*, p. 7.

28. "The Narrative of Alvar Nuñez Cabeza de Vaca," in Frederick W. Hodge and Theodore H. Lewis, eds., *Spanish Explorers in the Southern United States, 1528–1543* (1907; repr., New York: Barnes & Noble, 1946), pp. 18–30 (hereafter cited as *Cabeza de Vaca*).

29. Ibid., pp. 31–32. B. Calvin Jones established the probable location of Ivitachuco (interview, 3 August 1971).

30. *Cabeza de Vaca*, pp. 33–126.

31. The route of De Soto through Florida is discussed in detail, pp. 117–60, in *Final Report of the De Soto Expedition Commission*, John R. Swanton, chairman (Washington, D.C.: GPO, 1939). In the present account I generally rely on the route suggested by Swanton, although it is controversial.

32. "A Narrative of De Soto's Expedition Based on the Diary of Rodrigo Ranjel, His Private Secretary," in *Narratives of the Career of Hernando de Soto in the Conquest of Florida*, ed. Edward Gaylord Bourne, 2 vols. (1904; repr., New York: Allerton, 1922), vol. 2, p. 78 (hereafter cited as *Ranjel*).

33. "The Narrative of the Expedition of Hernando de Soto, by the Gentleman of Elvas," in *Spanish Explorers in the Southern United States*, p. 160 (hereafter cited as *Elvas*).

34. Garcilaso de la Vega, *The Florida of the Inca*, trans. and ed. John Grier Varner and Jeanette Johnson Varner (Austin: University of Texas Press, 1951), p. 175 (hereafter cited as *Garcilaso*).

35. "Relation of the Conquest of Florida Presented by Luys Hernandez de Biedma in the Year 1544," in *Narratives of the Career of De Soto*, vol. 2, p. 6 (hereafter cited as *Biedma*).

36. *Ranjel*, p. 78.

37. B. Calvin Jones, interview, 3 August 1971.

38. *Garcilaso*, pp. 175–81.

39. *Elvas*, p. 161; *Garcilaso*, p. 182.

40. *Garcilaso*, pp. 182–83.

41. B. Calvin Jones, interviews, 7 July, 15 September 1987, 1 April 1988.

42. Ibid.

43. Paisley, *Cotton to Quail*, n., p. 9; Leon Deed Book N, pp. 114, 475.

44. *Ranjel*, p. 82; *Garcilaso*, pp. 187–92; *Biedma*, p. 7; *Elvas*, p. 162; *De Soto Commission*, pp. 114–16.

45. *Garcilaso*, pp. 342, 627.

46. Ibid., p. 260.

3. The Cross in the Hills

1. Charlton W. Tebeau, *A History of Florida* (Coral Gables: University of Miami Press, 1971), pp. 33–34, 43–48.

2. *Francisco Pareja's 1613 Confessionario: A Documentary Source for Timucuan Ethnography*, ed. Jerald T. Milanich and William C. Sturtevant, trans. Emilio F. Moran (Tallahassee: Florida Division of Archives, History, and Records Management, 1972), pp. 23, 29, 34.

3. Luis Gerónimo de Oré, *The Martyrs of Florida, 1513–1616* [1619?], repr., ed. and trans. Maynard J. Geiger, Franciscan Studies, no. 18 (New York: J. F. Wagner, 1936), pp. 112–13.

4. Ibid., pp. 114–17.

5. Horruytiner to the King, 15 November 1633, WL, transcribed from the Archivo General de Indias, Library of Congress, Microfilm 502, DOCS.

6. *Pirates, Indians, and Spaniards: Father Escobedo's "La Florida,"* ed. James W. Covington (St. Petersburg: Great Outdoors, 1963), p. 152.

7. Michael V. Gannon, *The Cross in the Sand: The Early Catholic Church in Florida, 1513–1870* (Gainesville: University of Florida Press, 1965), p. 37.

8. Horruytiner to the King, 24 June 1637, WL.

9. Governor Damián de la Vega Castro y Pardo to the King, 22 August 1639, in Manuel Serrano y Sanz, ed., *Documentos Históricos de la Florida y la Luisiana Siglos XVI al XVIII* (Madrid: Suárez, 1912), pp. 198–201.

10. Ibid.; John Gilmary Shea, *History of the Catholic Church in the United States*, 4 vols. (New York: Shea, 1886), 1:164; B. Calvin Jones, *Archives and History News*, November–December 1970, pp. 1–2.

11. "Note on the Florida Missions, 1655," in Serrano y Sanz, *Documentos Históricos*, pp. 132–33.

12. Mark F. Boyd, Hale G. Smith, and John W. Griffin, *Here They Once Stood: The Tragic End of the Apalachee Missions* (Gainesville: University of Florida Press, 1951), n. 77, pp. 101–102. Boyd laid the basis for all subsequent archaeological investigations of the Apalachee missions. San Luis was the only known site when he started a search in 1939. Nearly all of the Apalachee missions have now been located.

13. Boyd, Smith, and Griffin, *Here They Once Stood*, pp. 10–13; Jones, *Archives and History News*, November–December 1972, pp. 1–2.

14. Boyd, Smith, and Griffin, *Here They Once Stood*, p. 111; B. Calvin Jones, interview, 3 August 1971. This interesting site, dug by Jones, deserves additional archaeological study and would lend itself, like San Luis, to restoration.

15. Boyd himself was instrumental in finding the site of this mission and participated with Smith and Griffin in digging it. See Boyd, Smith, and Griffin, *Here They Once Stood*, pp. 105–36.

16. Jones, interview; L. Ross Morrell, and B. Calvin Jones, "San Juan de Aspalaga (A Preliminary Architectural Study)," Florida Bureau of Historic Sites and Properties *Bulletin* no. 1 (Tallahassee: Division of Archives, History, and Records Management, 1970), pp. 25–43.

17. Jones, interview.

18. Ibid.

19. See my chapter 2.

20. Religious of the Province to the King, 10 September 1657, Rebolledo to the King, 18 October 1657, WL; Robert Allen Matter, "The Spanish Missions of Florida: The Friars versus the Governors in the 'Golden Age,' 1606–1690" (Ph.D. diss., University of Washington, 1972), pp. 146–49.

21. Matter, "Friars versus the Governors," p. 107.

22. Herbert E. Bolton, "The Mission as a Frontier Institution in the Spanish American Colonies," in John Francis Bannon, ed., *Bolton and the Spanish Borderlands* (Norman: University of Oklahoma Press, 1964), p. 200.

23. Governor Pablo de Hita Salazar to the king, 10 November 1678, trans. Swanton, in *Creeks and Their Neighbors*, pp. 299–304.

24. Verner W. Crane, *The Southern Frontier, 1670–1732* (Ann Arbor: University of Michigan Press, Ann Arbor Paperbacks, 1956), pp. 3–38.

25. Matter, "Friars versus Governors," pp. 271–75; Lucy L. Wenhold, "The First Fort of San Marcos de Apalache," *FHQ* 34 (April 1956):301–14.

26. Boyd, Smith, and Griffin, *Here They Once Stood*, pp. 20–24, 143–44.

27. Amy Bushnell, "The Menéndez Marquéz Cattle Barony at La Chua and the Determinants of Economic Expansion in Seventeenth Century Florida," *FHQ* 56 (April 1978):407–31; Bushnell, *The King's Coffer: Proprietors of the Spanish Florida Treasury, 1565–1702* (Gainesville: University Presses of Florida, 1981), pp. 14, 19. Bushnell's research is in a fruitful field of inquiry that was opened in 1961 by Charles W. Arnade in "Cattle Raising in Spanish Florida, 1513–1763," *Agricultural History* 35 (July 1961):116–24, reprinted as publication no. 21, St. Augustine Historical Society, 1965.

28. Boyd, Smith, and Griffin, *Here They Once Stood*, pp. 24–26.

29. Ibid., pp. 25, 26.

30. Crane, *Southern Frontier*, p. 74.

31. Ibid., pp. 71–79.

32. Boyd, Smith, and Griffin, *Here They Once Stood*, pp. 15–16, 48–50, 91–95.

33. Ibid., pp. 49–50, 74–80, 91–95.

34. Ibid., p. 78.

35. Ibid., pp. 50–53, 59.

36. Ibid., pp. 81–82.

37. Amy Bushnell, "Patricio de Hinachuba: Defender of the Word of God, the Crown of the King, and the Little Children of Ivitachuco," *American Indian Culture and Research Journal* 3, no. 3 (1979):1–21.

38. Boyd, Smith, and Griffin, *Here They Once Stood*, pp. 56–59.

4. The Old Fields of Apalachee

1. "Diego Peña's Expedition to Apalachee and Apalachicolo in 1716," ed. and trans. Mark F. Boyd, *FHQ* 28 (July 1949):13–19; Boyd, Smith, and Griffin, *Here They Once Stood*, p. 78; B. Calvin Jones, interview, 3 August 1971.

2. "Diego Peña's Expedition," pp. 5–7; Crane, *Southern Frontier*, p. 185; John Jay TePaske, *The Governorship of Spanish Florida, 1700–1763* (Durham: Duke University Press, 1964), pp. 204–205; Swanton, *Creeks and Their Neighbors*, p. 127. San Juan de Guacara was evidently a relocation of the one-time mission town on the Suwannee (Guacara) River. Suwannee seems to have been a corruption of "San Juan," while Guacara, as pronounced by the Indians, became Wakulla, the present name of the river in the county of the same name (J. Clarence Simpson, *A Provisional Gazetteer of Florida Place-Names of Indian Derivation*, Special Publication no. 1 [Tallahassee: FGS, 1956], pp. 101–102, 122).

3. Mark F. Boyd, "The Fortifications of San Marcos de Apalache," *FHQ* 15 (July 1936):11; Boyd, "Apalachee during the British Occupation," *FHQ* 12 (January 1934):114–16.

4. The British experience at St. Marks is related in the correspondence of its commandants, edited by Boyd, in "From a Remote Frontier" appearing in eight issues of *FHQ*, vols. 19, 20, 21, from January 1941 to October 1942.

5. "A Sketch of the Entrance From the Sea to Apalachy and Part of the Environs Taken by George Gauld, Esq., Surveyor of the Coast, and Lieutenant Philip Pittman, Assistant Engineer, 1767," the Gauld-Pittman Map, original, William M. Clements Library, University of Michigan, Ann Arbor, copy, DOCS.

6. The Stuart-Purcell Map, in the Public Records Office, London, is reprinted, along with descriptive notes of the mapmakers, in Mark F. Boyd, ed., "A Map of the Road from Pensacola to St. Augustine, 1778," *FHQ* 17 (July 1938):15–23 and nine plates.

7. Gauld-Pittman Map; interview with a store clerk, Wakulla, Florida, 2 February 1974.

8. Boyd, "A Map of the Road," p. 18.

9. Charles H. Fairbanks, *Ethnohistorical Report of the Florida Indians*, Indian Claims Commission Dockets 73, 151 (New York: Garland, 1974), pp. 4, 6, 49, 120–21, 131–32. The name "Seminole" came from the Spanish *Cimarrones*, or "wild ones," as this Spanish name was pronounced by the Indians and then spelled by the English (p. 4).

10. Mark F. Boyd and José Navarro Latorre, "Spanish Interest in British

Florida, and in the Progress of the American Revolution," *FHQ* 32 (July 1953):92–130.

11. David H. Corkran, *The Creek Frontier, 1540–1783* (Norman: University of Oklahoma Press, 1967), pp. 288–319.

12. Boyd and Latorre, "Spanish Interest in British Florida," pp. 94–97, 109–15.

13. Howard F. Cline, *Notes on Colonial Indians and Communities in Florida, 1700–1821*, Indian Claims Commission Docket 280 (New York: Garland, 1974), pp. 96–100.

14. Lawrence Kinnaird, "The Significance of William Augustus Bowles' Seizure of Panton's Apalachee Store in 1792," *FHQ* 9 (January 1931):156–92.

15. John Walton Caughey, *McGillivray of the Creeks* (Norman: University of Oklahoma Press, 1938), pp. 10, 20–24, 43.

16. J. Leitch Wright, Jr., *William Augustus Bowles, Director General of the Creek Nation* (Athens: University of Georgia Press, 1967), pp. 1–18, 32–34, 56–65.

17. Ibid., pp. 65–67, 74–75, 80–92; Caughey, *McGillivray of the Creeks*, p. 308. I quote Panton from Panton to McGillivray, Pensacola, 9 February 1792.

18. Wright, *William Augustus Bowles*, pp. 107–16.

19. Ibid., pp. 116, 124–25, 127–28.

20. Ibid., pp. 128–32. The pipe story was passed along by Ellen Call Long in *Florida Breezes; or, Florida, New and Old* (1883; repr. Gainesville: University of Florida Press, 1962), p. 41.

21. Wright, *William Augustus Bowles*, pp. 134–36, 145–49, 162–67, 170–71.

5. Andrew Jackson's Leisurely "Wolf Hunt" in the Red Hills

1. James F. Doster, *The Creek Indians and Their Florida Lands, 1740–1823*, 2 vols., Indian Land Claims Commission, Docket 280 (New York: Garland, 1974), 1:244–65.

2. Mark F. Boyd, "Events at Prospect Bluff on the Apalachicola River, 1808–1818: An Introduction to Twelve Letters of Edmund Doyle," *FHQ* 16 (October 1937):61–65; John C. Upchurch, "Aspects of the Development and Exploration of the Forbes Purchase," *FHQ* 48 (October 1969):117–39.

3. Hubert Bruce Fuller, *The Purchase of Florida: Its History and Diplomacy* (1906; repr., Gainesville: University of Florida Press, 1964), pp. 203–209.

4. Ibid., pp. 228–29; James Parton, *Life of Andrew Jackson*, 3 vols. (New York: Mason Brothers, 1860), 2:397–407.

5. Parton, *Andrew Jackson*, 2:407–10; John Spencer Bassett, *The Life of Andrew Jackson* (1911; repr., Hamden, Conn.: Archon Books, 1967), pp. 123–24.

6. Parton, *Andrew Jackson*, 2:391–97.

7. Ibid., pp. 411–21; Doster, *Creek Indians and Their Lands*, 2:192. Doster summarizes documentary material about the background of the First Seminole War and the events in it. Most of the documents can be found in *ASP, Military Affairs*, 1:673–769.

8. Doster, *Creek Indians and Their Lands*, 2:196–98. The quoted passages appear on pp. 197 and 198, respectively.

9. Ibid., p. 198.

10. Ibid., pp. 198–200.

11. Parton, *Andrew Jackson*, 2:428–29.

12. Ibid., pp. 429–31.

13. Ibid., pp. 432–43. Jackson's own readiness to undertake this "wolf hunt" is expressed in his letter of 16 December 1817 to Secretary of War Calhoun, *ASP, Military Affairs*, 1:689.

14. Mark F. Boyd brought to light and, with Gerald M. Ponton, edited Captain Young's "A Topographical Memoir on East and West Florida With Itineraries of General Jackson's Army, 1818," which was published in three issues (July and October 1934 and January 1935) of *FHQ*, 13:16–50, 82–104, and 129–64.

15. Parton, *Andrew Jackson*, 2:443–45.

16. "Young's Topographical Memoir," pp. 140–42.

17. Ibid., pp. 142–43. Information about Jackson's marching style appears in John Henry Eaton, *The Life of Andrew Jackson* (1824; repr., New York: Arno Press, 1971), p. 58.

18. "Young's Topographical Memoir," p. 88 and n. 25, p. 142.

19. Ibid., pp. 83–84. I quote page 84.

20. *ASP, Military Affairs*, 1:699–700.

21. Ibid., pp. 703–704; Parton, *Andrew Jackson*, 2:449–50; Doster, *Creek Indians and Their Lands*, 2:209.

22. Parton, *Andrew Jackson*, 2:450–53.

23. Ibid., pp. 459–63.

24. Ibid., 2:413–17, 431, 453–55. This Jackson biographer depends for much of his account of the events around St. Marks on J. B. Rodgers's diary (nn. p. 454 and 461).

25. Ibid., 2:455–58; Fuller, *The Purchase of Florida*, pp. 248–49.

26. Parton, *Andrew Jackson*, 2:462–80.

27. Ibid., pp. 480–83.

28. T. Frederick Davis, "Milly Francis and Duncan McKrimmon: An Authentic Florida Pocahontas," *FHQ* 21 (January 1943):254–65.

29. Parton, *Andrew Jackson*, 2:489, 498–504; Doster, *Creek Indians and Their Lands*, 2:210.

30. "Young's Topographical Memoir," pp. 33–34, 101–102.

31. Ibid., pp. 47–48.

32. Springtime Tallahassee, held annually, is no Mardi Gras, but is something of an imitation. At the head of a parade starting off the festive activities about 1 April rides "Andrew Jackson" instead of Rex.

6. The Spring Creek Trail

1. Wirt to John Coalter, 25 October 1819, *American Historical Review* 25 (July 1920):692–95.

2. "The Defences of the Floridas: A Report of Captain James Gadsden, Aide-de-camp to General Andrew Jackson, Nashville, 1 August 1818," *FHQ* 15 (April 1937):247.

3. Soil types found frequently in Jackson County west of the Chipola River are Red Bay, Orangeburg, and Dothan (former Jackson County Agent Leonard Cobb to the author, 7 December 1987).

4. Record Book 2, Proceedings of the Florida Land Claims Commission, Florida Division of State Lands, Title and Land Records Section, Tallahassee, pp. 104–44.

5. "Newnansville and Tallahassee Land Office Receivers' Receipts," WPA Typescripts, no. 33, DDR, Receipts nos. 271, 349, 392. In a few instances, such as that of John Williams, no claim was filed, but the testimony indicates that another claim would "interfere" with his settlement.

6. Thomas Perkins Abernethy, *The Formative Period in Alabama, 1815–1828*, 2d ed. (University: University of Alabama Press, 1965), pp. 34–40, 64–66.

7. Robert Preston Brooks, *History of Georgia* (1913; repr., Spartanburg, S.C.: Reprint, 1972), pp. 11–12, 188.

8. E. L. Williams of Valdosta, Ga., telephone interview, 5 January 1977, Williams to the author, 28 April 1984.

9. This manuscript census is in the Office of the Jackson County Circuit Court Clerk, Marianna.

10. Record Book 2. McDonald is included among these seventeen.

11. The late Mrs. Sam (Lora Richards Metcalf) Gay, Altha, Fla., to the author, 3 January 1977, and her sister, the late Mrs. Mary Blackman, Tallahassee, interview, 16 January 1977.

12. As reported by Governor William P. DuVal in 1826, the totals were Jackson County 2,236, Gadsden County 1,374, and Leon County 996; Dorothy Dodd, "The Florida Census of 1825," *FHQ* 22 (July 1943):34–40.

13. *Pensacola Gazette and West Florida Advertiser*, 9 April 1825.

14. J. Randall Stanley, *History of Jackson County* (Marianna, Fla.: Jackson County Historical Society, 1950), p. 72.

15. Floie Criglar (Mrs. John C.) Packard, Marianna, to the author, 22 February 1977; Stanley, *History of Jackson County*, p. 10 and n. 3.

16. Bettie D. (Mrs. C. M.) Dekle, Marianna, to the author, 2 January 1977.

17. *Pensacola Gazette and West Florida Advertiser*, 1 February 1826.

18. *Florida Territorial Acts, 1822*, p. 5; *Pensacola Floridian*, 8 March 1823.

19. *Pensacola Floridian*, 26 April, 3 May 1823.

20. Stanley, *History of Jackson County*, p. 43.

21. Ibid., pp. 43–49.

22. *ASP, Public Lands*, 4:448, 450; "General Plan of the Little River Survey in Forbes Purchase, Gadsden County" by Daniel McNeil, 1824. See front endpapers of Miles Kenan Womack, Jr., *Gadsden: A Florida County in Word and Picture* (Quincy, Fla.: Gadsden County Bicentennial Committee, 1976).

23. Herbert J. Doherty, Jr., *Richard Keith Call, Southern Unionist* (Gainesville: University of Florida Press, 1961), pp. 46–48, and T. Frederick Davis, "Pioneer Florida: First Militia Organization," *FHQ* 24 (April 1946):291.

24. Fifth Census, 1830, Florida, Manuscript Schedules, p. 143.

25. *Tallahassee Floridian*, 3 January 1832.

26. Ibid., 9 March 1833.

27. Ibid., 27 April 1830.

28. George M. Chapin, *Florida, 1513–1913: Past, Present, and Future*, 2 vols. (Chicago: S. J. Clarke, 1914), 2:87; Watt Marchman, "The *Florida Historical Quarterly*, 1856–1861, 1879, 1902–1940," biographical appendix, *FHQ* 19 (July 1940):59; *FHQ* 34 (October 1955):204.

29. Gadsden Probate, Old Book 7, inventories, pp. 58–80; Old Will Book, 1834–51, pp. 74–75.

30. *ASP, Public Lands*, 4:451; Record Book 2, p. 111; Stanley, *History of Jackson County*, pp. 19–20.

31. *ASP, Public Lands*, 4:448.

32. Ibid., p. 449; "Little River Survey"; Gadsden Probate Old Will Book, 1826–31, pp. 5–6.

33. *ASP, Public Lands*, 4:451.

34. W. H. Simmons and John Lee Williams, "The Selection of Tallahassee as the Capital," *FHQ* 1 (April 1908):34–35.

35. *Pensacola Floridian*, 13 April 1822, quoting the Darien *Gazette*.

36. Joy S. Paisley, *The Cemeteries of Leon County, Florida* (Tallahassee: Dominie Everardus Bogardus Chapter, Colonial Dames XVII Century, 1978), p. 120.

37. The information about Robinson and Lines comes principally from the late Sally Lines (Mrs. Edward E.) Thomas of Tallahassee and from Blucher Lines of Quincy (interview, 24 August 1976). See *Floridian*, 2 January 1832.

38. Gadsden Probate Old Record Book 5, County Court Proceedings, January 1832–February 1837, p. 39, Book 7, inventories, pp. 28–29.

39. Simmons and Williams, "Selection of Tallahassee," p. 18.

40. See Rowland H. Rerick, *Memoirs of Florida*, ed. Francis P. Fleming, 2 vols. (Atlanta, Ga.: Southern Historical Association, 1902), 1:722; Mrs. Fletcher Freeman, Havana, Fla., interview, 26 August 1976. Mrs. Freeman owns the White diary. The excerpts are from the Works Progress Administration Historical Records Survey typescript no. 22 of the WPA Typescripts, "Diary of D. L. White, July 1835–June 1842," DDR, pp. 39, 45, 50, 62, 67.

41. Charles Hentz, "My Autobiography," original in the Hentz Family Papers, Southern Historical Collection, Library of the University of North Carolina, Chapel Hill, gift of Hal Hentz. A photocopy and typescript by a grandson of Hentz, the late Charles T. Carroll of Maitland, Fla., are in SPC. The typescript, which I will cite hereafter, is in two volumes. The account of White's death appears in vol. 1, p. 338.

42. "Land Office Receipts," pp. 73–84; David A. Avant, Jr., *Illustrated Index, J. Randall Stanley's History of Gadsden County* (Tallahassee: L'Avant Studios, 1985), pp. 30–34 (hereafter cited as Stanley, *History of Gadsden County*).

43. George White, *Statistics of the State of Georgia* (1849; Spartanburg, S.C.: Reprint, 1972), pp. 364–65.

44. Steve Edwards, Tallahassee, interview, 10 April 1976; Stanley, *History of Gadsden County*, pp. 24–25.

45. Miss Sara May Love, Quincy, interview, 2 April 1976.

46. The late Miss Eloise McGriff, Tallahassee, interview, 25 August 1976.

47. Ibid., *Floridian*, 23 April 1840; Mrs. Fletcher Freeman, interview, 25 August 1976.

48. Fifth Census, 1830, Florida, Manuscript Schedules, pp. 142, 144, 147, 148, 149, 152.

7. The Complaint of Neamathla

1. Sidney Walter Martin, *Florida during Territorial Days* (Athens: University of Georgia Press, 1944), pp. 16–22; Robert V. Remini, *Andrew Jackson and the Course of American Empire, 1767–1821* (New York: Harper & Row, 1977), p. 408.

2. John B. Galbraith, "The History of Leon County," *Floridian*, 9 April 1853; Caroline Brevard, *A History of Florida from the Treaty of 1763 to Our Own Times*, ed. James A. Robertson, 2 vols. (Deland, Fla.: Florida State Historical Society, 1924–25), 1:50.

3. Andrew Jackson to the Secretary of War, Pensacola, 20 September 1821, with enclosures, *ASP, Indian Affairs*, 2:412–14.

4. "Treaty with the Florida Indians," 1823, *ASP, Indian Affairs*, 2:439.

5. Jackson to the Secretary of War, 20 September 1821, *ASP, Indian Affairs*, 2:413.

6. "Treaty with the Florida Indians," *ASP, Indian Affairs*, 2:429–35.

7. Ibid., pp. 436–42.

8. Martin, *Florida during Territorial Days*, pp. 35–36, 56, 60; Simmons and Williams, "Selection of Tallahassee," *FHQ* 1 (April 1908), Act of the Legislative Council, pp. 26–27 (quoted), journal of Commissioner W. H. Simmons, p. 35 (quoted).

9. Simmons and Williams, "Selection of Tallahassee," *FHQ* 1 (July 1908):19–20, journal of Commissioner John Lee Williams.

10. Ibid., p. 21; Simmons's journal, April 1908, p. 36.

11. Williams's journal, July 1908, p. 23; Williams, Pensacola, to Call, 20 November 1823, in Brevard, *History of Florida*, 1:265–66.

12. David Y. Thomas, "Report on the Public Archives of Florida," *Annual Report of the American Historical Association for the Year 1906*, 2 vols. (Washington, D.C.: GPO, 1908), 2:149–58. Thomas found a letter of 3 August 1824 in a file of DuVal's letters at the capitol. Since these were subsequently lost, Thomas's brief summary of this one is important in establishing the reason why the site of Tallahassee was picked for the territorial capital.

13. *Pensacola Gazette and West Florida Advertiser*, 24 September 1825.

14. Ibid., 11 December 1824.

15. See *Tallahassee Floridian*, 11, 18 May 1850, about Wyatt; *Pensacola Gazette and West Florida Advertiser*, 26 June, 24, 31 July 1824, 26 February 1825.

16. Leon Deed Book A, p. 183; *Pensacola Gazette and West Florida Advertiser*, 26 February 1825.

17. *Pensacola Gazette and West Florida Advertiser*, 22 May, 26 June, 21 August, 23 October, 20 November 1824. See also Leon Deed Book A, p. 56, agreement of 20 December 1824, SW 1/4 Section 1 1S1W.

18. "Plan for the City of Tallahassee," ca. 1829, Library of Congress, copy in DOCS. This, an inset in what is usually called the "Searcy Map of Florida," is the only authority for the precise location of DuVal's house. The archaeologist B. Calvin Jones, fitting the Searcy Map to a modern-day one, suggested that the Myers Park site might have been the governor's residence (interview, 5 November 1974). The controversy over DuVal's acquisition of this land is related in Mary Lamar Davis, "Tallahassee through Territorial Days," *Apalachee* 1 (1944):47–61, and is briefly mentioned in documents associated with selection of Tallahassee as the capital in *FHQ* 1 (July 1908):33–35. See *Pensacola Gazette and West Florida Advertiser* of 7 August 1824, about "Mount Aventine."

19. Galbraith, "The History of Leon County." Also see Washington Irving, *Wolfert's Roost and Other Papers* (New York: G. P. Putnam, 1855); *Pensacola Gazette and West Florida Advertiser*, 17 April and 26 June 1824.

20. Leon Superior Court Minute Book 1, p. 1, 4 October 1824.

21. Frank B. Woodford, *Mr. Jefferson's Disciple: A Life of Justice Woodward* (East Lansing: Michigan State University Press, 1953); John W. Reps, *The Making of Urban America: A History of City Planning in the United States* (Princeton: Princeton University Press, 1965), pp. 263–71.

22. *Pensacola Gazette and West Florida Advertiser*, 11 December 1824 and 8 January 1825; Reps, *Making of Urban America*, pp. 160–63.

23. Governor DuVal to Secretary of War Calhoun, Pensacola, 12 January 1824; DuVal to Secretary of War, Pensacola, 11 April 1824; DuVal to Secretary of War, Pensacola, 18 June 1824, *ASP, Indian Affairs*, 2:615–18. "The Conspiracy of Neamathla" is a chapter in *Wolfert's Roost*, pp. 297–304.

24. DuVal to Secretary of War, St. Marks, 12 July 1824; DuVal to Secretary of War, Tallahassee, 22 July 1824; DuVal to Secretary of War, St. Marks, 29 July 1824, *ASP, Indian Affairs*, 2:618–21.

25. DuVal to Secretary of War, 29 July 1824, *ASP, Indian Affairs*, 2:620–21. In *Wolfert's Roost* Irving said that DuVal "seized him [Neamathla] by the hunting shirt" to make his point. Caroline Brevard said DuVal "sprang upon him, seized him by the throat, and thrust him out of the council" (*History of Florida*, vol. 1, p. 80).

26. Walton to DuVal, Tallahassee, 26 May 1825, *ASP, Indian Affairs*, 2:629; Walton to Colonel Thomas L. McKenney, superintendent of Indian Affairs, Tallahassee, 6 October 1825, ibid., pp. 636–37.

27. James D. Horan, *The McKenney-Hall Gallery of American Indians* (New York: Crown, 1972), p. 260.

28. Grant Foreman, *Indian Removal: The Emigration of the Five Civilized Tribes of Indians*, rev. ed. (Norman: University of Oklahoma Press, 1953), p. 148. The place is apparently in Russell County. See William A. Read, *Indian Place-*

Names in Alabama, rev. ed. (University: University of Alabama Press, 1984), p. 34.

29. Foreman, *Indian Removal*, pp. 140–53. The quoted passage comes from *Army and Navy Chronicle* 3, p. 126.

30. Foreman, *Indian Removal*, pp. 154–57.

8. Tallahassee and the "Old Dominion"

1. *Pensacola Gazette and West Florida Advertiser*, 26 February 1825.

2. Ibid.; *Niles' Register*, 1 October 1825.

3. Tallahassee *Florida Intelligencer*, 24 February 1826.

4. Ibid., 22 July 1826; "Compte de Castelnau in Middle Florida, 1837–1838," trans. Arthur R. Seymour, *FHQ* 26 (April 1948):316 and picture facing p. 316.

5. From an address by E. L. T. Blake, November 1878, in the "Pi" Williams Collection, compiled by Arthur Williams for the Tallahassee Centennial, 1924, DDR.

6. Tallahassee *Florida Intelligencer*, 22 July 1826.

7. *Niles' Register*, 18 March 1826.

8. *Floridian*, 7 December 1830.

9. Charles Joseph Latrobe, *The Rambler in North America, 1832–1833*, 2 vols. (New York: Harper & Brothers, 1835), 2:44.

10. Guyte McCord, Sr., "A Glimpse at the Labors of the Court of Appeals of the Territory of Florida," *Apalachee* 4 (1956):90–91.

11. Searcy, "Plan for Tallahassee."

12. Leon Deed Book E, p. 458.

13. The late Mrs. W. M. Macklin, among Tallahasseans who were brought together in 1971 to record their turn-of-the-century recollections of the once beautiful waterfall, said: "It wasn't a cascade at all, just a dangerous sinkhole" (*Tallahassee Democrat*, 6 April 1975).

14. Leon Deed Books B, p. 544, C, p. 64; Tallahassee *Florida Intelligencer*, 14 April 1826; *Floridian*, 28 March 1829.

15. Bertram Groene, *Ante-Bellum Tallahassee* (Tallahassee: Florida Heritage Foundation, 1971), pp. 19–21.

16. "Original Owners of Lots in the Northern Addition to the City of Tallahassee as shown by the books of Thomas Brown, trustee for the commissioners," photocopy, DOCS.

17. Searcy, "Plan for Tallahassee." The map had many mistakes. The two-hundred-foot-wide boulevard on the west side of town was called "Bolivard Street" (did Searcy tell the Baltimore printer of the map that this street should be named for Simon Bolivar, or did he just mean to call it "Boulevard"? In either case the printed map corrupted the name to "Bolivard"). For 150 years people with embarrassment tried to explain how "Boulevard Street" got such a peculiar name. The name was finally changed in 1984 to Martin Luther King, Jr., Boulevard.

18. T. Stanton Dietrich, *The Urbanization of Florida's Population: An Historical Perspective of County Growth, 1830–1970* (Gainesville: Bureau of Economic and Business Research, 1978), pp. 11–13; *Fifth Census, 1830* (Washington, D.C.: Duff Green, 1832), pp. 156–59; *Floridian*, 7 December 1830.

19. "A Tallahassee Alarm of 1836," William Chandler, Georgetown, D.C., to Julia J. Yonge, 17 May 1886, *FHQ* 8 (April 1930):197.

20. Tallahassee *Florida Intelligencer*, 24 February 1826; *Floridian*, 7 December 1830.

21. "Diary of Robert Raymond Reid, 1833 and 1835," WPA typescripts, No. 47, DDR, p. 64.

22. Ibid., pp. 4, 61–65; Joy S. Paisley, *Cemeteries of Leon County*, p. 64.

23. Susan Bradford Eppes, *The Negro of the Old South* (Chicago: Joseph G. Branch, 1925), pp. 64–72.

24. "R" in *Floridian*, 18 September 1883 (possibly Dr. James Randolph); Ulrich Bonnell Phillips and James David Glunt, eds., *Florida Plantation Records from the Papers of George Noble Jones* (St. Louis: Missouri Historical Society, 1927), pp. 531–32; Jefferson Deed Book A, p. 116.

25. Alfred Jackson Hanna, *A Prince in Their Midst: The Adventurous Life of Achille Murat on the American Frontier* (Norman: University of Oklahoma Press, 1946), pp. 7–10, 115–22; "R."

26. Gadsden's house is said to have stood on Barrington Road about one mile east of State Road 259.

27. Jerrell H. Shofner, *History of Jefferson County* (Tallahassee: Sentry Press, 1976), p. 26.

28. Alexander Brown, *The Cabells and Their Kin* (Richmond, Va.: Garrett and Massie, 1905), p. 627.

29. *Biographical Directory of the American Congress, 1774–1971* (Washington, D.C.: GPO, 1971), p. 1911.

30. Often a favorite stop on the popular home tours conducted every spring by the Jefferson County Historical Society.

31. William R. Taylor, *Cavalier and Yankee: The Old South and American National Character* (New York: Harper & Row, Harper Torchbooks, 1969), pp. 70–73, 78–79.

32. Jefferson Deed Book A, p. 3; Jerrell H. Shofner, *History of Jefferson County*, pp. 26–27.

33. Dumas Malone, *The Sage of Monticello*, vol. 6: *Jefferson and His Times* (Boston: Little, Brown, 1981), pp. 15, 287–90.

34. Randolph Whitfield and John Chipman, comps., "The Florida Randolphs," photocopy of typescript, 1978, DDR, records much of the experience of Eppes and Randolph and a little of that of Samuel Parkhill, on pp. 18, 32, 35–36, 41–44, 57 (quoted).

35. Ibid., pp. 35–36; David Y. Thomas, "A History of Banking in Florida," unpublished typescript, no date, SPC, pp. 24, 73; petition of the widow of Samuel Parkhill, Martha Ann, and newspaper advertisement 31 March 1842, for sale of the estate, File No. 163, DDR.

36. Amy Goodbody (Mrs. G. Lester) Patterson to the author, 7 August 1977.

37. Joy S. Paisley, *Cemeteries of Leon County*, p. 140.

38. Herbert J. Doherty, *Richard Keith Call*. This beautiful place has long been the home of former governor LeRoy Collins and his wife, Mary Call Collins, a great-granddaughter of the original owner. The state expects eventually to turn it into a museum. See *Tallahassee Democrat*, 15 January 1985.

39. Paisley, *Cotton to Quail*, p. 4.

40. *Floridian*, 28 February, 29 May 1832, 20 December 1834.

41. G. Lester Patterson, interview, 3 April 1977; Paisley, *Cotton to Quail*, p. 4.

42. In 1977 I received an inquiry from Mary Anne Brown of Chillicothe, Ohio, about this return address on letters of David Macomb. A search led me to Deed Book C, pp. 147–50, 512, for the location, and she and I exchanged information. This land, together with Southwood Plantation and Verdura, is part of the St. Joe Paper Company's Southwood Farm. The company announced plans in 1987 to turn its ninety-five hundred acres here into the largest residential, office, commercial, and industrial development in Leon County.

43. Tallahassee *Florida Intelligencer*, 22 July 1826.

44. "R," in *Floridian*, 18 September 1883; Hanna, *A Prince in Their Midst*, p. 153.

45. The *Floridian*, 17 March 1831, lists suits by eight creditors. Leon Superior Court Minute Book 1, p. 386, and Law File 540 record the saving of Eleanor's piano.

46. Andrew Forest Muir, "David Macomb, Frontiersman," *FHQ* 32 (January 1954):189–201.

47. *Pensacola Gazette and West Florida Advertiser*, 2 May 1828; *Niles' Register*, 4 July 1829.

48. *Floridian*, 7 January 1837.

49. Leon Superior Court Minute Book 1, p. 36.

50. Ibid., pp. 34, 40, 41, 46, 61, 62, 64, 66, 76; *Pensacola Gazette and West Florida Advertiser*, 26 October 1827, 16 May 1828.

51. Minute Book 1, pp. 34, 41, 43, 62, 64, 74, 75, 85, 87, 103, 111; *Floridian*, 25 October 1826, 18 November 1828; Nancy Cone Hagan's Poems, photocopy and typescript transcribed by James C. Bryant, SPC.

52. *Floridian*, 7, 28 July, 4, 11 August 1831.

53. Ibid., 11 August 1831.

54. Ibid., 1, 8, 15 May, 19, 26 June, 14, 21 August 1832; Superior Court Minute Book 1, pp. 408, 409, 410, 411, 418, 419, 427, 428, 429.

55. *Floridian*, 11 December 1834; *Autobiography of Peggy Eaton* (New York: Charles Scribner's Sons, 1932), pp. 170–71.

56. *Floridian*, 25 July, 22 August 1835; Thomas, "A History of Banking in Florida," SPC, p. 24. The Union Bank of Florida had 285 stockholders in 1840, who were entitled to loans amounting to two-thirds of their stock; Leon

County had 106 of these, who owned 13,727 of the approximately 28,000 shares of stock.

9. Those Seminoles Again

1. John K. Mahon, *History of the Second Seminole War, 1835–1842* (Gainesville: University of Florida Press, 1967), pp. 75, 85–106.

2. Ibid., pp. 103, 107–13; Doherty, *Richard Keith Call*, pp. 96–97.

3. Mahon, *Second Seminole War*, pp. 162–63, 168–89.

4. Ibid., pp. 321–27.

5. "Territorial Census of 1838," *Floridian*, 14 July 1838; Dorothy Dodd, "Florida's Population in 1845," *FHQ* 24 (July 1945):28–29.

6. *Floridian*, 11 November, 30 December 1837, 6 January 1838.

7. Ibid., 10 November 1838, 21 December 1839, 8 February 1840.

8. Ibid., 29 December 1838, 9 February, 30 March, 15 June, 16 November 1839, 18 April, 16 May, 11 July 1840.

9. Mahon, *Second Seminole War*, p. 188; "Tennessee Volunteers in the Seminole Campaign of 1836: The Diary of Henry Hollingsworth," ed. Stanley F. Horn, *Tennessee Historical Quarterly* 1 (December 1942):346–49.

10. Mahon, *Second Seminole War*, pp. 259, 272.

11. *Floridian*, 22 March 1834, quoting the *North Carolina People's Press*.

12. See Dorothy Dodd, "Horse Racing in Middle Florida, 1830–1843," *Apalachee* 3 (1950):20–29; *Floridian*, 19 January 1830, 13 March, 18 September 1832, 23 March 1833.

13. *Floridian*, 20 March 1841, said that, when the U.S. marshal arrived at the bank to execute a judgment for $1,195, the bank, which had gone off specie, *did* this time pay off in cash, a third of the amount in five and ten cent pieces. The building, formerly on Adams Street next door to a house called The Columns, was saved from destruction and was moved to Apalachee Parkway in 1971 largely through the efforts of the Florida Society of Colonial Dames XVII Century and its president, Mrs. T. Aubrey Morse. The Columns, the oldest house in original Tallahassee, was also moved and became the headquarters of the Tallahassee Chamber of Commerce.

14. *Floridian*, 20 May 1837, 29 June 1839, 25 January, 18 April, 11 July 1840.

15. Thomas, "History of Banking," pp. 48–49.

16. Doherty, *Richard Keith Call*, pp. 78, 99; Mahon, *Second Seminole War*, pp. 159–60.

17. *Floridian*, 13 October 1838; Arthur W. Thompson, *Jacksonian Democracy on the Florida Frontier* (Gainesville: University of Florida Press, 1961), pp. 7–16.

18. Thompson, *Jacksonian Democracy*, pp. 23–28, 66–68.

19. *Floridian*, 6 February 1836; Thompson, *Jacksonian Democracy*, pp. 67–68; Doherty, *Richard Keith Call*, p. 78; St. Augustine *Florida Herald and Southern Democrat*, 11 September 1840.

20. St. Augustine *Florida Herald and Southern Democrat*, 11 September 1840.

21. *Floridian*, 29 August, 5, 12, 19 September 1840.

22. *Floridian*, 1 May 1841.

23. *Floridian*, 12, 18 June 1841.

24. D. H. Redfearn, "Presumption as to Order of Death in a Common Disaster: The Steamboat *Home*," *Florida Bar Journal* 37 (February 1963):78–99; see also letters in *Smith and Armistead* v. *B. Croom et al.*, Leon Superior Court Chancery File 1214, as follows: H. B. Croom to John Torrey, 17 October 1836; Croom to Mrs. Croom, 23 January 1837; Croom to Torrey, 4 April 1837; see also Alvan Wentworth Chapman in *Botanical Gazette* 10 (1885):251–54.

25. *Floridian*, 7 May 1836.

26. *Floridian*, 25 June 1836.

27. *Floridian*, 14 May 1836.

28. *Floridian*, 4 March 1837.

29. *Floridian*, 7 April 1838.

30. *Floridian*, 28 July, 4, 18 August 1838.

31. *Floridian*, 4, 11 August 1838.

32. *Floridian*, 25 August 1838.

33. "The Charles Hutchinson Letters from Territorial Tallahassee, 1839–1843," ed. James T. Campbell, *Apalachee* 4 (1956):19–20.

34. See James W. Covington, "Federal Relations with the Apalachicola Indians, 1823–1838," *FHQ* 42 (October 1963):125–41.

35. Joy S. Paisley, *Cemeteries of Leon County*, p. 65.

36. Reid diary in Stephen F. Miller, *The Bench and Bar of Georgia*, 2 vols. (Philadelphia: Lippincott, 1858), 2:221–25.

37. Ibid., p. 226.

38. "Diary of Robert Raymond Reid, 1833 and 1835," p. 62 (quoted); *Floridian*, 10 April, 12 June, 3, 10 July 1841.

39. *Floridian*, 17, 24 July 1841; Joy S. Paisley, *Cemeteries of Leon County*, p. 65.

40. DuVal, Tallahassee, to postmaster general, 13 November 1841, in Carter, *Territorial Papers*, 26:398–99; William Wilson, Tallahassee, to Lucretia Dutton, 31 March 1846, in William Wilson Letters, University of Vermont Archives, Burlington, copies, SPC.

41. Testimony of R. A. Shine, 31 July 1857, in *Smith and Armistead* v. *Bryan Croom et al.*, Leon Superior Court File 1203.

42. Groene, *Ante-Bellum Tallahassee*, pp. 59–67 and appendix, pp. 171–75.

43. Wilson to Dutton, 31 March 1846, William Wilson Letters.

44. Mary Lamar Davis, "Tallahassee through Territorial Days," *Apalachee* 1 (1944):61.

10. King Cotton Takes Control, 1845–1850

1. Daisy Parker, "The Inauguration of the First Governor of the State of Florida," *Apalachee* 2 (1946):59–67.

2. Lee H. Warner, *Building Florida's Capitol* (Tallahassee: Historic Tallahassee Preservation Board, 1977), pp. 6–12.

3. *Floridian*, 11 January 1851.

4. *Floridian*, 1 December 1849; Groene, *Ante-Bellum Tallahassee*, p. 66.

5. *Floridian*, 13 March 1847.

6. Parker, "Inauguration of First Governor," pp. 61–62; Lee H. Warner and Mary B. Eastland, *Tallahassee: Downtown Transitions* (Tallahassee: Historic Tallahassee Preservation Board, 1976), pp. 21–26.

7. Warner and Eastland, *Downtown Transitions*, pp. 20–21.

8. *Floridian*, 1 December 1849, 11 September 1858.

9. See picture, Hampton Dunn, *Yesterday's Tallahassee* (Miami: E. A. Seamann, 1974), p. 28.

10. Mary Margaret Pichard Rhodes, "From Mission Bells to Cathedral Chimes," *Apalachee* 9 (1984):70–72.

11. *Floridian*, 26 June 1858.

12. Warner and Eastland, *Downtown Transitions*, p. 28.

13. Ibid., pp. 14, 15.

14. *Floridian*, 2 January, 17 April 1847.

15. *Floridian*, 21 September 1850, 23 August 1851, 17 July 1852.

16. *Floridian*, 27 September 1851, 27 October 1855. Lloyd was also well known as a caterer and was expert in conducting barbecues. There was presumably some loss to the public in his change of jobs. Above Barnard's he had directed his advertising at "ladies and gentlemen visiting the capital of the Land of Flowers and Pretty Women," who he said "will have a favored opportunity at having the human face divine transferred to the silver and ivory plate in an artistical manner."

17. Seventh Census, 1850, Manuscript Schedules. Tallahassee's population appears marginally in the Leon County schedules.

18. See J. George Anderson, Tallahassee, to Colonel Robert Gamble, chairman, reporting contributions, *Floridian*, 15 May 1847, also issues of 6, 13, 27 March.

19. *Seventh Census*, 1850, 1:401; *Compendium, Seventh Census* (Washington, D.C.: Beverley Tucker, 1854), p. 377.

20. *Sentinel*, 5 May 1846.

21. Ibid.

22. Ibid.

23. *Sentinel*, 4, 11, 18 August 1846; *Charleston Courier*, 21 August 1846 (reprinted in Womack, *Gadsden*, pp. 61–62).

24. *Sentinel*, 18 August 1846; *Floridian*, 3, 10 October 1846.

25. *Floridian*, 11 July 1846.

26. *Floridian*, 28 November 1846; Joy S. Paisley, *Cemeteries of Leon County*, pp. 128, 163. Despite the fact that several Revolutionary War veterans were in Leon County, this grave alone has been found.

27. *Floridian*, 14, 21 August, 2 October 1847, 27 May, 19 August 1849; *Laws of Florida*, 1849, p. 122, Resolution no. 23.

28. *Floridian*, 16 February 1850; *Sentinel*, 19 February 1850.

29. *Seventh Census*, 1850, 1:380, 408. Thirteen counties in Alabama exceeded the production in Leon (*Seventh Census*, 1:431).

30. *Floridian*, 7 March 1846, 9 November 1850.

31. These interesting old storebooks, covering the period 1843–63, were brought to the author's attention by Angus Laird of Tallahassee. They were given to Strozier Library by Mr. and Mrs. Claude Groom of Jefferson County. In about 1930 Groom participated in the razing of an old store building at this location and did historians a great service by rescuing them.

32. *Sentinel*, 1 January 1850; Clifton Paisley, "Tallahassee through the Storebooks, 1843–1863: Antebellum Cotton Prosperity," *FHQ* 50 (October 1971):126.

33. *Floridian*, 2 November 1850.

34. Paisley, "Tallahassee through Storebooks," pp. 125–27.

35. *Floridian*, 11 January 1840, 18 December 1852. The size of the mercantile community is indicated by a list of twenty-seven establishments that closed for Thanksgiving in 1854 (*Floridian*, 18 November 1854).

36. *Floridian*, 3 November 1849.

37. *Floridian*, 26 January 1850.

38. *Seventh Census*, 1850, 1:401.

39. *Floridian*, 4 August 1849, 10 May 1851.

40. See B. G. Thornton's report in *Sentinel*, 22 January 1850.

41. Ibid., and *Sentinel*, 22 October 1850.

42. *Floridian*, 15 December 1849; *Sentinel*, 1 January 1850.

43. *Floridian*, 17 April, 1 May 1847.

44. See will of Jesse Coe, Jackson Probate Will Book D, pp. 395–97.

45. *Floridian*, 22 January 1848, 7 October 1854.

46. Groene, *Ante-Bellum Tallahassee*, pp. 54–55.

47. *Floridian*, 27 May 1848, 29 September 1849, 23 August 1851.

48. *Floridian*, 19 June 1852.

49. *Floridian*, 8, 22 December 1849 (quoted), 12 January 1850.

50. *De Bow's Review* 12 (March 1852):279; *Floridian*, 12 January 1850.

51. *Floridian*, 12 January 1850.

52. *Sentinel*, 5 February 1850.

53. *Floridian*, 7, 15 December 1849.

54. *Floridian*, 11, 18 May 1850.

11. The Florida Cotton Kingdom, 1850:
Jackson and Gadsden Counties

1. *Seventh Census*, 1850, 1:408. All but six of the twenty-eight Florida counties grew some cotton; the nearest rivals to any of the Red Hills counties were Columbia, 802 bales, and Marion, 701.

2. Hentz, "Autobiography," 1:228.

3. Ibid., pp. 159–78.

4. Ibid., pp. 178–80.

5. Jackson Deed Book C, p. 946. Seventh Census, 1850, Florida, Manuscript Schedules, Agriculture, DOCS, are used in determining crop production and other details of farming in this chapter and the two that follow. See appendixes 1 and 2 for tables listing the names, age, and state of birth (from population schedules) of Jackson and Gadsden County farmers with a production of fifty or more bales. Maps show the location of their farms.

6. Obituary, *Floridian*, 9 April 1859; Fifth Census, 1830, Alabama, Manuscript Schedules, p. 28, DOCS; James Covington, "Federal Relations with the Apalachicola Indians, 1823–1838," p. 138; Hentz, "Autobiography," 1:226–27, 241–50.

7. Harry P. Owens, "Port of Apalachicola," *FHQ* 48 (July 1969):14.

8. *Seventh Census*, 1850, 1:408, and Manuscript Schedules, Agriculture, Calhoun County.

9. Hentz, "Autobiography," 1:224–25, 248. The house was moved across the Apalachicola to Torreya State Park in the 1930s.

10. Hentz, "Autobiography," 1:234–35; Mrs. Bill Milton Wynn, Marianna, to the author, 20 October 1984.

11. Jackson Deed Books A, p. 26, B, p. 292; *Floridian*, 20 December 1834.

12. Caroline Hentz, *Marcus Warland; or, The Long Moss Spring* (Philadelphia: A. Hart, 1852), pp. 58–59.

13. Jackson Deed Book A, p. 63; Hardy Bryan Croom to Bryan Croom, 20 July 1833, in *Smith and Armistead* v. *Croom et al.*, Box 452, files of the Florida Supreme Court; *Floridian*, 27 May 1837, and Hardy Bryan Croom to Samuel C. Bellamy, 27 June 1837, in *Smith and Armistead* v. *Croom et al.*, Leon Superior Court Chancery File 1214; "*Edward C. Bellamy* v. *Administrator, Samuel C. Bellamy,*" *Florida Reports* 6 (1855):62–142; *Floridian*, 21 January 1854; *Sentinel*, 2 December 1851; Jackson Deed Book B, p. 292.

14. Jackson Deed Book A, pp. 159, 160, 161, 162, 163 (J. L. G. Baker); pp. 421, 422, 423, 424, 425, 427 (S. J. Baker); pp. 376, 377, 379 (S. Baker, Jr.); William S. Powell, ed., *Dictionary of North Carolina Biography*, vol. 1 (Chapel Hill: University of North Carolina Press, 1979), pp. 92–93.

15. Stanley, *History of Jackson County*, pp. 20, 132–33; Jackson Deed Book A, pp. 128, 129, 130, 131, 133, 142, 143, 298, 412, 465.

16. Jackson Deed Books A, p. 176, B, pp. 177, 719, 723, 787; Eighth Census, 1860, Manuscript Schedules, Agriculture.

17. Jackson Deed Book D, p. 701; John H. Wheeler, *Historical Sketches of North Carolina From 1584 to 1851* (Philadelphia: Lippincott, Grambo, 1851), pp. 207–12; will of William B. Wynns, Jackson Probate file 1150; Jackson Deed Book A, pp. 66, 380, 513, 515, 516, 518, 519, 520, 522; Mrs. Wynn to the author, 20 October 1984; Eighth Census, 1860, Manuscript Schedules, Agriculture.

18. *Seventh Census*, 1850, 1:400, 407–408; *Compendium, Seventh Census*, p. 208; *Eighth Census*, 1860, vol. 1, Population (Washington, D.C.: GPO, 1864), p. 54, vol. 2, Agriculture (Washington, D.C.: GPO, 1864), pp. 19, 195.

19. Biographical material on the Munroe and related families was furnished by the late Sally Lines (Mrs. Edward) Thomas, Tallahassee.

20. Gadsden Deed Book B, p. 58.

21. Sarah E. Munroe, Quincy, to Mrs. Virginia Fitzgerald Irby, undated typescript in the hands of Mrs. Abner Avirett, Tallahassee; *Floridian*, 9 February 1856; Mrs. Munroe to Mrs. Irby, 26 December 1856, Avirett collection.

22. *Floridian*, 21 February 1857; Womack, *Gadsden*, p. 155, pictures, Thomas Munroe house, p. 153, William Munroe house, p. 150.

23. *Floridian*, 23 January 1846, 5 May 1849; Gadsden Deed Book A, p. 94.

24. The late Miss Eloise McGriff, Tallahassee, interview, 13 February 1986.

25. Gadsden Probate Old Will Book, 1831–, pp. 69–71; Gadsden Deed Book B, pp. 204, 308, 323.

26. Gadsden Deed Book A, pp. 91, 109, 122.

27. Gadsden Deed Book C, p. 437; Gadsden Probate Old Will Book, 1831–, pp. 61–62.

28. Virginia Laing (Mrs. Clayton) Wilkie, Tallahassee, interviews, 10 April 1982, 15 February 1986; Gadsden Deed Book A, p. 58; *Floridian*, 9 April 1853. Mrs. Wilkie said Augustus was a distant kinsman of Sidney Lanier, who (according to family tradition) visited Augustus's son Joseph W. Lanier while he was in Tallahassee in 1874.

29. See obituary, *Floridian*, 25 August 1855, advertisement, 15 November 1856; Clifton Paisley, "Tallahassee through the Storebooks, 1843–1863," pp. 111–27.

30. See *"Sarah A. Lines v. Henry D. Darden and wife," Florida Reports* 5 (1853):51–83.

31. Gadsden Deed Book A, pp. 97, 116.

32. Ibid., pp. 420, 421.

33. Ibid., p. 87.

34. Ibid., p. 587; Eighth Census, 1860, Manuscript Schedules, Agriculture, Calhoun County.

35. A mid-nineteenth-century courthouse fire destroyed many Gadsden County records. In the absence of appropriate deeds, an eight-foot-long land ownership map of Gadsden County north of the Forbes Purchase, drawn in the 1840s or 1850s, is an aid in locating plantations. The map may be found in DOCS and is handily displayed in Womack, *Gadsden*, pp. 310–23. See, in Sections 29, 30, 2N 5W, some of the Kilcrease land. See also Eighth Census, 1860, Manuscript Schedules, and *"Samuel B. Stephens et al. v. Rhoda E. Gibbes," Florida Reports* 14 (1873):331–62.

36. Hentz, "Autobiography," 1:240–41; *Floridian*, 19 November 1853.

37. *Floridian*, 5, 12 May, 16 June 1860.

38. See Albert W. Gilchrist to C. P. Gilchrist, 12 March 1909, in the Gilchrist Papers, SPC.

39. *Floridian*, 12 April 1851, 4 December 1852. Forty years of experiments in wheat breeding on what was White's land at the North Florida Research and Education Center have at last helped make wheat a successful crop in Florida, 160,000 acres having been planted in 1985. The biggest wheat-growing

counties today are Escambia and Santa Rosa, but Jackson had 15,000–20,000 acres, Gadsden 5,000, and Jefferson and Madison a considerable acreage among Red Hills counties (Ronald D. Barnett, plant breeder at the center, interview, 20 February 1986).

40. *Seventh Census*, 1850, 1:380, 407–408.

41. Stanley, *History of Gadsden County*, pp. 55–56.

42. "Florida and Spanish Tobacco," an address by Arthur I. Forman, in *De Bow's Review* 18 (January 1855):36–39.

43. See Sections 2, 3, 9, 10, and 11, 3N, 5W, Land Ownership Map.

44. Sections 13, 14, 23, and 24, 3N, 5W, ibid.

45. Text of a paper by Glover reported in the *National Intelligencer* and reprinted in the *Floridian*, 23 February 1856. In connection with Wood's experiment, Glover reported that young Dr. John Gamble of Tallahassee, "assisted by myself, dissected one female bollworm moth or millar (an insect which in its caterpillar stage is most destructive of cotton) and we discovered a mass of eggs, which when counted amounted at the least calculation to 500."

46. Gadsden Deed Book A, pp. 207, 244, 267, 496; Sections 23, 24, 25, 26, Land Ownership Map.

47. Forman, "Florida and Spanish Tobacco," p. 39.

48. C. H. DuPont, "History of the Introduction and Culture of Cuba Tobacco in Florida," address delivered before the Florida Fruit Growers Convention, Jacksonville, 20 January 1875, reprinted in *FHQ* 6 (January 1928):151–55.

12. The Florida Cotton Kingdom, 1850:
Leon County

1. Leon Deed Books K, p. 586, M, p. 559; *Floridian*, 26 November 1859; Hanna, *A Prince in Their Midst*, pp. 241–45.

2. Leon Deed Book I, p. 70; Dunn, *Yesterday's Tallahassee*, p. 21; *Floridian*, 20 November 1847; Paisley, *Cotton to Quail*, p. 73n.

3. Leon Deed Book K, p. 349; *Floridian*, 7 January 1854, for the name "Buena Vista."

4. Leon County Deed Book K, p. 152; Paisley, *Cotton to Quail*, pp. 56–57.

5. *Floridian*, 13 August 1853; Leon Deed Book E, p. 225.

6. Leon Deed Book M, p. 583; open letter of Robert Butler, 4 July 1849, in *Floridian*, 28 July 1849.

7. Long, *Florida Breezes*, pp. 116–19.

8. Leon Deed Book K, p. 189; Eighth Census, 1860, Manuscript Schedules, Agriculture; *Floridian*, 10 October 1857.

9. Leon Deed Books K, p. 194, M, p. 556; *Floridian*, 9 October 1858. This interesting country house, later that of the late Millard F. Caldwell and Mrs. Caldwell on their plantation Harwood, was moved nine miles to the heart of

Tallahassee in July 1986 to a "village green" of the Florida State University College of Law.

10. Leon Deed Books I, p. 520, K, pp. 168, 437.

11. Leon Deed Books C, p. 138, F, p. 489, G, p. 179, K, pp. 114, 157.

12. *Floridian*, 12 February, 7 April 1855.

13. Leon Deed Books A, pp. 151, 152, K, p. 490; see Shepard's obituary, *Floridian*, 2 July 1853; also *Floridian*, 24 January 1846, 26 June 1847; *Sentinel*, 10 February 1846.

14. *Floridian*, 23 October 1847, 12 September 1857; Leon Deed Books M, p. 591, N, p. 155.

15. *Solon Robinson, Pioneer Agriculturist, Selected Writings*, 2 vols., ed. Herbert Anthony Kellar, vol. 2: 1846–1851 (Indianapolis: Indiana Historical Bureau, 1936), p. 462.

16. Leon Deed Books D, p. 622, K, pp. 277, 462. See the outline of Live Oak as "the Case Place" in Ball and Bradford, "Land Ownership Map of Leon County, 1883," and Deed Books D, p. 614, P, p. 386.

17. William S. Hoffman, *Andrew Jackson and North Carolina Politics* (Chapel Hill: University of North Carolina Press, 1958), pp. 47–48; *Floridian*, 10 January 1857; Eppes, *Through Some Eventful Years* (1926; repr., Gainesville: University of Florida Press, 1968), pp. 48–50.

18. Leon Deed Book M, pp. 152, 196; the late George Lester Patterson, a great-grandson of Bradford, interview, 28 February 1977.

19. Eppes, *Through Some Eventful Years*, p. 30; Leon Deed Books C, p. 214, D, pp. 284, 503, E, pp. 319, 322, 372, 415, 567, 577, 592.

20. Leon Deed Books K, p. 392, N, p. 382; *Floridian*, 29 December 1855.

21. Leon Deed Books L, p. 101, M, p. 238; *Solon Robinson, Pioneer Agriculturist*, 2:460–63.

22. Leon Deed Books H, p. 331, I, pp. 263, 265, 608, K, pp. 45, 300, 585, L, p. 12; see Paisley, *Cotton to Quail*, pp. 12, 83.

23. Paisley, *Cotton to Quail*, pp. 12–13, picture of the house between pp. 52–53.

24. Ball and Bradford, "Land Ownership Map of Leon County, 1883," provides the outline of nineteenth-century Chemonie. See Phillips and Glunt, *Florida Plantation Records*, pp. 6–9, 17–22.

25. Leon Deed Book K, p. 432.

26. Ibid., p. 482.

27. Ibid., I, p. 595.

28. Leon Deed Books E, p. 514, F, p. 399; Long, *Florida Breezes*, p. 95; "*Isaac W. Mitchell* v. *Frederick R. Cotten, executor of John W. Cotten*," *Florida Reports* 2 (1849):136–58.

29. "*Barrow* v. *William Bailey, Administrator of the Estate of John Bellamy*," *Florida Reports* 5 (1853):10–50; Leon Deed Books E, pp. 462, 550, 552, 553, H, pp. 452, 467. The *Floridian*, 30 July 1853, shows W. N. Taylor as the agent of Barrow.

30. Leon Deed Book K, p. 347.

31. Ibid., G, p. 124; promissory note, Leon Probate File 211; Leon Deed

Books F, pp. 277–81, I, pp. 150, 160, 174; John Evans to George Noble Jones, 31 August 1854, in *Florida Plantation Records*, p. 94.

32. Leon Deed Books G, pp. 508, 509, I, pp. 204, 297, K, p. 463.

33. Ibid., D, pp. 608, 623, E, p. 172, F, p. 265, L, pp. 105, 138, 425, M, p. 383; Redfearn, "The Steamboat *Home*," pp. 78–99; *Floridian*, 25 July 1857. Heirs of Mrs. Hardy Croom filed suit shortly after the sinking of the *Home* in 1838. The case dragged along, and after nearly twenty years the Florida Supreme Court, with the adversary, winner-take-all logic of lawyers, decided that a son was the last of the five members of the family to drown and Mrs. Croom's mother and sister, who were next of kin of the son, should get the bulk of the estate, principally Leon County land and slaves. (See "*Smith and Armistead* v. *Bryan Croom*," *Florida Reports* 7 [1857]: 81–207.)

34. Leon Deed Books K, pp. 463, 662, M, p. 383; Paisley, *Cotton to Quail*, pp. 7–8; Eighth Census, 1860, Manuscript Schedules, Agriculture; testimony of Joseph John Williams, 13 November 1871, House Reports, No. 22, *Affairs in the Insurrectionary States*, pt. 13, Florida, 42d Cong., 2d sess. (1871–72), ser. 1541, pp. 237, 239.

35. Leon Deed Book F, p. 287.

36. Ibid., M, pp. 141, 458.

37. Ibid., C, p. 369, D, pp. 559, 607, E, pp. 126, 152, F, p. 238.

38. Leon Probate File 411A, George W. Parkhill.

39. Leon Deed Book M, p. 70; *Floridian*, 2 October 1858.

40. By 1860 Ward was the third most productive cotton planter in the county with a crop of five hundred bales. Paisley, *Cotton to Quail*, pp. 8–9.

41. Leon Deed Book F, p. 367.

42. Ibid., E, p. 110, F, pp. 18–25.

43. *Compendium, Seventh Census*, 1850, p. 208.

44. *Eighth Census*, 1860, vol. 2, Agriculture, pp. 18–19; Manuscript Schedules, Agriculture.

13. The Florida Cotton Kingdom, 1850:
Jefferson and Madison Counties

1. See chapter 10, *Laws of Florida*, 1831, pp. 79–83.

2. J. William Yon, Jr., *Geology of Jefferson County, Florida*, Geological Bulletin no. 48 (Tallahassee: FGS, 1966), pp. 16–18.

3. *Floridian*, 12 January 1850, 13 March, 1 May 1852.

4. Jefferson Deed Book D, p. 490.

5. Ibid., I, p. 123; R. E. Clark, Casa Bianca, interview, 31 May 1980.

6. "Florida White," a sketch of Ellen Adair Beatty by Mary E. Bryan in the *Monticello Constitution*, 9 June 1892, photocopy of clipping loaned by Mrs. R. E. Clark.

7. Margaret Anderson Uhler, " 'Florida White,' Southern Belle," *FHQ* 55 (January 1977):304.

8. Jefferson Deed Book G, p. 284.

9. Thompson, *Jacksonian Democracy*, p. 86.

10. Brown, *The Cabells and Their Kin*, pp. 271, 280–81, 627–37; Jefferson Deed Book E, p. 512; Herbert J. Doherty, Jr., *The Whigs of Florida, 1845–1854* (Gainesville: University of Florida Press, 1959), pp. 18–56.

11. Jefferson Deed Book C, pp. 383, 384, F, pp. 14, 632; *Floridian*, 15 February 1851.

12. Jefferson Deed Book D, pp. 452–54. See also the Gamble Family Papers, photocopies, SPC.

13. *Tallahassee Democrat*, 8 March 1985.

14. Jefferson Deed Book A, p. 3.

15. Shofner, *History of Jefferson County*, pp. 1, 27; Hale G. Smith, "A Spanish Mission Site in Jefferson County, Florida," in Boyd, Smith, and Griffin, *Here They Once Stood*, pp. 107–36 and n. 7, p. 135.

16. Jefferson Deed Books C, p. 217, D, p. 492; *DAB*, 7:83–84.

17. Jefferson Deed Books G, p. 384, H, p. 422, I, p. 52.

18. Phillips and Glunt, *Florida Plantation Records*, pp. 543–44.

19. *Floridian*, 5 September, 17 October 1840; Jefferson Deed Book E, p. 446.

20. *DAB*, 3:190.

21. Bryan, "Florida White."

22. *Floridian*, 14 August 1847, 23 December 1848.

23. Jefferson Deed Book C, pp. 417, 456, 482; see *Floridian*, 30 July 1853, offer of this and the Barrow Place in Leon County for sale.

24. *National Cyclopaedia of American Biography* (New York: White, 1892), 11:377.

25. Paisley, *Cotton to Quail*, pp. 10–11, 20.

26. Doherty, *Whigs of Florida*, pp. 14–15, 25–29.

27. *Floridian*, 21 April 1855; *De Bow's Review* 13 (June 1855).

28. Jefferson Deed Book I, p. 271.

29. Jefferson Deed Book C, p. 593, D, p. 581, F, pp. 114, 115.

30. *Seventh Census*, 1850, 1:400, 408; *Compendium, Seventh Census*, p. 208.

31. Rerick, *Memoirs of Florida*, 2:554; Madison Deed Book A, p. 108.

32. Madison Deed Book B, pp. 27, 30, 31, C, p. 123, D, p. 135; order by Judge G. M. T. Brinson, 8 February 1861, Madison Probate Dower Record, 1848–1915, pp. 30–33; Dan Collins of Tallahassee, a great-great-great-grandson, to the author, 15 December 1979.

33. *Floridian*, 13 October 1860.

34. Madison Deed Books C, p. 92, D, pp. 5, 84, 148, 173, 197, 371, 385, 417, 422; Huxford, *Pioneers of Wiregrass Georgia*, vol. 3 (Pearson, Ga.: published by the author, 1957), pp. 250–51; vol. 6 (Jesup, Ga.: published by the author, 1971), p. 201; Madison Probate Record of Annual Returns, 1847–73, pp. 25, 36; Julia Floyd Smith, *Slavery and Plantation Growth in Antebellum Florida, 1821–1860* (Gainesville: University of Florida Press, 1973), pp. 14–15, 165.

35. Smith subsequently moved to Madison and died in 1891. He was buried in Oak Ridge Cemetery. This cemetery was an expansion of the Parramore family cemetery, indicated by an iron fence enclosing the graves of Parramore (1799–1851) and his wife, Mary Ann, who died in 1897 at age seventy-four.

36. *Floridian*, 3 December 1853. However, he noted this drawback in growing Sea Island: "The best roller gins now used will not give over 300 pounds of lint a day."

37. Clifton Paisley, "Madison County's Sea Island Cotton Industry, 1870–1916," *FHQ* 54 (January 1976):285–87; "W" of Tallahassee, Fla., 16 October 1844, in the *Southern Agriculturist*, 4 n.s.(December 1844):450, 452 (microfilm, DOCS). However, the agricultural census in 1850 found a production of only 560 bales of cotton of all kinds in Hamilton and 802 in Columbia counties (*Seventh Census*, 1850, 1:408).

38. More than anyone else, Edwin B. Browning (1904–81), sometime county superintendent of schools for Madison County and historian, has preserved the name of Richard Mays of Clifton Plantation. See Madison County Historical Society, "Second Annual," mimeographed, 1941, pp. 49–51 (SPC).

39. Madison Deed Books E, p. 412, G, p. 621; *Floridian*, 17 February 1855.

40. Madison County, "Second Annual," pp. 23–25; Madison Deed Book C, p. 311.

41. Madison Deed Book C, p. 417, D, p. 303, E, p. 428; Madison County, "Second Annual," p. 23; Chapin, *Florida, 1513–1913*, 2:61.

42. Margaret Watson, *Greenwood County Sketches* (Greenwood, S.C.: Attic Press, 1970), p. 288; John A. Chapman, *History of Edgefield County, S.C. . . . to 1897* (1897; repr., Spartanburg, S.C.: Southern Historical Press, 1976), p. 95.

43. Madison Deed Books B, pp. 101, 215, C, p. 395.

44. Smith, *Slavery and Plantation Growth*, pp. 147–48. See also his will, recorded in Madison Probate Will Book B, pp. 1–8.

45. *Floridian*, 22 October 1859.

46. Watson, *Greenwood County Sketches*, p. 307; Chapman, *History of Edgefield County*, p. 182; *Floridian*, 25 January 1834.

47. "Diary of Robert Raymond Reid, 1833, 1835," pp. 5–6.

48. *Floridian*, 25 January 1834; Watson, *Greenwood County Sketches*, pp. 31, 307.

49. Rosa Galphin, "John C. McGehee," *FHQ* 4 (April 1926):186–91.

50. Through the efforts of Leroy Cruce, who lives nearby, Mrs. Paisley and I found another neighbor, Marvin E. Bass, who took us to the site of McGehee's house, Chuleotah, and the graveyard on 11 May 1985. Only two broken-up stones remain. A marble one for John McGehee proclaims: "An honest man is the noblest work of God." D. J. Gossett of Brooksville, Fla., who has owned 460 acres here since 1971, plans to restore the stones and enclose the cemetery (Gossett to the author, 22 February 1988).

51. Madison Deed Books A, pp. 54, 171, 173, 174, 186, C, p. 94; Galphin, "John C. McGehee," p. 187.

52. Madison Deed Books H2, p. 846, J, p. 325.

53. Madison Deed Books A, p. 157, B, pp. 346, 397, 410, 418, 447, C, pp. 246, 248, D, pp. 10, 12, 13, 16, 51, 52, 54, 55.

54. Madison Deed Books C, pp. 244, 252, 430, D, pp. 153, 331, 363, 430.

55. Madison Probate Record Book of Annual Returns, 1847–73, pp. 259, 263, 270, 310.

56. Leon Deed Book K, p. 742.

57. *State* v. *Cade Godbold*, 23 March 1855, Leon Superior Court Minute Book 5; *Floridian*, 24 March 1855.

58. Quoted in the *Floridian*, 14 April 1855.

59. "Elijah Swift's Travel Journal from Massachusetts to Florida, 1857," ed. Virginia Steele Wood, *FHQ* 55 (October 1976):186.

60. *Floridian*, 10 April 1858.

61. Madison Probate Record Book of Annual Returns, 1847–73, p. 264; *Floridian*, 22 November 1856, 12 December 1857; Madison Deed Book F, p. 376.

62. *Floridian*, 8 March 1856; Leon Deed Book L, p. 425.

63. *Floridian*, 17 March 1855.

64. "An Actual Settler," in *Floridian*, 22 June 1850.

65. *Seventh Census*, 1850, 1:400, 407–408.

14. The Railroad-Building Boom

1. *Floridian*, 15 January 1853; Ulrich Bonnell Phillips, *History of Transportation in the Eastern Cotton Belt to 1860* (1908; repr., New York: Octagon Press, 1968), pp. 252–334.

2. Harry P. Owens, "Port of Apalachicola," *FHQ* 48 (July 1969):1–25.

3. *Floridian*, 15 January 1853.

4. *Floridian*, 13 January 1849.

5. *Floridian*, 29 January 1853.

6. *Floridian*, 7, 21 May 1853, 11 February 1854.

7. Alexander Brown, *Cabells and Kin*, pp. 627–34; Florida Senate *Journal*, 1852, Appendix, pp. 1–24.

8. *Laws of Florida*, 1854, pp. 9–19.

9. *Floridian*, 17 February, 17 November 1855.

10. *Floridian*, 27 May, 16 June, 27 October 1855, 2 February, 11 October 1856.

11. *Floridian*, 20 December 1856.

12. *Floridian*, 6 December 1856.

13. Bertram H. Groene, "Lizzie Brown's Tallahassee," *FHQ* 48 (October 1969):157. After the cascade was destroyed, water in the sink into which it fell became deeper and the sink became an "attractive nuisance." Two black boys, Charley, eight, and Lewis, nine, jumped in and drowned in 1859 (*Floridian*, 9 July 1859).

14. *Floridian*, 3 November 1855, 11 July 1857.

15. *Floridian*, 10 October, 28 November, 5 December 1857, 25 September 1858.

16. *Floridian*, 12, 19 December 1857, 26 May 1860.

17. *Floridian*, 19 December 1857.

18. *Floridian*, 17 November 1855, 3 January 1857, 19 February 1859, 21 July 1860.

19. *Floridian*, 9 May 1857, 12 February, 9 April 1859.

20. *Floridian*, 30 June, 25 August 1860.

21. *Floridian*, 8 December 1860.

22. William Warren Rogers, *Ante-Bellum Thomas County, 1825–1861*, Florida State Univ. Studies, no. 39 (Tallahassee: Florida State University, 1963), p. 49.

23. *Floridian*, 1 January 1859, 14 January, 25 February 1860.

24. *Floridian*, 6 September 1856.

25. Atlantic and Gulf Central Railroad, *Minutes of the Proceedings with the Report of the President and Directors at Their Meeting Held in Jacksonville July 5, 1859* (Jacksonville: C. Drew, 1859), pp. 17–18.

26. *Floridian*, 23 December 1856, 14 February 1857, 10 July 1858, 16 July 1859. The population was nevertheless 441 in 1860.

27. *Floridian*, 25 July 1857, 14 May, 24 November 1859.

28. *Floridian*, 29 December 1855, 12 December 1857, 23 January 1858.

29. *Floridian*, 8 September 1860.

30. *Floridian*, 3 July 1858.

31. Map of the State of Georgia compiled by James R. Butts, late surveyor general, 1859, DOCS.

32. National Oceanic and Atmospheric Administration Hydrographic Maps, U.S., Gulf Coast, Apalachee Bay, no. 11405 (Washington, D.C.: NOAA, 1984).

33. The George K. Walker Papers, SPC; Harry Gardner Cutler, *History of Florida Past and Present*, 3 vols. (New York: Lewis Publishing, 1923), 3:190; Franklin County Office of Circuit Court Clerk, Apalachicola, Deed Book A, p. 74, 5 January 1859.

34. *Floridian*, 1 December 1855. The George K. Walker Papers note that two children were born at Highwood, David Meade in 1850 and Annie Helen in 1857.

35. *Floridian*, 16 July 1859, 28 April, 5 May 1860.

36. Seventh Census, 1850, Population Schedules, Leon County; *Eighth Census*, 1860, vol. 1, Population, p. 54; *Floridian*, 20 June 1857, 7 January 1860.

37. *Eighth Census*, 1860, vol. 3, Manufactures, pp. 57, 58, 59.

38. *Floridian*, 31 January 1852, 3 December 1853, 14 February 1857.

39. *Floridian*, 26 November, 24 December 1853, 3 May 1856; Dorothy Dodd, "The Manufacture of Cotton in Florida before and during the Civil War," *FHQ* 13 (July 1934):1–15.

40. *Eighth Census*, 1860, vol. 1, Population, pp. 50–57; *Floridian*, 14 November, 12 December 1857. For background about Williams, see Paisley, *Cotton to Quail*, pp. 7–8.

41. *Floridian*, 28 August 1858.

42. *Floridian*, 10 July 1858.

43. Nita Katherine Pyburn, *The History of the Development of a Single System*

of Education in Florida, 1822–1903 (Tallahassee: Florida State University, 1954), pp. 57–65.

44. *Floridian*, 2, 30 March, 21, 28 September 1850, 20 December 1851; Seventh Census, 1850, Manuscript Schedules, Population, Leon County.

45. *Floridian*, 3 January 1857.

46. *Floridian*, 18 February, 1 April 1854, 31 January, 12 September 1857, 26 June 1858; William G. Dodd, *History of West Florida Seminary, 1857–1901, and Florida State College, 1901–1905* (Tallahassee: Florida State University, 1952), p. 59; *Laws of Florida*, 1856, pp. 28–29.

47. *Floridian*, 18 February, 1 April 1854.

48. Fenton Garnett Davis Avant, *My Tallahassee*, ed. David A. Avant, Jr. (Tallahassee: L'Avant Studios, 1983), pp. 163–75.

49. Ibid., pp. 167–68. The fine Harrison House mentioned by Mrs. Avant was saved by the late Mrs. Rainey Cawthon in the 1960s and was restored at the Cawthon home on Ocala Road. Now it has been moved again to become part of a "village on the green" at the College of Law at Florida State University (*Tallahassee Democrat*, 8 July 1985, 20 April 1986).

50. Clifton Paisley, "Tallahassee through the Storebooks: War Clouds and War, 1860–1863," *FHQ* 51 (July 1972):37–51.

51. *Floridian*, 26 November 1859, 29 September, 24 November 1860.

15. The Blacks

1. "Memoirs of Helen M. Edwards," printed and bound pamphlet, no date, SPC, pp. 1–3, 5; Jefferson Deed Book D, p. 477.

2. Leon Deed Books K, p. 730, L, pp. 547, 569, N, p. 324.

3. *Slave Narratives: A Folk History of Slavery in the United States, from Interviews with Former Slaves* (1939; repr. St. Clair Shores, Mich.: Scholarly Press, 1976, from mimeographed copies of interviews, 1936–1938, of the Federal Writers Project, vol. 17, Florida Narratives), pp. 242–44.

4. *Slave Narratives*, 17:347–49; Hayward's house stood at 322 North Adams Street, occupying the block now used by the Greyhound and Trailways bus terminals (Leon Deed Books K, p. 386, L, p. 100). See Evelyn Whitfield Henry, "Old Houses of Tallahassee," Tallahassee Historical Society *Annual*, vol. 1, 1934, mimeographed, SPC, p. 53.

5. *Seventh Census*, 1850, 1:400–401.

6. Phillips and Glunt, *Florida Plantation Records*, p. 55.

7. *Slave Narratives*, 17:259.

8. Ibid., p. 243.

9. Ibid., pp. 250–54.

10. Ibid., pp. 327–31.

11. Ibid., pp. 257–58.

12. Phillips and Glunt, *Florida Plantation Records*, pp. 53, 404–406, 410.

13. *Slave Narratives*, 17:165–66.

14. Ibid., p. 166.

15. Ibid., pp. 250, 252, 253.

16. *Floridian*, 21 January 1854.

17. Donald G. Mathews, *Slavery and Methodism: A Chapter in American Morality, 1780–1845* (Princeton: Princeton University Press, 1965), pp. 6–7, 18, 264, 279.

18. Richardson, *Lights and Shadows of Itinerant Life: An Autobiography* (Nashville: Barbee and Smith, 1901), pp. 159, 179.

19. See chapter 11.

20. Jefferson County Tax Rolls, 1858, DDR.

21. Madison County Tax Rolls, 1858, DDR.

22. Cooper Clifford Kirk, "A History of the Southern Presbyterian Church in Florida, 1821–1891" (Ph.D. diss., Florida State University, 1966), pp. 197–98.

23. Smith, *Slavery and Plantation Growth*, p. 96.

24. *Floridian*, 14 February 1846.

25. Kirk, "History of the Southern Presbyterian Church," pp. 226–27.

26. *Slave Narratives*, 17:212, 214–15.

27. Helen Edwards, "Memoirs," p. 5.

28. *Sentinel*, 15 February 1853.

29. Jonathan Roberson to G. Noble Jones, 12 May 1852, in Kathryn T. Abbey, "Documents Relating to El Destino and Chemonie Plantations," pt. 3, *FHQ* 8 (July 1929):12.

30. *Slave Narratives*, 17:244–45.

31. Pat Harbolt in *Tallahassee Democrat*, 15 October 1978.

32. Eppes, *Negro of the Old South*, pp. 3–4, 57–63.

33. *Floridian*, 6 November 1858.

34. *Floridian*, 20 November 1858.

35. *Floridian*, 4, 18 December 1858.

36. *Floridian*, 6, 13 December 1856.

37. *Floridian*, 17 January 1857, 10 November 1860; Sarah Munroe to Jennie, Quincy, 26 December 1856, Mrs. Abner Avirett Collection.

38. *Floridian*, 8 November 1856.

39. Ibid., 7 April 1849; Phillips and Glunt, *Florida Plantation Records*, p. 110.

40. Frank Hatheway Diary, SPC.

41. Eppes, *Negro of the Old South*, pp. 30–37.

42. *Slave Narratives*, 17:254.

43. *Floridian*, 6 March 1847.

44. *Floridian*, 20 December 1851.

45. *Floridian*, 22 January 1853.

46. *Floridian*, 9 September 1848.

47. *Floridian*, 8 June 1833. Lovelace was a "tolerable bright mulatto, his teeth out before, has a down look when spoken to, about thirty-five. Took with him an old shot gun." Having a "downcast look" and stuttering have been found to be characteristics of many runaways. Eugene D. Genovese suggests that these slaves may have been "seething with hostility toward those who commanded the paternalistic relationship in which they found

themselves embedded" (Eugene D. Genovese, *Roll Jordan Roll: The World the Slaves Made* [New York: Random House, 1972], pp. 646–47).

48. *Floridian*, 20 December 1851.

49. *Floridian*, 10 November 1860.

50. *Floridian*, 8 March 1856.

51. *Floridian*, 27 October 1849.

52. *Floridian*, 3 November 1855.

53. *Floridian*, 20 May 1854.

54. *Floridian*, 25 July 1846.

55. *Floridian*, 11 March 1837.

56. *Floridian*, 28 January 1854.

57. *Floridian*, 1 November 1851.

58. Eppes, *Negro of the Old South*, pp. 98–101.

59. *Slave Narratives*, 17:62–63.

60. *Floridian*, 23 November 1850.

61. "*Sarah A. Lines* v. *Henry D. and Eloiza Darden*," *Florida Reports* 5 (1853):54.

62. "*John G. Powell, Administrator of Simon Partridge, Deceased*, v. *Thomas K. Leonard*," *Florida Reports* 9 (1861):359–66.

63. "*Cato, a Slave, Plaintiff in Error*, v. *The State*," *Florida Reports* 9 (1860):163–87.

64. "*Samuel S. Sibley* v. *Maria, a Woman of Color*," *Florida Reports* 2 (1849):553–66.

65. "*William Clark* v. *Thomas N. Gautier in behalf of Dick, a Person of Color*," *Florida Reports* 8 (1859):360–69.

66. *Seventh Census*, 1850, 1:400, and Manuscript Schedules.

67. *Floridian*, 7 July 1855.

68. Rosalind Parker, "The Proctors—Antonio, George, and John," *Apalachee* 2 (1946):19–29; unpublished manuscript by Lee H. Warner about George Proctor, including his career in California; Lee H. Warner, Asolo Performing Arts Center, to the author, 8 December 1988.

69. Dorothy Dodd, "The Schooner Emperor: An Incident of the Illegal Slave Trade in Florida," *FHQ* 13 (January 1935):117–28.

70. *Floridian*, 3, 17 November 1849.

71. *Floridian*, 28 September 1850, 7 June 1851.

72. *Floridian*, 19 February 1859.

16. "A Slight Touch of Ashby de la Zouche" and Secession

1. *Floridian*, 7, 14 August 1847.

2. *Floridian*, 18 September 1847.

3. Resolution no. 1, approved 13 January 1849, *Laws of Florida*, 1848.

4. *Floridian*, 27 January 1849.

5. *Floridian*, and 16 February, 2 March, 14 May 1850.

6. *Floridian*, 2 March 1850.

7. *Floridian*, 2 March, 6 April 1850.

8. Allan Nevins, *Fruits of Manifest Destiny, 1847–1852*, vol. 1 of *Ordeal of the Union*, 8 vols. (New York: Charles Scribner's Sons, 1947), pp. 315–45.

9. *Floridian*, 7 June 1851.

10. *Floridian*, 19 July 1851.

11. Ibid.

12. *Floridian*, 11 October 1851.

13. Kirk, "History of the Southern Presbyterian Church," pp. 150–53, 192.

14. *Floridian*, 15 July 1854.

15. Raimondo Luraghi, *The Rise and Fall of the Plantation South* (New York: Franklin Watts, New Viewpoints, 1978), pp. 20–34, 64–102.

16. Paisley, "Tallahassee through the Storebooks, 1843–1863: Antebellum Cotton Prosperity," *FHQ* 50 (October 1971):113–14. Recalling turn-of-the-century social life in Tallahassee, Miss Clare Bowen said in 1972 that "we were all a dancing set—everybody loved to dance" (interview, 22 April 1972), typescript, Florida Archives).

17. *Floridian*, 8 May 1847.

18. "Spectator," in *Floridian*, 12 May 1849.

19. "Bend," in *Floridian*, 19 May 1849.

20. *Floridian*, 3 May 1851.

21. *Floridian*, 6 May 1854. The May Oak lasted for a quarter of a century after the end of the May parties, then toppled to the ground in a 1986 windstorm (*Tallahassee Democrat*, 11 August 1986).

22. *Floridian*, 5 May 1860.

23. *Sentinel*, 23 December 1851.

24. *Floridian*, 20 December 1851, 3 January 1852; *Sentinel*, 30 December 1851.

25. *Sentinel*, 30 December 1851.

26. Ibid.

27. *Floridian*, 28 February 1852, Leon Superior Court law file 5707, *Samuel Carroll* v. *William G. Moseley*.

28. *Sentinel*, 30 December 1851.

29. *Pars Fui*, in *Floridian*, 25 February 1854; "Public Notice" by C. H. Austin, in ibid.

30. *Floridian*, 13, 27 June, 11, 25 July, 29 August 1857, 12 March 1859.

31. *Pars Fui*, in *Floridian*, 26 February 1854.

32. *Floridian*, 26 December 1857, 16 January, 20 February, 3 April 1858, 22 January 1859.

33. *Floridian*, 7 August, 13, 29 November, 4 December 1852.

34. *Floridian*, 20 November 1852.

35. *Floridian*, 18 August 1855.

36. *Floridian*, 29 November 1856.

37. *Floridian*, 22 October, 3 December 1859, 18 February, 21 March 1860.

38. *Floridian*, 23 June 1860.

39. *Floridian*, 23 June, 25 August, 1 September, 17 November 1860.

40. *Floridian*, 24 November 1860.

41. *Floridian*, 1 December 1860.

42. Jacksonville *Florida Times-Union*, 13 September 1981.

43. *Floridian*, 1 December 1860.

44. *Floridian*, 17 November 1860; Paisley, "Tallahassee through the Storebooks: War Clouds and War," p. 42; William Watson Davis, *The Civil War and Reconstruction in Florida* (1913; repr., Gainesville: University of Florida Press, 1964), p. 50.

45. *Journal of the Proceedings of the Convention of the People of Florida Begun . . . on Thursday, Jan. 3, 1861* (Tallahassee: printed by Dyke & Carlisle, 1861), pp. 6, 12; *The Diary of Edmund Ruffin*, vol. 1, 1856–1861, ed. William Kauffman Scarborough (Baton Rouge: Louisiana State University Press, 1972), pp. 523–24.

46. *Floridian*, 15 December 1860.

47. *Journal of Proceedings*, pp. 28–32.

48. *Diary of Ruffin*, pp. 528–29, 588.

49. *Journal of Proceedings*, pp. 32–34; Eppes, *Through Some Eventful Years*, pp. 143–45.

17. The Civil War

1. Fred L. Robertson, comp., *Soldiers of Florida in the Seminole Indian, Civil, and Spanish-American Wars*, prepared and published under the supervision of the Board of State Institutions (Live Oak, Fla.: Democrat Book & Job, [1903?]), SPC, pp. 38, 58–71. The Red Hills units were Companies A and D, Leon; E, Jackson; F, Madison; G, Gadsden; and I, Jefferson.

2. Davis, *Civil War and Reconstruction in Florida*, pp. 74–94.

3. Ibid., pp. 114–33. See also John E. Johns, *Florida during the Civil War* (Gainesville: University of Florida Press, 1963), pp. 50–53. The official reports of the battle are in *War of the Rebellion: A Compilation of the Official Records of the Union and Confederate Armies* (Washington, D.C.: GPO, 1880–1901), ser. 1, vol. 6, pp. 438–63 (hereafter cited as *OR*).

4. Eppes, *Through Some Eventful Years*, pp. 151–52. Long, *Florida Breezes*, reported an additional local casualty: "Our city, for the first time, has the reality of the war brought home. Three of the flower of our young men were killed" (p. 332).

5. Davis, *Civil War and Reconstruction*, pp. 146–49.

6. Robertson, *Soldiers of Florida*, p. 39.

7. Ibid., pp. 327–28; James Patton Anderson, "Civil War Letters of Major General James Patton Anderson," ed. Margaret Anderson Uhler, *FHQ* 56 (October 1977):150, 153.

8. Robertson, *Soldiers of Florida*, pp. 39–40, 99–102, 118–19.

9. Ibid., pp. 153–55, 170.

10. Ibid., p. 331; Mary Lamar Davis, "Brigadier General William G. M. Davis," *Florida Bar Journal* 23 (January 1949):36–39.

11. Robertson, *Soldiers of Florida*, pp. 332–33.

12. Davis, *Civil War and Reconstruction*, pp. 142–49.

13. Captain George Washington Parkhill, Fort Spottswood, Va., to his wife Lizzie, 17 March 1862, in George Washington Parkhill, Civil War Letters, 1861–62, SPC. The forty Parkhill letters were among the possessions of a grandson, the late Parkhill Mays, of Monticello, Fla., who at my suggestion generously gave them to Strozier Library in 1976.

14. Parkhill, Camp Sycamore, Va., to Lizzie, 4 May 1862.

15. Robertson, *Soldiers of Florida*, pp. 77–79 and *OR*, ser. 1, vol. 11, pt. 1, pp. 403, 406.

16. David E. Maxwell, "Some Letters to His Parents by a Floridian of the Confederate Army," ed. Gilbert Wright, *FHQ* 36 (April 1958):358–60.

17. In Parkhill, Civil War Letters.

18. Francis P. Fleming to Aunt Tilly, 28 July 1862, in "Soldiering with the Second Florida Regiment," ed. John P. Ingle, *FHQ* 59 (January 1981):336–37.

19. Richard S. Nichols, "Florida's Fighting Rebels: A Military History of Florida's Civil War Troops" (master's thesis, Florida State University, 1967), pp. 82–89, 125–29.

20. Robertson, *Soldiers of Florida*, pp. 336–38.

21. Wilbur Gramling, Civil War Diary, original in the hands of Owen I. Gramling, Tallahassee, photocopy and typescript by Clifton Paisley, SPC; Clay W. Holmes, *The Elmira Prison Camp: A History* (New York: G. P. Putnam, 1912), p. 131 (death toll); Macon, Ga., *Southern Christian Advocate*, 25 January 1871.

22. Robertson, *Soldiers of Florida*, pp. 119, 189.

23. Ibid., p. 335.

24. *Official Records of the Union and Confederate Navies in the War of the Rebellion* (Washington, D.C.: GPO, 1894–1922), ser. 1, vol. 16, pp. 526–27, 545, 584–89 (hereafter *ORN*).

25. Ibid., p. 585.

26. Davis, *Civil War and Reconstruction*, pp. 197–203.

27. Parkhill to Lizzie, 22 May 1862, in Parkhill, Civil War Letters.

28. Eppes, *Through Some Eventful Years*, pp. 220, 236.

29. Interview by Clifton Paisley, 22 April 1972, typescript, Ms. no. M77-167, Florida State Archives, Tallahassee.

30. *Eighth Census*, 1860, vol. 2, Agriculture, pp. 18–19.

31. Joe A. Akerman, Jr., *Florida Cowman: A History of Florida Cattle Raising* (Kissimmee Fla.: Florida Cattlemen's Association, 1976), pp. 84–96.

32. Jerrell H. Shofner and William Warren Rogers, "Confederate Railroad Construction: The Live Oak to Lawton Connector," *FHQ* 43 (January 1965):217–28; Davis, *Civil War and Reconstruction*, pp. 193–96.

33. Mark F. Boyd, "The Federal Campaign of 1864 in East Florida," *FHQ* 29 (July 1950):3–37.

34. Davis, *Civil War and Reconstruction*, p. 212, n. 1, pp. 245–46, 257.

35. Eppes, *Through Some Eventful Years*, p. 206.

36. Davis, *Civil War and Reconstruction*, pp. 260–61.

37. Charlotte Corley Farley, "Florida's Alamo: The Battle of Marianna As 'Twas Told to Me," bound photocopy of typescript, DDR, pp. 26–27. The

author is a great-granddaughter of James H. Brett, a homeguard participant who was killed. Other accounts, in addition to those in *OR*, appear in Stanley, *History of Jackson County*, pp. 187–96; Mark F. Boyd, "The Battle of Marianna," *FHQ* 29 (April 1951):225–42; and Jerrell H. Shofner, *Jackson County, Florida: A History* (Marianna: Jackson County Heritage Association, 1985), pp. 242–46.

38. Farley, "Florida's Alamo," p. 27 and n. 6.

39. Boyd, "Battle of Marianna," pp. 235–41.

40. Ibid., pp. 232–34. Stanley called the battle "the most tragic event in the history of Jackson County, as it was the most memorable" (*History of Jackson County*, p. 187).

41. William Miller, "The Battle of Natural Bridge," ed. Mark F. Boyd, *Apalachee* 4 (1956):85, n. 1.

42. Ibid., pp. 78–79.

43. Mark F. Boyd, "The Joint Operations of the Federal Army and Navy near St. Marks, Florida, March 1865," *FHQ* 29 (October 1950):96–124. Official reports of the Battle of Natural Bridge are in *OR*, ser. 1, vol. 49, pt. 1, pp. 57–70, pt. 2, pp. 1134–36; *ORN*, ser. 1, vol. 17, pp. 813–21.

44. Miller, "Battle of Natural Bridge," pp. 80–81. This account by Miller of his activities after his return from the Tennessee battlefront and including his detailed report on the battle to Major General Jones was delivered before the Anna Jackson Chapter of the United Daughters of the Confederacy, probably in 1901.

45. Marion B. Lucas, "Civil War Career of Colonel George Washington Scott," *FHQ* 58 (October 1979):130–35, 142; Scott, "How to Escape the Yankees: Maj. Scott's Letter to His Wife at Tallahassee, March 1864," ed. Clifton Paisley, *FHQ* 50 (July 1971):53–61.

46. *Floridian*, 11 March 1865, photocopy of a clipping given the author by J. J. Scott of Scottsdale Mills, Ga.; Samuel Jones to the Superintendent, Savannah, Albany & Gulf Railroad, Thomasville, Ga., 5 March 1865, *OR*, ser. 1, vol. 49, pt. 1, p. 1029; Newton to Headquarters, Military Division of West Mississippi, 19 March 1865, ibid., pp. 58–62.

47. Newton to Headquarters, 6 April 1865, *OR*, ser. 1, vol. 49, pt. 1, p. 64; Miller, "Natural Bridge," p. 81.

48. Miller, "Natural Bridge," pp. 81–82; Boyd, "Joint Operations," pp. 17–18.

49. Hentz, "Autobiography," 1:353–55.

50. B. Byrd Coles, Clayton, Ala., to the *Tallahassee Daily Democrat*, 4 December 1918.

51. "Reminiscences of the Battle of Natural Bridge," written by Miss Susan Archer for the UDC chapter in 1911 and enclosed in a letter published in the *Tallahassee Daily Democrat*, 7 November 1918. Devoting eight pages to an investigation of the cadets' part in the battle, Boyd said their role "has begun to assume the character of folk-lore" (Boyd, "Joint Operations Near St. Marks," pp. 117–24).

52. Hentz, "Autobiography," 1:361–62.

53. Ibid.; Stanley, *History of Jackson County*, p. 181.

54. Eppes, *Through Some Eventful Years*, pp. 265–66.

Epilogue

1. Paisley, *Cotton to Quail*, pp. 23, 29–30 and n. p. 30; *Floridian*, 11 May 1869; testimony of Joseph John Williams, 13 November 1871, House Reports, No. 22, *Affairs in the Insurrectionary States*, pt. 13, Florida, 42d Cong., 2d sess. (1871–72), ser. 1541, p. 226.

2. Paisley, *Cotton to Quail*, pp. 25–38 and n. p. 38; pp. 72–98.

3. Stanley, *History of Jackson County*, pp. 263–65; Stanley, *History of Gadsden County*, pp. 151–73; Paisley, "Madison County's Sea Island Cotton Industry, 1870–1916."

4. *Florida Statistical Abstract*, 20th ed., ed. Anne H. Shoemyen (Gainesville: University Presses of Florida, 1986), pp. 138–40.

5. Ibid., pp. 4–11; *Twelfth Census*, 1900, vol. 1, pt. 1 (Washington, D.C.: U.S. Census Office, 1901), pp. 2, 94; *Sixteenth Census*, 1940, vol. 1 (Washington, D.C.: GPO, 1942), 219; Evelyn Whitfield Henry, "Old Houses of Tallahassee," Tallahassee Historical Society "Annual," vol. 1, 1934, mimeographed, SPC, pp. 39–55.

6. Torrey, *A Florida Sketch-Book*, pp. 167, 210–11.

Bibliography

Documents, Manuscript Records, and Unpublished Studies

The *Tallahassee Floridian* (published under various names, for example as the *Floridian & Advocate*), is available on microfilm at DOCS and is the principal primary source for history of the Red Hills after American settlement and until the Civil War. For two long Spanish periods that preceded American settlement, the historical documents are mostly preserved in Spanish archives. Many of the Spanish-language records are available on microfilm in the Woodbury Lowery Transcripts and the East Florida Collection, PKY and DOCS; PKY also has photocopies of the extensive Stetson Collection. Many translations will be found under "Books" and "Articles" in this bibliography. Other primary sources are variously classified below in this section.

Natural Setting

Publications of FGS (DOCS)

Cooke, C. Wythe. *Scenery of Florida Interpreted by a Geologist.* Bulletin no. 17, 1939.
———. *Geology of Florida.* Bulletin no. 29, 1945.
Harper, Roland M. "The Geography and Vegetation of Northern Florida." In *Sixth Annual Report*, 1914, pp. 163–437.
Hendry, Charles W., Jr., and Sproul, Charles R. *Geology and Ground-water Resources of Leon County, Florida.* Bulletin no. 47, 1966.
Moore, Wayne E. *Geology of Jackson County, Florida.* Bulletin no. 37, 1955.
Yon, J. William, Jr. *Geology of Jefferson County, Florida.* Bulletin no. 48, 1966.

Publications of USDA (DOCS)

Fippin, Elmer O., and Aldert S. Root. "Soil Survey of Gadsden County, Florida." *Field Operations of the Bureau of Soils*, 1903, pp. 331–53. Washington, D.C.: GPO, 1904.

Jones, Grove B., E. E. Tharp, and H. L. Belden. "Soil Survey of Jefferson County, Florida." *Field Operations of the Bureau of Soils*, 1907, pp. 345–79. Washington, D.C.: GPO, 1909.

Wilder, Henry J., J. A. Drake, Grove B. Jones, and W. J. Geib. "Soil Survey of Leon County, Florida." *Field Operations of the Bureau of Soils*, 1905, pp. 363–88. Washington, D.C.: GPO, 1907.

Maps (DOCS)

Ball, Le Roy D., and John Bradford. "Land-ownership Map of Leon County, 1883." Library of Congress. Inset is a redrawing of the DuVal Plan for the Town of Tallahassee, 1868, with numbered lots.

"Gadsden County Land Ownership Map [1850]." An eight-foot-long map of the part of Gadsden County that lies north of the Forbes Purchase, ca. 1840–50.

Purcell, Joseph. "A Map of the Road from Pensacola in West Florida to St. Augustine in East Florida, from a Survey Made by Order of the late Hon. John Stuart." The Stuart-Purcell Map. Public Records Office, London.

"A Sketch of the Entrance From the Sea to Apalachy and Part of the Environs Taken by George Gauld Esq., Surveyor of the Coast, & Lieutenant Philip Pittman, Assistant Engineer, 1767." Clements Library, University of Michigan, Ann Arbor.

THE NATIVE POPULATIONS (DOCS)

See also "Books" and "Articles."

Bulletins no. 1–6, Bureau of Historic Sites and Properties of the Florida Division of Archives, History and Records Management, published by the Department of State, 1970–80.

Tesar, Louis Daniel. *The Leon County Bicentennial Survey Report: An Archaeological Survey of Selected Portions of Leon County, Florida*. Florida Bureau of Historic Sites and Properties Miscellaneous Project Report Series, no. 49. Duplicated and bound in two volumes. Florida Division of Archives, History, and Records Management, 1979, revised 1980.

PUBLIC HISTORICAL DOCUMENTS AND RECORDS

U.S. Documents (DOCS)

American State Papers, Indian Affairs. Vol. 2. Washington, D.C.: Gales & Seaton, 1834.

American State Papers, Military Affairs. Vol. 1. Washington, D.C.: Gales & Seaton, 1832.

American State Papers, Public Lands. Vol. 4. Washington, D.C.: Gales and Seaton, 1859.

Carter, Clarence Edwin, ed. *The Territorial Papers of the United States.* Vols. 22, *Florida, 1821–24* (Washington, D.C.: GPO, 1956), to 26, *Florida, 1839–45* (Washington, D.C.: National Archives, 1962).

Official Records of the Union and Confederate Navies in War of the Rebellion (ORN). Washington, D.C.: GPO, 1894–1922.

War of the Rebellion: A Compilation of the Official Records of the Union and Confederate Armies (OR). Washington, D.C.: GPO, 1880–1901.

Florida Territorial and State Documents (DOCS)

Florida Reports [of the Supreme Court of Florida, published biennially], vols. 1–10, 1846–64.

House Journal, 1840–60 (after 1845 of the General Assembly of the State of Florida).

Journal of the Proceedings of the [Secession] Convention of the People of Florida Begun . . . on Thursday, Jan. 3, 1861. Tallahassee: Dyke & Caldwell, 1861.

Journal of the Proceedings of the Legislative Council of the Territory of Florida, 1821–39.

Laws of Florida, 1845–60.

Robertson, Fred L., comp. *Soldiers of Florida in the Seminole Indian, Civil and Spanish-American Wars.* Prepared and published under the supervision of the Board of State Institutions, as authorized by Chapter 2203, Laws of Florida, approved May 14, 1903. Printed Live Oak, Fla.: Democrat Book & Job, [1903?]. (SPC)

Senate Journal, 1840–60 (after 1845 of the General Assembly of the State of Florida).

Territorial Acts, 1821–44.

Miscellaneous Manuscripts

The following manuscripts, useful for their maps and other records to historians examining early American settlement in the Red Hills, may be found in the Florida Division of State Lands, Title and Land Records Section, Commonwealth Building, Tallahassee.

Official U.S. Survey township plats, 22 vols.

Record Book, vol. 2 of 13 vols., Proceedings of the Commissioners, Florida Land Claims Commission, Reported to Congress, West Florida, Secretary's Book, 1824.

State of Florida Tract Books, 31 vols.

Census Records and Tax Rolls

Of particular interest for the Red Hills region, which comprised the cotton belt of Florida in 1850, are the records of the U.S. Census Bureau, Census of Agriculture for 1850 and 1860. The original schedules for all of Florida, by county, appear in two heavy volumes in DOCS. This section also has microfilm of manuscript county-by-county records for Florida of the Fifth Census (1830), Sixth Census (1840), Seventh Census (1850), and Eighth Census (1860).

The Territory of Florida made censuses beginning in 1825, when county property tax assessors were asked to count the population, black and white. Only the detailed returns of the 1825 census from Jackson and Leon counties survive. The valuable manuscript schedules for Jackson County may be found in the Office of Circuit Court Clerk, Marianna. The Leon schedules are reproduced by Dorothy Dodd in "The Florida Census of 1825," *Florida Historical Quarterly* 22 (July 1943):34–40. Territorial and state censuses thereafter provide much material about the population at mid-decade, between the decennial U.S. censuses.

Tax rolls, by county, may be found in manuscript form in the Florida State Archives. They are also on microfilm, the form most easily used in DDR.

County Repositories

A wealth of information about individuals, particularly their land ownership, may be found in the office of the circuit court clerk in the courthouses of the county seats: Marianna (Jackson County), Quincy (Gadsden County), Tallahassee (Leon County), Monticello (Jefferson County), and Madison (Madison County). Deed books are filed here, along with tract books, whereas probate court files are particularly rich with the detail of wills and estates. In some of the offices, such as that of the clerk in Leon County, the civil case files of Superior Court are complete and intact for the earliest days, as are most minute books from the time the court opened in October 1824.

DIARIES, LETTERS, OTHER PRIVATE MANUSCRIPTS AND ORAL HISTORY INTERVIEWS BY LIBRARIES OR ARCHIVES

Florida State University

Bannerman, Charles. "Iamonia Lake Plantation Journal, 1837–61." Original in PKY. Microfilm of a typescript in James D. Glunt, "Plantation and Frontier Records of East and Middle Florida, 1789–1868" (Ph.D. diss., University of Michigan, 1930), vol. 2 of microfilm no. 4266, pp. 2–145. (DOCS)
Gamble Family Papers. Photocopies, including Plantation Records, 1833–53. (SPC)

Gramling, Wilbur. "Civil War Diary, 1864–65." Photocopy and typed tran-
    script made by Clifton Paisley from the original. (SPC)
Hatheway, Frank. "The Frank Hatheway Diary, 1845–53." (SPC)
Hentz, Charles. "My Autobiography." In Southern Historical Collection, Li-
    brary of the University of North Carolina, Chapel Hill, part of the Hentz
    Family Papers #332, a gift of Hal Hentz, Photocopy in SPC, also a bound
    and duplicated typescript by Charles T. Carroll of Maitland, Fla., 2 vols.
Parkhill, George Washington. Forty "Civil War Letters, 1861–62."(SPC)
Tallahassee Merchants' Account Books, 1843–63. (SPC)
"William Wilson Letters." Original, University of Vermont Archives. Photo-
    copies, SPC.
William Wirt Papers. Originals, Maryland Historical Society. Microfilm no.
    3543. (DOCS)

State Library of Florida

"Receivers' Receipts of the Tallahassee and Newnansville Land Office Re-
    ceivers." Works Progress Administration Typescripts, no. 33, 3 vols. (DDR)
Reid, Robert Raymond. "Diary of Robert Raymond Reid, 1833, 1835." Works
    Progress Administration Typescripts, no. 47 (DDR). Another part of Reid's
    diary appears in Stephen F. Miller, *The Bench and Bar of Georgia*, 2 vols.
    (Philadelphia: Lippincott, 1858), 2:204–26 (12 June 1825 to 11 June 1841).
    (SPC)
White, David L. "Diary of D. L. White, July 1835–June 1842." Works Progress
    Administration Typescripts, no. 22. (DDR)

Florida State Archives

Bowen, Nettie Clare. Tallahassee, Florida. Typescript of interview by Clifton
    Paisley, April 22, 1972. M77-167.
Scott, George Washington. Papers, 1850–1904. Civil War Letters and Maps,
    typescript of Diary, 1850–51, in possession of J. J. Scott, Wheaton, Ill. Pho-
    tocopies. M87-022.

Unpublished Studies and Compilations

Farley, Charlotte Corley. "Florida's Alamo: The Battle of Marianna As 'Twas
    Told to Me." Bound photocopy of typescript, Miami, 1980. (DDR)
Kirk, Cooper Clifford. "A History of the Southern Presbyterian Church in
    Florida, 1821–1891." Ph.D. diss., Florida State University, 1966. (SPC)
Matter, Robert Allen. "The Spanish Missions of Florida: The Friars versus the
    Governors in the Golden Age, 1606–1690." Ph.D. diss., University of Wash-
    ington, 1972. (SPC)
Thomas, David Y. "A History of Banking in Florida." Typescript, undated.
    (SPC)

Newspapers and Journals

De Bow's Review, 1846–80
Harper's Weekly, 1857–1916
Leslie's Illustrated Weekly, 1855–1922
Niles' Register, 1811–49
Pensacola Gazette, 1821–53
St. Augustine Florida Herald & Southern Democrat, 1823–48
Tallahassee Democrat, 1910–
Tallahassee Florida Sentinel, 1841–61
Tallahassee Floridian, 1828–93

Books

Abernethy, Thomas Perkins. *The Formative Period in Alabama, 1815–1828.* 1922. 2d ed. University: University of Alabama Press, 1965.

Arnade, Charles W. *Florida on Trial, 1593–1602.* University of Miami Hispanic American Studies, n. 16. Coral Gables: University of Miami Press, 1959.

Avant, David A., Jr., ed. *Illustrated Index, J. Randall Stanley's History of Gadsden County.* Tallahassee: L'Avant Studios, 1985.

Bassett, John Spencer. *The Life of Andrew Jackson.* 1911. Repr. Hamden, Conn.: Archon Books, 1967.

Bonner, James C. *A History of Georgia Agriculture, 1732–1860.* Athens: University of Georgia Press, 1964.

Bourne, Edward Gaylord, ed. *Narratives of the Career of Hernando De Soto in the Conquest of Florida* [by the Gentleman of Elvas, vol. 1, pp. 3–223, and Luis de Biedma, vol. 2, pp. 3–40, and based on the diary of Rodrigo Ranjel, vol. 2, pp. 43–149]. 2 vols. 1904. Repr. New York: Allerton Book, 1922.

Boyd, Mark F., Hale G. Smith, and John W. Griffin. *Here They Once Stood: The Tragic End of the Apalachee Missions.* Gainesville: University of Florida Press, 1951.

Brevard, Caroline Mays. *A History of Florida from the Treaty of 1763 to Our Own Times.* 2 vols. Ed. James Alexander Robertson. DeLand: Florida Historical Society, 1924–25.

Bushnell, Amy. *The King's Coffer: Proprietors of the Spanish Florida Treasury, 1565–1702.* Gainesville: University Presses of Florida, 1981.

Calderón, Gabriel Díaz Vara. *A Seventeenth Century Letter of Gabriel Díaz Vara Calderón, Bishop of Cuba, Describing the Indian Missions of Florida.* Trans. Lucy L. Wenhold, with an introduction by John R. Swanton. Smithsonian Miscellaneous Collections, vol. 95, no. 16. Washington, D.C.: Smithsonian Institution, 1936.

Chapin, George M. *Florida, 1513–1913: Past, Present, and Future.* 2 vols. Chicago: S. J. Clarke, 1914.

Cline, Howard F. *Notes on Colonial Indians and Communities in Florida, 1700–1821.* Indian Claims Commission Docket 280. New York: Garland, 1973.

Collins, LeRoy. *Forerunners Courageous: Stories of Frontier Florida.* Tallahassee: Colcade Publishers, 1971.

Corkran, David H. *The Creek Frontier, 1540–1783.* Norman: University of Oklahoma Press, 1967.

Crane, Verner W. *The Southern Frontier, 1670–1732.* 1929. Rev. ed. Ann Arbor: University of Michigan Press, Ann Arbor Paperbacks, 1956.

Cushman, Joseph D., Jr. *A Goodly Heritage: The Episcopal Church in Florida, 1821–1892.* Gainesville: University of Florida Press, 1965.

Davis, William Watson. *The Civil War and Reconstruction in Florida.* 1913. Repr. Gainesville: University of Florida Press, 1964.

Doherty, Herbert J., Jr. *The Whigs of Florida, 1845–1854.* University of Florida Monographs in the Social Sciences, no. 1. Gainesville: University of Florida Press, 1959.

———. *Richard Keith Call, Southern Unionist.* Gainesville: University of Florida Press, 1961.

Doster, James F. *The Creek Indians and Their Florida Lands, 1740–1823.* Indian Claims Commission Docket 280. 2 vols. New York: Garland, 1974.

Eppes, Susan Bradford. *The Negro of the Old South.* Chicago: Joseph G. Branch, 1925.

———. *Through Some Eventful Years.* 1926. Repr. Gainesville: University of Florida Press, 1968.

Escobedo, Alonso de. *Pirates, Indians, and Spaniards: Father Escobedo's "La Florida."* Ed. James W. Covington. St. Petersburg: Great Outdoors, 1963.

Fairbanks, Charles H. *Ethnohistorical Report of the Florida Indians.* Indian Claims Commission, Dockets no. 73, 151. New York: Garland, 1974.

Federal Writers Project. *Slave Narratives: A Folk History of Slavery in the United States from Interviews with Former Slaves.* Vol. 17: *Florida.* St. Clair Shores, Mich.: Scholarly Press, 1976.

Foreman, Grant. *Indian Removal: The Emigration of the Five Civilized Tribes of Indians.* 1932. Rev. ed. Norman: University of Oklahoma Press, 1953.

Fuller, Hubert Bruce. *The Purchase of Florida: Its History and Diplomacy.* 1906. Repr. Gainesville: University of Florida Press, 1964.

Gannon, Michael V. *The Cross in the Sand: The Early Catholic Church in Florida, 1513–1870.* Gainesville: University of Florida Press, 1965.

Geiger, Maynard J. *The Franciscan Conquest of Florida, 1573–1618.* Washington, D.C.: Catholic University of America Press, 1937.

Gergel, Thomas J., and Morton D. Winsberg. *A Tour Guide of the Newer Coastal Plain South of Tallahassee, Florida.* Tallahassee: Florida State University Department of Geography, 1969.

Groene, Bertram H. *Ante-Bellum Tallahassee.* Tallahassee: Florida Heritage Foundation, 1971.

Hann, John H. *Apalachee: The Land between the Rivers.* Ripley P. Bullen Monographs in Anthropology and History, No. 7, Florida State Museum. Gainesville: University Presses of Florida, 1988.

Hanna, Alfred Jackson. *A Prince in Their Midst: The Adventurous Life of Achille*

Murat on the American Frontier. Norman: University of Oklahoma Press, 1946.

Hodge, Frederick W., and Theodore H. Lewis, eds. *Spanish Explorers in the United States, 1528–1543*. The narratives of the expeditions of Panfilo de Narváez by Alvar Nuñez Cabeza de Vaca, pp. 12–126; of Hernando De Soto by the Gentleman of Elvas, pp. 132–272; and of Francisco de Coronado by Pedro de Castañeda, pp. 281–387. 1907. Repr. New York: Barnes & Noble, 1946.

Jahoda, Gloria. *The Other Florida*. New York: Charles Scribner's Sons, 1967.

Johns, John Edwin. *Florida during the Civil War*. Gainesville: University of Florida Press, 1963.

Johnson, Malcolm B. *Red, White, and Bluebloods in Frontier Florida*. Tallahassee: Rotary Clubs of Tallahassee, 1976.

Lanier, Sidney. *Florida: Its Scenery, Climate, and History*. 1875. Repr. Gainesville: University of Florida Press, 1973.

Long, Ellen Call. *Florida Breezes; or, Florida New and Old*. 1883. Repr. Gainesville: University of Florida Press, 1962.

Luraghi, Raimondo. *The Rise and Fall of the Plantation South*. New York: Franklin Watts, New Viewpoints, 1978.

McRory, Mary Oakley, and Edith Clark Barrows. *History of Jefferson County*. Monticello: Kiwanis Club, 1935.

Mahon, John K. *History of the Second Seminole War, 1835–1842*. Gainesville: University of Florida Press, 1967.

Martin, Sidney Walter. *Florida during Territorial Days*. Athens: University of Georgia Press, 1944.

Milanich, Jerald T., and Charles H. Fairbanks. *Florida Archaeology*. New York: Academic Press, 1980.

Nevins, Allan. *Fruits of Manifest Destiny, 1847–1852*. Vol. 1 of an 8-book series, *Ordeal of the Union* (1947–1971). New York: Charles Scribner's Sons, 1947.

Oré, Luis Gerónimo de. *The Martyrs of Florida, 1513–1616*. [1619?] Repr., ed. and trans. Maynard J. Geiger. Franciscan Studies, no. 18. New York: J. F. Wagner, 1936.

Paisley, Clifton. *From Cotton to Quail: An Agricultural Chronicle of Leon County, Florida, 1860–1967*. Gainesville: University of Florida Press, 1968.

Paisley, Joy S. *The Cemeteries of Leon County, Florida: Rural White Cemeteries, Tombstone Inscriptions and Epitaphs*. Tallahassee: Dominie Everardus Bogardus Chapter, Colonial Dames XVII Century, 1978.

Pareja, Francisco. *Francisco Pareja's 1613 Confessionário: A Documentary Source for Timucuan Ethnography*. Ed. Jerald T. Milanich and William C. Sturtevant. Trans. Emilio F. Moran. Tallahassee: Florida Division of Archives, History, and Records Management, 1972.

Parton, James. *Life of Andrew Jackson*. 3 vols. New York: Mason Brothers, 1860.

Phillips, Ulrich Bonnell. *History of Transportation in the Eastern Cotton Belt to 1860*. 1908. Repr. New York: Octagon Press, 1968.

Phillips, Ulrich Bonnell, and James David Glunt, eds. *Florida Plantation Records from the Papers of George Noble Jones*. St. Louis: Missouri Historical Society, 1927.

Reese, J. H. *The Lands of Leon*. New Era ed. Supplement of the *Tallahassee Weekly True Democrat*. Tallahassee: Milton A. Smith, 1911.

Remini, Robert V. *Andrew Jackson and the Course of American Empire, 1767–1821*. New York: Harper & Row, 1977.

Reps, John W. *The Making of Urban America: A History of City Planning in the United States*. Princeton: Princeton University Press, 1965.

Rerick, Roland H. *Memoirs of Florida*. Ed. Francis P. Fleming. 2 vols. Atlanta: Southern Historical Association, 1902.

Richardson, Simon Peter. *Lights and Shadows of Itinerant Life: An Autobiography*. Nashville: Barbee & Smith, 1901.

Roberts, William. *An Account of the First Discovery and Natural History of Florida*. 1763. Repr. Gainesville: University of Florida Press, 1976.

Robinson, Solon. *Solon Robinson, Pioneer Agriculturist, Selected Writings*. 2 vols. Ed. Herbert Anthony Kellar. Vol. 2: 1846–51. Indianapolis: Indiana Historical Bureau, 1936.

Rogers, William Warren. *Ante-Bellum Thomas County, 1825–1861*. Florida State Univ. Studies, no. 39. Tallahassee: Florida State University, 1963.

———. *Thomas County during the Civil War*. Florida State University Studies, no. 41. Tallahassee: Florida State University, 1964.

———. *Thomas County, 1865–1900*. Tallahassee: Florida State University Press, 1973.

Romans, Bernard. *A Concise Natural History of East and West Florida*. 1775. Repr. Gainesville: University of Florida Press, 1962.

Ruffin, Edmund. *The Diary of Edmund Ruffin*. Vol. 1: 1856–61. Ed. William Kauffman Scarborough. Baton Rouge: Louisiana State University Press, 1972.

Serrano y Sanz, Manuel, ed. *Documentos Históricos de la Florida y la Luisiana Siglos XVI al XVIII*. Madrid: Suarez, 1912.

Shofner, Jerrell H. *History of Jefferson County*. Tallahassee: Sentry Press, 1976.

———. *Jackson County, Florida: A History*. Marianna: Jackson County Heritage Association, 1985.

Simpson, J. Clarence. *A Provisional Gazetteer of Florida Place-Names of Indian Derivation*. Florida Geological Survey Special Publication no. 1. Tallahassee: FGS, 1956.

Sims, Elizabeth H. *A History of Madison County, Florida*. Madison: Madison County Historical Society, 1986.

Stanley, J. Randall. *History of Jackson County*. Marianna, Fla.: Jackson County Historical Society, 1950.

———. *History of Gadsden County*. 1948. Ed. David A. Avant, Jr. Tallahassee: L'Avant Studios, 1985.

Swanton, John R. *Early History of the Creek Indians and Their Neighbors*. Smithsonian Institution Bureau of American Ethnology Bulletin No. 73. Washington, D.C.: GPO, 1922.

————. *Final Report of the DeSoto Expedition Commission.* John R. Swanton, Chairman. Washington, D.C.: GPO, 1939.

————. *The Indians of the Southeastern United States.* Smithsonian Institution Bureau of American Ethnology Bulletin No. 137. Washington, D.C.: GPO, 1946.

Taylor, William R. *Cavalier and Yankee: The Old South and American National Character.* 1961. New York: Harper & Row, Harper Torchbooks, 1969.

Tebeau, Charlton W. *A History of Florida.* Coral Gables: University of Miami Press, 1971.

TePaske, John Jay. *The Governorship of Spanish Florida, 1700–1763.* Durham: Duke University Press, 1964.

Thompson, Arthur W. *Jacksonian Democracy on the Florida Frontier.* University of Florida Monographs in Social Science, no. 9. Gainesville: University of Florida Press, 1961.

Thompson, Maurice. *A Tallahassee Girl.* Boston: Houghton Mifflin, 1881.

Torrey, Bradford. *A Florida Sketch-Book.* Boston: Houghton Mifflin, 1894.

Varner, John Grier, and Jeanette Johnson Varner, eds. and trans. *The Florida of the Inca.* Austin: University of Texas Press, 1951. An account of the De Soto expedition by Garcilaso de la Vega, published in Madrid in 1605.

Warner, Lee H. *Building Florida's Capitol.* Tallahassee: Historic Tallahassee Preservation Board, 1977.

Warner, Lee H., and Mary B. Eastland. *Tallahassee: Downtown Transitions.* Tallahassee: Historic Tallahassee Preservation Board, 1976.

White, George. *Statistics of the State of Georgia.* 1849. Repr. Spartanburg, S.C.: Reprint, 1972.

Willey, Gordon R. *Archeology of the Florida Gulf Coast.* Smithsonian Miscellaneous Collections, vol. 113. Washington, D.C.: GPO, 1949.

Williams, John Lee. *The Territory of Florida.* 1837. Repr. Gainesville: University of Florida Press, 1962.

————. *A View of West Florida.* 1827. Repr. Gainesville: University Presses of Florida, 1976.

Womack, Miles Kenan, Jr. *Gadsden: A Florida County in Word and Picture.* Quincy: Gadsden County Bicentennial Committee, 1976.

Woodford, Frank B. *Mr. Jefferson's Disciple: A Life of Justice Woodward.* East Lansing: Michigan State University Press, 1953.

Wright, J. Leitch, Jr. *William Augustus Bowles, Director General of the Creek Nation.* Athens: University of Georgia Press, 1967.

————. *The Only Land They Knew: The Tragic Story of the Indians in the Old South.* New York: Free Press, 1981.

Articles

Abbey, Kathryn T. "Documents Relating to El Destino and Chemonie Plantations, Middle Florida, 1828–1868." 4 pts. *FHQ* 7:179–213, 291–329; 8:3–46, 79–111 (January–October 1929).

Anderson, James Patton. "Civil War Letters of Major General James Patton Anderson." Ed. Margaret Anderson Uhler. *FHQ* 56 (October 1977):150–75.

Arnade, Charles W. "Cattle Raising in Spanish Florida, 1513–1763." *Agricultural History* 35 (July 1961):116–24. Repr. as publication no. 21, St. Augustine Historical Society, 1965.

Bolton, Herbert E. "Spanish Resistance to the Carolina Traders in Western Georgia (1680–1704)." *Georgia Historical Quarterly* 9 (June 1925):115–30.

———. "The Mission as a Frontier Institution in the Spanish American Colonies." *Bolton and the Spanish Borderlands*, ed. John Francis Bannon, pp. 187–211. Norman: University of Oklahoma Press, 1964.

Boyd, Mark F. "The Fortifications of San Marcos de Apalache." *FHQ* 15 (July 1936):3–34.

———. "Events at Prospect Bluff on the Apalachicola River, 1808–1818: An Introduction to Twelve Letters of Edmund Doyle." *FHQ* 16 (October 1937):55–96.

———. "A Map of the Road from Pensacola to St. Augustine, 1778, with Nine Plates." *FHQ* 17 (July 1938):15–23.

———. "Spanish Mission Sites in Florida." *FHQ* 17 (April 1939):255–80.

———. "From a Remote Frontier: Letters and Documents Pertaining to San Marcos de Apalache, 1763–1769, During the British Occupation of Florida." *FHQ* 19:179–212, 402–412; 20:pp. 82–92, 203–9, 293–310, 382–97; 21:44–52, 135–46 (January 1941–October 1942).

———. "Enumeration of Florida Missions in 1675." *FHQ* 27 (October 1948):181–88.

———. "The Federal Campaign of 1864 in East Florida." *FHQ* 29 (July 1950):3–37.

———. "The Joint Operations of the Federal Army and Navy Near St. Marks, Florida, March 1865." *FHQ* 29 (October 1950):96–124.

———. "The Battle of Marianna." *FHQ* 29 (April 1951):225–42.

Boyd, Mark F., and José Navarro Latorre. "Spanish Interest in British Florida and in the Progress of the American Revolution." *FHQ* 32 (July 1953):92–130.

Brown, Frances Elizabeth. "Lizzie Brown's Tallahassee." Ed. Bertram H. Groene. *FHQ* 48 (October 1969):155–75.

Burch, Daniel L. "The First American Road in Florida: Papers Relating to the Survey and Construction of the Pensacola–St. Augustine Highway." Ed. Mark F. Boyd. *FHQ* 14 (October 1935):73–106; (January 1936):139–92.

Bushnell, Amy. "The Menéndez Marquéz Cattle Barony at La Chua and the Determinants of Economic Expansion in Seventeenth Century Florida." *FHQ* 56 (April 1978):407–31.

———. "Patricio de Hinachuba: Defender of the Word of God, the Crown of the King, and the Little Children of Ivitachuco." *American Indian Culture and Research Journal* 3, no. 3 (1979):1–21.

Castelnau, Francis de la Porte, Comte de. "Essay on Middle Florida, 1837–1838, by Comte de Castelnau." Ed. Mark F. Boyd. Trans. Arthur R. Seymour. *FHQ* 26 (January 1948):199–255.

———. "Compte de Castelnau in Middle Florida, 1837–1838." Trans. Arthur R. Seymour. *FHQ* 26 (April 1948):300–24.

Chandler, William. "A Tallahassee Alarm of 1836: Letter of William Chandler, Georgetown, D.C., 17 May 1886, to Julia J. Yonge." *FHQ* 8 (April 1939):197–99.

Clausen, C. J., and others. "Little Salt Spring, Florida: A Unique Underwater Site." *Science* (16 February 1979):609–14.

Covington, James W. "Federal Relations with the Apalachicola Indians, 1823–1838." *FHQ* 42 (October 1963):125–41.

Davis, Mary Lamar. "Tallahassee through Territorial Days." *Apalachee* 1 (1944):47–61.

———. "Brigadier General William G. M. Davis." *Florida Bar Journal* 23 (1949):36–39.

Davis, T. Frederick. "Milly Francis and Duncan McCrimmon: An Authentic Florida Pocahontas." *FHQ* 21 (January 1943):254–65.

Dodd, Dorothy. "The Manufacture of Cotton in Florida before and during the Civil War." *FHQ* 13 (July 1934):1–15.

———. "The Schooner Emperor: An Incident of the Illegal Slave Trade in Florida." *FHQ* 13 (January 1935):117–28.

———. "The Florida Census of 1825." *FHQ* 22 (July 1943):34–40.

———. "Florida's Population in 1845." *FHQ* 24 (July 1945):28–29.

———. "Horse Racing in Middle Florida, 1830–1843." *Apalachee* 3 (1950):20–29.

Fleming, Francis P. "Francis P. Fleming in the War for Southern Independence: Soldiering with the Second Florida Regiment." Ed. Edward Williamson. *FHQ* 28:38–62, 143–55, 205–10 (July 1949–January 1950).

———. "Soldiering with the Second Florida Regiment." Ed. John P. Ingle. *FHQ* 59 (January 1981):335–39.

Forman, Arthur I. "Florida and Spanish Tobacco." *De Bow's Review* 18 (January 1855):36–39.

Gadsden, James. "The Defences of the Floridas: A Report of Captain James Gadsden, Aide-de-Camp to General Andrew Jackson, Nashville, 1 August 1818." *FHQ* 15 (April 1937):242–48.

Galphin, Rosa. "John C. McGehee." *FHQ* 4 (April 1926):186–91.

Griffin, John W. "The Historic Archaeology of Florida." *The Florida Indian and His Neighbors*. Ed. John W. Griffin, pp. 45–48. Winter Park, Fla.: Inter-American Center, 1949.

———. "Test Excavation at the Lake Jackson Site." *American Antiquity* 16 (October 1950):99–112.

Henry, Evelyn Whitfield. "Old Houses of Tallahassee." *Tallahassee Historical Society Annual* 1 (1934):39–55. Mimeographed, with pictures, SPC.

Hollingsworth, Henry. "Tennessee Volunteers in the Seminole Campaign of 1836: The Diary of Henry Hollingsworth." Ed. Stanley F. Horn. *Tennessee Historical Quarterly* 1:269–74, 344–62; 2:61–73, 163–78, 236–56 (September 1942–September 1943).

Hutchinson, Charles. "The Charles Hutchinson Letters from Territorial Tallahassee, 1839–1843." Ed. James T. Campbell. *Apalachee* 4 (1956):13–28.

Kurz, Herman. "Secondary Forest Succession in the Tallahassee Red Hills." *Proceedings of the Florida Academy of Sciences* 7 (1945):59–100.

Lucas, Marion B. "Civil War Career of Colonel George Washington Scott." *FHQ* 58 (October 1979):130–49.

Matter, Robert A. "Economic Basis of the Seventeenth-Century Florida Missions." *FHQ* 52 (July 1973):18–37.

Maxwell, David E. "Some Letters to His Parents by a Floridian of the Confederate Army." Ed. Gilbert Wright. *FHQ* 36 (April 1958):353–72.

Milanich, Jerald T. "Life in a Ninth Century Indian Household: A Weeden Island Fall-Winter Site on the Upper Apalachicola River, Florida." Florida Bureau of Historic Sites and Properties *Bulletin* no. 4, pp. 1–44. Tallahassee: Fla. Division of Archives, History, and Records Management, 1974.

Miller, William. "The Battle of Natural Bridge." Lecture before the Anna Jackson Chapter, United Daughters of the Confederacy, Tallahassee, circa 1901. Ed. Mark F. Boyd. *Apalachee* 4 (1956):76–86.

Olsen, Stanley J. "The Wakulla Cave." *Natural History* 67 (August 1958):396–98, 401–403.

Owens, Harry P. "Port of Apalachicola." *FHQ* 48 (July 1969):1–25.

Paisley, Clifton. "Tallahassee through the Storebooks, 1843–1863: Antebellum Cotton Prosperity." *FHQ* 50 (October 1971):111–27.

———. "Tallahassee through the Storebooks: War Clouds and War, 1860–1863." *FHQ* 51 (July 1972):37–51.

———. "Madison County's Sea Island Cotton Industry, 1870–1916." *FHQ* 54 (January 1976):285–305.

Parker, Rosalind. "The Proctors—Antonio, George, & John." *Apalachee* 2 (1946):19–29.

Peña, Diego. "Diego Peña's Expedition to Apalachee and Apalachicolo in 1716." Trans. and ed. Mark F. Boyd. *FHQ* 28 (July 1949):1–27.

———. "Documents Describing the Second and Third Expeditions of Lieutenant Diego Peña to Apalachee and Apalachicolo in 1717 and 1718." Trans. and ed. Mark F. Boyd. *FHQ* 31 (October 1952):109–39.

Pittman, P. "Apalachee during the British Occupation: A Description Contained in a Series of Four Reports by Lieut. Pittman, R.E." Ed. Mark F. Boyd. *FHQ* 12 (January 1934):114–22.

Portier, Michael. "From Pensacola to St. Augustine in 1827: A Journey of the Rt. Rev. Michael Portier." *FHQ* 26 (October 1947):135–66.

Scott, George Washington. "How to Escape the Yankees: Major Scott's Letter to His Wife at Tallahassee, March, 1864." Ed. Clifton Paisley. *FHQ* 50 (July 1971):53–61.

Shofner, Jerrell H., and William Warren Rogers. "Confederate Railroad Construction: The Live Oak to Lawton Connector." *FHQ* 43 (January 1965):217–28.

Simmons, W. H., and Jno. Lee Williams. "The Selection of Tallahassee as the

Capital: Journals of W. H. Simmons and John Lee Williams, Commissioners, 1823." *FHQ* 1 (April 1908):26–44 and (July 1908):18–38.

Thomas, David Y. "Report on the Public Archives of Florida." *Annual Report of the American Historical Association for the Year 1906*. 2 vols. Vol. 2. Washington, D.C.: GPO, 1908.

Upchurch, John C. "Aspects of the Development and Exploration of the Forbes Purchase." *FHQ* 48 (October 1969):117–39.

Wenhold, Lucy L. "The First Fort of San Marcos de Apalache." *FHQ* 34 (April 1956):301–14.

Young, Captain Hugh. "A Topographical Memoir of East and West Florida with Itineraries of General Jackson's Army, 1818." Ed. Mark F. Boyd and Gerald M. Ponton. *FHQ* 13, pp. 16–50, 82–104, and 129–64 (July 1934– January 1935).

Index